SECOND EDITION

HEALTH PROMOTION AND HEALTH COUNSELING

Effective Counseling and Psychotherapeutic Strategies

LEN SPERRY

Florida Atlantic University and Medical College of Wisconsin

JON CARLSON

Governors State University

JUDY LEWIS

Governors State University

MATT ENGLAR-CARLSON

California State University at Fullerton

PEARSON

Boston ■ New York ■ San Francisco
Mexico City ■ Montreal ■ Toronto ■ London ■ Madrid ■ Munich ■ Paris
Hong Kong ■ Singapore ■ Tokyo ■ Cape Town ■ Sydney

Executive Editor: *Virginia Lanigan*
Series Editorial Assistant: *Scott Blaszak*
Executive Marketing Manager: *Amy Cronin Jordan*
Editorial-Production Service: *Omegatype Typography, Inc.*
Composition and Prepress Buyer: *Linda Cox*
Manufacturing Buyer: *Andrew Turso*
Cover Administrator: *Joel Gendron*
Electronic Composition: *Omegatype Typography, Inc.*

For related titles and support materials, visit our online catalog at www.ablongman.com.

Between the time Web site information is gathered and then published, it is not unusual for some sites to have closed. Also, the transcription of URLs can result in typographical errors. The publisher would appreciate notification of where these errors occur so they may be corrected in subsequent editions.

Library of Congress Cataloging-in-Publication Data

Health promotion and health counseling : effective counseling and psychotherapeutic
    strategies / Len Sperry . . . [et al.].—2nd ed.
      p. ; cm.
    Rev. ed. of: Health counseling / Judith A. Lewis. c1993.
    Includes bibliographical references and index.
    ISBN 0-205-34420-8 (alk. paper)
    1. Health counseling. 2. Health promotion. 3. Health education. 4. Psychotherapy. I.
Sperry, Len. II. Lewis, Judith A., 1939–. Health counseling.
    [DNLM: 1. Health Education. 2. Counseling–methods. 3. Health Promotion. 4. Models,
Educational. WA 590 H43812 2005]
R727.4.H427 2005
362.1'04256—dc22

                                                 2004049409

Printed in the United States of America

10 9 8 7 6 5 4 3 2 1   09 08 07 06 05 04

CONTENTS

CHAPTER SIX

Drug and Alcohol Abuse   161

CHAPTER NINE

Sexual Health   241

CHAPTER TEN

Chronic Pain   273

CHAPTER ELEVEN

Chronic Disease and Other Illness-Related Concerns   299

PREFACE

Health counseling has grown and developed dramatically in the years since this book's first edition was published in 1993. When we began talking about drafting that book in 1990, there were hints that major changes in health care were coming and that health counseling would be a necessary strategy; however, we had little sense of the enormity of change that would ensue. At that time, there were no competing health counseling books and very limited resources to meet the needs of counselors and other health and mental health care professionals or students in training. A few books on health psychology and a few more on health education were available, but none of them adequately addressed the process and the strategies of health counseling.

Accordingly, based on our clinical and academic experience—Len Sperry's training and practice in preventive medicine with a focus on health promotion, Judy Lewis's health-focused counseling practice for clients dealing with substance-abuse issues, and Jon Carlson's experience with running a wellness center—we decided to write and publish such a book. As educators, we recognized the need for a book that could teach students how to use counseling skills to address problems related to physical health. As clinicians, we wanted to write a book that would build a bridge between theory and practice, reviewing the literature on health issues but also focusing on clinical applications. We knew that counselors were being asked to help clients with common health concerns, such as weight control, smoking cessation, substance abuse, and sleep difficulties. We also knew that health-care professionals, trained to deal with physical problems, needed to add counseling to their skills repertoire. We felt that a comprehensive text on health counseling, with a good balance of theory, research, and application, could help achieve these separate but complementary goals, and it was this belief that led us to plan and conceptualize *Health Counseling* in the early 1990s.

In 2000, when the Surgeon General announced the rollout of *Healthy People 2010,* the decade-long master plan for the nation's health, he noted that health counseling is necessary to achieve acceptable levels of health and well-being on the Leading Health Indicators—physical activity, substance use, weight control, tobacco use, and responsible sexual behavior. Subsequently, programs in medicine, nursing, and other allied health professions were directed to emphasize training in health counseling. The Surgeon General's directive came at a time when health care was beginning to shift to a more integrative and relational model of practice. Most obvious was the emergence of complimentary and alternative medicine (CAM), with its emphasis on the provider–patient relationship and on patient self-care. Less obvious was the emerging focus of medical schools on the doctor–patient relationship, spirituality, and nutrition.

As health care continues to change and evolve, health professionals are being challenged to expand the services they provide. While primarily trained to deal with psychological issues, counselors and psychotherapists are increasingly being asked to help with clients' health concerns. Providers recognize the need to increase their repertoire of counseling skills to be able to more effectively deal with these health concerns. Similarly, while trained to deal with physical problems, health-care professionals are beginning to recognize the need to add counseling to their skills repertoire. Trends such as these represent a *felt need*. History shows that felt needs are inevitably translated into action; in this case, an increasing demand for education and training in health counseling theory and practice.

Although associated with traditional health-care settings, such as hospitals and clinics, rehabilitation programs, human service agencies, and private practices, health promotion and health counseling are becoming more common in other settings—the workplace and the community, including schools. In traditional settings, health counseling is often provided in a one-to-one format. On the other hand, health promotion workplace and community programs tend to emphasize group-based interventions over one-to-one interventions. Irrespective of the setting, however, we believe that the relationship, assessment, intervention, maintenance, and prevention strategies provided in this book are applicable in both health care and other settings.

So what kind of changes can the reader expect in this edition of *Health Promotion and Health Counseling*? A new Chapter 1 contains an overview of the evolving field of health counseling; it describes and differentiates five types of health counseling. An important feature here is our attention to defining and differentiating the key concepts related to health counseling, including general health, disease, acute disease, chronic disease and its process levels, illness, chronic illness and its phases, impairment, disability, health education, health promotion, wellness, as well as specific health counseling issues. A critical distinction between health promotion and wellness provides both a measure of hope and strategies for working with clients and patients with progressively debilitating and terminal illnesses. Chapter 11 has been completely rewritten to emphasize chronic disease and illness. Every chapter's content and references have been significantly updated. Each chapter emphasizes the assessment of cultural factors and their influence on health and suggests ways of tailoring health counseling interventions to incorporate the multicultural dimension. We are indebted to Matt Carlson and the multicultural counseling and health expertise that he brings to this revision.

Part I, The Basics of Health Counseling, introduces the book's conceptual framework and discusses practical strategies and skills that can be used to help clients initiate and maintain health-oriented behavior changes. In Part II, Health Counseling in Action, we apply the health counseling model to a number of specific issues: weight control, smoking cessation, substance abuse, exercise, sleep, sexual health, chronic pain, and chronic disease and other illness-related conditions. Part II's applications chapters survey the theoretical and research literature related to a topic and also provide clinical input on relationship development, assessment, intervention, treatment maintenance, and prevention. Each of the applications' chapters also includes case materials, available health counseling resources, and detailed descriptions for the assessment and planning of psychotherapy and several preventive strategies for various health problems and issues.

Health Promotion and Health Counseling is directed primarily at mental health professionals; those who are in training to be professional counselors, counseling and clinical psychologists, and marriage and family therapists; and to clinicians who want or need to expand the scope of their practice. This book should also be helpful to social workers who need to increase their knowledge and clinical skills for working with clients who have health-related issues. It may be of interest to health educators and health-promotion specialists, as well as physicians, nurses, and other health-care professionals.

The need for professionals who are trained in health counseling continues to increase. With additional training, health professionals already skilled in individual counseling or psychotherapy can be prepared to practice effective health counseling.

ACKNOWLEDGMENTS

The authors would like to thank the reviewers: Paul Blisard, Southwest Missouri State University; Craig Demmer, Lehman College, City University of New York; Joseph Donnelly, Montclair State University; Paul Granello, The Ohio State University; and Jane E. Myers, University of North Carolina, Greensboro.

THE BASICS OF HEALTH COUNSELING

Health counseling as this book conceives it is essentially an attitude or perspective rather than a new approach or counseling specialty. This perspective reflects an integrative, biopsychosocial, and proactive way of viewing and working with clients. Part I's three chapters describe this perspective and provide an overview and an introduction to the practice of health counseling. Chapter 1 covers the increasing demand for health counseling, basic definitions and different types of health counseling, as well as cultural and professional training issues. Chapter 2 describes six key theories and models of health behavior and several key concepts that underlie the practice of health counseling. Chapter 3 discusses the process of health counseling and highlights some of its important strategies, skills, and concepts.

· · · · · ██

CHAPTER ONE

AN OVERVIEW OF HEALTH PROMOTION, WELLNESS, AND HEALTH COUNSELING

Health promotion is the science and art of helping people change
their lifestyle to move toward a state of optimal health.

—M. O'Donnell, Ph.D.

Increasingly, clients are seeking help from counselors and psychotherapists to achieve healthier lifestyles or to adapt to changes for their physical well-being. They may be otherwise healthy and successful individuals who are experiencing flagging energy levels and/or find that coffee or caffeine is ruining their sleep. They have just been diagnosed with high blood pressure or high cholesterol levels and don't really want to take medications. They may be trying to cope with a chronic illness. Or, they may need to stop smoking or need help in sticking with an exercise prescription that their health-care provider has given them. Whatever the reason, the clients want and need health counseling.

Health counseling is a process of assisting people to make the kinds of changes necessary to enhance their physical health and psychological well-being. This chapter introduces health promotion and health counseling by describing the increasing need for counseling and some reasons for the rapid development of the health counseling specialty and then defines health, heath promotion, wellness, and health counseling. After that there are profiles of the five types of health counseling: medical care counseling, patient care counseling, health promotion counseling, health-focused counseling, and health-focused psychotherapy. Finally, the discussion turns to cultural factors as they relate to health counseling and to the professional preparation needed for those who want to practice health counseling.

THE NEED FOR HEALTH COUNSELING

The profession of health counseling has grown and developed dramatically during the past decade; there are several reasons for this phenomenon. This section describes three of them:

personal health awareness, public health awareness, and changes in health-care delivery and the health-care professions.

Personal Health Awareness

Individuals in the prime of their lives today have greatly different views and expectations of health than individuals who were in their prime at the beginning of the twentieth century. For instance, in 1900, a 45-year-old businessowner living in an urban community might wake up with arthritis pain and think nothing of it and then read the newspaper while eating a hearty breakfast of bacon, ham, grits, and eggs. The newspaper would contain local and national news, but have little if anything about medical treatments or health issues. He would then travel in silence to his place of business in a horse-drawn carriage—accompanied only by indigestion, heartburn, or some symptom of a chronic illness—thinking how good it was to be alive given that many of his social and business acquaintances had already died. It is unlikely that he would consider seeing a physician or stopping by a hospital for tests or treatment. At that time hospitals were still largely places for the poor with life-threatening illnesses, and because of the high rates of infection and death associated with health care and hospitals, most people stayed away from medical treatment except as a last resort. Our businessowner would be grateful to have lived to the age of 45 since he already had exceeded the life expectancy for males. Smiling as he looks forward to the wedding of his youngest daughter and the birth of his next grandchild, he muses: "Life sure has been good to me."

Today, a business executive might wake up and immediately get on her treadmill while watching a morning news program on which a prominent researcher is being interviewed about the latest advances in some medical treatment. She compliments herself on following a friend's advice to take glucosamine sulfate, which really has helped, for the joint pain she has been experiencing lately. She then eats a breakfast consisting of foods specifically tailored to her metabolism and body type, including a handful of specially formulated vitamins and nutrients for a 45-year-old premenopausal female. Following that she takes a commuter train to work while reading newspaper stories about new medications and health procedures and checks the NASDAQ index to see how her biotech stock is doing. Throughout the day, she is bombarded with health information on billboards, the Internet, TV and radio, as well as in face-to-face conversations with friends and business associates. She leaves work early and arrives at a hospital-based clinic just in time for the full-body CT scan that promises to "detect any hidden heart disease, tumors, cancers, or other problematic health conditions." She is relieved when the radiologist tells her that the exam detected no indication of heart disease or cancer; nevertheless, she schedules a follow-up scan for next year.

Unlike previous generations, members of today's baby-boom generation expect to live vibrant lives well into their 80s and 90s. This expectation is largely fueled by the prospect of increased life expectancy; by the promise of age-defying supplements, prescribed medications, and medical procedures; and, particularly, by alternative medicine and counseling to promote health. People have begun to understand that many of the leading causes of death are related to lifestyle; accordingly, many are attempting to make lasting lifestyle changes.

For this generation, health education and health counseling may be the keys to living life to the fullest. These individuals do not welcome the later-life experiences that they witnessed their parents having. That generation, and others before it, accepted old age as synonymous with an inevitable array of chronic degenerative diseases. The current more health-conscious generation rejects the prospect of 20 or more years of progressively disabling illness and a limited quality of life. They hope to live full, vibrant lives until moments before death. People now understand the value of making lifestyle changes and have been sold on the prospect of defying the aging process. Not surprisingly, they constantly seek opportunities to learn more about improving their health and well-being. Needless to say, the baby-boom generation and those to come are prime candidates for and soon-to-be consumers of health counseling.

Public Health Awareness and *Healthy People 2010*

While an increasing number of highly educated adults in the United States are attempting to pursue the dream of life with few or no diseases related to lifestyle, many others are experiencing unprecedented levels of lifestyle-related acute and chronic diseases. As part of its agenda for promoting the nation's health, the federal government has targeted certain acute and chronic illnesses. *Healthy People 2010* represents the third time that the U.S. Department of Health and Human Services (USDHHS) has developed 10-year national objectives (USDHHS, 2000). The indicators in the plan reflect the scientific advances that have taken place over the past 20 years in preventive medicine, disease surveillance, vaccine and therapeutic development, and information technology. It specifies 467 objectives in 28 focus areas to achieve two goals: increase quality and years of healthy life and eliminate health disparities.

Unlike previous plans, *Healthy People 2010* includes a set of Leading Health Indicators to help researchers and practitioners target and track the success of actions to improve health. Similar to the Leading Economic Indicators used to measure the economy's health, these benchmarks provide a concise means for measuring the health of people in the nation. Five of the health indicators are lifestyle indicators: physical activity, being overweight or obese, tobacco use, substance abuse, and responsible sexual behavior; the other five in the set are health system service indicators: mental health, injury and violence, environmental quality, immunization, and access to health care. Underlying each of the indicators is the significant influence of income and education.

The plan's indicators are intended to facilitate the development of strategies and action plans for health promotion and disease prevention efforts and to encourage wide participation in improving people's health during the first decade of the new millennium. It is important to note that most of the indicators are behavioral rather than medical in nature, and they are lifestyle-related. Accordingly, such indicators lend themselves to modification by changes in lifestyle. Unlike other editions, *Healthy People 2010* emphasizes the importance of health counseling.

It was designed in such a way that it would be implemented and so that *Healthy People 2010*'s goals and health indicators could be carefully monitored. Furthermore, it was designed to have an impact not only on health-care practice but also on research on health care. Presumably, medical, nursing, and other training programs for health providers who receive federal funding will incorporate education in health counseling. This kind of training should have a positive influence on the clinical practice patterns of health-care providers.

Presumably, grant applications to the National Institutes of Health (NIH) would not be funded unless applications specified how the proposed research would relate to one or more of the 467 objectives.

Changes in Health-Care Delivery and the Health-Care Professions

In addition to personal and public health awareness, there are four related social trends. The first involves the enormously far-ranging and often wrenching changes occurring in health-care delivery and the scientific and technological breakthroughs and advances in medicine that are fueling these changes. However managed care evolves, it is sure to retain its focus on accountability, effectiveness, and patient satisfaction. Because patient satisfaction is closely related to the feeling that health care is responsive and caring—hallmarks of effective health counseling—the demand for such counseling is likely to increase significantly.

The second trend involves the intensity of the movement toward professionalization that has gripped many of the helping professions during the past two decades. This movement has been marked by basic changes in the very identity and sense of autonomy of some of the professions. For instance, the American Psychological Association recently "refashioned" the identity of psychology from a mental health profession to a primary health-care profession. Professional counselors have enlarged their identity and scope of practice to: "licensed counselors specializing in mental health and marital and family therapy." Nurse practitioners who get necessary certification have gained prescription-writing privileges and the option to practice independent of physicians. New credentialed health-care specialties have also emerged, including physician assistants and certified health education specialists.

The third major social trend involves the baby-boom generation, which continues to redefine demands and expectations for the scope of health-care services as this generation's oldest members move into their late 50s. Boomers appear to be more health conscious than any previous generation and have come to expect that health-care services can and should be able to maintain their sense of youthfulness and well-being into to their later years.

The fourth trend has been evolving for some time. For more than 50 years, Western medicine was based on an acute care model that emphasized a high-tech, low-touch focus on rapid symptom relief and "cure." The low-touch, or nonrelational, aspect of this model for acute care has been bothersome to many individuals, patients and providers alike. Furthermore, the fact that greater numbers of Americans are concerned and affected more by chronic diseases than acute diseases has challenged the standard medical practice model. Fortunately, health care is beginning to show signs of a slow but steady shift to an integrative and relational practice model. This newly emerging health-care model is being called *complimentary and alternative medicine* (CAM), which focuses more on a high-touch, low-tech approach. CAM and other humanistic and integrative approaches to medicine emphasize "healing," health promotion, and wellness. With this emerging model, there needs to be more focus on education, attitude, and behavior change than was the case with the acute care model. Models such as CAM will also require highly trained professionals who can provide skillful and effective health counseling to an increasing number of patients and clients.

DEFINITIONS OF BASIC TERMS

Since this book is about health, health education, health promotion, wellness, and health counseling, it may be useful to begin the discussion here by defining and describing these terms as they are used throughout this book. Table 1.1 provides a capsule summary of the definitions.

Health

There are a number of ways in which *health* can be defined. Just ask three individuals, and you are likely to get three different definitions. For example, one person might define health as "not feeling sick." But that seems be a rather limited definition because one can feel perfectly well and be harboring a serious or even fatal condition such as cancer. Another person may say health is "the absence of symptoms and signs of disease"; however, having no symptoms is not the same as radiant or optimal health. Someone else may define it in broader, more holistic terms, a definition that may be close to the way the Word Health Organization (WHO) defined health more than 50 years ago. The WHO defined health as "a state of complete physical, mental, and social well-being and not merely the absence of disease or infirmity" (Word Health Organization, 1948, p. 1). This definition represents a vision that few individuals, much less nations, have attained. An even more inclusive definition would add the spiritual dimension. It may be useful to think of the

TABLE 1.1   Definitions of Basic Terms

TERM	DEFINITION
Health	Attaining and maintaining a state of complete physical, mental, and social well-being, not merely the absence of disease or infirmity.
Health education	Learning experiences that assist individuals in making informed decisions in order to increase their health status.
Health promotion	The science and art of helping individuals change their lifestyles to reflect a state of optimal health, which involves balancing the physical, emotional, social, spiritual, and intellectual aspects of life.
Wellness	A way of life oriented toward the optimal level of health and well-being that an individual is *capable* of achieving. It is related to, but independent of, health; as such wellness is a continuum ranging from low to high that is *parallel* to health, which is also a continuum ranging from low to high.
Health counseling	A broad, encompassing term that describes various approaches and methods for assisting individuals to reduce or to prevent the progression of disease processes, as well as to improve and to promote health status and functioning. There are five types: medical care counseling, patient care counseling, health promotion counseling, health-focused counseling, and health-focused psychotherapy.

definitions of health as spanning a continuum from "absence of symptoms" to "complete, optimal well-being."

Implications for Health Care.   The way the term *health* is viewed and defined is more than a matter of semantics. Definitions are important because the way health is viewed has a direct bearing on the type and extent of health care that will be authorized and provided. For example, when health is viewed as the absence of the symptoms of disease, "disease management" is the type of health care that is provided. Not surprisingly, most health maintenance organizations (HMOs) define health as the absence of symptoms and will authorize and pay for disease management–oriented treatment but, typically, will not pay for health-promotion services. A few more-enlightened HMOs, however, will authorize and pay for some types of preventive and health-promotion services because they recognize that such services are cost-effective.

Health Education

Health education has been defined in several ways. The Glanz, Lewis, and Rimer book (1999) surveys several definitions, including:

- Griffin (1972)—"attempts to close the gap between what is known about optimum health practice and that which is actually practiced"
- Simond (1976)—"bringing about behavioral change in individuals, groups and larger populations from behaviors that are presumed to be detrimental to health, to behaviors that are conducive to present and future health"
- Green (1980)—"any combination of learning experiences designed to facilitate voluntary adaptations of behavior conducive to health"

Common to these definitions are instruction, voluntary involvement, informed behavior change, and the goal of health status improvement. Beyond informing people about instructional activities to improve health status, health education can also include organizational, environmental, economic, and policy components. For the purpose of this book, however, health education is viewed as "learning experiences that assist individuals in making informed decisions in order to increase their health status."

Health Promotion

The term *health promotion* is used with increasing frequency today. What does it mean? *Health promotion* has been defined as "the science and art of helping people change their lifestyle to move toward a state of optimal health. Optimal health is defined as a balance of physical, emotional, social, spiritual, and intellectual health" (O'Donnell, 1989, p. 3). It is interesting to note that this rather holistic definition reflects the editorial policy of the *American Journal of Health Promotion*. *Physical health* refers to nutrition, medical self-care, and control of substance abuse. *Emotional health* refers to care for an emotional crisis and stress management. *Social health* refers to communities, families, and friends, while *intellectual health* refers to educational achievement and career development. Finally, *spiritual health* refers to self-transcendence and includes love, hope, and charity.

Unlike disease management, which addresses the symptoms and signs of actual disease processes, health promotion addresses the personal, modifiable lifestyle habits and practices that lead to disease processes. Almost half of all premature deaths in the United States are the result of lifestyle-related problems. Many of these deaths could be prevented and the quality of life for millions can be enhanced through lifestyle changes such as regular exercise, eating nutritious foods, avoiding tobacco and excess alcohol, learning to manage stress, clarifying lifestyle values, and achieving a sense of fulfillment in life. Health counseling is a primary means of accomplishing this goal.

Lifestyle change can be facilitated through a combination of efforts to enhance awareness, change behavior, and create environments that support good health practices. Of the three, supportive environments seem to have a significant impact on bringing about lasting changes. Effective health counseling involves all three.

Wellness

Wellness and health promotion are often used interchangeably, which is unfortunate because each represents different, although related, realities. Halbert Dunn, M.D., who has been called the architect of the modern wellness movement, defines *wellness* as "an integrated method of functioning which is oriented toward maximizing the potential of which the individual is capable" (Dunn, 1961, p. 4). William Hettler, M.D. (1984), known as the father of modern wellness, views wellness as a process of making choices for a successful existence. More recently, Myers, Sweeney, and Witmer (2000) define wellness as "a way of life oriented toward an optimal state of health and well-being . . . that each individual is capable of achieving" (p. 252). Common to all three definitions are choice and capability, where *capability* refers to the extent to which an optimal state of well-being is possible and achievable.

Pilch (1985) emphasizes that both choice and capability are essential to understanding wellness. Interestingly, he distinguishes health from wellness and envisions *wellness* as a continuum ranging from low to high that is *parallel* to health, which is also a continuum ranging from low to high. Accordingly, Pilch contends that individuals who are successful, conditioned athletes but use their strength to abuse and intimidate others might have achieved a high level of health but would only be considered to have achieved a low level of wellness. This is because such individuals have not chosen to "put their lives in proper perspective . . . to discover the true meaning of life" (1985, p. 2). For Pilch, abusiveness would be incompatible with a wellness perspective wherein life is viewed as sacred.

Wellness is related to, but is independent of, health and health status. Wellness and health status might be compared to two parallel sets of train tracks on which two trains—health and wellness—can move in the same or opposite directions at the same speed or at different speeds. The contention in this book is that while wellness is similar to health status, wellness can coexist with chronic disease or even terminal illness. Thus, individuals can choose to experience a high level of wellness irrespective of their health status. The basic *choice* to be made is to adopt, or not to adopt, a positive, life-giving attitude and to endeavor to integrate, or not integrate, the past with the present.

Another contention here is that individuals with high-level wellness can engage in preventive health behaviors (e.g., eating a healthy diet and exercising) to the extent to which they are able, but that such behaviors are not necessarily essential to wellness. Rather, wellness reflects an individual's life-affirming attitudes toward his or her body and others, and the integration of these attitudes into a philosophy of life.

Furthermore, the basic goal of all health counseling interventions should be to improve health status and/or wellness, whichever the client is capable of achieving, to the degree to which it is possible for him or her to do so. Thus, *capacity* and *choice* are two key determinants of wellness. To this end, it is essential for both clients and health counselors to come away from any such a discussion with the following four basic understandings:

1. There is basic a difference between health status and wellness, even though there are similarities.
2. Wellness can coexist with chronic disease or even terminal illness.
3. The wellness perspective described here allows every individual irrespective of their health status—whether mentally retarded, chronically ill, or terminally ill—to achieve a high level of wellness.
4. The primary goal of health counseling is always to increase wellness, although optimizing health status, cure, or stabilization may be related goals.

Figure 1.1 illustrates the relationship between one's health status level and wellness. Individual A manifests a high level of both health status and wellness. On the other hand, individual B manifests a high level of health status and a low level of wellness. For example, B might be a highly conditioned professional athlete who is in top physical shape and practices excellent health behaviors. At the same time, however, this athlete uses his physical strength to intimidate other players and forces himself sexually on women, so he would be considered to have achieved low-level wellness despite having high-level health status.

Implications for Health Care.   Typically, corporate- and community-sponsored health-promotion programs are called "wellness programs" or "wellness centers." But how many of these programs actually adopt the wellness perspective as articulated by Pilch and others? Observations show that many such programs are more health-focused than wellness-focused. Often, a program's facilities, activity schedule, and staff qualifications are reflective of whether it is health- or wellness-focused. True wellness programs, in the sense described here, can include fitness equipment, swimming pools, and exercise rooms; offer aerobic dance classes, hatha yoga, and nutrition courses; and are staffed by exercise physiologists, nutritionists, and personal trainers. While health-focused programs typically have

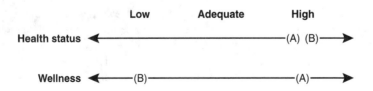

FIGURE 1.1   The Relationship between Health Status Level and Wellness

such equipment, programs, and/or staff, these things are not essential for wellness programs. The essential and defining feature of a true wellness program is that it assists individuals—irrespective of whether they have a chronic degenerative illness, a terminal illness, or are able-bodied—to achieve more life-affirming attitudes toward their bodies; in other words, they attain a higher level of wellness.

A necessary tension exists between the wellness and the health-promotion perspectives that presents a formidable challenge to health-care providers. Individuals whose training and professional identity is principally in exercise physiology or nutrition are unlikely to find this challenge interesting and comfortable. However, those who are competent to provide health counseling have the training and experience to find this challenge not only interesting but gratifying.

Counseling for Wellness.   Healthy life attitudes, positive health behaviors, and an individual's willingness can be fostered by the health counseling process, particularly the counselor's encouragement and modeling of health and wellness. Health counseling can facilitate the expression of healthful life attitudes and a change toward positive health behaviors, fostering wellness. The primary goal of health counseling is to increase wellness while a related goal is to increase health status to the extent that it is possible. A counselor's expertise in dealing with one's barriers to change and in tailoring interventions both changes and validates the client's adoption of the wellness perspective in his or her life.

Culture and Wellness.   It is important to note that the concept of wellness itself rests within a set of cultural expectations and values. Considerable variation may exist between the concepts underlying Western ideas of wellness and the concepts underlying other traditional systems of healing. "American" culture, for example, has been viewed as overemphasizing the role of the individual at the expense of cultural, social, and political factors beyond an individual's control, which nonetheless strongly affect wellness (Bishop, 1998). Differing from an individualistic perspective, clients with an Afrocentric worldview may believe that wellness and health spring from a harmony and balance with the natural order that come from a connection and awareness with one's cultural heritage (Phillips, 1990).

Health counselors, in looking to understand their clients, need to be open to the variety of wellness perspectives that exist. Cultural factors influence biopsychosocial processes in the etiology, symptom manifestation and report, diagnosis, assessment, intervention, and success of treatment outcomes (Mukherji, 1995). Traditional forms of wellness recognize that illness can influence one's sense of self and emphasize the holistic concept of healing. The holistic concept of health can extend beyond the individual to incorporate members of one's family and community. From this perspective, the health of an individual is virtually indistinguishable from the health of one's community (Garrett & Myers, 1996). If a culture or community is experiencing distress, members of it invariably will suffer. Therefore, across diagnosis and intervention, health counselors need to be continually aware of the larger cultural context and social climate that surround clients and the distress they are experiencing. From a health counseling perspective, however, most interventions in the clinical realm occur at the individual level.

Health Counseling

So what exactly is health counseling? First of all, health counseling is a form of health education. *Health counseling* is a broad, encompassing term that describes various approaches and methods for assisting individuals to reduce or to prevent the progression of disease processes, as well as to improve and to promote health status and functioning. Rather than being a new or separate health-care specialty, health counseling is more an attitude and orientation toward health and well-being. The next section describes the five types.

THE FIVE TYPES OF HEALTH COUNSELING

Were it simply a matter of providing patients with health-related information about lifestyle change, the task of health counseling would be relatively simple. Unfortunately, studies of the effectiveness of lifestyle change programs indicate that there is no one-to-one relationship between a client's knowledge about the need and the means for change and a client's subsequent behavior change (Janis, 1983). While health information is necessary for those providing health counseling aimed at proper nutrition, exercise, management of stress, smoking cessation, and control of alcohol intake, it is seldom sufficient to achieve health behavior change (Jordan-Marsh, Gilbert, Ford, and Kleeman, 1984). Effective health counseling requires an understanding of the barriers to change and the requisite counseling and psychotherapy strategies and skills to accomplish such change.

There are at least five different approaches to the practice of health counseling. The first and second approaches or types, medical and patient care counseling, are provided by physicians and physician extenders in a medical or clinic setting. A third approach, health-promotion counseling, is used by specialists who provide counseling in private practice or corporate or community settings. Health-focused counseling provided by the behavioral health professions on a referral basis is the fourth type. The fifth approach, health-focused psychotherapy, is a variant of the fourth. Table 1.2 summarizes the focus/concern, conditions of change, and the intervention strategies associated with each type.

Medical Care Counseling

In the medical setting, physicians typically broach a health matter, ask a few questions, give focused information, and prescribe some behavior change, all within a very short time frame. Usually, patients are given the prescription to change behaviors (e.g., lose weight, stop smoking, take up exercise). The goal of this type of counseling is to improve health status by having patients implement the health prescription or recommendation. Change or improvement is assumed to occur because the patient follows the provider's prescription. This approach also assumes that patients comply with health prescriptions because of their confidence and belief in the provider's expertise and authority. Typically this type of counseling involves some limited advice as to the need for the change and some general guidelines to follow. There usually is a minimal degree of education and little or no monitoring. If the patient is not able to follow the prescription, for whatever reason, referral may be made for "patient education"—patient care counseling.

TABLE 1.2   Types of Health Counseling

COUNSELING TYPE	FOCUS/CONCERN	CHANGE CONDITIONS	CHANGE STRATEGIES
Medical care counseling	improve health status by implementing a health prescription	change occurs because the patient follows the provider's health prescription based on the patient's confidence in the providers' expertise and authority	health provider recommends or prescribes a course of treatment; involves minimal degree of education and monitoring
Patient care counseling	improve patient understanding, skill, and compliance with health prescription	change occurs because the patient sufficiently understands and has practiced/mastered the prescribed change	individual and/or group educational methods; may include assessment of understanding, skill mastery, and monitoring compliance
Health-promotion counseling	improve lifestyle, health behaviors and/or health status in light of psychological principles	change occurs because the client collaborates in process of establishing, practicing, and monitoring a tailored intervention	assessment; establishing a collaborative relationship with client; and interventions tailored to client need/expectations; relapse prevention
Health-focused counseling	improve lifestyle, health behaviors and/ or health status by increasing adherence to a health prescription when barriers are present or anticipated	change occurs because the client is sufficiently engaged and collaborates with the tailored intervention process, and barriers (intrapersonal, interpersonal, social and/or cultural) are recognized and dealt with	assessment of client need, strengths, and readiness; engaging client in the treatment process; focus on tailored interventions; relapse prevention; use of cognitive restructuring and other strategies to reduce barriers to change;
Health-focused psychotherapy	improve health status or acceptance of life-threatening or progressively debilitating illness	change, usually acceptance of illness, occurs because relevant current and early life conflicts, trauma, and failed expectations are psychotherapeutically processed sufficiently	formal psychotherapeutic strategies and tactics such as clarification, confrontation, interpretation, cognitive restructuring, and working through

Case Example

A recent physical examination indicated that Jack Impana's blood pressure and his choles-terol level were in abnormal ranges. In addition, Jack's weight had creeped up to 220 pounds, 35 more than his ideal weight. Because of these risk factors and a family history of cardiovascular disease—his father had high blood pressure and died following a heart attack—his physician, Dr. Jonas Simonton, told Jack that his risk for stroke and heart attack were very high. During a scheduled 30-minute appointment, Dr. Simonton described two treatment options that Jack could pursue. The first was a conservative approach—exercise, weight loss, and dietary restriction of salt and fatty foods. The second was a more aggressive approach involving two cardiac medications. Although Jack wasn't initially all that keen about exercise and weight loss, Dr. Simonton suggested that if Jack made a commitment to a program of moderate exercise, he could reduce or delay the onset of cardiovascular disease and possibly forgo the need for medication. Jack opted to begin with the conservative approach and if that didn't work he would take the medication route.

Jack was given a detailed diet plan and a handout with information on a suggested exercise plan. He agreed to follow the diet plan and exercise 4 times a week for 30 minutes and to lose approximately 1 pound per week. He was to meet with his physician again in 4 weeks to review his progress. During the first week Jack bought an exercise bike and started eating a more sensible diet. At his next appointment Jack was somewhat embarrassed and discouraged to report that he hadn't really followed the diet or exercise plan—he couldn't find time to exercise except on weekends and had lost no weight. Jack's physician complimented him on the efforts he had made, such as getting and using the exercise bike a little, but suggested that daily walking might be better. He urged Jack to continue on the diet and exercise plan for another 2 weeks.

■ ■ ■ ■ ■

Jack's response to medical care counseling is not unusual. Some individuals are ready, willing, and able to achieve lifestyle changes based on the general guidelines provided by Dr. Simonton during medical care counseling. However, many others fail or are only partially successful in achieving their goal. For that reason, physicians often refer individuals like Jack to patient care counseling.

Patient Care Counseling

Patient education, also called psychoeducation, is related to medical care counseling and typically is provided by physician extenders such as nurses, nurse practitioners, or a medical assistant in a clinical setting. Patient education provided by physician extenders tends to be longer in duration, more specific, and focused on content. It may or may not be based on an assessment but is usually directed at a specific health concern that the physician deems problematic. Less often the assessment involves a formal health-risk appraisal, which may or may not be tailored to the patient's needs and expectations. More properly, health counseling provided by a health-promotion specialist is known as *patient care counseling.*

Patient education encompasses any health education experience planned by both the health-care provider and the client to meet the client's specific learning needs, interests, and capabilities (Squyres, 1980). It is a process of education and activity based on an intentional exchange and sharing of information such that the patient's behavior is positively affected. Patient care counseling is best explained as a communication activity that occurs within the context of a counselor/client encounter that influences client behavior toward improved health. It includes a variety of strategies designed not only to facilitate behavioral change, but also to help individuals to identify their social support system and to maintain their change achievement over a long period of time. It is much more complex than the printed handouts or audiovisual aids so often associated with patient care counseling; in short, personal interaction is a key dimension.

The purpose of patient education is to improve patient understanding, skill, and compliance with a health prescription. It provides patients with sufficient information in order to understand the factors that promote or threaten health so that they have a better opportunity to make informed choices in their lives (Levant, 1986). In addition, patient care counseling provides the support, as well as the technical assistance necessary, to help individuals carry out their choices. It is assumed that change occurs because the patient sufficiently understands and has adequately practiced or mastered the prescribed change regimen. Assessment typically involves estimating the patient's understanding of the need for treatment, the treatment regimen, and the degree of mastery of any requisite skills necessary for compliance with the regimen. A variety of intervention strategies can be used, including individual or group educational methods. Monitoring compliance is essential for success. As compared to medical care counseling, there is considerably more education, assessment, and monitoring during patient care counseling.

Case Example

Melissa Garcia, a 39-year-old married mother of three, was taken by ambulance to the emergency room at Community General Medical Center after her husband found her on the floor of their home, clutching her throat and gasping for breath. The ER physician who evaluated her for acute respiratory distress diagnosed her with bronchial asthma. Within a minute or two of injecting her with corticosteroids, the asthma attack stopped. This was the first time Mrs. Garcia had experienced such an attack. The physician wrote an order for oral corticosteroids and left an order for a nurse to teach her how to use an inhaler; since using it correctly is a challenge for many, instruction is mandatory. A nurse gave her a brief lesson. After three tries, Mrs. Garcia seemed to be able to use the inhaler adequately. She was sent home with an inhaler, another medication, and written instructions to follow.

Up to this point, essentially this patient was provided medical care counseling. However, because this type of counseling—and in particular the use of an inhaler—took place in an emergency room situation amid the distress associated with an asthma attack, medical care counseling is usually insufficient to ensure effective adherence to a treatment regimen. Practically speaking, this means that most patients taught how to use an inhaler for the first time in an ER setting have trouble using it correctly when at home. Accordingly, it is Community General's policy to provide patient care counseling for all patients who come to the emergency room with their first acute asthma attack.

Patient care counseling for asthma involves one or more follow-up home visits by a Community General nurse/patient care counselor. Sydney Rosen, RN, met with Mrs. Garcia the next afternoon in her home and followed a standard asthma control counseling protocol. He reviewed the diagnosis and treatment of asthma; went over the patient's instruction sheet regarding medications, inhaler use, and preventive measures; and answered the patient's questions. Then he asked Mrs. Garcia to show him how she had used the inhaler earlier that day. The nurse then gave feedback and more instruction and modeled correct use of the inhaler. Mrs. Garcia was asked to practice using the inhaler under the watchful eye of the patient care counselor who provided corrective feedback until she felt fully confident in the effective use of the inhaler. Many ERs use a similar patient care counseling acute asthma protocol because learning to use an inhaler in familiar and less stressful surroundings significantly increases patient success and greatly reduces the incidence of relapse and return to the emergency room for further costly treatment.

■ ■ ■ ■ ■

Health-Promotion Counseling

Quite different from both physicians and physician extenders, health-promotion specialists usually begin with a general screening assessment such as a formal health-risk appraisal instrument. Individuals being assessed may not see themselves in the patient role nor present with signs or symptoms of disease. At its best, this approach to health counseling should be tailored to individuals' needs and expectations and also identify their level of readiness for change and barriers to adherence to lifestyle change. More properly, health counseling provided by health-promotion specialists could be called *health-promotion counseling.*

The purpose of such counseling is to improve lifestyle and health behaviors. It is assumed that change will occur because of clients' collaboration in the process of establishing, practicing, and monitoring a tailored health-promotion intervention. Commonly interventions are tailored to clients' needs and expectations. Increasingly, relapse prevention is a component in successful health-promotion endeavors.

Lifestyle changes usually involve the development of health-oriented behaviors; development of these behaviors depends as much on specific skills as it does on factual information. Although individuals need to know something about the health issues they are addressing, they also need to believe that they know *how* to change their behaviors. Because personal skills are so crucial, health-promotion counseling uses educational methods aimed toward skill building.

The literature on changing health behaviors suggests that a sense of personal control seems to be at the heart of success in optimizing one's health. Because this sense of control seems basic to health enhancement, health-promotion counseling uses interventions designed to increase clients' perceptions of control and self-efficacy.

Case Example

Tom Baroni was referred by Jefferson Sims, Tom's financial advisor, to Jennifer Chen, Ph.D., for health-promotion counseling. Mr. Sims, who had engaged in a course of counseling with Dr. Chen, was quite pleased with the results. Tom said he wanted help to better manage stress in his life and to improve his overall health and well-being. Baroni, a general contractor who builds 10 to 15 office buildings a year, is 41, has been married for 14 years, and has two children. He is also a part-time soccer coach at his children's school.

For the past year he has not had the energy and stamina that marked his earlier years. Tom admits his job is stressful, but no more so than it has been for several years. In addition to his declining energy levels, and occasional periods of moodiness and irritability, he logged 7 sick days during the past year for various maladies, compared with previous years when he took only 2 sick days. Needless to say, sick days are very costly for self-employed individuals, and because he is the boss and coordinates employees' work, missed days means lower productivity and less profit for Tom's company. Being away from work only increases his stress levels to which he responds by eating, subsequently gaining weight. Tom loves his family, his job, and coaching soccer and is hoping Dr. Chen can help him find more energy and balance in his life.

■ ■ ■ ■ ■

Health-Focused Counseling

Behavioral health professionals, such as social workers, professional counselors, psychologists, psychiatric nurses, and psychiatrists, with formal training and experience in counseling and psychotherapy, tend to approach health counseling in a different way than health-promotion specialists, physicians, and patient education personnel do. Usually, clients referred for this type of health counseling have been unsuccessful with patient care counseling or health-promotion counseling. Invariably, such individuals have problems adhering to a change program because of internal or external barriers.

The goal of health-focused counseling is to reduce symptoms and to improve health status, to improve lifestyle and positive health behaviors, and/or to increase adherence to a health prescription. It is assumed that change occurs because the client is sufficiently engaged and collaborates with the tailored intervention process, and because barriers to change (e.g., intrapersonal, interpersonal, social, and/or cultural) have been recognized and dealt with. Effective health-focused counseling requires that the client's readiness for change be sufficient before proceeding with the prescribed change effort. Accordingly, the counselor must be proficient in the use of motivational counseling strategies to promote readiness (Miller & Rollnick, 1991). The assessment done using this approach to health counseling is more extensive than in the first two approaches and includes an evaluation of personality patterns, motivation and readiness for change, strengths, and barriers—psychological, relational, situational, and cultural—that have or could impede adherence to a change program. The emphasis of health-focused counseling is on tailored interventions and relapse prevention. Several psychotherapeutic interventions, such as reframing and cognitive restructuring as well as other systemic strategies, are used to reduce barriers to change. More properly, health counseling provided by a behavioral health professional is known as *health-focused counseling.*

Because health is impacted by social environment, health-focused counseling tends to broaden the scope of the counseling process beyond the individual to include the social system. Interventions are designed to help the client build social support and, if possible, lessen environmental stressors. Furthermore, the aim of health-focused counseling is to build up the individual's ability to engage in self-management, which in turn requires a repertoire of health-oriented skills, a belief in one's own ability to address life's challenges, and an environment that encourages positive development.

There is much more to be said about the theoretical basis and actual practice of health-focused counseling; the section that follows the next case example briefly differentiates it from health-focused psychotherapy. A subsequent chapter describes and illustrates the curative elements and stages and the actual practice of this approach to health counseling.

Case Example

During his follow-up appointment with Dr. Simonton 2 weeks later, Jack Impana indicated that while he really did make an effort to adhere to the health changes, at least on some days, he thought he needed something more than a diet plan and exercise prescription. Dr. Simonton agreed and referred him for health-focused counseling. Jack met with James Dietrich, a licensed professional counselor specializing in health-focused counseling, for 10 minutes later that afternoon. Mr. Dietrich briefly described his philosophy for counseling, outlined how they would work together to achieve the health changes, answered Jack's questions, and scheduled 6 weekly individual sessions. One group session, a relapse-prevention group consisting of other health counseling clients, was also scheduled.

During their first session, Mr. Dietrich completed a health education assessment which consisted of Jack's health beliefs and readiness for change. Jack and Mr. Dietrich worked collaboratively to tailor a plan for meeting specific weight, diet, and exercise objectives for each upcoming week. For the most part, Jack was able to meet those objectives and was heartened to see his blood pressure and cholesterol levels drop into the normal range by the sixth session. Monthly booster sessions were scheduled with Mr. Dietrich for the next 4 months and then quarterly after that for the next year. Jack also continued to see Dr. Simonton for medical checkups every 4 to 6 months. Needless to say, Dr. Simonton was pleased with Jack's progress.

■ ■ ■ ■ ■

Health-Focused Psychotherapy

A related approach to health counseling offered by some behavioral health providers, particularly psychotherapists, is known as *health-focused psychotherapy.* Here the individuals referred for this type of intervention have difficulty coping with the pain or disability associated a severe or life-threatening illness or have difficulty accepting their health condition or status. This type of health counseling has little or no concern for health promotion or disease prevention. Psychotherapeutic interventions tend to focus more on core personality dynamics than health-focused counseling does. Assessment is more consistent with traditional psychotherapeutic parameters than is health-focused counseling. Nevertheless, education on health matters is a part of this approach.

There are a number of similarities as well as differences between health-focused psychotherapy and health-focused counseling. This section explores the similarities and differences as they relate to strategies, skills, and concepts. Briefly stated, strategies for individual psychotherapy center on formal, ongoing, scheduled appointments—usually 50-minute sessions—in a private practice or mental health office or consulting room. On the other hand, strategies for health counseling are much more diverse, ranging from scheduled and ongoing encounters in a private practice or physician's office to unscheduled, occasional sessions at someone's bedside or in a hospital clinic. Although the specific counseling skills and interventions of psychotherapy and health counseling are quite similar, their focus tends to be different. Even though concepts, such as adherence, psychoeducation, relapse prevention, and systems influence, are common to both psychotherapy and health counseling, they are seldom discussed in the psychotherapy literature. Since these four concepts are so important to health counseling, they will be discussed further in subsequent chapters in reference to topics such as nutrition, exercise, and smoking cessation.

In psychotherapy, a confidential and more intense relationship develops between a client with emotional and behavioral symptoms and/or dysfunction and the skilled therapist. The therapist uses verbal and nonverbal methods to effect symptom relief and to improve the client's ability to cope with internal and external stressors and with his or her relationships with others. Frank (1984) believes that the majority of psychotherapy patients are demoralized and that encouragement is the primary nonspecific therapeutic effect of treatment. Specific treatment methods are described as supportive, diagnostic, analytic, and reconstructive in nature. Although "talking therapy" is the mainstay of treatment, it may be supplemented with adjuncts such as dream analysis, biofeedback, hypnosis, or psychological testing. In addition, some medically trained psychotherapists may prescribe medications or other adjunctive somatic treatments. Traditional approaches to psychotherapy usually involve regularly scheduled sessions with the same therapist for months or even years. However, newer, brief therapy approaches involve shorter time frames often only 8 to 20 sessions.

Compared to health-focused psychotherapy, health-focused counseling involves a more action-oriented and participative relationship between a client who needs to reduce health risks or change lifestyle patterns and the skilled counselor who can facilitate acquisition and maintenance of the health changes. The duration of treatment is usually short term. This approach is more oriented toward prevention than is either medical care counseling or health-focused psychotherapy. Treatment methods not only involve information-giving and prescriptions for lifestyle change but also include a number of traditional psychotherapeutic interventions as well as interventions unique to health counseling.

Case Example

Mary Seagraves was in a rage and wasted no time letting her coworkers know about the just-posted corporate policy and its implications for her and them. Employees would no longer be allowed to smoke in the building where she had worked and puffed for more than 10 years. Several times, Mary had tried to quit smoking on her own, but she had not been successful. She had tried hypnosis, nicotine gum, nicotine patches, Zyban—an antidepressant reportedly helpful in smoking cessation—and group counseling geared to smoking cessation. The only thing she remembered about that group was others' insistence that she was an "angry woman." She believed that she was now at a turning point. She was unwilling to step outside during rain- and snowstorms when the urge to smoke overtook her, but she didn't believe that smokers' complaints would bring about a reversal in the new policy.

But it wasn't just the new policy. At her last annual physical exam, her physician had told her there appeared to be a spot on her chest X-ray that could be malignant. She never followed up for additional tests to rule out lung cancer. Now she felt she really had to do something. She needs help in making one of the most difficult life changes—giving up cigarettes forever. But hadn't she lost enough already, her infant son and her husband in a fiery car accident. That was nearly 5 years ago but she was still angry and rageful. Given the history of several failed attempts to quit smoking, what appears a grief reaction or complicated bereavement, and an anger-prone personality, Mary's problem is better-suited to a health-focused psychotherapy approach.

■ ■ ■ ■ ■

As described here, there a five somewhat different forms of health counseling practice. Each requires different skills, training, and experience. Nevertheless, all five counseling approaches share a common element, namely a focus on improvement of health and/or wellness.

Health-focused counseling is emphasized in this book since it is the type most commonly practiced by professional counselors and psychotherapists. Rather than imply or contend that it is a new theory or specialty, we simply suggest that health-focused counseling is essentially an *attitude* toward health counseling. This attitude reflects integrative, biopsychosocial, and proactive ways of viewing and working with patients and clients. A holistic and biopsychosocial orientation means that the focus is on the client's health status, interpersonal and social competence, as well as psychological and physical well-being. It is not just focused on the psychological and emotional aspects that tend to be the focus of the majority of theories and systems of counseling. The biopsychosocial perspective has been articulated by Engel (1977) and is clearly based on systems thinking; health-focused counseling is called biopsychosocial therapy (Sperry, 1988) when it relates to treatment issues. In addition to having this holistic perspective, health-focused counseling is proactive; that is, not only does it emphasize restoration of previous levels of health and well-being or adjustment, which is primarily a reactive function, but it also emphasizes prevention and increasing an individual's level of development and functioning.

PROFESSIONAL PREPARATION

Who is qualified to provide effective health counseling and what training and credentials are required? At this particular point in history, the matter of the training and credentialing of those providing health counseling is beginning to engender discussion, given the increasing movement toward professionalization of health care. Needless to say, while this section highlights some of the parameters of this discussion, it is not intended to provide a proposed set of qualifications and standards for the practice of health counseling, much less to offer the definitive or last word on what will surely be a spirited discussion for some time to come. The matter of professional training and credentialing involves both academic and political considerations. The criterion—"scope of practice is limited based on training and experience"—is one starting point for such a discussion. Unfortunately, while it seems to be have considerable face validity as a criterion, it is fraught with various interpretations and involves both academic and political considerations.

One value of describing the five different types of health counseling earlier in this chapter is being able to recognize that certain counseling forms have, for the most part, already addressed the question of scope of practice. For example, medical care counseling is within the scope of professional training for physicians and other designated licensed health-care professionals such as physicians assistants and nurse practitioners. Similarly, a case could be made that health-focused psychotherapy is already within the scope of practice of those licensed for the practice of psychiatry and psychotherapy (e.g., psychiatrists, clinical and counseling psychologists, social workers, mental health counselors). It seems that patient care counseling is usually provided by registered nurses, registered dieticians, nutritionists, and certified health education specialists. Others, such as physicians, physicians assistants, and licensed mental health-care professionals (e.g., psychologists), do not seem drawn to this type of health counseling.

Where the matter of training and credentialing and scope of practice is the least clear is with health-promotion counseling and health-focused counseling, at least in the form designated earlier for both. Individuals with a wide variety of training, credentialing, and experience are providing health-promotion counseling, including those with recognized licensure or certification (e.g., certified health education specialists, registered dieticians, registered nurses, nurse practitioners, licensed mental health counselors, and other licensed or certified psychotherapists). Whether health-promotion counseling, as described here, is within the scope of practice of these individuals, or is beyond that scope and requires additional training and supervised experience, has yet to be answered. Nevertheless, many others, such as nutritionists, health educators, human resource specialists, and so on, also do not have recognized licensure and credentials.

The question of adequacy of training and credentialing to provide health-focused counseling, at least as the preceding designates it, is similarly murky and uncertain. Health-focused counseling requires the capacity to use an extensive array of client assessment methods as well as sophisticated and tailored interventions. The methods and interventions include the use of psychotherapeutic strategies, such as cognitive restructuring, reframing, and even interpretation, to reduce intrapersonal and interpersonal barriers to change and to facilitate the attitude change process involved in fostering wellness. Arguably, this suggests that its scope of practice is probably limited to those with advanced training and licensure or certification in professional counseling and psychotherapy. In other words, providing health-focused counseling appears to be outside of the scope of practice for certified health education specialists, registered dieticians, and even physicians and nurse practitioners without the specialty certification in psychotherapy.

Again, as noted earlier, the intent of this section is simply to raise the question of training and credentialing within the context of the five designated approaches or types of health counseling. Our intention was not to provide a definite proposal or an answer to the question. Finally, further discussion of the question of qualifications for health counseling is beyond the scope of this book.

MULTICULTURAL ISSUES AND HEALTH COUNSELING

When considering health, individual differences, social issues and cultural variables are significant factors (Lewis, 2002). Cultural variables, such as racial background, ethnicity, gender, sexual orientation, socioeconomic status, and ability, are organizing factors of an individual's identity, lifestyle, and health status. Additionally, it is crucial for health counselors to know that any illness or health behavior occurs within a cultural context. The culture of a client can provide resources for coping with illness and hospitalization as well as influence a client's willingness to seeking counseling and accept interventions (Canino & Guarnaccia, 1997; Leong, Wagner, & Tata, 1995). Cultural context influences how pain and discomfort are caused, experienced, and expressed, as well as the consequences of suffering (Lewis, 2002). Any given health-associated factor is likely to vary across cultural groups.

Until very recently, the idea of actively including cultural variables within the assessment and intervention process has been disregarded. It is common for many health-care professionals to fail to take a client's cultural background into account, which can result in misattribution of a behavior and a lack of understanding between client and counselor. Nowadays, it is increasing clear that effective, ethical, and respectful treatment is accomplished through careful and purposeful inclusion and consideration of cultural factors and the cultural context of treatment. Those involved in health counseling and health-promotion counseling must ascertain where their own cultural biases lie and avoid centering treatment exclusively on themselves and their biased cultural position (Lewis, 2002).

CONCLUDING NOTE

This chapter has defined and described health, health promotion, wellness, the various types of health counseling, and three reasons why the need for health counseling has become increasingly evident during the past decade. Much of the emphasis here was on the contributions of theory and research to counseling and psychotherapy as effective ways of working with clients on health-related issues. It was noted that wellness, defined as the optimal state of health and well-being an individual is capable of achieving, differs from health and health status. It was described as a continuum ranging from low to high that is parallel to health, which is also on a continuum ranging from low to high. This means that wellness can coexist with chronic disease or even terminal illness. Thus, individuals can choose to experience a high level of wellness irrespective of their health status. The basic choice is to adopt, or not to adopt, a positive, life-giving attitude and to endeavor to integrate, or not integrate, the past with the present. Wellness depends on the individual's choice to adopt a healthy lifestyle and his or her capacity to achieve it.

Other key points about the practice of health counseling also were emphasized. One is that health counseling is a broad, encompassing endeavor that spans the continuum from medical care to patient education to psychoeducation to health-focused counseling to health-focused psychotherapy. While each of these types differs considerably, education (i.e., health education) is a central component of each type. Second, is that professional counselors and psychotherapists can, with some additional training and experience, extend the scope of their professional practices to provide all five types of health counseling; they are likely to find the practice of health-focused counseling and/or health-focused psychotherapy the most professionally challenging. Nevertheless, the other types of health counseling can be performed by other health-care providers, especially when those providers have the training, experience, and credentialing to extend their practices' scope.

Those who practice health counseling, regardless of the setting in which they are employed, need to be able to help clients make health-related attitude and behavioral changes involving both health promotion and wellness principles. Health counseling is an action-oriented process through which a helper enables a patient or client to make changes that will lead each person in the direction of improved health and well-being. This process depends less on the provider's job title or employment setting than it does on his or her point of view. Health counseling takes place in medical practices, human service agencies, private practices, workplaces, and a variety of other settings. In short, some form of health counseling can take place wherever a provider with a biopsychosocial perspective practices.

REFERENCES

Bishop, G. D. (1998). East meets West: Illness cognition and behavior in Singapore. *Applied Psychology: An International Review, 47,* 519–534.

Canino, G. & Guarnaccia, P. (1997). Methodological challenges in the assessment of Hispanic children and adolescents. *Applied Developmental Science, 1,* 124–134.

Dunn, H. (1961). *High-level wellness.* Arlington, VA: R. W. Beatty.

Engel, G. (1977). The need for a new medical model: A challenge to biomedical science. *Science, 196,* 129–136.

Frank, J. D. (1984). Therapeutic components of all psychotherapies. In J. Myers (Ed.), *Cures by psy-*

chotherapy. What affects change? New York: Praeger.

Garrett, M. T., & Myers, J. E. (1996). The rule of opposites: A paradigm for counseling Native Americans. *Journal of Multicultural Counseling and Development, 24,* 89–104.

Glanz, K., Lewis, F., & Rimer, B. (Eds.). (1999). *Health behavior and health education: Theory, research, and practice* (2nd ed.). San Francisco: Jossey-Bass.

Hettler, W. (1984). Wellness: Encouraging a lifetime pursuit of excellence. *Health Values, 8,* 13–17.

Janis, I. (1983). *Short-term counseling: Guidelines based on recent research.* New Haven: Yale University Press.

Jordan-Marsh, M., Gilbert, J., Ford, J., & Kleeman, C. (1984). Life-style intervention: A conceptual framework. *Patient Education and Counseling, 6,* 29–38.

Leong, F. T. L., Wagner, N. S., & Tata, S. P. (1995). Racial and ethnic variations in help-seeking attitudes. In J. G. Ponterotto, J. M. Casas, L. M. Suzuki, & C. M. Alexander (Eds.), *Handbook of multicultural counseling* (pp. 415–438). Thousand Oaks, CA: Sage.

Levant, R. (1986). *Psychoeducational approaches to family therapy and family counseling.* New York: Springer.

Lewis, M. (2002). *Multicultural health counseling: Special topics acknowledging diversity.* Boston: Allyn & Bacon.

Miller, W. R., & Rollnick, S. (1991). *Motivational interviewing: Preparing people for change.* New York: Guilford.

Mukherji, B. R. (1995). Cross-cultural issues in illness and wellness: Implications for depression. *Journal of Social Distress and the Homeless, 4,* 203–217.

Myers, J., Sweeney, T., & Witmer, J. (2000). The wheel of wellness: Counseling for wellness. *Journal of Counseling and Development, 78,* 251–266.

O'Donnell, M. (1989). Definition of health promotion: Part III: Stressing the impact of culture. *American Journal of Health Promotion, 3*(3), 1–8.

Pilch, J. (1985). *Wellness spirituality.* New York: Crossroad.

Prochaska, J., Norcross, J., & DiClemente, C. (1994). *Changing for good.* New York: Morrow.

Squyres, W. (1980). *Patient education: An inquiry into the state of the art.* St. Louis: Mosby.

U.S. Department of Health and Human Services (USDHHS). (2000). *Healthy people 2010: Understanding and improving health.* Washington, DC: Government Printing Office.

World Health Organization (WHO). (1948). *The first ten years of the World Health Organization.* Geneva: Author.

CHAPTER TWO

THEORIES, MODELS, AND CONCEPTS OF HEALTH BEHAVIOR AND HEALTH COUNSELING

He had much experience of physicians, and said "The only way to keep your health is to eat what you don't want, drink what you don't like, and do what you druther not."

—Mark Twain

Chapter 1 notes that counselors increasingly are finding that their clients are asking for something new: assistance as they try to achieve healthier lifestyles or adapt to changes in their physical wellness. Health counseling can be a very effective strategy for achieving the kinds of changes that can enhance physical health and well-being. Until recently, however, counselors and psychotherapists have focused on psychological and social issues, but they have not viewed themselves as competent to deal with their clients' physical well-being. In reality, it is a natural progression for counselors to move toward a more holistic approach. Mind and body are woven together so closely that counselors cannot realistically expect to focus on one at the expense of the other. Counselors can no more specialize in dealing with either the mind or the body than choose to work solely with emotions, solely with cognitions, or solely with overt behaviors. Each person's feelings, behaviors, and social milieu affect his or her physical health. At the same time, physical health can affect one's ability to cope with a variety of stressors. Because these factors are locked together, counselors can be most effective if they approach counseling from a biopsychosocial perspective (Engel, 1977; Schwartz, 1982), which recognizes the presence of biological, psychological, and social components in all aspects of individuals' well-being.

Counselors regardless of the setting in which they are employed, need to be able to help clients make health- and wellness-oriented changes and to cope with threats to their physical health. Health counseling is an action-oriented process through which a helper enables clients to make lifestyle changes that can lead them in the direction of optimal health. This process depends less on the helper's job title or employment setting than it does on his or her point of view. Health counseling takes place in schools, human service agencies, private practices, health-care organizations, and a variety of other settings. In short, it takes place wherever a helper with a biopsychosocial perspective can be found.

The practice of health counseling is informed by health behavior theories, models, concepts, strategies, skills, and processes. This chapter describes six key health behavior theories and models and several key concepts that underlie the practice of health counseling. Chapter 3 continues this discussion and focuses on the strategies, skills, and processes of health counseling.

THEORIES AND MODELS OF HEALTH BEHAVIOR

Several theories and models have been developed to explain and help understand health behavior and the changes that can occur in health behaviors. This section describes and evaluates six prominent theories and models. Table 2.1 previews and summarizes them.

Health Belief Model

The Health Belief Model is an explanation of individuals' health behavior based on their beliefs about the threat of ill health and the pros and cons of taking action—that is, the costs and benefits of the health behavior (Becker & Rosenstock, 1984). Specifically, this model is based on four beliefs about: susceptibility, severity, benefits, and barriers. Threat perception involves one's perceived *susceptibility* to illness or health breakdown (e.g., "How

TABLE 2.1   Six Health Behavior Change Theories and Models

THEORIES AND MODELS	DESCRIPTION
Health Belief Model	Based on beliefs—susceptibility, severity, benefits, and barriers—about the perceived threat of illness or injury and the costs and benefits of the health behavior
Theory of Reasoned Action	Health depends on intentions and intentions are based on attitudes and beliefs regarding the behavior and the subjective norm
Self-Efficacy	The belief that one has the necessary resources, capacity, and capability to achieve a specified change in health behavior
Theory of Planned Behavior	Health change depends on behavioral intentions regarding a specific behavior, subjective norm, and perceived behavioral control
Stages of Change Model	Describes readiness to change in terms of five stages: precontemplation, contemplation, preparation, action, and maintenance
Conviction–Confidence Model	Health change is dependent on both conviction—the change effort is in the one's best interest—and confidence—the belief that one has the capacity, self-efficacy, to make and/or maintain changes

likely am I to develop lung cancer if I keep smoking?") and the anticipated *severity* of the consequences of the illness or breakdown (e.g., "How bad would it be if I got lung cancer?"). The model also includes beliefs concerning the *benefits* or effectiveness of a recommended health behavior (e.g., "Will I live longer?" "What will I gain if I give up smoking?") and the costs or *barriers* (e.g., "Will I gain weight if I give up smoking?"). Two other factors are *cues to action,* which trigger health behavior when individuals are aware of a health threat and are convinced of the effectiveness of the action, such as advice from physicians; and general *health motivation,* that is, how much the individual values good health. Attitudes toward a specific behavior or behavior change are assessed by asking individuals to respond to various belief statements based on the four beliefs.

Janz and Becker (1984) review several studies involving the degree to which the four basic beliefs of the Health Belief Model can be distinguished among individuals who adopted or failed to adopt suggested health behaviors. Their review separated studies of sick role behaviors (e.g., those involving medication usage) from studies of the adoption of health-promoting behaviors (e.g., regular breast self-exams). The article indicates that perceived costs or barriers were particularly important, suggesting that minimizing the degree to which health behaviors are thought to be painful, expensive, time-consuming, or embarrassing helps promote them. The review also notes that perceived severity was less important in health promotion than responses to medical advice or symptoms. This seems to suggest that emphasizing susceptibility to health problems is more effective in promoting health behavior changes than the severity of the threat.

Theory of Reasoned Action

There are a number of modifications or extensions to the Health Belief Model. One of them is the Theory of Reasoned Action; this health behavior theory is based on two premises. The first is that individuals decide their intentions in advance of most voluntary behaviors, such as quitting smoking; the second is that intentions are the best predictor of an individual's action (Ajzen & Fishbein, 1980).

So what determines an individual's intention to perform a behavior? Intention is determined by two attitudes: attitudes regarding the behavior and attitudes about a subjective norm. One's attitudes regarding the suggested behavior changes are essentially judgments as to their perceived positive or negative value (i.e., outcome and reward). For instance, the outcome might be "If I stop smoking I will be more healthy and attractive" while the reward is "Being healthy and more attractive is gratifying and pleasant."

One's attitudes about a subjective norm reflect the impact of social influence regarding the behavior's acceptability and appropriateness and provide the motivation to comply with a given norm. For example, the attitude that others' opinions are important (e.g., "My family says that quitting smoking is best for me.") combines with the motivation to comply (e.g., "I want to do what they think is best.") and results in the intention to change a specified behavior.

These two types of attitudes combine to produce an intention. Accordingly, the Theory of Reasoned Action is an explanation of how individuals' health is dependent on their intentions, wherein intentions are based on their attitudes and beliefs regarding the behavior and the subjective norm.

In this theory, assessment follows a sequence of statements about attitudes. The individual is queried by a set of attitude statements about the behavior in terms of specific expectations as well as the desirability of the behavior change. Expectations are assessed with statements such as: "Stopping smoking will enable me to breathe easier" or "Stopping smoking will make me more irritable." The desirability of the behavior change can be assessed with statements such as: "Stopping smoking will make me gain weight" and "Gaining weight would not be good for me." Determining an individual's subjective norms is accomplished by assessing the extent to which important persons (e.g., spouse, child, parent, physician) want someone to quit smoking. The individual would also be asked how much he or she wants to meet the others' wishes and expectations.

Self-Efficacy Theory

Self-efficacy is a key construct in Bandura's social cognitive theory (Bandura, 1986). Self-Efficacy Theory is the belief or expectation that one has the necessary resources and capacity to achieve a specified health behavior change. Expectation is central to social cognitive theory and Bandura distinguishes between "outcome expectations" and "behavioral expectations." Outcome expectations signify an individual's beliefs about whether an outcome is internally determined (e.g., personal responsibility) or externally determined (e.g., by chance or luck). On the other hand, behavioral expectations, more commonly called *self-efficacy,* signify an individual's belief that he or she can implement the behavior and achieve a desired outcome. An example of a behavioral expectation is: "I can stop smoking even if my friends continue to smoke." This is in contrast with a related outcome expectation: "I got lung cancer because I smoked for thirty years." Even though Joe, a smoker, may take responsibility for his actions and their consequences (outcome expectation), it does not mean the smoker believes he can or will stop smoking (behavioral expectation).

Theory of Planned Behavior

Self-efficacy is one of the most highly regarded theoretical constructs in not only health counseling but also in all of the behavioral sciences. As a result, many theorists have attempted to incorporate this construct into their theory or model. A case in point is the Theory of Planned Behavior, which is an extension of the Theory of Reasoned Action (Ajzen & Fishbein, 1980). Proposed by Ajzen (1988), the Theory of Planned Behavior adds "perceived behavioral control" (e.g., "I can go without smoking after eating breakfast") as the third determinant of intention to change behavior. As noted earlier, the first two determinants of intention are attitudes regarding the behavior itself and perceived behavioral control was influenced by Bandura's research on self-efficacy (Bandura, 1977; 1988).

According to the Theory of Planned Behavior, perceived behavioral control predicts behavior independent of intentions in situations where no actual control over the behavior is possible. Thus, the more individuals perceive that they have control over a behavior the more likely they are to engage in that behavior even if they did not intend to do so.

Assessment in this theory follows the same sequence of questions about attitudes as in the Theory of Reasoned Action, with the addition of questions with regard to perceived behavioral control. The individual is queried using a set of attitude statements about the difficulty or ease of changing or modifying a specified behavior (e.g., "I am confident I can stop smoking whenever I choose," "I can resist smoking in situations where other individuals are smoking").

Stages of Change Model

As noted earlier, effective health counseling is usually a collaborative venture. What does this really mean? It means that both the counselor and the client must be ready and willing to become fully involved in the health counseling process. Irrespective of the extent of the counselor's experience and expertise, unless the client is really invested in the counseling process, expected outcomes will not be achieved. A readiness and willingness to engage in the process (i.e., to change) cannot be taken for granted. In fact, readiness for change probably accounts for most failures in counseling. This is also true for other change efforts whether they be quality, continuous quality-improvement, or work teams.

Readiness for change and the dynamics of this stage of change were developed by Prochaska, Norcross, and DiClemente (1994); they identified six stages of change: precontemplation, contemplation, preparation, action, maintenance, and recycling and relapse. Those practicing health counseling would do well to have a working knowledge of these stages and the underlying construct of readiness for change. As those being counseled cycle through the stages, the counselor needs to not only understand the stage of readiness, but must know how to respond appropriately to facilitate the individual moving to a higher stage of readiness.

Precontemplation.   In this first stage there is a denial or lack of awareness of the need for change. In terms of counseling, this means that the individual refuses to even talk about having a problem or needing health counseling. Precontemplation represents the lowest level of readiness for change. At this stage, the best strategy is to provide information, establish trust, and create doubt. A key question to pose here is: "What's wrong with the way things are right now?"

Contemplation.   There may be an awareness that a problem exists but at this second stage, there is no perceived need to do something it. As with the first stage, insisting that an individual who needs to change begin a counseling process, or referring the individual to a counselor, is not only premature but could also be counterproductive. It would be much better to actively listen to the individual and perhaps identify the positives and negatives of making a change. A reasonable question at this stage is: "Will making a change be worth it?"

Preparation.   The third stage is when a decision or preparation is necessary. The individual not only recognizes the problem and the need for doing something about it, but decides to change and begins to make plans to change. While a higher level of readiness exists here than in the first two stages, there is no guarantee that the individual will actually engage in the counseling process. Nevertheless, helping him or her consider the what and how of counseling and providing information on the types and process of counseling can facilitate movement to the next stage of change.

Action.   The fourth stage is action in which the individual actually engages in the change process. In terms of counseling, this stage represents the optimal level of readiness for change. It is only here that the client can work collaboratively with the counselor to assess, plan, and implement a counseling plan. Among other things, the counselor's primary responsibilities are to support the change efforts and to affirm the client's commitment and involvement. A basic question to pose at this stage is: "What will you do?"

Maintenance.   The plan for change is still in process at the fifth stage, but the expected outcome has not yet been achieved or the change does not feel "natural" to individuals. It is important for counselors to recognize clients' uncomfortableness at this stage and to support them. Possibly, some clients will even need help with the so-called "soft skills" (e.g., assertive communication, problem solving, or other relational skills) that could provide new ways of viewing their lives and attaining necessary skills to increase their sense of empowerment during this uncomfortable stage. A basic question to ask at this stage is: "What could help?"

Recyling and Relapse.   While the original formulation of the Readiness for Change Model ended with maintenance, a sixth stage, which takes into account the inevitable backsliding or relapse that occurs, can also be considered (Prochaska, Norcross, & DiClemente, 1994). Relapse means that the change outcome was not sustained because the individual was involved in a high-risk situation where relapse was inevitable, experienced a lack of social support, and so on. The result is that the individual slips back to a lower stage, usually contemplation. During this stage the client is decidedly ambivalent about trying again and generally is full of excuses to explain the failure. He or she needs help in resolving this ambivalence, evaluating the commitment to change, identifying and eliminating obstacles to successful change, and recycling back to the action stage. A key question to ask at this stage is: "What's your intention with regard to change today?"

The Readiness for Change Model has been widely used in all areas of health counseling ranging from smoking cessation to medication compliance as well as substance abuse treatment and psychotherapy. Assessment for this change theory can be accomplished by self-report instruments (cf. McConnaughy, DiClimente, Prochaska, & Velicer, 1989).

Conviction–Confidence Model

This health change model is based on three observations. The first observation is that there are three groups of troublesome health behavior: self-destructive, nonadherence, and avoidance. Self-destructive behaviors include smoking, alcohol consumption, and substance abuse or dependence. Nonadherence behavior involves treatment regimens such as failure to monitor blood pressure levels or not completing a course of antibiotics. Avoidance of healthy behavior includes poor management of stress, failure to exercise, and overeating. The second observation is that health change involves two separate processes: conviction and confidence. The third observation is that other health change models are too complex and/or not user-friendly. Accordingly, the Conviction–Confidence Model was developed to be easy for health providers to use to address all three troublesome health behaviors. Not surprisingly, this model emphasizes the two dimensions of conviction and confidence that Keller and White (1997) describe.

Conviction refers to the belief that undertaking a given change effort will be in the client's best interest. When individuals have conviction, they engage in "a thoughtful assessment and decision-making process involving the change itself: 'Do I believe that making this change will enhance my well-being?'" (p. 35). Assessment focuses on either the positive benefits that may accrue with the change or on the danger of not making the change.

Confidence refers to individuals' belief that they have the capacity to actually make the change. With confidence, individuals engage in "a self-evaluation of their capacity to work through the change: 'Do I believe I can make this change?'" (p. 35). Several factors, such as a previous history of success or failure with behavior change, the adequacy of social support, and the nature of the provider–patient relationship, affect confidence. Keller and White note that confidence is the equivalent of self-efficacy.

Both conviction and confidence can be easily assessed through two simple questions asked by the provider. Conviction is assessed by asking: "On a 1 to 10 scale, how convinced are you that stopping smoking is in your best interest?"; while confidence is assessed by asking: "On a 1 to 10 scale, how confident are you that you will succeed in giving up smoking?" Based on responses to the two questions, four response patterns are possible: low conviction and low confidence, high conviction and low confidence, low conviction and high confidence, or high conviction and high confidence.

By knowing which pattern applies, the provider can use specific interventions to increase the individual's conviction, confidence, or both. For example, for an individual with low conviction and low confidence, the provider might accept the situation and the individual without judging either: "If I understand what you are saying, you don't believe that you could do any exercise right now and you are not sure that it would benefit you at your age." The provider would then add: "If that changes, I would like to help in any way I can" (p. 35). Or, for someone with high conviction and low confidence, the provider could emphasize the importance of making choices about the issue, rather than treating the issues as something beyond [his or her] volition: 'These are difficult choices, but you have made hard choices in your life before. How did you make those decisions?" (p. 36). (For suggested interventions for all four patterns, see Keller and White's 1997 article.)

Evaluation of the Health Behavior Models and Theories

Providers need to know whether individuals they are working with have the necessary and sufficient conditions to succeed in making suggested or needed changes. These conditions include adequate motivation and perseverance to engage in the change process as well as the determination to maintain the gains achieved. In the language of change, this reflects (1) the readiness to begin and engage in the change process, (2) the desire and conviction to make the change, and (3) the capacity or ability to achieve the change. In other words, individuals must be "ready," "willing," and "able." Experience indicates that lacking one or more of the three reduces the probability that the change will be achieved and maintained in a timely fashion. In short, the model must be comprehensive.

Providers have an additional concern; they want, and need, a model that is brief and easy to use or implement, meaning that it should provide a straightforward protocol of guidelines and, of course, be effective. Researchers, on the other hand, would require that the model be both reliable and empirically validated. At the very least, an ideal health behavior model—one that reflects both the necessary and sufficient conditions—would encompass the following four criteria:

1. Comprehensive (i.e., include all three dimensions—"ready, willing, and able")
2. Easy to use and provider-friendly
3. Empirically validated and reliable
4. Able to accurately predict change outcomes

Using these criteria to evaluate the models previously described shows that some do not appear to meet any of them, while others meet one or two of the criteria.

Health Belief Model. While this model has considerable face validity, it does not appear to meet any of the four criteria, certainly not the comprehensiveness one. The four underlying beliefs do not appear to be related to the "ready, willing, and able" criterion. The actual use of this model is not particularly provider-friendly given that no protocols for its use are available. Finally, although there is some research on the Health Belief Model (Janz & Becker, 1984), it cannot yet be considered empirically validated and appears to have low predictive value.

Theory of Reasoned Action. The major shortcoming of the this theory is that intentions do not always lead to actions. Individuals do not always do what they plan, or claim, to do. The theory is also incomplete in that it omits the important role of the individuals' prior experience with attempts to change the behavior. Like the Health Belief Model, the Theory of Reasoned Action assumes that individuals deliberate in detail about health risks; weigh the perceived costs and benefits; and then, based on this reasoning, act according to the outcome of the analysis. In actuality, individuals change health behaviors for a variety of vague and apparently nondeliberated reasons such as "My physician said that smoking was bad for me." Nevertheless, this theory is considerably better at predicting behavior than the Health Belief Model (Schwarzer, 1992).

The Theory of Reasoned Action does not appear to directly address the comprehensiveness criterion with regard to readiness, willingness, or ability to change. While a provider can assess the two determinants of intention with a series of belief statements, there is no protocol for using that assessment's finding to tailor interventions. Although there is some research on this model, it cannot yet be considered empirically validated. However, it does appear to have some predictive value, as noted in a metaanalysis of 56 studies done by Godin and Kok (1996) in which they found that 41 percent of intentions were explained by this theory.

Self-Efficacy Theory. Technically speaking, self-efficacy is more a construct than a theory or model. In this section on evaluation of the theories, the construct of self-efficacy has been incorporated into both the Theory of Planned Behavior and the Conviction–Confidence Model. Thus, this construct should be evaluated and critiqued in the context of the theory or the model.

Theory of Planned Behavior.   Similarly, this theory is far from being an ideal theory or model of behavior change. Nevertheless, the Theory of Planned Behavior does address at least one of the comprehensiveness dimensions, namely, perceived behavioral control/ self-efficacy (i.e., "able"). Although a provider can assess the three determinants with a series of belief or attitude statements, there is no protocol for using the assessment findings to tailor interventions. Finally, even though there is some research on this model, it cannot yet be considered empirically validated; however, it appears to have more predictive power than the Theory of Reasoned Action (Schwarzer, 1992). The metaanalysis of Godin and Kok (1996) found that 41 percent of intentions, 34 percent of future behaviors, and an additional 11.5 percent of perceived behavioral control were explained by the Theory of Planned Behavior.

Stages of Change Model.   Even as the most commonly known and promising health behavior model, this model comes up short when evaluated by the four criteria. For instance, while the Stages of Change Model initially may appear to meet the criterion of being reasonably easy to use, this book's authors and others (Miller & Rollnick, 1991) have found that it requires considerable skill to use. Moreover, the model seems to focus only on readiness for change (i.e., the "ready" dimension) and does not formally address confidence or self-efficacy (i.e., the "able" dimension) nor conviction (i.e., the "willing" dimension). Although probably the most researched health change model, its validity and reliability data are still insufficient.

Conviction–Confidence Model.   This model can also be evaluated in terms of the four criteria. While the Conviction–Confidence Model is reasonably comprehensive in that it addresses the "willing" (conviction) and "able" (confidence) dimensions, it has yet to be empirically validated nor can it predict change outcomes. In addition, the model fails to meet the second criterion of being easy to use and provider-friendly. "The difficulty with the Conviction–Confidence Model, however, is that significant time and energy are necessary to learn and implement it" (Liang, 1998, p. 37).

At this point, it appears that all of these health behavior change theories and models have limitations and that further research and development are needed. In the meantime, it would not be unreasonable to combine the dimensions of the Stages of Change Model with the Conviction–Confidence Model. This would result in a more comprehensive model that includes all three "ready," " willing," and "able" dimensions. Granted, the counselor would need to develop some skills in assessing and then, when indicated, help the individual increase his or her readiness, willingness, and capacity for change.

HEALTH BEHAVIOR CONCEPTS RELEVANT TO HEALTH COUNSELING

The importance of health counseling becomes especially apparent when the direct linkages between both behavior and health and personal and social characteristics and health are considered.

Linkages between Behavior and Health

The most pressing health problems U.S. society faces today stem from the health-compromising actions of individuals. A century ago, infectious diseases were the leading cause of death. Now, although diseases, such as tuberculosis, measles, poliomyelitis, influenza, and pneumonia, are still present, they can be treated through the various medical means at our disposal. In contrast, illnesses and disabilities related to lifestyles show few signs of abatement. As Matarazzo (1982) points out, the reduction in the incidence of infectious diseases "has occurred along with an increase during the same years in conditions such as lung cancer, major cardiovascular disease, drug and alcohol abuse, and motorcycle and alcohol-related automobile accidents" (p. 3). Even the most serious outbreaks of infectious diseases, such as the Acquired Immune Deficiency Syndrome (AIDS) epidemic, occur in the presence of high-risk behaviors. Undoubtedly, the afflictions that affect the largest number of people today are of the type that are more likely to be affected by behavioral interventions than by strict reliance on traditional medicine. Behavioral interventions are clearly in the counselor's bailiwick.

In the latter years of the 1980s, nine chronic diseases—all largely preventable or controllable—accounted for more than half of the deaths in the United States ("Preventable diseases . . . " 1990). These chronic diseases—stroke, heart disease, diabetes, obstructive lung disease, lung cancer, breast cancer, cervical cancer, colorectal cancer, and cirrhosis of the liver—tend to be associated with various risk factors, including cigarette smoking, poor diet, and insufficient exercise. Unintentional injury is another behaviorally affected cause of death that claims an untold number of people, especially the youngest members of the population. Among adolescents, the primary causes of mortality are accidents, homicide, and suicide; disabilities related to vehicular accidents also take a high toll on the individual well-being of members of this age group (Millstein, 1989). In addition, adolescents are at risk for death or long-term disability because of lifestyle-related problems such as sexually tramsmitted diseases (STDs), early pregnancy, and substance abuse. In fact, problems related to adolescent health behaviors may be even more severe than anyone realizes. The public tends to be aware of the immediate health risks of substance abuse and accidents but unaware of the degree to which other behaviors can affect long-term health. As Millstein (1989) points out, 50 percent of the mortality among adults is a direct result of modifiable behavioral factors, many of which have their onset during adolescence" (p. 837).

In U.S. society, people of all ages are at risk for the development of health-related problems associated with their behaviors and lifestyles. According to Michael (1982), most Americans can improve their health and extend their lifespans through "elimination of cigarette smoking, reduction of alcohol misuse, moderate dietary changes to reduce intake of excess calories and excess fats, moderate exercise, periodic screening for major disorders such as high blood pressure and certain cancers, adherence to traffic speed laws, and use of seat belts" (p. 937). Clearly, the association between behavior and health is well documented, direct, and—most important—amenable to intervention.

In addition to the overt mind–body connection, there is another set of interactions that is less likely to be readily understood but that, in the future, may turn out to be just as important. The relationship between diet and heart disease or between smoking and lung cancer are clear and understandable to most everyone. Far less obvious is the notion that the immune system itself can be "compromised behaviorally" (Borysenko, 1984, p. 248). Promising research conducted by Ader and his associates (Ader, 1981; Ader, 1989; Ader & Cohen, 1984) indicates that the immune system is not as autonomous as has generally been believed; rather, it is influenced by the central nervous system, which may act as a mediator between psychosocial factors and disease processes. Ader (1989) found that it was possible to condition immunosuppression in animals. Although comparable evidence is not available for humans, research that focuses on infectious diseases indicates that "psychosocial factors appear to be capable of influencing both the likelihood of developing disease and the course of disease" (Ader & Cohen, 1984, p. 118).

A number of studies, some going back several decades, have identified linkages between social or personality factors and health problems such as streptococcal disease (Meyer & Haggerty, 1962), respiratory illness (Boyce et al., 1977; Jackson et al., 1960; Jacobs et al., 1970), and infectious mononucleosis (Greenfield, Roessler, & Crosley, 1959; Kasl, Evans, & Neiderman, 1979). Moreover, some accumulated evidence indicates that people affected by stressful events, such as loss of a loved one, show measurable changes in immune responses (Bartrop et al., 1977; Schleifer et al., 1983).

It is difficult to identify the specific mechanisms through which such linkages occur. It is increasingly apparent, however, that health is determined through interactions among genetic predisposition, environment, and behavioral factors (Borysenko, 1984). Of course, psychoneuroimmunology cannot, at this stage of its development, point counselors in the direction of preventive interventions, but the existence of the research does help to support the notion that psychosocial and biological factors are absolutely inseparable.

Linkages between Personal and Social Characteristics and Health

The inseparability of the mind and the body is also brought to light when the developing body of research linking personal characteristics and health is considered. Again, current findings are not so definitive that they point toward very specific interventions. Yet, counselors need to be aware of the literature that identifies linkages between personality factors and health outcomes, if only because such research provides further evidence of the need for a holistic approach.

Researchers in health-related disciplines have been somewhat successful in identifying characteristics that may relate to positive or negative health events. Some individuals demonstrate characteristics that could make them vulnerable to the development of disease or dysfunction, whereas others exhibit attitudes or behaviors that seem to play a protective role. Among the personal factors that can affect general health are a "hardy personality style" (Kobasa, 1979; Kobasa, Maddi, & Courington, 1981), a "sense of coherence" (Antonovsky, 1987), a disposition toward optimism (Scheier & Carver, 1987), and a number of factors related to cognition and coping mechanisms. In addition, there appears to be a differentiation among the personality characteristics most closely associated with specific illnesses.

Hardiness.   Kobasa (1979) used the concept of *hardiness* to explain the results of her study of business executives who had experienced a large number of stressful life events. Some of the individuals succeeded in maintaining their health despite high stress levels.

What seemed to differentiate them from their less healthy peers was a collection of factors that she called the "hardy personality style." The components of this personality style include *commitment,* as opposed to alienation; *control,* as opposed to powerlessness; and *challenge,* as opposed to threat (Kobasa, Maddi, & Courington, 1981).

Hardy individuals show a high degree of commitment, involving themselves fully in life and work. They tend to believe in the importance and have an inherent interest in whatever they are doing. Far from feeling alienated, they maintain their curiosity about all aspects of life; these individuals have a sense of purpose and believe that their lives are meaningful. Their sense of commitment is closely related to their belief in the possibility of control. Hardy individuals perceive that they can influence events. They tend to take responsibility for their lives, showing an internal locus of control (Rotter, 1966; 1989) rather than attributing events to chance or to the actions of powerful others.

This attitude toward life tends to make hardy individuals welcome challenge and change. Such people assume that change will always be a part of life and that the result will be positive growth and development. Far from seeing change as a threat, hardy individuals see it as a challenge and a source of stimulation.

The variables of commitment, control, and challenge are closely associated with one another. "Thus a hardy person's attempt to influence the course of some event (control) includes curiosity about how it happened and interest in what it is (commitment), plus an attempt to learn from it whatever will enhance personal growth (challenge)" (Kobasa, Maddi, & Courington, 1981, p. 369). This energetic approach to life may help hardy people choose positive interpretations of life events that might prove stressful and health-compromising for others. In contrast, individuals with a low level of hardiness may be bored or threatened by the environment, feel powerless to do anything about their lives, and uncomfortable with change. "Because their personalities provide little or no buffer, the stressful events are allowed to have a debilitating effect on health" (Kobasa, Maddi, & Courington, 1981, p. 369). Constitutional predisposition and stressful life events contribute to the development of illness, but hardiness can play a role in mediating that relationship.

Kobasa (1987) points out that, because the subjects of her original study included 900 male executives and only 20 females, "hardiness studies are essentially studies of personality and stress resistance in men" (p. 322). However, some subsequent studies have dealt with women and gender differences. Hardiness did appear to mediate the effects of stress on the well-educated, middle-class women who made up the sample in other studies. On the other hand, in a study of female secretaries, Kobasa (1987) found no such effect.

> Business executives may find themselves in jobs that allow them to exercise, and perhaps even to grow in, commitment, control, and challenge. Secretaries, on the other hand, may confront jobs which limit their expression of hardiness. It may indeed be the case, for example, that some bosses enjoy expressions of control at the expense of their secretaries' sense of control. (pp. 324–325)

Thus, the construct of hardiness, like any factor, should be examined while keeping in mind questions about the effects of gender, culture, and economics.

Sense of Coherence. Antonovsky's (1979, 1984, 1987) concept of the sense of coherence also combines several variables to define a global, health-enhancing orientation. Antonovsky's work is based on an assumption that, given the stressfulness of life, health is more surprising and more mysterious than illness. "We all, by virtue of being human, are in a high-risk group" (1984, p. 117). Thinking "salutogenically," Antonovsky points out that, at any one time, all people can be placed somewhere on a continuum between total wellness and total illness. The question that needs addressing is not what causes illness (the pathogenic approach), but what facilitates an individual's position or movement along the health–illness continuum toward the wellness pole. Antonovsky's (1987) research identifies a general way of viewing the world that he termed the *sense of coherence.*

> The sense of coherence is a global orientation that expresses the extent to which one has a pervasive, enduring though dynamic feeling of confidence that (1) the stimuli deriving from one's internal and external environments in the course of living are structured, predictable, and explicable; (2) the resources are available to one to meet the demands posed by these stimuli; and (3) these demands are challenges, worthy of investment and engagement. (p. 19)

The components that make up the sense of coherence include comprehensibility, manageability, and meaningfulness. *Comprehensibility* involves the degree to which individuals feel able to understand (to comprehend) themselves and the world. A person with a high sense of comprehensibility believes that future events, if not predictable, are at least ordered and explainable. He or she finds that stimuli make cognitive sense rather than being "chaotic, disordered, random, accidental, [and] inexplicable" (Antonovsky, 1987, p. 17). *Manageability* implies a belief that events are not only predictable but also controllable. The person with a high sense of manageability believes that resources for meeting life's demands can somehow be obtained. If he or she cannot control events, then legitimate others can. *Meaningfulness* is Antonovsky's emotional counterpart to comprehensibility. "People who are high on meaningfulness feel that life makes sense emotionally, that at least some of the problems and demands posed by living are worth investing energy in, are worthy of commitment and engagement, and are challenges that are welcome rather than burdens" (Antonovsky, 1984, p. 119).

Antonovsky's conceptualization is that people who develop a strong sense of coherence are more likely to maintain or improve their health than are those with a weak sense of coherence. A number of explanations are possible. Perhaps the individual with a strong sense of coherence is more active in avoiding threat, more involved in health-promoting activities, more inclined to do the work needed to develop good coping mechanisms, and/or more likely to gather and exploit effective resources. In any event, such individuals are unlikely to give up in the face of health-endangering stimuli.

Dispositional Optimism. Scheier and Carver (1987) suggest that many of the characteristics that have been identified as differentiating between positive and negative health outcomes may in fact be the result of a pervasive sense of optimism, or "generalized expectations that good things will happen" (p. 171). One plausible explanation for this phenomenon lies in the notion that people's behaviors are strongly affected by their beliefs in the outcomes that can be expected.

In our view, people who see desired outcomes as attainable continue to exert efforts at attaining those outcomes, even when doing so is difficult. When outcomes seem sufficiently unattainable (whether through personal inadequacies or through externally imposed impediments), people reduce their efforts and eventually disengage themselves from pursuit of the goals. Thus, we see outcome expectancies as a major determinant of the disjunction between two classes of behavior: (a) continued striving versus (b) giving up and turning away. (Scheier & Carver, 1987, p. 170)

The Scheier and Carver reviews of several studies seem to bear out their conceptualization of the link between optimism and physical well-being. One of their studies (Scheier & Carver, 1985) tracked college students during a particularly stressful time: the last four weeks of an academic semester. The subjects completed the Life Orientation Test, which provides a score for optimism, and were also asked to report on their physical symptoms both at the outset of the study and on the last day of classes. Optimism was negatively correlated with symptom reporting: People who scored high on optimism showed fewer symptoms over time.

The tentative conclusions of another study (Scheier & Carver, 1987) also pinpoints the possible importance of dispositional optimism. After undergoing coronary artery bypass surgery, optimists showed better recovery rates than pessimists. Optimists were judged by members of the cardiac rehabilitation team as showing a faster rate of recovery, reaching recovery milestones more quickly, and showing healthier physiological responses. Six months after surgery, the high correlation between optimism and self-reported quality of life remained.

A later study by Carver and Pozo (cited in Adler, 1991) traced the progress of 60 women with breast cancer. Preliminary results indicated that optimists reported less distress than pessimists did throughout their medical ordeals. The researchers suspect that optimism made its contribution through its affect on coping techniques. Optimists used acceptance, humor, planning, reframing the situation in an active light, and active coping; pessimists tended to cope with distress through denial and behavioral disengagement.

Reker and Wong (1983) studied an elderly population. They, too, found a correlation between optimism and physical health. People who had been assessed as optimists two years earlier showed a higher degree of physical, psychological, and general well-being and reported fewer negative symptoms in comparison with pessimists.

The mechanism through which optimism acts on physical health is unclear, but the linkage of optimism with the use of effective, problem-focused coping strategies appears to be a promising line of research (Scheier, Weintraub, & Carver, 1986). "When confronting adversity optimists keep trying, whereas pessimists are more likely to get upset and give up" (Scheier & Caver, 1987, p. 191).

Cognitive Factors.   Cognitive factors appear to play a central role in the individual's success in maintaining health and preventing or minimizing disease. As J. Seeman (1989) points out: "If there is one dominant subsystem in its impact on health, it is the cognitive subsystem. Study after study [has] reported the commanding role of self-definition, self-perception, and sense of control in the maintenance and enhancement of health" (p. 1108).

A belief in one's ability to exert control over events seems especially important. Both Kobasa's hardiness construct and Antonovsky's concept of the sense of coherence highlight the centrality of the healthy person's sense of control. Research findings focused specifically on the issue of control also provide support for the notion that a sense of control helps individuals stay healthy. For example, M. Seeman and T. Seeman (1983) conducted multiple interviews over a yearlong period with more than 1,000 individuals. On the basis of this study, these researchers were able to measure correlations between sense of control and a number of health indices. The Seemans (1983) found that sense of control was associated with the following health-status measures:

> (1) [p]racticing preventive health measures, [that is], diet, exercise, alcohol moderation; (2) making an effort to avoid the harm in smoking (by quitting, trying to quit, or simply not smoking); (3) being more sanguine about early medical treatment for cancer; (4) achieving higher self-ratings on general health status; (5) reporting fewer episodes of both chronic and acute illness; (6) evidencing a more vigorous management style with respect to illness; [that is], staying in bed less once a bed-confinement occasion has occurred; and (7) showing less dependence on the use of the physician. (p. 155)

Research conducted by Rodin, Langer, and Buie (Rodin & Langer, 1977; Rodin, 1986; Buie, 1988) indicates that experiences and perceptions of control affect the health status of older people. In one study, nursing home residents, who were given choices and who were able to maintain control of day-to-day events, showed greater health gains than did members of a control group whose needs were met through caring attention by staff members. Rodin and her associates also studied a group of older people who were not currently living in nursing home settings. For these people as well, control predicted immune function and a number of other health-related variables. A sense of personal control may be important not just in preventing illness, but also in improving individuals' ability to cope effectively with the presence of a disease or disability. Taylor, Lichtman, and Wood (1984), for instance, found that cancer patients who believed that they had personal control over the progression of the disease were able to make better adjustments and had better outcomes than those who expressed a sense of helplessness or denial.

In general, control seems to be an important factor for both men and women. Some studies, however, have shown gender differences sufficient to question whether generalizations about sense of control as a protection against stress can be made with impunity. Possibly, there are differences in the kind and degree of control exerted by men and women, according to Kobasa (1987):

> One can argue for a difference between control conceived of as (1) a sense of personal competence or mastery; and that defined as (2) generalized expectancies regarding control within oneself (rather than in others or fate) over a variety of personal, interpersonal, and broad sociopolitical domains. It may be that the former—that is, feeling effective in what it is that one has to do in life—is more important for women's stress resistance than it is for men's. (pp. 317–318)

Bandara's (1982) concept of self-efficacy is closely related to questions of individual control. Efficacy involves a general ability to manage one's environment by mobilizing the cognitive and behavioral skills necessary for dealing with challenging situations. An individual's perceived self-efficacy involves his or her judgment about the adequacy of these skills; this judgment affects every aspect of the individual's performance. The person who lacks a sense of self-efficacy concerning a particular task is likely to give up quickly or even avoid the challenge altogether. In contrast, the person with a strong sense of self-efficacy is likely to meet difficult challenges and maintain positive behavior changes.

> In any given activity, skills and self-beliefs that ensure optimal use of capabilities are required for successful functioning. If self-efficacy is lacking, people tend to behave ineffectually even though they know what to do. . . . The higher the level of perceived self-efficacy, the greater the performance accomplishments. Strength of efficacy also predicts behavior change. The stronger the perceived efficacy, the more likely are people to persist in their efforts until they succeed. (Bandura, 1982, pp. 127–128)

The perception of self-efficacy regarding health-enhancing behaviors may have a strong influence on well-being. Self-efficacy has been shown to affect people's ability to quit smoking and maintain the nonsmoking state (DiClemente, 1981; Curry, 1989), to avoid relapse in addictive behaviors (Marlatt & Gordon, 1985), and to exert self-regulation regarding a range of preventive health measures (Schunk & Carbonari, 1984). "When knowledge of health risks is combined with a strong sense of efficacy for avoiding them, long-term maintenance of healthy lifestyles results" (Schunk & Carbonari, 1984, p. 244).

Although individuals' perceptions of control and self-efficacy are important, a number of other beliefs, especially about the nature of the situation being faced, can have a major impact on health-related behaviors and thereby on outcomes. The Health Belief Model (HBM), which was developed in the 1950s and had received major research attention by the early 1970s (Becker, 1974), has been the focus of a number of studies since that time. The HBM was first developed by the U.S. Public Health Service in an attempt to determine why so few people participated in programs designed to prevent disease. The model is based on the notion that behavior is affected by the value that an individual places on a particular goal and by his or her estimate of the likelihood that a specific action will help in the achievement of that goal. The model addresses the following cognitive dimensions (Janz & Becker, 1984):

1. *Perceived susceptibility*—the individual's feeling of vulnerability with regard to a particular illness or disability
2. *Perceived severity*—the person's evaluation of the seriousness of the medical or social consequences of the illness
3. *Perceived benefits*—the individual's belief that a specific action would be effective in preventing or overcoming the threat
4. *Perceived barriers*—the person's perception of negative effects that might balance the positive aspects of the specific behavior

The social psychologists who developed the model also took into account the importance of internal or external cues to action. They recognized the impact of the demographic and psychosocial variables that might influence behavior indirectly through their effects on perception. Thus, the Health Belief Model posits that demographic and psychosocial variables affect the individual's perceptions concerning the seriousness of a disease and his or her susceptibility to it. If one perceives that he or she is at risk, the individual is more likely to adopt health-oriented behaviors. Whether this cue is internal, such as a symptom or physiological warning sign, or external, such as a public health media campaign, the likelihood that action will be taken depends on the person's perception of the actions, benefits, and liabilities. This perception may also be affected by a number of demographic and psychosocial variables.

Although the Health Belief Model originally focused on preventive behavior, it has also been studied in relation to health-related behaviors initiated after the onset of an illness. Janz and Becker (1984) reviewed HBM studies published between 1974 and 1984 that focused on sick-role behaviors as well as on preventive behaviors. With regard to preventive health behavior, the findings consistently supported the notion that individual perceptions of susceptibility, benefits, and barriers were significantly related to behavioral outcomes; perceived severity of the illness in question was less important. Studies of behaviors to aid recovery among people already diagnosed with illnesses showed that perception of severity was most important, second only to perceived barriers. The Janz and Becker summary of all Health Belief Model studies up to 1984 indicates that "each HBM dimension was found to be significantly associated with the health-related behaviors under study; the significance–ratio orderings (in descending order) are 'barriers' (89%), 'susceptibility' (81%), 'benefits' (78%), and 'severity' (65%)" (1984, p. 41).

Other conceptualizations have been developed in an attempt to learn how cognitive factors might affect people's health-related behaviors. For instance, Leventhal and his associates (Leventhal, Meyer, & Nerenz, 1980; Leventhal, Zimmerman, & Gutmann, 1984) conceptualized the relationship between people's representations of illnesses and the likelihood that they would adhere to medical regimens. According to their conceptualization, each individual is likely to have a cognitive representation of illness that includes both abstract and concrete components. Included in the individual's mental construction are perceptions about the symptoms associated with the disease, beliefs about the causes and consequences of the disease, and expectations concerning its duration (acute, cyclic, or chronic). These researchers found that help-seeking behaviors and treatment compliance are affected by the patient's mental representation of the disease in question. For instance, people who believed that they could recognize their own hypertension by monitoring symptoms tended to take their medication only when they perceived symptoms of elevated blood pressure, despite the fact that hypertension is, in reality, asymptomatic. Similarly, patients who believed that hypertension was a chronic disease were more likely to remain in treatment than those who believed it to be an acute illness.

Meichenbaum and Turk (1987) suggest that a large number of patient beliefs, either rational or irrational, can affect decisions concerning adherence to treatment. Among the possible reasons for noncompliance are factors such as uncertainty or even pessimism about the efficacy of the treatment being suggested; prior experiences with illness or with health-care providers; belief that inconvenience or negative side effects of the treatment may outweigh the benefits; perceived stigma of being in treatment; a desire to maintain a sense of control; competing demands that are seen as more important; and a "view of adherence as interfering with lifelong belief systems, future plans, family relationship patterns, social roles, self-concept, emotional equilibrium, or daily life patterns" (p. 51).

Clearly, individuals' perceptions and beliefs have a major effect on health behaviors, even in situations where treatment adherence would appear to be the only rational decision.

Preventive health maintenance, which is characterized by vagueness in goals and a lower level of perceived need, presents an even greater challenge.

Coping Mechanisms.   It is a generally accepted truism that stress plays an important role in health outcomes. This relationship is complex, however, because a number of factors mediate the effects of stressful events on individuals. One of the most important of these modifiers involves the ways in which people cope with stress (Cohen, 1984).

Lazarus and Folkman (1984) define coping as "the process of managing demands (external or internal) that are appraised as taxing or exceeding the resources of the person" (p. 283). This conceptualization makes it clear that stress-related problems occur only when individuals interpret events or situations as demanding. Whether people find situations threatening depends on a number of factors: their view of their competence to handle the new demand, their previous success in dealing with similar situations, the degree to which they feel in control of events, their perceptions of being overloaded or of having conflicting needs, and the standards they set for their own performance. It is only when individuals perceive an event to be stressful that they react physiologically, activating stress responses that can, over time, have negative effects on their health. "Broadly speaking, degree of stress depends mainly on the appraisal of how much appears to be at stake in the transaction . . . and the relative power of the environmental demand to do harm, compared with the power of the person to prevent or manage such harm" (Lazarus & Folkman, 1984, p. 290).

Stress-related problems are a result of a combination of three variables: external demands, individual perceptions, and physiological responses. Therefore, individuals can cope by making changes at any of these three points. First, they can alter their stress levels by exerting control over their environments and using problem-solving skills to confront potential stressors and to make their life situation less demanding. Second, they can alter their mental processes, learning to change their appraisals in a purposeful way. People who tend to see many stimuli as threatening can try to monitor their reactions and to substitute positive self-statements for their maladaptive cognitions. Finally, people can alter their physiological responses by learning relaxation techniques that can help them control the stress response and avoid the negative health consequences associated with long-term stress.

Any one of a number of coping strategies can be used at any of these points. In general, however, coping tends to be either "problem-focused" or "emotion-focused" (Folkman & Lazarus, 1980; Lazarus & Folkman, 1984). *Problem-focused coping* involves taking some kind of constructive action to mitigate conditions that are perceived as threatening, whereas *emotion-focused coping* attempts to regulate the individual's emotional response and thus to alleviate distress. The emotion-regulating responses category includes denial of the existence or of the seriousness of the threat, as well as attempts to control nervous system activation. In fact, another way to categorize coping strategies is to make a distinction between active and avoidant strategies (Cohen, 1984).

Stress may affect people's health differentially, depending on the appropriateness and effectiveness of the coping strategies they choose. Because control, commitment, and optimism are associated with positive health, it is often assumed that active, problem-focused coping styles are the most adaptive. In fact, it appears that there is no one coping mechanism that is always preferred. Suls and Fletcher (1985) found that avoidant strategies were associated with poor outcomes over the long term; in the short term, however, denial played a helpful role. Similarly, problem-focused coping strategies are adaptive when situations are amenable to change, whereas emotion-focused coping strategies are more effective when stressors are not subject to control. Thus, the coping mechanisms that succeed in mediating the effects of stress are the ones that work best in the situation at hand. The people who adapt the most effectively may be the ones with several types of coping skills in their repertoires.

Characteristics Associated with Specific Illnesses

In their questions about the relationship between personal characteristics and health, researchers have been following two parallel lines. A number of studies used what Antonovsky calls a *salutogenic* approach in an attempt to identify the positive characteristics that help to maintain health. This line of investigation has led to a growing awareness of the importance of attributes such as a sense of control, a tendency toward optimism, and an ability to cope effectively with stress. At the same time, researchers continue to examine the relationships between specific personal attributes and disease-proneness, asking what characteristics might increase individuals' vulnerability to particular health problems.

The Type A behavior pattern, which is thought to have a relationship to coronary heart disease among both men and women, is the most widely accepted and extensively researched example of such a behavioral risk factor (Spielberger, 1989). Type A individuals (Friedman & Rosenman, 1974) are characterized by hard-driving competitiveness, impatience, aggressiveness, hostility, overinvolvement in work, a strong need for control across all situations, and a sense of time urgency. The Type A personality is recognizable through overt behaviors such as excessive anger, irritability, and rapid speech and body movements; thus can be contrasted with the Type B pattern, which is characterized by a more relaxed approach to life. The usefulness of recognizing Type A behavior as a risk factor has become more apparent with the beginnings of some success in changing Type A individuals' behaviors and cognitions, thereby preventing recurrences of myocardial infarction (Thoresen & Eagleston, 1985).

Other studies have led in the direction of increased precision in measuring and addressing the Type A pattern by showing that some of the characteristics associated with its behaviors overshadow others. In particular, it seems that the Type A individual's intense job involvement is not associated with heart disease (Spielberger, 1989), but that anger and hostility are more salient factors in placing him or her at risk for cardiac disease (Friedman & Booth-Kewley, 1987; Matthews, 1988; Spielberger, 1989).

Attempts have also been made to determine relationships between personality characteristics and cancer. The relationship between risk behaviors and the development of some cancers is known, but the role of personality as a predisposing factor is less clear. Temoshok and her colleagues (Temoshok et al., 1985) posit a cancer-prone personality, which they have labeled Type C. The individual whom they view as vulnerable to cancer is emotionally repressed, apathetic, and even hopeless. Although other researchers report similar findings, those studies largely focused not on the initial development of cancer but on survival rates. For instance, Pettingale (1984) found that breast cancer patients who displayed helplessness and passive acceptance of the disease were more likely to have recurrences than those with more hopeful and expressive personalities. Jensen (1987) also followed up on breast cancer patients and found that, over two years, cancer was more likely to spread if an individual demonstrated repression and an inability to express emotions.

Social Factors

The health of individuals is drastically affected by their membership in specific populations. Consider, for example, the effects of gender on health and illness. On average, women live longer than men, but women are more likely to be subject to chronic illnesses and to have other health problems (Public Health Service, 1985; Strickland, 1988; Rodin & Ickovics, 1990). Women use health-care services more frequently, either because of the presence of more health problems or because of gender-driven differences in sick-role behaviors. Of course, there are also some problems that are unique to women, such as concerns related to pregnancy or breast disease; and some that affect women disproportionately, such as lupus, osteoporosis, and eating disorders (Rodin & Ickovics, 1990). Unlike men, women are also subject to differences in how they are treated by medical personnel, are more likely to receive prescriptions for psychoactive medications, and possibly undergo unnecessary surgeries. At the same time, they are less likely than men to receive careful diagnostic workups when presenting the same symptoms—"Men get medical workups; women get tranquilizers" (Holt, 1990). Women have also been vastly underrepresented in health research, making the recent opening of the National Institutes of Health Office of Research on Women's Health a necessity.

Health problems are further exacerbated for minority women, who "suffer a disproportionate share of illness" and "experience higher infant and maternal mortality rates; greater prevalence [for] chronic diseases such as diabetes, hypertension, cardiovascular disease, and certain types of cancer; and a lower life expectancy than their White counterparts" (Manley et al., 1984, p. II–37). The differences between African American males and White males are just as clear, with mortality rates for Black males remaining 50 percent higher than those for White males (Rene, 1987). African American older people are more likely than the White older age group to be sick and disabled and to see themselves as being in poor health. They have higher rates of chronic disease, functional impairment, and risk factors such as high blood pressure (AARP, 1995). Cutting across ethnic and gender lines are the major barriers to health brought about by poverty, according to Albino and Tedesco (1984):

> It is indisputable that health suffers when nutrition is poor; when living conditions are crowded and unsanitary, when the environment is polluted; when there is no respite from noise, when there is no meaningful work; when there is continuing stress related to unequal social treatment; and [when] there are few ties to other human beings who are able to provide comfort, esteem, and mutual support. Until we can begin to change this total situation, poor health will be just another symptom of poverty, and resources will continue to be poured into secondary- and tertiary-level care for chronic health problems that are to a high degree preventable. (p. 170)

At the microsystem level, access to social support of any kind is often considered to be as important as any other factor—including psychological state—that affects health. Studies that examine the relationships between social support and health indicate that social support affects both the onset of health problems (S. Cohen, 1988; Gentry & Kobasa, 1984) and recovery from serious illnesses (DiMatteo & Hays, 1981).

Particular attention has been paid to the interactions among stress, social support, and health outcomes. Gentry and Kobasa emphasize the role of social support as a buffer, protecting people from the harmful effects of high and chronic levels of stress. Cohen, however, makes a distinction between (1) stress-buffering models, which posit social-support systems as protectors against the pathogenic influences of stressful events; and (2) main-effect models, which see support as an important predictor of health regardless of current stress levels. Cohen's (1988) conceptualization emphasizes that the individual's perception that social support is available is the most likely source of the stress-buffering effect, whereas social integration (the number and strength of social ties) is the primary cause of the more general main effects. In either situation, the links between social resources and health can be explained by the availability of useful information and advice; the role of social support in enhancing feelings of self-esteem, identity, and motivation; the presence of social controls and encouragement of health-enhancing behaviors; or the existence of tangible assistance in solving problems.

The preponderance of evidence indicates that social support, along with personality variables, cognitions, and coping mechanisms, can have a major impact on health outcomes. These personal factors may have direct, biological effects or may work more indirectly through their influence on health-related behaviors. Although these pathways may as yet be unclear, their results are certain. Psychosocial factors have a major impact on physical outcomes, and some psychosocial factors are amenable to change through interpersonal processes, making health-focused counseling a necessity.

Multicultural Considerations

The health of an individual can be impacted and influenced by a variety of beliefs, expectations, and behaviors rooted within one's cultural development and context. Behavior does not exist within a vacuum, but is influenced, created, and maintained by multiple factors, including cultural variables. Counselors in the mental health field have become increasingly aware of the role of cultural factors, such as race, ethnicity, gender, social class, religion, and sexual orientation, in psychological and social development and functioning (Atkinson, Morten, & Sue, 1998). At the same time, over the past three decades the counseling field has recognized multiculturalism as a significant force in the treatment process.

Numerous authors have argued that traditional psychology and counseling approaches and techniques are ineffective when they minimize or ignore the importance of variables such as age, gender, race, ethnicity, sexual orientation, and disability (e.g., Casas, Ponterotto, & Gutierrez, 1986; Enns, 1997; Malgady, 1996; Olkin, 1999; Perez, DeBord, & Bieschke, 1999). As a result, assessment and treatment literature has emerged with specific considerations for clients from particular cultural groups (e.g., Aponte & Wohl, 2000; Enns, 1997; Olkin, 1999; Perez, DeBord, S. Bieschke, 1999). When understood and appropriately applied, sensitivity to multicultural issues greatly facilitates the health counseling process and leads to treatments that are more specific and effective.

The United States traditionally has been considered a "melting pot" in which diverse populations were assumed and expected to assimilate to mirror "mainstream" White America. Through experiences commonly associated with daily living and working together, it was thought that people of diverse cultures would acculturate or adopt "American" customs and values. For a number of reasons, however, many groups have opted to hold onto their cultural heritages, traditions, identities, and customs; they wanted their cultural characteristics and values recognized as legitimate rather than inferior or wrong (Baruth & Manning, 1999). Considerable evidence suggests that the melting-pot metaphor does not provide an accurate description of the many cultural groups living in the United States. Cultural pluralism is now recognized as a fact. The assumed expectation to become "Americanized," or the belief that all cultures naturally gravitate toward an "American culture," has been replaced with greater sensitivity to preserving, recognizing, and celebrating cultural differences. With this acceptance has come the understanding that effective health counseling should be based on the adaptation of treatment to meet the cultural needs and expectations of all clients.

Individuals from ethnic and racial minority groups and/or with a biracial, multiethnic, or multiracial identity represent the largest growing populations in the United States (Judy & D'Amico, 1997; Wehrly, Kenney, & Kenney, 1999). The changing U.S. demographic landscape promises a richness of diversity and multiple perspectives, but also many difficult challenges that everyone in the United States continues to struggle with and address. Historically, minority populations have found themselves at the bottom of the economic and social order in comparison to the White majority. Persons of color are disproportionately represented among the poor, the unemployed, the homeless, and the sick.

Hand in hand with these concerns, systemic and societal issues of racism and oppression continue to be a significant aspect of U.S. life (Thompson & Neville, 1999) Although these demographic trends have been recognized and discussed since the 1990 U.S. Census, educational institutions, employers, government agencies, health-care agencies, and other professional bodies are only now beginning to engage in systemic approaches to become more knowledgeable, effective, and culturally sensitive and responsive to all groups within the population (APA, 2001). The challenge facing mental health-care practitioners is to provide effective service that is accessible for all people while being sensitive enough to be tailored to meet the cultural needs of each ethnic or social group member.

Within the mental health field and counseling, incorporating and considering multicultural factors is no longer viewed as a separate approach or type of treatment. All counseling at its core is multicultural counseling (Pedersen, 1990); however, not all counselors purposefully address and explore the cultural context. Currently, the generally accepted and promoted effective and ethical treatment of any one individual needs to consider the cultural factors and diversity of the treatment process (APA, 2001). Multicultural counseling should include direct and purposeful consideration and exploration of the cultural context and worldview of both the counselor and the client.

One's cultural background and experiences within the majority culture provide a framework through which current experiences and information are processed and behavior is produced, according to Hughes, (1993). As such, health-related behavior has a cultural component encompassing not only both the creation and maintenance of behavior, but also the process of behavior change. From this perspective, it must be clearly noted that all counseling about health issues can also be viewed as multicultural health counseling. Not so long ago the idea that clients are embedded within a cultural context that dramatically influences clinical treatment would only have been accepted by a small group of counselors.

Currently, however, this very same idea is a cornerstone and necessity for effective treatment planning.

Health behaviors are significantly influenced by a variety of multicultural factors. Cultural expectations around diet, use of drugs and alcohol, sexual behavior, and illness can all influence people's health behaviors. Even the expression of symptoms can have a cultural component, as some "symptoms" are not recognized as such because may be so widely experienced in a given culture (Zola, 1973).

Another area in which cultural differences are clearly apparent is with regard to access to health and mental health services and health-care utilization rates. The Health Belief Model (discussed earlier in this chapter) states that whether a person seeks treatment for a symptom can be predicted by two factors: the extent to which one perceives a threat to his or her health and the extent to which he or she thinks that a particular health measure will be effective in reducing that threat. Needless to say, however, the HBM does not adequately address socioeconomic factors for those without access to health services or insurance or funds to pay for them. Yet the Health Belief Model focuses on the cognitive component related to cultural mistrust of mental health services and practitioners.

Clients from some ethnic groups may question whether clinicians will adequately understand their concerns in a manner that honors and respects their cultural background; therefore they may not even try to access services, believing that counselors will not be responsive (Sue et al., 1991). Previous research found that misclassification of mental health disorders of ethnic clients (e.g., African American, Latino, Asian American) was due to the counselor's lack of understanding of cultural and/or linguistic differences (Huertin-Roberts & Snowden, 1993). Other population groups may rely on traditional folk remedies or laypersons for care as opposed to obtaining health-care services through majority culture-endorsed, help-seeking pathways (e.g., primary care doctor, emergency room, mental health services), according to Chung and Lin (1994).

THE HEALTH COUNSELING APPROACH

The traditional medical model maintains an emphasis on physical symptomatology and a focus on illness rather than on wellness. This model no longer seems adequate to meet society's health needs now that the interactions among psychosocial and physical factors have been recognized and now that most common ailments are amenable to prevention or control through behavior change. To augment the work of the medical establishment, a strategy to help people maintain or improve their health through their own efforts is needed. The health counseling approach attempts to accomplish this task by helping people develop and practice health-enhancing behaviors.

The development of health-oriented behaviors seems to depend as much on specific skills as it does on factual information. Although people need to know something about the health issues that they are addressing, they also need to believe that they know *how* to change their behaviors. Because personal skills are so crucial, health counseling uses psychoeducational methods aimed toward skill building.

The literature concerning linkages between personal characteristics and health outcomes is equivocal, or conflicted, in some areas, but one clear message does emerge: A sense of personal control seems to be at the heart of many people's success in optimizing their health. Because this sense of control seems basic to health enhancement, counselors need to use interventions designed to increase clients' perceptions of control and self-efficacy.

It is also clear that health is at least partly a function of the interaction between an individual and his or her social environment. For this reason, health counseling tends to broaden the scope of the counseling process beyond the individual to include the social system. It is best to have interventions that are designed to help the client build social support and, if possible, lessen environmental stressors.

The health counseling approach clearly acknowledges the salience of multicultural factors—including culture-specific beliefs, values, and behaviors—and recognizes human universalities; but it also views as significant the differences among individuals within various groups. A health counselor's view of diversity is broadened to include ethnographic and racial factors, demographic factors (e.g., age, gender, and sexual orientation), affiliation (e.g., religious), and status (e.g., socioeconomic). Within this broader multicultural view, a health counselor's sensitivity to clients' worldview and their responsiveness to each individual client's varying needs becomes a salient feature of therapeutic interaction. As such, health concerns and questions are framed within the client's contextual lens in which concerns are viewed as impacted by his or her cultural experiences. Therefore, the mandate for all counselors is to recognize that multicultural health counseling is a combination of two converging worldviews, both of which contribute to the counseling process. It is up to the counselor, however, to ensure that he or she is operating in a manner that is respectful of a client's cultural context.

The aim of health counseling is to build up the individual's ability to engage in self-management, which, in turn requires a repertoire of health-oriented skills, a belief in one's ability to address life's challenges, and an environment that encourages positive development. Thus, the following three general emphases permeate the process of health counseling:

- A focus on skill building
- A focus on self-efficacy and personal control
- A focus on social and systemic interventions

Skill Building

Thoresen (1984) points out that the health-enhancement literature tends to assume that people will be able to take better care of their health if they have information and encouragement:

> Behaving in personally responsible ways—that is, exercising effective selfmanagement—requires a number of skills that are not necessarily inherent in everyone's repertoire. . . . People need to be taught how to be more caring and more responsible for their own health and well-being, especially when the social environment commonly promotes irresponsible or nonhealthy behavior. (p. 300)

Whether a client is working toward general health maintenance, toward risk reduction, or toward stabilization of an existing condition, he or she needs help with skill development, not just with cognitive input. Yet, as Thoresen has implied, health professionals frequently depend on the provision of information as their only psychoeducational vehicle. Consider, for example, current practices regarding drug and alcohol abuse interventions that Lewis, Dana, and Blevins (1988) describe:

> "Educational" approaches in the form of lectures about the dangers of drugs and alcohol are used very widely, both as preventive tools and as treatment methods. In inpatient alcoholism treatment programs, for instance, a great deal of time is likely to be spent on lectures concerning the disease concept and the negative effects of alcohol. Although this approach may affect cognitive knowledge, it does not appear to have any measurable effect on behavior. (p. 182)

In view of the evidence that information alone neither prevents nor interrupts substance abuse, health counselors should implement other educational options. People who have not yet developed problems related to substance use might benefit by developing life skills that emphasize a preventive function. For instance, stress-management and relaxation skills might be good replacements for alcohol or drugs for dealing with anxiety; problem-solving and decision-making skills might forestall the impulsiveness of drug use; interpersonal and life-planning skills might encourage participation in nonsubstance-related recreation; and assertiveness skills might help young people avoid the pressure to drink or use drugs in social settings. Clients being treated for existing drug or alcohol problems also need help in developing these skills, along with more intensive training that might help them avoid risk-for-relapse situations, identify and practice methods for coping in social situations, and deal with personal cravings and external pressures to use.

Self-Efficacy and Personal Control

The example of substance abuse also helps to illustrate the importance of strategies designed to enhance self-efficacy, or an individual's belief in his or her ability to meet a specific challenge effectively. "With regard to drinking, self-efficacy refers to a problem drinker's degree of confidence in his or her ability to control his or her drinking in situations that are generally associated with problem drinking" (Curry & Marlatt, 1987, p. 118). Whether the individual client's primary drug of choice is alcohol or another substance, he or she can be expected to deal with the problem most effectively if the person's sense of self-efficacy is high.

> When coping skills are underdeveloped and poorly used because of disbelief in one's efficacy, a relapse will occur. Faultless self-control is not easy to come by for pliant activities, let alone for addictive substances. Nevertheless, those who perceive themselves to be inefficacious are more prone to attribute a slip to pervasive self-regulatory inefficacy. Further coping efforts are then abandoned, resulting in a total breakdown in self-control. (Bandura, 1982, pp. 129–130)

Unfortunately, many of the strategies in use in current treatment programs for alcohol- and/or drug-dependent clients emphasize powerlessness and loss of control, rather than power and self-efficacy.

> It is ironic that the major strength of the disease model, absolving the addict of personal responsibility for the problem behavior, may also be one of its shortcomings. . . . If an alco-

holic has accepted the belief that it is impossible to control his or her drinking (as embodied in the AA slogan that one is always "one drink away from a drunk"), then even a single slip may precipitate a total, uncontrolled relapse. Since drinking under these circumstances is equated with the occurrence of a symptom signifying the reemergence of the disease, one is likely to feel as powerless to control this behavior as one would with any other disease symptom. (Marlatt & Gordon, 1985, pp. 7–8)

It is possible to work with substance-abusing clients in ways that emphasize the development of self-efficacy and that avoid notions of powerlessness. Such strategies begin at intake, with the counselor encouraging clients to take responsibility for their own treatment. Clients begin to build a sense of the possibility of control when they are allowed to decide on goals, beginning with the decision about whether to make any changes at all in their drinking or drug use. Once the commitment to change has been made, clients enhance their sense of the possibility of control as they identify situations that place them at risk for substance use and as they learn how to use coping methods that work for them. Each time coping strategies are used successfully, self-efficacy is enhanced and long-term maintenance of the new behavior becomes a more likely outcome.

Clearly, an emphasis on skill building and a focus on control and self-efficacy are complementary. Effective implementation of skills enhances self-efficacy and this sense in turn encourages attempts to develop new competencies. If those practicing health counseling think in terms of the example of substance abuse, it is possible to see that the client who learns how to cope with situations previously associated with drinking or drug use may become more aware of his or her efficacy and more optimistic about the possibility of control with each success. At the same time, a client who is treated as a responsible person, and as capable of making positive decisions, is likely to be motivated to perform the hard work involved in embarking on new behaviors. A sense of self-efficacy may elicit an optimistic view that is often missing in treatments that emphasize powerlessness.

A self-management approach that focuses on skills and self-efficacy can be useful for a variety of health-related issues. One client may be learning to manage a chronic disease such as diabetes, another may be attempting weight control or smoking cessation, and still another may be addressing behavioral variables that put him or her at risk for heart disease. As does the substance-abusing client, these clients need to come to a believe in the possibility of control. Regardless of the specific health problem being addressed, the general principles underlying self-management hold true.

The self-management strategy also cuts across the methods used by the health counselor and the contexts in which service is provided. It is an appropriate goal of an educational intervention that focuses on general life skills for people who have not shown signs of any particular health problems. Self-management is just as applicable when the method being used is individual counseling for a client trying to cope with a serious illness, or for group counseling for people attempting to support one another in the eradication of health-jeopardizing behaviors. An examination of the usual processes involved makes clear the generalizability of this approach; according to Kanfer (1980):

Training in self-management requires strong early support from the helper, with the client gradually relying more and more on his [or her] newly developed skills. These include skills in (1) self-monitoring; (2) establishment of specific rules of conduct by contracts with oneself or others: (3) seeking support from the environment for fulfillment; (4) self-evaluation;

and (5) generating strong, reinforcing consequences for engaging in behaviors which achieve the goals of self-control. (p. 344)

The focus, then, is on personal power and competence, not on dependence on professional assistance.

Social and Systemic Interventions

Although individual competence is important, "social environments can either facilitate or restrict people's competence development and adaptation" (Cowen, 1985, p. 38). Each person's health is affected by the environment, both directly through the presence or absence of health hazards, and indirectly through the effects of the setting on individual behaviors. If services that focus on clients' self-management skills are to have maximum impact, they should be joined by attempts to affect the wider social systems as well. Ideally, both macrosystem and microsystem interventions should be considered. Macrosystems "refer to the overarching institutions of the culture or subculture, such as the economic, social, educational, legal, and political systems. . . ." Microsystems involve "the complex of relations between the developing person and environment in an immediate setting containing that person (e.g., home, school, workplace)" (Bronfenbrenner, 1976, p. 3).

Interventions directed toward macrosystems occur largely at the policy-formation level, and they involve strategies such as imposing economic incentives or sanctions, creating barriers between individuals and risky products or situations, and placing controls on the advertisement or promotion of products related to unhealthful behaviors (Jeffrey, 1989). Smoking behavior, for instance, is affected on a populationwide basis through strategies, such as taxation, limitations on settings in which smoking is allowed, and controls on cigarette advertising, which also have more direct effects on nonsmokers' health because of the affect on the air around them.

In the context of health counseling, microsystem interventions focus on the healthy or unhealthy aspects of those environments that have the most immediate effect on individuals' lives. The workplace and the family are two examples of such influential microsystems.

The importance of the workplace in enhancing individual health has become more and more apparent as corporate wellness programs continue to proliferate. Employers' recognition of their stake in maintaining employee health has fueled the growth of wellness and health-promotion programs, with the workplace being "recognized as an appropriate site for the encouragement of healthy lifestyles" (Lewis & Lewis, 1986, p. 139). Currently, most programs to promote health offer at least some activities that focus on specific risk factors. Smoking-cessation clinics, weight-loss groups, drug and alcohol information, and exercise classes or facilities are elements of many programs. Just as basic, however, is a general orientation toward wellness. Most programs try to encourage employees to take control of their own health by offering help with self-assessment and planning, along with encouragement aimed toward maintaining health improvements.

The element that should be added to workplace wellness programs is a recognition that: "Identifying the effects of environmental factors on employees' health is just as important as strengthening individual coping mechanisms and self-responsibility" (Lewis & Lewis, 1986, p. 145); in fact this is complementary to self-management programs. For instance, if a wellness program includes training in stress-management techniques, it should also address questions related to the stressful aspects of the workplace itself. Focus should be placed not just on increasing the adaptiveness of individual employees, but also on enhancing the organizational climate, on building social support mechanisms into the corporate environment, and on lessening physical stressors (e.g., inadequate light, extreme temperatures, excessive noise, or noxious fumes). Similarly, if a company offers smoking-cessation programs as part of its wellness effort, it should also examine its policies concerning the locations where smoking is allowed.

The family is even more closely involved with individual health and well-being. Turk and Kerns (1985) say that the family is "the major context in which illness occurs and health is maintained" (p. 2). The power of the family to affect individual well-being becomes especially apparent when health problems occur, with family support serving as an important component in recovery (Roback, 1984; Turk & Kerns, 1985). In fact, "[W]hen patients are faced with disharmony in their families, family instability, or social isolation, they are less likely to cooperate with their medical regimens" (Friedman & DiMatteo, 1989, p. 77). Conversely, the illness or disability of a family member has a major impact on the family's functioning. There is no doubt that health counseling strategies should include work with the families of people who are facing chronic or acute health problems.

AN INTEGRATED APPROACH

Health counseling combines direct, skill-building strategies with environmental interventions. This integrated approach is helpful in dealing with a variety of health-related issues. Most of this book's chapters are devoted to specific health-related problems and/or behaviors and are meant to serve primarily as examples to illustrate the potential applications of health counseling. Any number of additional health-risk behaviors and problems exist and can be approached through similar combinations of strategies. In chapter 3 we describe details the specific strategies and skills that underlie the health counseling approach.

REFERENCES

Ader, R. (Ed.). (1981). *Psychoneuroimmunology.* New York: Academic.

Ader, R. (1989, August). *Psychoneuroimmunology.* Paper presented at the 97th annual convention of the American Psychological Association, New Orleans.

Ader, R., & Cohen, N. (1984). Behavior and the immune system. In W. D. Gentry (Ed.), *Handbook of behavioral medicine* (pp. 117–173). New York: Guilford.

Adler, T. (1991, February). Optimists coping skills may help beat illnesses. *The APA Monitor,* 22(2), 12.

Ajzen, I., & Fishbein, M. (1980). *Understanding attitudes and predicting social behavior.* Englewood Cliffs, NJ: Prentice-Hall.

Ajzen, I. (1988). *Attitudes, personality and behavior.* Chicago: Dorsey Press.

Albino, J. E., & Tedesco, L. A. (1984). Women's health issues. In A. U. Rickel, M. Gerrard, & I. Iscoe (Eds.), *Social and psychological problems of women: Prevention and crisis intervention* (pp. 157–172). Washington, DC: Hemisphere Publishing Corporation.

American Association of Retired Persons (AARP). (1995). *A portrait of older minorities.* Long Beach, CA: Author.

American Psychological Association (APA). (2001). *Guidelines for multicultural counseling proficiency for psychologists: Implications for education and training, research and practice.* Washington, DC: Author.

Antonovsky, A. (1979). *Health, stress, and coping.* San Francisco: Jossey-Bass.

Antonovsky, A. (1984). The sense of coherence as a determinant of health. In J. D. Matarazzo, S. M. Weiss, J. A. Herd, N. E. Miller, & S. M. Weiss (Eds.), *Behavioral health: A handbook of health enhancement and disease prevention* (pp. 114–128). New York: Wiley.

Antonovsky, A. (1987). *Unraveling the mystery, of health: How people manage stress and stay well.* San Francisco: Jossey-Bass.

Aponte, J. F., & Wohl, J. (Eds.). (2000). *Psychological intervention and cultural diversity.* Boston: Allyn & Bacon.

Atkinson, D. R., Morten, G., & Sue, D. W. (1998). *Counseling American minorities* (5th ed.). Boston: McGraw-Hill.

Bandura, A. (1982). Self-efficacy mechanism in human agency. *American Psychologist, 37,* 122–147.

Bandura, A. (1977). Self-efficacy: Toward a unifying theory of behavior change. *Psychological Bulletin, 84,* 191–215.

Bandura, A. (1986). *Social foundations of thought and action: A social cognitive theory.* Englewood Cliffs, NJ: Prentice-Hall.

Bandura, A. (1997). *Self-efficacy.* New York: Freeman.

Bartrop, R. W., Luckhurst, E., Lazarus, L., Kiloh, L. G., & Penny, R. (1977). Depressed lymphocyte function after bereavement. *Lancet, 1,* 834–836.

Baruth, L. G., & Manning, M. L. (1999). *Multicultural counseling and psychotherapy: A lifespan perspective* (2nd ed.). Upper Saddle River, NJ: Merrill.

Becker, M. H. (1974). The health belief model and personal health behavior. *Health Education Monographs, 2,* 324–508.

Becker, H. & Rosenstock, I. (1984). Compliance with medical advice. In A. Steptoe & A. Mathews (Eds.), *Health care and human behavior* (pp. 167–294). London: Academic.

Borysenko, J. (1984). Stress, coping, and the immune system. In J. D. Matarazzo, S. M. Weiss, J. A. Herd, N. E. Miller, & S. M. Weiss (Eds.), *Behavioral health: A handbook of health enhancement and disease prevention* (pp. 248–260). New York: Wiley.

Boyce, W. T., Cassel, J. C., Collier, A. M., Jensen, E. W., Ramey, C. T., & Smith, A. H. (1977). Influence of life events and family routines on childhood respiratory tract illness. *Pediatrics, 60,* 609–615.

Bronfenbrenner, U. (1976). Reality and research in the ecology of human development. *Master lectures on developmental psychology.* Washington, DC: American Psychological Association.

Buie, J. (1988, July). "Control" studies bode better health in aging. *APA Monitor,* p. 20.

Casas, J. M., Ponterotto, J. G., & Gutierrez, J. M. (1986). An ethical indictment of counseling research and training: The cross-cultural perspective. *Journal of Counseling and Development, 64,* 347–349.

Chung, R. C-Y, & Lin, K. M. (1994). Help-seeking behavior among Southeast Asian refugees. *Journal of Community Psychology, 22,* 109–120.

Cohen, F. (1984). Coping. In J. D. Matarazzo, S. M. Weiss, J. A. Herd, N. E. Miller, & S. M. Weiss (Eds.), *Behavioral health: A handbook of health enhancement and disease prevention* (pp. 261–274). New York: Wiley.

Cohen, S. (1988). Psychosocial models of the role of social support in the etiology of physical disease. *Health Psychology, 7,* 269–297.

Cowen, E. L. (1985). Person-centered approaches to primary prevention in mental health: Situation focused and competence-enhancement. *American Journal of Community Psychology, 13,* 31–48.

Curry, S. (1989, August). Motivation for behavior change: Testing models with smoking cessation. Paper presented at the 97th annual convention of the American Psychological Association, New Orleans.

Curry S. G., & Marlatt, G. A. (1987). Building self-confidence, self efficacy and self-control. In W. M. Cox (Ed.), *Treatment and prevention of alcohol problems: A resource manual* (pp. 117–137). New York: Academic.

DiClemente, C. C. (1981). Self-efficacy and smoking-cessation maintenance: A preliminary report. *Cognitive Therapy and Research, 5,* 175–187.

DiMatteo, M. R., & Hays, R. (1981). Social support and serious illness. In B. H. Gottlieb (Ed.), *Social networks and social support.* Newbury Park, CA: Sage.

Engel, G. L. (1977). The need for a new medical model: A challenge for biomedicine. *Science, 196,* 129–136.

Enns, C. (1997). *Feminist theories and feminist psychotherapies: Origins, themes, and variations.* New York: Haworth Press.

Folkman, S., & Lazarus, R. S. (1980). An analysis of coping in a middle-aged community sample. *Journal of Health and Social Behavior, 21,* 219–239.

Friedman, H. S., & Booth-Kewley, S. (1987). The disease-prone personality: A meta-analytic view of the construct. *American Psychologist, 42,* 539–555.

Friedman, H. S., & DiMatteo, M. R. (1989). *Health psychology.* Englewood Cliffs, NJ: Prentice-Hall.

Friedman, M., & Rosenman, R. H. (1974). *Type A behavior and your heart.* New York: Knopf.

Gentry, W. D., & Kobasa, S. C. O. (1984). Social and psychological resources mediating stress illness relationships in humans. In W. D. Gentry (Ed.), *Handbook of behavioral medicine* (pp. 87–116). New York: Guilford.

Godin, G., & Kok, G. (1996). The theory of planned change: A review of its application to health-related behaviors. *American Journal of Health Promotion, 11*(2), 87–98.

Greenfield, N. S., Roessler, R., & Crosley, A. P. (1959). Ego strength and length of recovery from infectious mononucleosis. *Journal of Nervous and Mental Disease, 128*, 125–128.

Holt, L. H. (1990, October). *How the medical care system has failed to meet women s needs.* Paper presented at the Rush/North Shore Medical Center Women and Mental Health conference, Evanston, IL.

Huertin-Roberts, S., & Snowden, L. (1993). *Comparison of ethnographic descriptors of depression and epidemiological catchment area data for African-Americans.* Paper presented at the 18th annual American Anthropology Association meeting, Washington, DC.

Hughes, C. G. (1993). Culture in clinical psychiatry. In A. C. Gaw (Ed.), *Culture, ethnicity, and mental illness* (pp. 3–41). Washington, DC: American Psychiatric Press.

Jackson, G. G., Dowling, H. F., Anderson, T. O., Riff, L., Saporta, M. S., & Turck, M. (1960). Susceptibility and immunity to common upper respiratory viral infections—The common cold. *Annals of Internal Medicine, 53*, 719–738.

Jacobs, M. A., Spilken, A. Z., Norman, M. M., & Anderson, L. S. (1970). Life stress and respiratory illness. *Psychosomatic Medicine, 32*, 233–242.

Janz, N. K., & Becker, M. H. (1984). The Health Belief Model: A decade later. *Health Education Quarterly, 11*(1), 1–47.

Jeffery, R. W. (1989). Risk behaviors and health: Contrasting individual and population perspectives. *American Psychologist, 44*, 1194–1202.

Jensen, M. R. (1987). Psychobiological factors predicting the course of breast cancer. *Journal of Personality, 55*, 317–342.

Judy, R. W., & D'Amico, C. (1997). *Workforce 2020.* Indianapolis: Hudson Institute.

Kanfer, F. H. (1980). Self-management methods. In F. H. Kanfer & A. P. Goldstein (Eds.), *Helping people change* (pp. 334–389). New York: Pergamon.

Kasl, S. V., Evans, A. S., & Neiderman, J. C. (1979). Psychosocial risk factors in the development of infectious mononucleosis. *Psychosomatic Medicine, 41*, 445–466.

Keller, V., & White, M. (1997). Choices and changes: A new model for influencing patient health behavior. *Journal of Clinical Outcomes Management, 4*(6), 33–36.

Kobasa, S. C. (1979). Stressful life events, personality and health: An inquiry into hardiness. *Journal of Personality and Social Psychology, 37*, 1–11.

Kobasa, S. C. (1987). Stress responses and personality. In R. C. Barnett, L. Biener, & G. K. Baruch (Eds.), *Gender and stress* (pp. 308–329). New York: Free Press.

Kobasa, S. C., Maddi, S. R., & Courington, S. (1981). Personality and constitution as mediators in the stress–illness relationship. *Journal of Health and Social Behavior, 22*, 368–378.

Lazarus, R. S., & Folkman, S. (1984). Coping and adaptation. In W. D. Gentry (Ed.), *Handbook of behavioral medicine* (pp. 282–325). New York: Guilford.

Leventhal, H., Meyer, D., & Nerenz, D. (1980). The commonsense representation of illness danger. In S. Rachman (Ed.), *Contributions to medical psychology* (pp. 7–30). Oxford, England: Pergamon.

Leventhal, H., Zimmerman, R., & Gutmann, M. (1984). Compliance: A self-regulation perspective. In W. D. Gentry (Ed.), *Handbook of behavioral medicine* (pp. 369–436). New York: Guilford.

Lewis, J. A., Dana, R. Q., & Blevins, G. A. (1988). *Substance abuse counseling: An individualized approach.* Pacific Grove, CA: Brooks/Cole.

Lewis, J. A., & Lewis, M. D. (1986). *Counseling programs for employees in the workplace.* Pacific Grove, CA: Brooks/Cole.

Liang, B. (1998). Commentary on Keller and White's choices and changes: A new model for influencing patient health behavior. *Hospital Physician* (April), 37–38.

Malgady, R. G. (1996). The question of cultural bias in assessment and diagnosis of ethnic minority clients: Let's reject the null hypothesis. *Professional Psychology: Research and Practice, 27*, 73–77.

Marlatt, G. A., & Gordon, J. R. (1985). Relapse prevention. *Maintenance strategies in the treatment of addictive behaviors.* New York: Guilford.

Matarazzo, J. D. (1982). Behavioral health's challenge to academic, scientific, and professional psychology. *American Psychologist, 37*, 1–14.

Matthews, K. A. (1988). Coronary heart disease and Type A behaviors: Update on and alternative to the Friedman and Booth-Kewley (1987) quantitative review. *Psychological Bulletin, 104*, 373–380.

McConnaughy, E., DiClemente, C., Prochaska, J., & Velicer, W. (1989). Stages of change in psychotherapy: A follow-up report. *Psychotherapy, 20*, 368–375.

Meichenbaum, D., & Turk, D. C. (1987). *Facilitating treatment adherence: A practitioner's guidebook.* New York: Plenum.

Meyer, R. J., & Haggerty, R. (1962). Streptococcal infections in families: Factors altering individual susceptibility. *Pediatrics, 29,* 539–549.

Michael, J. M. (1982). The second revolution in health: Health promotion and its environmental base. *American Psychologist, 37,* 936–941.

Miller, W. R. & Rollnick, S. (1991). *Motivational interviewing: Preparing people for change.* New York: Guilford.

Millstein, S. G. (1989). Adolescent health: Challenges for behavioral scientists. *American Psychologist, 44,* 837–842.

Olkin, R. (1999). *What psychotherapists should know about disability.* New York: Guilford.

Perez, R. M., DeBord, K. A., & Bieschke, K. J. (Eds.). (1999). *Handbook of counseling and psychotherapy with lesbian, gay, and bisexual clients.* Washington, DC: American Psychological Association.

Pettingale, K. W. (1984). Coping and cancer prognosis. *Journal of Psychosomatic Research, 28,* 363–364.

Preventable Diseases Take High Toll. (1990, January 19). *Chicago Tribune,* p. 4.

Prochaska, J., Norcross, J., & DiClemente, C. (1994). *Changing for good.* New York: William Morrow.

Public Health Service (1985). *Women's health: Report of the Public Health Service task force on women's health issues.* Washington, DC: Government Printing Office.

Reker, G. T., & Wong, P. T. P. (1983, April). *The salutary effects of personal optimism and meaningfulness on the physical and psychological well-being of the elderly.* Paper presented at the 29th annual meeting of the Western Gerontological Society, Albuquerque.

Rene, A. A. (1987). Racial differences in mortality: Blacks and Whites. In W. Jones & M. F. Rice (Eds.), *Health care issues in black America: Policies, problems, and prospects* (pp. 21–42). New York: Greenwood Press.

Roback, H. B. (Ed.). (1984). *Helping patients and their families cope with medical problems.* San Francisco: Jossey-Bass.

Rodin, J. (1986). Aging and health: Effects of the sense of control. *Science, 223,* 1271–1276.

Rodin, J., & Ickovics, J. R. (1990). Women's health: Review and research agenda as we approach the twenty-first century. *American Psychologist, 45,* 1018–1034.

Rodin, J., & Langer, E. (1977). Long-term effects of a control-relevant intervention with institutionalized aged. *Journal of Personality and Social Psychology, 35,* 897–902.

Rotter, J. B. (1966). Generalized expectancies for internal versus external control of reinforcement. *Psychological Monographs, 80* (1, Whole No. 609).

Rotter, J. B. (1989, August). *Internal versus external control of reinforcement: A case history of a variable.* Paper presented at the 97th annual convention of the American Psychological Association, New Orleans.

Scheier, M. F., & Carver, C. S. (1985). Optimism, coping, and health: Assessment and implications of generalized outcome expectancies. *Health Psychology, 4,* 219–247.

Scheier, M. F., & Carver, C. S. (1987). Dispositional optimism and physical well-being: The influence of generalized outcome expectancies in health. *Journal of Personality 55*(2), 169–210.

Scheier, M. F., Weintraub, J. K., & Carver, C. S. (1986). Coping with stress: Divergent strategies of optimists and pessimists. *Journal of Personality and Social Psychology, 51,* 1257–1264.

Schleifer, S. J., Keller, S. E., Camerino, M., Thornton, J. C., & Stein, M. (1983). Suppression of lymphocyte stimulation following bereavement. *Journal of the American Medical Association, 250,* 374–377.

Schunk, D. H., & Carbonari, J. P. (1984). Self-efficacy models. In J. D. Matarazzo, S. M. Weiss, J. A. Herd, N. E. Miller, and S. M. Weiss (Eds.), *Behavioral health: A handbook of health enhancement and disease prevention* (pp. 230–247). New York: Wiley.

Schwartz, G. E. (1982). Testing the biopsychosocial model: The ultimate challenge facing behavioral medicine? *Journal of Consulting and Clinical Psychology, 50,* 1040–1053.

Schwarzer, R.(1992). Adaptation and maintenance of health behaviors: A critical review of theoretical approaches. In R. Schwarzer (Ed.), *Self-efficacy: Thought control of actions.* New York: Hemisphere.

Seeman, J. (1989). Towards a model of positive health. *American Psychologist, 44,* 1099–1109.

Seeman, M., & Seeman, T. E. (1983). Health behavior and personal autonomy: A longitudinal study of the sense of control in illness. *Journal of Health and Social Behavior, 24,* 144–160.

Spielberger, C. (1989, August). Stress, emotions, and health. Paper presented at the 97th annual convention of the American Psychological Association, New Orleans.

Strickland, B. R. (1988). Sex-related differences in health and illness. *Psychology of Women Quarterly, 12,* 381–399.

Sue, S., Fujino, D., Hu, L., Takeuchi, D., & Zane, N. (1991). Community mental health services for eth-

nic minority groups: A test of the cultural responsiveness hypothesis. *Journal of Consulting and
Clinical Psychology, 59,* 533–540.

Suls, J., & Fletcher, B. (1985). The relative efficacy of
avoidant and nonavoidant coping strategies: A
meta-analysis. *Health Psychology, 4,* 249–288.

Taylor, S. E., Lichtman, R. R., & Wood, J. V. (1984). Attributions, beliefs about control, and adjustment to
breast cancer. *Journal of Personality and Social
Psychology, 46,* 489–502.

Temoshok, L., Heller, B. W., Sagebiel, R., Blois, M., Sweet,
D. M., DiClemente, R. J., & Gold, M. L. (1985). The
relationship of psychosocial factors to prognostic
indicators in cutaneous malignant melanoma. *Journal of Psychosomatic Research, 29,* 139–154.

Thompson, C. E., & Neville, H. A. (1999). Racism, mental health, and mental health practice. *The Counseling Psychologist, 27,* 155–223.

Thoresen, C. E. (1984). Overview. In J. D. Matarazzo, S. M.
Weiss, J. A. Herd, N. E. Miller, & S. M. Weiss
(Eds.), *Behavioral health: A handbook of health
enhancement and disease prevention* (pp. 297–307).
New York: Wiley.

Thoresen, C. E., & Eagleston, J. R. (1985). Counseling for
health. *Counseling Psychologist, 13*(1), 15–87.

Turk, D. C., & Kerns, R. D. (Eds.). (1985). Health, illness,
and families: *A lifespan perspective.* New York:
Wiley.

Wehrly, B., Kenney, K. R., & Kenney, M. E. (1999).
Counseling multiracial families. Thousand Oaks,
CA: Sage.

Zola, I. K. (1973). Pathways to the doctor: From person to
patient. *Social Science and Medicine, 7,* 677–689.

CHAPTER THREE

STRATEGIES AND SKILLS OF THE HEALTH COUNSELING PROCESS

Health and intellect are the two blessings of life.
—Menander

In this book, health counseling is described more as an attitude toward counseling than as a new theory system or even as a counseling subspecialty. This *attitude about health counseling* reflects integrative, biopsychosocial, and proactive ways of viewing and working with clients. This holistic and biopsychosocial orientation means that the focus is on the whole client—physical health status, interpersonal and social competence, as well as psychological and emotional well-being—not just on the psychological and emotional aspects that tend to be the focus of the majority of theories and systems of counseling. The biopsychosocial perspective has been articulated by Engel (1977) and is clearly based on systems thinking; it is called biopsychosocial therapy (Sperry, 1988; 2001) when related to treatment issues. In addition to having this holistic perspective, health counseling is proactive, meaning that it not only emphasizes restoration of previous levels of health and well-being or adjustment, which is primarily a reactive function, but also emphasizes prevention and increasing an individual's level of development and functioning.

This chapter describes the process of health counseling and highlights some of its important strategies, skills, and concepts. It begins with a discussion of the curative factors of health counseling, then presents two different strategies for relating to patients, or clients: formal and less formal. Subsequent sections focus on 13 counseling skills commonly used in both strategies, as well as on the concepts of treatment adherence, psychoeducation or patient education, relapse prevention, and systems influences. A detailed, continuing case example illustrates these points and provides the prospective health counselor with a "feel" for the process of health counseling.

CURATIVE ELEMENTS IN
HEALTH-FOCUSED COUNSELING

The field of counseling and psychotherapy has much to offer the practice of health counseling. This section contains a brief overview of four curative factors that are operative in the practice of counseling. Based on his review of several outcome studies, Michael Lambert (1992) proposed that these four common elements are central to all forms of psychotherapy irrespective of counselors' theoretical orientation; modality of treatment (e.g., individual, group, family); or the frequency, duration, and number of sessions. Some argue that the curative elements represent a common, unifying language for the practice of psychotherapy (Miller, Duncan, & Hubble, 1997). The subsections that follow describe the four factors: (1) client resources, (2) therapeutic relationship, (3) intervention strategies and tactics, and (4) expectations (Lambert, 1992).

Client Resources

Clients do not come for treatment in a vacuum; they come with symptoms, worries, conflicts, and predicaments. Clients come with a unique developmental histories and the cultural roots that define them. In addition, they come with certain resources—both personal and environmental—that can significantly contribute to the outcome of therapy. In both medical and psychological research literature, clients' contributions to outcome are related to the phenomenon called *spontaneous remission*. Similar to the spontaneous remission of a cancerous tumor or the debilitating symptoms of multiple sclerosis, the client who is in psychotherapy can experience a remission of their depressive or anxious symptoms. Some experience such a remission after simply making their first therapy appointment, but not before keeping that appointment. On the other hand, some clients can be in therapy for months or years with little or no discernible change. What accounts for this difference? It's a matter of the absence or presence of certain kinds of client resources.

The presence of such resources is estimated to amount to about a 40 percent improvement, which occurs with any treatment (Lambert, 1992). Client resources refers to both inner and outer factors, which the client brings to therapy, that aid in recovery *irrespective* of an individual's actual participation in the treatment process. Inner resources include readiness for change, coping and personal and/or social skills, motivation, ego strength, intelligence, achievements, psychological-mindedness, courage, and history of success with change efforts. Outer resources are specific environmental resources that impact the client, including his or her social support system, financial resources, and even fortuitous events. The four client resources that can have the greatest impact on health counseling are: biological individuality, self-efficacy, optimism, and readiness for change.

Biological Individuality.   There is a growing awareness that, just as there are individual differences in a person's emotional makeup and identity, there are individual differences in a person's biological and biochemical needs and processes. But while medical science has long recognized that unique personality differences among individuals exist, people have been slow to recognize and accept the unique biological differences. Take the "food pyramid," which all students are being taught is the framework for a healthy and balanced diet for every American, similar to the "one-size-fits-all" health prescriptions—the "myth of uniformity." Among others, noted scientist Roger Williams, Ph.D., challenged this myth with research studies that have convincingly shown that there are wide structural and biochemical variations among individuals of the same age, sex, and body size. He was convinced that every individual has distinct biological needs programmed into their unique genetic makeup. He coined the term "biochemical individuality" (Williams, 1956) to describe this biological uniqueness—biological individuality—phenomenon.

What are the implications of biological individuality for health counseling? The main implication is that there can be no uniform, *one-size-fits-all* health prescription (e.g., diet, exercise plan, or stress-management program) that will be effective for everyone. In other words, all health prescriptions must be tailored to individuals' unique biological needs as well as their expectations.

Self-Efficacy.   As discussed in chapter 2, self-efficacy is the individual's belief in his or her ability to meet a specific challenge effectively (Bandura, 1997). Whether it is losing weight, increasing fitness through exercise, or stopping smoking or substance use, self-efficacy—a sense of self-control—is critical to any successful lifestyle change.

Clients begin to build a sense of the possibility of control when they are allowed to decide on their own goals, beginning with the decision about whether to make any lifestyle changes. Once the commitment to change has been made, clients enhance their sense of the possibility of control as they identify situations that place them at risk for relapse and as they learn how to use coping methods that work for them. Each time coping strategies are used successfully, self-efficacy is enhanced and long-term maintenance of new behaviors becomes a more likely outcome.

Optimism.   Clearly, an emphasis on skill building and a focus on control and self-efficacy are complementary. Effective implementation of skills enhances self-efficacy, and a sense of self-efficacy in turn encourages attempts to develop new competencies. Think in terms of the example of a substance abuser: Experience shows that the client who learns how to cope with situations previously associated with drinking or drug use becomes more aware of his or her efficacy and more optimistic about the possibilities of controlling other things with each success. At the same time, a client who is treated as a responsible person and as capable of making positive decisions is likely to be motivated to perform the hard work involved in embarking on new behaviors. His or her sense of self-efficacy may elicit an optimistic view of the possibility of control that has been missing in treatments that emphasize powerlessness.

Readiness for Change.   As noted earlier, effective health counseling is usually a collaborative venture. What does this really mean? It means that both the counselor and the client must be ready and willing to become fully involved in the health counseling process. Irrespective of the extent of the counselor's experience and expertise, unless the client is really invested in the counseling process, expected outcomes will not be achieved. This readiness and willingness to engage in the counseling (i.e., to change) cannot be taken for granted. In fact, a lack of readiness for change probably accounts for most counseling failures. This is also true for other change efforts whether it be quality, continuous quality-improvement, or work teams.

Readiness for change and the dynamics of this change stage were developed by Prochaska, Norcross, and DiClemente (1994) who identified six stages of change: precontemplation, contemplation, preparation, action, maintenance, and recycling. Those practicing health counseling would do well to have a working knowledge of the stages and the underlying construct of readiness for change. As those being counseled cycle through the stages, the counselor needs to not only understand the stage of readiness, but also how to respond appropriately to facilitate the individual's movement to a higher stage of readiness.

The first stage is *precontemplation* in which there is a denial or lack of awareness of the need for change. The second stage is *contemplation* in which, although there may be an awareness that a problem exists, there is no perceived need to do something about it. As with the first stage, insisting that an individual in need of counseling begin the process, or referring the individual to a counselor, is not only premature, it may be counterproductive.

The third stage is decision or *preparation* in which the individual not only recognizes the problem and the need to do something about it, but also decides to change and begins to make plans to change. While there is a higher level of readiness than in the first two stages, there is no guarantee that the individual will actually start to engage in the counseling process. The fourth stage is *action* in which the individual actually engages in the change process. This stage represents the optimal level of readiness for change. The fifth stage is *maintenance* in which the plan for change is still in process but the expected outcomes have not yet been achieved or the change does not feel "natural" to the individual. The sixth stage is *recycling* or relapse; the counseling outcome was not able to be sustained because of a lack of support from top management; the counseling ended prematurely; or the individual has relapsed, slipping back to a lower stage, usually contemplation: "What's your intention to change today?"

This readiness for change model has been widely used in all areas of health counseling ranging from smoking cessation to medication compliance to substance-abuse treatment and psychotherapy. Readiness can be assessed by interview as well as by paper-and-pencil instruments.

Therapeutic Relationship

The therapeutic relationship is the context in which the process of therapy is experienced and enacted. Although there are notable differences in the way this relationship is described among the various psychotherapy approaches, most acknowledge the importance of this relationship. Across these various approaches, a correlation has been found between the therapeutic relationship and psychotherapy outcome. Lambert (1992) estimates that about 30 percent of the variance in psychotherapy outcome is due to "relationship factors" as compared to 40 percent attributible to "client resources" or "spontaneous remission" factors. Based on his analysis of psychotherapy research, Strupp (1995) concludes that the therapeutic relationship is "the sine qua non in all forms of psychotherapy" (p. 70). Furthermore, the research of Orlinsky, Grawe, and Parks (1994) suggests that the quality of the client's participation in the therapeutic relationship is the essential determinant of outcome. In short, a client who is motivated, engaged, and collaborates in the process with the counselor benefits the most from the experience.

Core Conditions.   Important to the formation of a strong therapeutic alliance is what Carl Rogers called the "core conditions" of effective counseling and psychotherapy: empathy, respect, and genuineness (Rogers, 1951). It appears that when clients feel understood, safe, and hopeful, they are more likely to take the risk of disclosing painful affects and the intimate details of their lives, as well as risk thinking, feeling, and acting in more adaptive and healthful ways. However, the core conditions must actually be felt by clients and are experienced differently by clients depending on their internal dynamics and cultural matrix. Duncan, Solovey, and Rusk (1992) contend that the most helpful alliances are likely to develop when counselors establish a therapeutic relationship that matches clients' definitions of empathy, respect, and genuineness.

Transference and Countertransference.   Of the various facets of the client–counselor relationship in health counseling, the matter of transference and countertransference bears mentioning in this chapter. While transference and countertransference are phenomena usually associated with the practice of psychotherapy, particularly dynamically oriented psychotherapy, they are also present in health-care settings. In psychotherapy, transference is identification of a figure in the present (i.e., the therapist) with a figure from the past (i.e., parent or caretaker). As it relates to health counseling, *transference* is used in a less restrictive sense to refer to the emotional reactions that patients and clients have toward health-care providers. Transferences can be positive or negative and can impact the process and outcome of health counseling.

On the other hand, countertransference is a transference reaction on the part of the provider to a patient or client. *Countertransference* refers to all the emotional reactions, positive or negative, elicited in a health-care provider by someone (cf. Goodheart, 1997; Fennell, 2001). Although health counselors and other health-care providers may not recognize their countertransference feelings toward a client, the feelings and the counselor's or provider's response can significantly impact the relationship with the client and therefore the course of treatment. Whether positive or negative, feelings can blind providers to important information that the patient is trying to communicate. For instance, the provider with feelings of disapproval or revulsion about a patient's behavior (e.g., what appears to be drug-seeking behavior for pain management) may reflexively pull back from or make non-empathic or even threatening comments. When providers refuse to continue seeing certain patients, summarily refer them elsewhere, or dismiss their concerns as psychological or "all in their minds," countertransference is probably operative.

Then too, positive transference feelings can blind or distract providers from properly gathering and evaluating information needed to competently treat patients and clients. For example, admiring a patient's courage in the face of the intense pain associated with bone cancer can blind a provider to subtle indicators of depression or to treatment noncompliance. Because of its impact on process and outcome, it behooves those practicing health counseling to learn to recognize and deal with countertransference.

Countertransference seems to be more common in health-focused counseling and health-focused psychotherapy for chronic illnesses because of their very nature than with other forms of or treatment foci in health counseling. Chapter 11 discusses some factors that seem to trigger countertransference in counseling those with chronic illness and some suggestions for dealing with it.

Intervention Strategies and Tactics

One of the defining features of psychotherapeutic approaches is a unique set of strategies and tactics used in explaining the change process and socializing clients to become receptive and responsive to various technical interventions. Such strategies and tactics include clinical interpretation, free-association, confrontation, cognitive restructuring, medication, empty-chair technique, biofeedback, systematic desensitization, reframing, family sculpting, "miracle" questions, and/or other solution-focused techniques. The content and process of therapeutic sessions are ostensibly different depending on the counselor's theoretical perspective and orientation.

Despite the field's fascination—and near obsession—with specific intervention strategies and tactics, the overall impact of intervention on the outcome of treatment is rather minimal. In a seminal review of psychotherapy outcome research, Lambert (1992) estimates that a clinician's therapeutic perspective and intervention strategies and tactics contribute only about 15 percent of the variance in psychotherapy outcome. Miller, Duncan, and Hubble (1997) observe that, by and large, clients are much less impressed with their counselors' interventions than are their counselors. These authors contend that an immediate implication of Lambert's research finding is "that counselors spend less time trying to figure out the right intervention or practicing the right brand of therapy and spend more time doing what they do best: understanding, listening, building relationships, and encouraging clients to find ways to help themselves" (p. 30). Subsequent chapters of this book detail a number of specific intervention strategies and tactics for various health conditions.

Expectations

Lambert (1992) notes that the remaining 15 percent of the variance of psychotherapy is attributed to the phenomenon known as the *placebo effect.* It is that proportion of treatment outcomes related to clients' belief in their counselor or care provider, as well their belief in and hopefulness about the efficacy of the specific treatment to make a difference in their lives. Much continues to be written about the dynamics of the placebo effect and the negative placebo or *nocebo effect,* which can actually diminish or neutralize the effect of a powerful treatment (Harrington, 1997). Benson (1996) and Matthews and Clark (1998) describe the placebo effect as the "faith factor," suggesting that an individual's belief in the cure or in the clinician who provides the cure has healing or curative powers. Related to this belief are specific expectations about how, when, and why change will occur.

Research indicates that simply expecting therapy to be helpful somehow reverses demoralization, mobilizes hope, and facilitates improvement (Frank & Frank, 1991). Presumably, the creation of such hope is strongly influenced by the counselor's attitude toward the client at the outset of treatment. When doubt about positive outcomes because of the severity or chronicity of the condition or the limitations of client or treatment resources are conveyed, even in subtle ways, the placebo effect is unlikely to be "triggered" nor will the client's sense of hopelessness be easily reversed. However, when the clinician instills hope and the belief that the treatment is likely to work—verbally and/or nonverbally—improvement and positive treatment outcomes tend to occur. In other words, fostering a positive expectation for change appears to be a prerequisite for successful treatment (Snyder, Irving, & Anderson, 1991).

A STRATEGY FOR FORMAL HEALTH COUNSELING

Formal, planned health counseling sessions, particularly health-focused counseling and health-focused psychotherapy, often last about 30 minutes and may be scheduled weekly for six or more sessions depending on the nature of the change program and the type of collaboration between the health counselor and the referring health provider. In some cases, health counseling sessions are scheduled in tandem with actual change program participation; in other cases, sessions are separate and distinct. In almost all cases, follow-up contacts or sessions are arranged at 6-, 12-, and 18-month intervals after the last session to evaluate progress, deal with compliance and relapse issues, and encourage permanency of the lifestyle change.

Four phases of the counseling and psychotherapy process are applicable to the health counseling process (Dinkmeyer & Sperry, 2000). The following section describes a formal strategy for health-focused counseling that involves engaging the client and developing the relationship, conducting the assessment, selecting and implementing interventions, and maintaining or consolidating the lifestyle-change process (see Table 3.1).

Engagement and Relationship

The relationship between the counselor and the client is developed in a fashion similar to that in individual psychotherapy; however, there are some important differences involving timing and intentionality. In psychotherapy, the task of developing the relationship can be leisurely accomplished over the course of the first three or four sessions, but because of the very brief and focused nature of health counseling, achieving cooperation and negotiating a treatment agreement is the primary goal of the first session. Typically scheduled for 60 to 90 minutes, the first session is the most important of all sessions. Its purpose is to engage the client in the change process by establishing a cooperative relationship between counselor and client and by negotiating a mutually acceptable change program. During this time, the health counselor must come to understand the client's reasons and degree of motivation for making the particular lifestyle change. If the change is sought primarily to appease a spouse, the employer, or the family physician, this needs to be dealt with at the outset. If little or no intrinsic motivation can be elicited, the probability of noncompliance and limited success need to be openly discussed; also, considering whether to continue or stop treatment is best done at this time. Next, the client should be asked the following three important questions.

The first question involves a functional assessment: "How does your (obesity, smoking, pain, and so on) interfere with your daily life?" This question is followed by asking about the life tasks of work, love, and friendship, including the individual's level of functioning and degree of satisfaction in each of these. The extent of distress and impairment is often related to receptivity to change. The more distressed the individual, the more receptive he or she will be to a treatment program to relieve that distress and impairment. The

TABLE 3.1   Stages of Health-Focused Counseling

STAGE	DESCRIPTION
Engagement and relationship development	Engagement involves the development of a working relationship between counselor and client based on trust and mutual respect and a commitment to collaborate on establishing and achieving realistic goals. Unless the client is sufficiently engaged (i.e., in the action stage of readiness), goals are unlikely to be achieved and maintained. Therefore, the first goal of counseling is to effect a substantial level of engagement. Motivational counseling strategies can be used to increase the client's readiness.
Assessment	Assessment involves identifying the biological, psychological, and/or social–cultural factors that led to the development and maintenance of the client's unhealthy patterns. It should include the client's needs and expectations for change, strengths and previous successes in making personal changes, as well as the motivation and readiness for change; an assessment also should include identification of barriers to change (e.g., intrapersonal, interpersonal, social, and cultural factors).
Intervention	Intervention refers to the treatment goals to improve health patterns. Several counseling processes and interventions can be used to achieve the goals, including instruction, advice, modeling, skill-building, and practice. Since there are often barriers to adopting a new health pattern, various psychotherapeutic and systemic strategies may be required. Cognitive restructuring and reframing are commonly used when intrapersonal barriers, such as negative core beliefs or schemas, have been identified.
Maintenance and relapse prevention	Once a new pattern has been established, it is necessary to maintain that new change and prevent relapse. Monitoring progress is a key strategy at this stage, as is establishing a relapse-prevention plan. As clients are weaned from sessions and assume more responsibility for maintaining the new health patterns, occasional relapses can occur and their level of readiness may shift downward, sometimes to precontemplative or contemplative. Scheduling follow-up sessions after termination is a common to relapse-prevention plans.

counselor must be alert to the payoff or gain that a dysfunction may provide the client that thus may interfere with change efforts.

The second question involves the client's personal explanation of the symptom or condition: "What do you believe is the reason for your (obesity, stress, and so on)?" The answer to this and the follow-up questions begins to suggest the individual's health beliefs, as well as the extent of the factual accuracy that the person has of his or her condition and prognosis. This will be an important indicator of the amount of information and education that the counselor will need to provide at a later time.

Third is a set of questions to elicit the person's treatment expectations in terms of his or her, as well as the counselor's, involvement of time and effort, expected outcome, and satisfaction: "What specific changes are you expecting? By when? What kind of involvement are you willing to make to see that change occurs? What kind of involvement do you expect of me?" In addition, it would be good for the counselor to evaluate the client's previous efforts to make lifestyle changes. Specific information about number of attempts, length of time devoted, extent of success, outside help accessed, and reasons for quitting or noncompliance are important determiners of the client's current success or failure expectations.

On the basis of the counselor's understanding of background information—particularly the client's expectations for treatment and outcome—the counselor can propose a realistic change program that states broad time lines, level of involvement, and expected outcomes; the counselor should discuss them in relation to the client's expectations, which constitutes the negotiation process. The purpose of the negotiation is to achieve a mutually agreed-on contract for change; often, this agreement is put in writing, couched in performance-based language. Here's an example of this phase.

Case Example

Eleanor S. is a 38-year-old mother of three who was referred by her doctor to a health counseling specialist at the behavioral medicine clinic of Excel Health Plan, a local HMO. Her physician, who had assumed care for Eleanor when she and her husband switched to the HMO some 2 months before, determined that Eleanor was 55 pounds over her ideal weight and placed her on a daily 1,200 calorie diet. He provided her with detailed instructions for this high-protein diet and indicated that if she followed the program closely, she could expect to lose 2 to 3 pounds per week. She was told to see her physician biweekly to monitor her weight, vital signs, and certain blood levels. After 4 weeks there was a slight weight increase, so the referral for health counseling was made. During the first session, the counselor learned that Eleanor had gained 45 pounds over the past 8 years of marriage, and most of that gain had occurred in the last 18 months while working part-time for a local realtor. She related that her husband had encouraged her to develop a career once the children were in school, but now she felt that he was subtly discouraging her.

Eleanor's answers to the three screening questions suggested that she had good insight and motivation for change. Her obesity did not seem to affect her daily life unduly. She attributed her recent weight gain to the stressfulness of keeping up with all her home duties while trying to keep on top of new realty listings. She also noted that although on weekdays she was successful at following most of the diets she tried, including the Blackburn diet, she would "fall off" on weekends. Usually, her husband "rewarded" her by taking her to exotic restaurants on Saturday night, and there was a standing invitation for a seven-course meal at a relative's home on Sundays. She noted that her parents did not understand why she wanted to lose weight. She believed that she probably would be successful on her doctor's diet if she could "control my cravings better" and find time for the exercise part of the prescribed program.

A specific change program was then negotiated between the counselor and Eleanor—they would meet for 20 weekly sessions and then for follow-up sessions at 6-month intervals for 2 years. A goal of 45 pounds of weight loss over the 20 sessions, approximately 2 to 3 pounds per week, was negotiated. She also committed herself to a graduated exercise program along with a behavioral and cognitive restructuring plan. At least three conjoint sessions with Eleanor's husband were also planned. She would continue to be monitored medically by her Excel Health Plan physician who would confer regularly with the counselor.

■ ■ ■ ■ ■

Assessment

The term *assessment* is used here in a very focused fashion—assessment of the client's health and personality patterns. *Pattern* refers to the client's unique biological individuality as well as his or her predictable and consistent style of health beliefs and behaviors, including the manner in which the client thinks, feels, acts, copes, and defends the self in both stressful and nonstressful situations. Also assessed are the individual's readiness for change, strengths, and previous successes in making health behavior or other personal changes that counterbalanced dysfunctions. Finally, barriers and facilitators for successful adherence to a health prescription are assessed. Barriers include intrapersonal, interpersonal, social, and cultural factors that can hinder client progress. In short, the assessment phase of treatment needs to concentrate on specific health and personality patterns, readiness for change, strengths, barriers, and facilitators.

The health counseling assessment phase tends to be more focused and, in many cases, is briefer than the psychotherapy assessment phase. Here, the counselor attempts to understand the person's present health behaviors in terms of personal and contextual factors. As such, the standard procedure for obtaining a complete social and developmental history and assessment of personality and cognitive factors may not be possible or even necessary.

At a minimum, it is useful to do at least a brief assessment of personality style, health beliefs, and past and recent gains or payoffs for the current health condition or symptoms. In addition, it is useful to evaluate the extent and accuracy of the individual's knowledge about his or her condition. The client's earliest recollection of health or experience of illness is useful for assessing his or her health beliefs and attitudes toward health and illness (Sperry, 1986). This is done by asking the person to recall singular experiences when he or she was ill or when another family member or relative was ill. Responses often provide valuable insights into the person's body image and personality regarding cognitions or beliefs about self and others, particularly about themes of entitlement, superiority/martyrdom, and authority figures.

In terms of contextual factors, it would be helpful to do a brief assessment of the client's family of origin, with a focus on values related to health and illness behaviors, and to learn about the health and illness behaviors of other family members or relatives who could have served as social models for the client. It is essential for the counselor to assess the client's cultural health status, which, according to Allen (1981), involves the "silent" attitudes and norms of one's family, social and ethnic group, and the community that influences and reinforces certain health behaviors and not others. Allen indicates that everyone is influenced by cultural norm indicators for exercise, smoking, stress, weight control, nutrition, alcohol use or alcohol abuse, safety, and mental health; he has developed several paper-and-pencil inventories to elucidate these cultural norms. Let's return to the case example.

Case Example

On the basis of Eleanor's early recollections, health beliefs, family health values, spousal behavior, and cultural norms, the health counselor developed the following formulation. Eleanor views her inner self as small and incapable yet encapsulated in a large, outer body shell that makes her appear strong and competent in some situations but vulnerable to external influences in other situations. She views the world as demanding and sometimes cruel, especially to the sick and obese, and believes that women are to be subservient to authority figures, particularly men. Therefore, her goal is to strive to be strong and competent, yet to avoid conflict and displeasing others at all costs. Thus, overeating serves as a safety valve for the conflict between her expectations and those of authority figures. Her payoffs for being obese as a child involved special parental attention and rewards of desserts for her unquestioned obedience. Modeling for overweight was universal in Eleanor's family of origin.

Turning to contextual factors, it became clear that Eleanor's spouse was a negative support system for her weight-management program because he subtly and not so subtly sabotaged her efforts to lose weight by taking her out for high-calorie meals. A conjoint session revealed his jealousies and fears that he might lose her to another man if she lost too much weight; Mr. S. himself was moderately overweight. He also was not particularly happy about her success in the realty business, but the thought that she might leave him was the most unbearable. On the other hand, Eleanor has a college friend, with whom she now works, who was successful with a weight-loss and management program and was willing to provide Eleanor with the social support necessary. Eleanor's eastern European roots and a tradition believes that "You're not worthwhile unless you're strong enough to work; and you're not strong and healthy unless you're stout and proud of it." She checked the following items on the inventory of cultural norms (Allen, 1981), which undoubtedly reinforce her self-view and worldview:

- "It's expected that if you lose weight through dieting you'll gain it back sooner or later."
- "Sweets are a special reward for good behavior."
- "Everybody loves a fat person."
- "Sweets are just as nutritious as other food types."

■ ■ ■ ■ ■

Intervention

The goal of the *intervention* phase is quite straightforward—modify or transform the client's maladaptive pattern into a more adaptive pattern. Potentially, intervention methods include all of the therapeutic intervention strategies and tactics—focused pattern-interruption strategies, cognitive restructuring, and interpretation and/or reframing methods. A significant, obvious intervention method is often overlooked in discussions such as this: elicit and support internal and external "client resources."

In clinical settings, maladaptive patterns often manifest themselves with symptomatic distress and functional impairment; thus, decreasing symptomatology and/or increasing life functioning are usually treatment goals related to intervention. Individuals and couples who present for psychological treatment because of symptomatic distress are seeking relief from symptoms, which they have not been able to reduce by their own efforts. Therefore symptom reduction or removal should be one of the first goals of treatment. Usually, this goal is achieved with behavioral and/or medication interventions. Research indicates that as symptoms increase one or more areas of life functioning decrease; and therapeutic efforts to increase functional capacity tend to be thwarted until symptomatology is decreased (Sperry, Brill, Howard, & Grissom, 1996).

The two main levels of intervention are the individual level and the systems, or family, level. At the individual level, encouragement is the basic, nonspecific intervention. Specific interventions involve information and instruction-giving; cognitive restructuring; and behavior modification, including setting behavior goals, monitoring, pattern identification, stimulus-control, reinforcement, and relapse-prevention training.

Intervention at the systems level has the express purpose of increasing client compliance and minimizing relapse. Dropout rates from lifestyle-change programs are as high as 80 percent when no health counseling is provided. Enlisting the aid of social-support systems, such as family members, coworkers, or friends, is a critical task for both client and counselor. Not surprisingly, the more uninvolved and dysfunctional the family or the marital partner is, the more the health counselor should anticipate problems in implementing any change program. To the extent that family members can be incorporated in a change program, the more likely it is to be successful. For example, Brownwell (1984) reports that when the obese client's spouse attended sessions at which he or she was also encouraged to modify eating habits, success with weight loss and maintenance was greater than for the control group studied. Brownwell also found that an unwilling spouse can, and often does, sabotage the client's treatment program. Similarly, it has been shown that for exercise programs, the spouse's attitudes toward the change program are probably more important than the client's (Dishman, Ickles, & Morgan, 1980). If family members can be directly involved in individual or group sessions, they should be encouraged or even required to participate. If this is not possible, the family's indirect support should be enlisted.

Doherty and Baird (1983) describe "family compliance counseling" as one way of enlisting this support, and they list the following steps. After the change program has been negotiated, the client is asked to come to the next session with his or her family. The counselor begins the session by providing information about the client's health condition to all family members and answers whatever content questions they may have. This is done to develop a common mind-set and to set the stage for the family's commitment to the change program. The counselor then asks for reactions to the client's health problem and the proposed change program. Next, the counselor helps the family make a contract for compliance with the program, by first asking whether the client would like help from the family. If the response is affirmative, the counselor asks the client questions about what kind of help he or she would like and continues until a family contract emerges. The counselor can provide specific health-promotion literature to clarify and increase family members' involvement in the program. Finally, a follow-up session is scheduled for the purpose of evaluating the client's progress and the family's adherence to the support contract. Now, let's return to the case example.

Case Example

Eleanor and the counselor have already negotiated the contract for change and the assessment has specified the strategies. At the behavioral level, Eleanor was quick to learn, and she applied a number of methods for changing her eating behavior and for learning and practicing some relapse-prevention skills. Because lack of assertiveness, especially in the marriage, was defined as a major issue, skill training was begun during the third session.

Stimulus prevention or environmental engineering was stressed from the beginning. Eleanor had to avoid situations in which she would be "forced" by social convention to overeat (e.g., Sunday meals with her overeating relatives). She partially solved this by scheduling social activities with her children during that time and inviting relatives to her house for a light dinner that she prepared. She and her friend joined a beginner's aerobics class at a local YWCA.

At the cognitive level, Eleanor worked with the counselor to challenge and restructure some of her personality-style cognitions and health beliefs in a more socially useful direction. The counselor renamed her occasional relapses as "slips" rather than failures. At the social-support level, three conjoint marital sessions were helpful in reducing Mr. S.'s fears about Eleanor leaving him should she slim down. And, after some communication and skill training, he became more sensitive to her need to assert her independence. He further supported her when both sets of parents were upset with the change in their Sunday schedule. By the fifth session, Mr. S. was willing to go on the same diet plan as his wife, which aided in her compliance with the program. Eleanor's friend was invaluable in helping her stick to her weight-loss and maintenance program on the job, as well as in helping her with menu planning.

At the physiological level, she continued to be monitored biweekly by her physician who conferred periodically with the counselor. By session 20, Eleanor had shed 55 pounds, and 12 months later she was within 8 pounds of her ideal weight. Her husband was also approximately to his ideal weight, and both reported improved personal and marital functioning.

■ ■ ■ ■ ■

Maintenance and Relapse Prevention

The last phase of health counseling is maintenance and relapse prevention. The goals of this phase are to maintain the newly acquired adaptive pattern, to prevent relapse, and to reduce and/or eliminate the client's reliance on the treatment relationship. Technically, *relapse* refers to a continuation of the "original" behavior, while *recurrence* is the instigation of a "new" episode of the same problem. In this text, both terms are used synonymously. In order to prevent relapse, therapists must assess the client's risk factors and potential for relapse, and incorporate relapse-prevention strategies into the treatment process.

Relapse Prevention.   Relapse prevention is described as an intervention consisting of specific skills and cognitive strategies that prepare the client in advance to cope with the inevitable slips, or relapses, in compliance to change programs (Marlatt & Gordon, 1985; Sperry, 1986). Health counseling that does not recognize and emphasize the importance of relapse education and prevention is ineffective counseling. Subsequent chapters of this book each include a section on relapse, education, and prevention strategies specific to the chapter's content, be it weight management, smoking cessation, or exercise. This section briefly reviews four relapse education and prevention training models (Daley, 1989): recovery training, cognitive-behavioral, Marlatt's relapse-prevention, and psychoeducational. These different relapse-prevention models grew out of both inpatient and outpatient programs, often from those involving substance dependence; however, experience shows that the concepts embodied in the models have relevance to many other lifestyle-change and health-promotion programs.

Recovery Training Model.   This relapse-prevention model assumes that addiction, besides being a disease, is a way of life within a distinct subculture. Further, it assumes that recovery requires the addict not only to stop substance use but also to develop a new way of life, which includes the development of new skills and a program that can respond to several critical recovery challenges.

To avoid relapse, the client must learn to handle substance cravings, to socialize differently in order to build a new social network, to adjust to substance-free activities and to be satisfied with them, to cope with physical pain or stress without returning to substance use, to initiate and to sustain interpersonal relationships to meet intimacy needs, to refuse offers of substances, and to respond to occasional slips without succumbing to full-blown relapse. An aftercare program for meeting these challenges consists of four components: (1) recovery-training sessions, (2) fellowship meetings, (3) substance-free social and community activities, and (4) a network of long-time ex-addicts; Zackon, McAuliffe, and Chien (1985) is the primary source of the addict aftercare information.

Recovery-training sessions should focus on particular recovery issues. They are meant to be educational rather than a substitute for therapy or a 12-step program. Sessions need to help addicts examine their experiences and learn facts and ideas about recovery and healthy lifestyles. Usually, groups consist of between 6 and 30 members who meet for a minimum of an hour and a half. To actively involve all members, written handouts and group exercises are used. The sessions' primary purpose is to prepare members for predictable difficulties and to teach appropriate responses to inevitable relapses.

As do other relapse-prevention models, addict aftercare addresses the reality of relapse by discussing it before trouble arises. The developmental model encourages honest reporting of actual substance-use episodes. Relapses are carefully assessed and discussed so that members can develop strategies to forestall substance use. Systematic research on addict aftercare discloses that 32 percent of participants were abstinent during the yearlong follow-up sessions, in contrast to the 18 percent abstinence of those not in a program.

Cognitive-Behavioral Model.   The relapse-prevention model developed by Dr. Helen Annis and her colleagues at the Addiction Research Foundation of the University of Toronto incorporates tenets of Bandura's self-efficacy theory; the information here is adapted from their research (Annis, 1986). The two important elements of this cognitive-behavioral model are efficacy expectation and outcome expectation. *Efficacy expectation* refers to the belief that one has the ability to execute a certain behavior pattern. Clients who believe that they can cope with substance-related situations are more likely to do so than those who lack this belief. An *outcome expectation* refers to a judgment about the likely consequences of such a behavior change. For instance, the judgment of an alcoholic may control his or her desire to drink because of a belief that this will result in acceptance by the spouse.

According to self-efficacy theory, procedures for helping clients to begin changing may not be the most effective ones for generalizing behavior change or for maintaining long-range treatment effects. Self-efficacy theory presumes that treatment interventions are effective only if the client's expectations of personal efficacy are increased. Treatment effects that generalize into the future would be the result of strong efficacy expectations—for example, the client's confidence that he or she can successfully cope with alcohol-related situations. Conversely, low-efficacy expectations indicate poor coping behaviors in difficult situations.

The behavioral model treatment concentrates on two phases: initiating behavior change and maintaining and expanding the positive change. During the second phase, the client takes a more active role in designing performance paths that will lead to self-directed mastery experiences. As treatment progresses, the client assumes greater personal responsibility for change.

This relapse-prevention program involves 6 hours of assessment, followed by 8 outpatient sessions over a 3-month period. Outpatient treatment consists of a 1½-hour group session involving 4 to 7 clients. This group is followed by 10 to 15 minutes of individual counseling for each client during which previously assigned homework for performance tasks is reviewed and new performance tasks are planned.

Early research findings from two randomized control trials show that the cognitive–behavioral model for relapse prevention was effective in helping most clients dramatically reduce alcohol consumption. Also, these studies revealed that clients who received this kind of specialized relapse prevention improved in several personal and social functioning areas.

Marlatt's Relapse-Prevention Model.   Marlatt and his colleagues (Marlatt & Gordon, 1985) from the Addictive Behaviors Research Center at the University of Washington developed one of the most comprehensive theoretical and clinical models of relapse prevention. The model has been applied to impulse-control problems, such as sexual compulsions, and to impulsive aggressive acts, such as child abuse and rape, as well as to chemical dependency and weight control; the information that follows is adapted from the Marlatt and Gordon 1985 book.

Marlatt and Gordon believe that addictive behaviors are acquired habit patterns that can be changed by learning new procedures. Essentially, they view relapse prevention as a self-management program that helps the individual maintain changes in substance as well as behavioral addictions. A relapse-prevention approach effectively engages the client in the recovery process, giving him or her the primary responsibility for making changes. In short, recovery from addictive behaviors is a learned task that involves acquiring new skills.

This model of relapse prevention is predicated on three key assumptions about human behavior change. The first assumption is that the cause of the addictive habit and the process of behavior change are governed by different principles. The second assumption is that changing an addictive habit involves three distinct stages: Stage 1, making a commitment and becoming motivated to change; Stage 2, implementing change; and Stage 3, achieving long-term maintenance of change. The third key assumption is that maintenance accounts for the greatest proportion of variance in long-term treatment outcomes. In other words, clients have a much easier time getting sober than staying sober for a long time. Relapses most often occur during the maintenance stage.

Marlatt and his colleagues have identified several relapse determinants, which fall into one of two general categories: intrapersonal and interpersonal factors. Examples of intrapersonal factors include negative emotional states, urges, and temptations; examples of interpersonal factors include conflicts in relationships and social pressure to use substances. These researchers found that the majority of adult relapses occur in response to stressful situations—while the individual is in a negative emotional state—and following some interpersonal conflict or social pressure.

The first step in relapse prevention is to help the client anticipate high-risk situations and predict how she or he will cope. An individual's risk level can be identified by examining past situations, by discussing the problem behavior (i.e., the substance or behavioral addiction), or by talking about imaginary relapse situations.

Recovery strategies should address each client's unique high-risk factors. The counselor first helps him or her identify situations that pose future relapse risks. Self-monitoring records, self-efficacy ratings, autobiographical data, and a review of past relapses are some of the materials that can be used to assess risk. It is also helpful for the counselor to assess the client's coping skills by observing him or her in an actual problem situation. Simulation and role-playing have been effectively used as assessment tools.

Three cognitive factors interact in the relapse process: self-efficacy, outcome expectancy, and attribution of causality. Self-efficacy and outcome expectancy are similar to the Annis relapse-prevention model. Attribution of causality refers to a cognitive process that becomes important only when a person engages in a taboo behavior such as a substance or behavioral addiction. It is the person's perception of the cause of the initial lapse into the addictive behavior; the addiction or relapse may be attributed to internal or external factors. Attributions of causality are important because they influence subsequent behaviors. For example, an individual who believes that an initial lapse will lead to a total loss of control and that this was caused by personal weakness—known as the abstinence violation effect— is more likely to continue using substances. If this individual believes that the relapse began because he or she made the mistake of not applying relapse skills, he or she is more likely to stop the behavior before it gets out of control.

Marlatt and his colleagues indicate that both skill-training and cognitive-reframing strategies are important in relapse prevention. Skill-training strategies help clients learn to cope with high-risk situations through behavioral and cognitive responses. Dry runs, covert modeling, and relapse rehearsals are examples of useful skill-training methods for clients. Cognitive-reframing strategies teach clients techniques such as alternative cognitions, coping imagery, and reframing reactions to initial episodes of addictive response. Cognitive skills might include learning to think of the long-term—"seeing through the urges." If a relapse occurs, it can be framed optimistically, and with constant restructuring, a relapse can be viewed as a simple mistake rather than a fatal error or moral shortcoming. The Marlatt and Gordon book notes that those who view the relapse as a failure and blame themselves are more likely to have complete relapses; however, those who learn from the experience and act as "Monday-morning quarterbacks" have a greater chance of recovering from the relapse. Finally, their research notes that lifestyle-intervention techniques, such as exercise, meditation, or relaxation, are designed to strengthen total coping ability as well as to diffuse urges and cravings.

Psychoeducational Model.   Daley (1989) developed an educational model of relapse prevention based on his clinical experience with individuals, families, and groups in a residential chemical-dependency treatment program; his 1985 work is the primary resource for the information is this section. Such a program involves group sessions that are task-oriented and consist of a combination of lectures, large-group discussions, and structured and precisely focused small-group tasks. Written handouts are used to provide information and to engage clients in self-assessment and relapse-prevention planning activities.

The goal of the relapse-prevention groups is to provide clients with enough details on relapse prevention and intervention and to instill the attitude that sobriety in relapse prevention is a continuing process that requires a long-term commitment to recovery. As do the other relapse-prevention models, the psychoeducational model introduces clients to several cognitive and behavioral coping strategies.

Group sessions may be held daily and last between one and two hours. Topics covered in the course of them include understanding the relapse process, handling cravings to seek out and use substances, identifying and handling high-risk situations, using leisure time during sobriety, accessing relapse interventions, avoiding social pressure to use substances, and managing anger when sober.

A STRATEGY FOR LESS
FORMAL HEALTH COUNSELING

Health and mental health personnel can also use a strategy for health counseling that is particularly suited for less formal and less structured counseling encounters. When the client encounter is limited to only a few meetings and telephone calls, or even a single occasion, the ERIC—engaging the client and exploring the client's world, reformulating the client's concern, initial intervention, continued intervention—strategy has been particularly useful (Sperry, 1987).

ERIC is the acronym for four progressive levels or steps of therapeutic communication. Briefly, ERIC is a "mental map" that guides the counselor's relationship with the client so that each planned or unplanned encounter, such as returning telephone calls, can be primarily therapeutic not simply conversational. The rules for using this map are simple: (1) begin each client encounter at the first level of ERIC and move to subsequent levels only when the situation requires; and (2) in subsequent encounters with the same client, begin again at the first level, but expect to focus more time and effort at subsequent levels. The levels of ERIC can be described as follows.

- **E**—Refers to *engaging* the client in a relationship of respect and confidence and *exploring* the client's world. This is shown by the counselor's use of nonverbal and verbal cues such as active or empathic listening. During the engagement process, the client's problem or concern is explored. Such an exploration involves the antecedents and consequences of the problem along with the client's beliefs about and *expectations* for resolving it.
- **R**—Refers to *reformulating* the client's concern into a diagnostic category or solvable entity. Usually, this involves *reassurance* and *reframing*. It can require *renegotiation* when previous treatment plans did not account for the client's understanding and expectations, which may have set the stage for noncompliance or for a negative set for treatment outcomes. The purpose here is to come up with a mutually developed treatment plan or contract.

■ **I**—Refers to the *initial intervention* that follows from a mutually developed treatment plan. It usually involves information- and permission-giving; it may include *instructing* the patient in learning *"interference"* strategies to reverse, for example, anxious or dysphoric feelings or ruminative thoughts that significantly interfere with his or her daily functioning. Basic interference strategies, such as controlled breathing, affirmations, and thought stopping, can be taught to a client in a few minutes.

■ **C**—Refers to the *continued intervention* level that is needed only when initial interventions have not been sufficient or when compliance with the treatment plan is an issue. Outside *consultation* or referral may then be indicated; otherwise, other *counseling* interventions can be implemented.

As few as one or as many as four levels of progression may be used in a single encounter depending on client need or circumstance. For instance, the client's concern may be adequately addressed at the first level with simple engagement skills or processes, such as when the counselor's active listening allows the client to "get something off his chest" so that Tom feels understood and encouraged to go on with his life without further professional help. At other times, progression to the second level may be needed. For example, the counselor may need to reformulate Rosa's perception of certain physical symptoms into a diagnosable and easily treatable illness or to reframe her perceived "failure" in a behavior-modification program as a correctable "lapse." Let's now look at the ways the levels of therapeutic communication apply to health counseling.

In health-promotion counseling, the counselor engages the client by empathically listening and nonverbally attending to her or him. Usually, a preventive prescription for diet change, exercise, or stress management has already been tried, and counseling has been recommended because of noncompliance—that is, an inability to implement the prescribed change. The counselor explores the need for and reservations about lifestyle change, her or his explanation of the existing health predicament and previous compliance issues, and the specific expectations for the current treatment. Reformulating and negotiating a viable treatment contract are critical. Instances of noncompliance are inevitable when trying to change long-standing habits. Since clients frame these as failures, the counselor must reframe them as correctable lapses; such reframing encourages and supports the client's efforts to change. Relapse prevention is one of the most important initial interventions in this type of counseling (Marlatt & Gordon, 1985; Sperry, 1986). Contracting for change, attention to compliance issues, and specific skill training in self-monitoring and assertiveness, among others, are important continuing interventions.

Health counseling can also be incorporated into long-term psychotherapy. Some established psychotherapy models, such as multimodal therapy, actively address health issues and concerns within the formalized treatment plan; whereas other models may not directly assess and address clients' health concerns. When clinically appropriate, health counseling can be integrated into most forms of psychotherapy. Many clients enter psychotherapy with a single presenting problem in mind. As psychotherapy progresses and the therapeutic relationship becomes stronger, clients often bring up other concerns they have been thinking about or other aspects of their lives they would like to change. In addition, lifestyle and behavioral factors, such as exercise, sleep, stress, substance use, and weight management and diet, may be related to clients' presenting issues. A health or lifestyle intervention focused on behavioral change may provide clients with immediate and tangible symptom relief.

The ERIC model is an ideal strategy for integrating health counseling into personal counseling. When someone mentions health concerns, a psychotherapist can engage the client and determine if he or she would like to attempt to make a behavior change. It should be noted that when integrating health counseling into psychotherapy, the therapist probably should explicitly state that health counseling may be more didactic, behavioral, and action-oriented than the type of therapy the client is used to receiving. The psychotherapist and client can develop a treatment plan to address the health concern and negotiate how to use in-session time to monitor the behavior change in conjunction with ongoing therapy.

In addition, psychotherapists and mental health counselors may want to initiate health counseling with their clients. For example, the benefits of exercise on a variety of psychological disorders (e.g., depression, anxiety, somatoform disorders) have been noted in the literature (Tkachuk & Martin, 1999). For a client who has not exercised or recently stopped exercising, a psychotherapist may suggest adding exercise to a treatment plan. Psychotherapists may wish to augment other therapies with a health counseling approach; again the ERIC model provides a brief and effective framework for integrating health interventions into psychotherapy.

HEALTH COUNSELING SKILLS

A number of interviewing and other counseling skills are involved in health counseling. The five general interviewing skill categories are: empathic, exploring, engaging, reframing, and instructional responses. The following sections give descriptions and examples for 13 specific skills in these categories. Other skills are described in Sperry, Carlson, and Kjos (2003).

Empathic Responses

Empathy has been described as the ability to understand another individual's feelings and ideas and to communicate that understanding to the individual by nonverbal as well as verbal means (Riccardi & Kurtz, 1983). In a health-care setting, communicating empathy is an important means of establishing rapport, showing support, clarifying clients' problems, and collecting information. Here, the nonverbal means of conveying empathy is discussed first and then the verbal means.

The counselor asks a client, for example: "Have you been following your diet prescription regularly?" This rather straightforward and simple question can be expressed in several different ways, each conveying different meanings to the listener. The counselor could be frowning or looking expectantly at the client, standing over her or him or sitting at eye level, speaking in a businesslike tone of voice or one that is soothing and encouraging. Irrespective of the verbal message, communication on another level is occurring. It is estimated that only 7 percent of communication is transmitted through verbal speech; 22 percent is communicated through nonverbal speech, such as tone of voice and inflection; whereas 55 percent is communicated through what is popularly called "body language." DiMatteo and his associates (DiMatteo, Taranta, Friedman, & Prince, 1980) report that physicians who were judged to be more expressive of and sensitive to nonverbal communication skills received higher satisfaction ratings from their patients. This and other studies suggest that the counselor's nonverbal behavior can either facilitate the counselor–client relationship, and thus the treatment outcome, or detract from it.

Nonverbal communication can be either negative or positive. A counselor can communicate negative nonverbal messages through an expressionless, blank face; infrequent eye contact or staring; turning the body 45 degrees or more away from the client; and sitting far away from him or her, and/or slouching, with legs crossed and arms folded across the chest. Sitting or standing too close (within 2 feet) or too far away (9 feet) conveys a negative message to the client. Incongruence between verbal messages and nonverbal behaviors, such as saying "I'd really like to know more about your job" while sitting with arms across the chest and one's body turned away from the client, negates the message.

Positive nonverbal messages are communicated when counselors face their clients directly and at the same eye level, position themselves a comfortable distance—about 3 to 4 feet away—from patients, maintain eye contact without staring, lean forward, and assume a relaxed body posture. Interest in clients is also communicated when counselors gently nod and respond with animated facial expressions. Finally, responding in complete sentences without verbalized pauses ("uhs"), rambling, hesitation in delivery, and/or asking only one question at a time also communicates respect for clients.

The main verbal behaviors that convey empathy are called *active listening* because the counselor actively attends to a client's words and feelings rather than passively waiting for him or her to stop speaking. The four main active-listening skills are: clarifying, paraphrasing, reflecting, and summarizing responses.

Clarifying responses is a way in which the counselor makes a client's previous message explicit, confirms the accuracy of what was heard, or clears up any ambiguity of the message. Clarifying usually means that the counselor rephrases all or part of the client's previous message in a question that begins "Are you saying that . . . ?" or "Do you mean . . . ?" The following example illustrates how clarification helps clients clarify their own thinking.

> **Client:** "I wish I didn't have to fill out these diet forms! This doesn't make much sense to me."
>
> **Counselor:** "Are you saying that you don't see any purpose to filling out these forms?"
>
> **Client:** "No. I just don't think they can possibly help me with my problem at this point."

Paraphrasing is a way of rephrasing or reflecting the content of the client's message in the counselor's own words. By responding to the content of the message, a counselor helps a client focus on important information that could easily become clouded with emotions; for example:

> **Client:** "I can follow this diet when I'm at home, but with the kind of job I have that puts me on the road five or six days a month, I have to eat in restaurants, and then I really blow my diet."

> **Counselor:**   "You're saying that you have success on the diet when you can eat at home, but you're not very successful when you eat away from home."

Paraphrasing highlights the content of the statement, namely that diet compliance is situation-specific—it is not a response to the client's feelings about his or her job. Feelings may be very important but, in this exchange, they only detract from the important topic of compliance.

   Reflecting rephrases the affective or feeling component of the statement. When counselors respond to feelings, they encourage the client to express additional feelings or to experience the emotion more intensely.

> **Client:**   "I don't know. Staying on this diet seems so useless. I don't think I'll ever slim down."
>
> **Counselor:**   "You feel very discouraged about your prospects for slimming down."
>
> **Client:**   "Yeah. It really is discouraging. I've been thinking about dropping the diet. What's the use in kidding myself?"

The reflecting response unearthed the client's ambivalence about continuing with the diet. The counselor was provided with an opportunity to deal with the discouragement and ambivalence feelings before the lack of progress caused both the client and the counselor to become disheartened.

   Summarizing is a more complex skill than the previous ones, yet it builds on them. Here the counselor recognizes the patterns or themes in several of the client's messages and then links them into a single statement that reflects both feeling and content. Summarizing puts two or more paraphrases or clarifications together to condense several client messages or even the entire session; the following is an example.

> **Client:**   "I really want to stay on this diet. But, there are so many things that pull me back to food and my old ways of eating. I mean, my friends, the places I hang out, my family . . . you name it. But even so, I know it's best for me to lose weight, and I want to stick with this program."
>
> **Counselor:**   "You are really feeling torn. On the one hand, you want to lose weight and you know its best for you, but on the other hand, you're reluctant to part ways with people and circumstances that pull you toward food and overeating."

Exploring Responses

Exploring responses are the principal communication skills in the exploratory phase; they are counselor-oriented rather than client-oriented. These responses move beyond the client's frame of reference and help her or him see the need for action and behavior change through a more objective frame of reference (Egan, 1986). Two kinds of exploring responses are probing—open-ended, closed, and focused questioning—and confronting.

Probing.   The *probing response* uses questions to secure critical, specific information such as the effect that clients' problems have on their daily lives, clients' explanation for why they have these problems, their past attempts to change their health behavior, and their expectations for the current program. The three kinds of probing questions are all useful in health-care settings.

Open-ended questioning encourages clients to begin to talk and elaborate on their symptoms or their "stories." Questions usually begin with "What," "When," "Who," or "How" and are phrased in such a way that they cannot be answered easily with a yes or no. This kind of question is most effective at the beginning and during the early stages of the exploration; for example:

> **Counselor:**   "What problems (or concerns) bring you here today?"
>
> "How does being obese interfere with daily living?"
>
> "How did your diet charting go this week?"
>
> "What do you think keeps you from losing weight?"

Whereas general or open-ended questions broaden the focus of inquiry, *closed questioning* narrows the focus to specific information. Sometimes this kind of questioning is needed to probe for more explicit meaning or to clarify data. Questions are prefaced with words like "Do," "Is," "Did," "Can," or "Could" and are phrased to encourage one-word or short phrase answers. This form of questioning is very effective in the review of systems in a medical history or in screening examinations during which the purpose is to assess risk factors, precipitants (events that trigger a symptom or a condition), and social-support systems. This form of questioning has its place; however, when counselors use it exclusively, it inhibits discussion, fosters a dependent client role, and allows clients to avoid sensitive topics. Here are a couple examples:

> **Counselor:**   "Is your husband aware that taking you to restaurants frustrates your diet program?"
>
> "Do you see any solution to this particular frustration?"

Focused questioning narrows or defines a topic by asking for a specific response. These questions are used when patients have difficulty responding to an open-ended question, or when the goal is to characterize a symptom or to elicit descriptive data concerning a clinical sign or issue. Focused questions usually begin with "Have you . . . ," "Do you . . . ," or "Can you . . . "; for example:

> **Counselor:**   "Can you tell me more about the health status of your parents?"
>
> "Can you describe the sensation of bloating?"

Closed questions (e.g., "Are your parents obese?" or "Do you feel bloated?") do not elicit the quality of response that focused questions are likely to prompt.

There are some general guidelines for wording all types of probing questions; according to Cormier, Cormier, and Weiser (1984), questions should be phrased:

- Simply, avoiding medical jargon
- Concisely

- Singly—ask one question at a time rather than stringing two or three questions together
- Nonaccusatorily—begin with "What" or "How" rather than "Why"
- Unbiasedly, not as leading questions that suggest symptoms, illnesses, or diagnoses

Confronting.   A *confronting response* points out a distortion or discrepancy in the client's communication. In popular usage, the word *confrontation* often has hostile or punitive overtones, but it does not carry such a meaning or intent in health counseling. Counselors judge neither feelings nor behavior, and they do not imply that a client is wrong. Rather, they calmly and noncritically point out discrepancies in what the client is communicating. These discrepancies can be between a client's messages and actions or between a client's verbal statement and nonverbal message.

Since confronting responses can have a powerful effect on the client and on the course of the interview, they must be used carefully. Generally, confrontation is most helpful in the latter parts of the interview, after empathy and trust have been established. A confronting response should be descriptive and concrete rather than judgmental and vague. It should be directed toward situations and behaviors that can be changed rather than toward those beyond the client's control or means; for example, certain dietary changes or supplements may be unrealistic for clients with limited incomes. A confronting response should be a request, rather than a demand for change, made only when there is sufficient time to hear and to understand the client's reaction to the situation. Some clients react to confrontation in a variety of ways—denial, anger, confusion, feigned acceptance, or genuine acceptance. The following example of a confronting response points out the discrepancy between a verbal statement and behavior.

> **Client:**   (*a 35-year-old woman who has just admitted she has not completed the daily diet and exercise diary*) "I need to lose this weight because it's clear I was passed over for the promotion because of my obesity. Can't you do something to change this quickly?"
>
> **Counselor:**   "On the one hand, you're indicating you want to get your weight under control as soon as possible. But on the other hand, you've said you have had a hard time remembering to do the things that will help you achieve your goal."

Engaging Responses

It is usually necessary to orient clients to the treatment process and to the counselor's frame of reference. This involves what is called *engagement,* and one way of fostering this is with role-structuring responses.

Because much of the process and outcome of health counseling is affected by the client's attitudes at the start, it is important to describe the proposed program, its potential outcomes, and the roles and expectations of both client and counselor in the treatment process. Frank (1984) calls this process the "role induction interview." Clients who receive such an orientation are less likely to drop out of treatment and are more likely to benefit from it (Goldstein, 1973).

Counselor: "It will be helpful if I mention what I believe the weight-management program should involve. We will spend time together to discuss your concerns about your weight and what you would like to do about them. Then we will work as a team to try to meet your goals. The treatment plan we come up with, and that you carry out—with my assistance—both in and outside of the sessions can help you change your eating habits and other health behaviors that will result in weight loss and maintenance. This is not a 'quick-fix' approach, but it has been very successful. I'd like to know your reaction and your own expectations."

Reframing Responses

Reframing responses offer an alternative to the client's view of a situation, including the nature of the problem, the client's progress, and the client's expectation for success with the program. A standard medical diagnosis is an example of reframing—the physician reframes the symptoms and signs into a diagnosis. Reframing is a powerful tool because it redefines what appears to be an incomprehensible, unbearable, or untreatable concern into a comprehensible, bearable, and treatable problem. Reframing responses have a significant place in health-promotion counseling, particularly when clients feel that they have failed to adhere to a treatment regimen. The reframing of perceived failures as correctable lapses can reduce embarrassment and discouragement. This section describes only one form of reframing, the ability-potential response.

The *ability-potential response* points to the client's current potential for achieving something (Cormier & Cormier, 1979). This sort of encouragement is particularly valuable in health-promotion and lifestyle-change programs when clients become discouraged about the prospects for change. Ability-potential responses encourage clients who lack initiative or self-confidence to follow through with a desired change, and they can also expand their awareness of personal strengths.

This type of response should be reserved for times when a client has indicated a readiness for change but is hesitant to begin without some encouragement. It is best used when there is a basis for affirming the client's ability to pursue a desired goal rather than as a pep talk to counteract discouragement from a previous failure. In most cases, it is better to clarify and reflect feelings of discouragement before affirming the person's ability to change. In the example here, the counselor has used reflecting and paraphrasing before using the ability-potential response.

Client: (*a 45-year-old male who has tried several weight-loss plans*)   "Right now, I'm not sure I can drop this weight and keep it off. I've tried! But it's really getting to me, and it's affecting my family. I just don't feel I can do it, or for that matter, do anything else right."

Counselor: "You're really discouraged right now. And because of that, you're not sure you can be successful at anything. But the fact is that you've been tobacco-free for over 10 years, and you were able to lose and keep off 40 pounds for nearly ten months. With a track record like this, you've got a lot going for you, and a lot to build on."

Instructional Responding

A basic counseling skill that is directed at behavior change is called instructional responding; there are two kinds of instruction: information-giving and instruction-giving (Cormier & Cormier, 1979). Informing and instructing are the cornerstones of client education.

Information-Giving.   Communicating data or facts to someone at an appropriate time and in an effective manner serves to inform a client of possible options, to help him or her evaluate the options, and to correct inaccurate information. Information-giving involves much more than transmitting information; timing and delivery are critical. For each client, the counselor must identify what information to give and when and how to provide it.

Instruction-Giving.   Effective instruction-giving is a skill that can be learned; the following guidelines should be helpful. First, identify the kind of information that will be useful to the client, then assess the accuracy and the extent of his or her present knowledge. Second, wait for the client's readiness cues—don't force the instruction prematurely. Third, limit the amount of information given at one time, and deliver necessary instructions in a sensitive and friendly manner. Finally, ask for and discuss the client's feelings and biases about the information. Here is an example.

> **Counselor:**   *(after reviewing the client's clinical picture and lab results)* "Well, Mr. Burns, these results confirm both of our suspicions that you have diabetes. What's your reaction?" *(after counselor and client discuss this)* "Can you tell me what you know about diabetes?"
>
> **Client:**   "Sure. One of my friends has it so I know the symptoms and the causes. And, I know there is more than one way to treat it."
>
> **Counselor:**   "That's correct; there are generally three ways to treat diabetes: diet, exercise, and medication. Usually, we try diet and exercise first. Because there's so much information about all three, I'd just like to discuss diet for now, to see if it would be a reasonable approach to start. How does that sound to you?"
>
> **Client:**   "Well, I don't want to go to medication except as a last resort. What would diet be like?"
>
> **Counselor:**   *(counselor explains carbohydrate intake, insulin requirements, blood sugar levels, and their relationship to controlling diabetes)* "What is your reaction to all this information?"

Instructing means verbally directing a client on how to perform a specific task or follow a treatment regimen. As pointed out earlier, instructing must be integrated with other interpersonal skills if clients are to understand, cooperate with, profit from, and be satisfied with the treatment regimen and their relationship with the counselor. This skill is a major theme in the following chapters, so it will not be elaborated on here; however, note that to be effective, instructions must be specific, concise, and delivered as suggestions rather than as commands. Counselors should confirm that clients have understood the directions and, whenever possible, should give clear, written instructions for them to take home. When appropriate, oral instructions should be supplemented with demonstrations. Adherence to instructions is more likely if they are limited to positive or rewarding consequences such as sustained weight maintenance, social compliments, or an increased sense of self-control.

OTHER HEALTH COUNSELING STRATEGIES

This section describes a number of additional useful health counseling strategies and factors to consider; these include compliance and adherence improvement strategies, psychoeducational strategies, and accounting for social systems' factors.

Compliance and Adherence Improvement Strategies

Compliance refers to how faithfully a client follows the advice and direction of a treatment provider (Sperry, 1986). This term has acquired a pejorative connotation, implying a passive and subservient client in relation to an active, authoritarian health-care provider. As a result, adherence, cooperation, and mutual participation have become preferred designations. In any event, treatment compliance is a problem encountered by all health-care professionals and encompasses a wide variety of client behaviors, including failure to begin treatment, premature termination, or minimally completing the treatment regimen—particularly regarding medication or lifestyle-change prescriptions. Compliance also encompasses a number of treatment provider behaviors, such as emotional and time involvement with clients, clarity and specificity of language, and awareness of their needs and expectations for treatment. Statistics from the lifestyle-change literature suggest that treatment adherence is one of the most critical health-care issues. What is the practical significance of this issue for the counselor?

As more counselors become involved with lifestyle-change and other health-care programs, the issue of nonadherence, which presents numerous and perplexing concerns and challenges for health counselors, takes on new dimensions. Since financial compensation is often based on actual services provided to clients, nonadherence can dramatically affect a clinical practice. Increasing adherence increases not only the client's satisfaction with the treatment rendered but also the counselor's job satisfaction. It is not surprising, then, that research on adherence to lifestyle-change programs has increased significantly. Unfortunately, this work is not easily available to practicing counselors; thus, here's a brief review of medical and lifestyle-change programs.

Medical Programs.   Composite averages of more than 200 studies reviewed by Sackett and Haynes (1976) suggest that 50 percent of patients do not take prescribed medications in accordance with instructions. Furthermore, about 20 to 40 percent of recommended immunizations are not obtained, and about 20 to 50 percent of medical appointments are missed. Even being hospitalized does not guarantee treatment adherence. Under- and overdosage of medications and failure to follow prescribed diets are commonly reported in studies done at hospitals (Kirscht & Rosenstock, 1979).

Lifestyle-Change Programs.   These programs span the spectrum from smoking and weight-management treatment to exercise programs for health and for clients recovering from heart attacks. The statistics are as dismal as are those for medical compliance. Sachs (1982) found that the average dropout rate for all types of exercise programs is 30 to 70 percent. In spite of reported improvements in figure, mood, and a general sense of well-being, 50 percent of individuals who start an exercise program stop it within 6 weeks to 6 months (Ward & Morgan, 1984). Cox (1984) notes that corporate wellness programs typically recruit no more than 15 to 20 percent of employees and, of these, 50 percent or more drop out within the first 6 months—at considerable cost to the corporation. Smoking-cessation programs, by comparison, are considered unusually effective if more than one third of entrants have reduced their smoking at the end of 6 months (Kirscht & Rosenstock, 1979).

Statistics such as these often shock health-care providers who assume that good adherence is the norm. They reason that if treatment is worthwhile, its benefits cannot be gained in the absence of adherence. Various attempts have been made to explain nonadherence. Blackwell (1982b) notes that there is little consensus on features that consistently influence adherence, despite research on more than 200 variables. However, most would agree that the main determinant involves the client, the health conditions, the treatment regimen, the treatment setting, and the provider–client relationship.

The majority of adherence studies have focused on the characteristics of clients. Many researchers anticipated that a noncompliant personality type would be identified; unfortunately, as in the search for the cancer-prone personality, no such profile for nonadherence has been found (Blackwell, 1973). Rather, studies suggest that, under certain circumstances, every client is a potential defaulter. Clients' health beliefs, presence of aggressive or passive–aggressive behavior patterns, dependence, and denial are associated with nonadherence (Backeland & Lundwall, 1975). No single client attribute—with the possible exception of scores on the self-motivation inventory (Dishman, Ickles, & Morgan, 1980), which have adequately predicted compliance with exercise—combined with biological factors or with personality factors is as predictive as are situational variables and provider–client factors. One possible explanation for this abundance of studies that link adherence to client characteristics is the underlying belief that the client is basically to blame for nonadherence to treatment.

Blackwell's reviews (1973, 1982a, 1982b) suggest that there has been a recognition that adherence is multiply determined. Reviewing a number of situational variables, Blackwell indicates that the duration of the health conditions—as well as the repetition of relapse and the presence of specific kinds of symptoms—influences adherence, as does the complexity of the treatment regimen and its side effects. The more complicated and inconvenient the regimen and the more discomfort is perceived, the less the adherence. Adherence is also strongly influenced by perceived or actual shortcomings in the treatment setting, as well as by the extent of supervision, social support, and follow-up supplied by the health-care provider or team. Finally, Blackwell and others suggest that the provider's attitudes and behaviors, as evident in the provider–client relationship, may be critical among the multiple variables that predict adherence.

There is modest but growing research literature on the aspect of mutuality, collaboration, and/or cooperation in the provider–client relationship as it relates to treatment adherence. For the most part, these studies are descriptive or correlational rather than experimental in design. This, of course, poses considerable limits on statements of causality. One group of studies describes the informational techniques and the extent of explicitness regarding client behaviors that are necessary to ensure adequate levels of adherence. A second group of studies views compatibility of client and provider expectations for treatment as a critical variable for adherence; the studies' focus is on the behaviors necessary for this mutuality of goal expectations to occur. A third group of studies links the client's assumption of responsibility for treatment to maximal adherence. A final group of studies deals with the affective tone of the provider–client relationship before and during the treatment regimen. Adherence is seen as dependent on the social support supplied by the provider, as well as that provided by other clients and members of the treatment team (Garrity, 1982).

Psychoeducational Strategies

Psychoeducation, also known as patient education, encompasses any health education experience planned by both health-care provider and client to meet clients' specific learning needs, interests, and capabilities (Squyres, 1980). Thus, psychoeducation is a process of education and activity based on an intentional exchange and sharing of information such that the clients' behavior is positively affected. It is best explained as a communication activity occurring within the context of a counselor and client encounter that influences client behavior toward improved health. Psychoeducation includes a variety of strategies designed not only to facilitate behavioral change, but also to help individuals identify their social support and to maintain their achieved behavior over a long period of time. It is much more complex than the printed handouts or audiovisual aids so often associated with it. In short, *personal interaction* is the key dimension.

The purpose of psychoeducation is to provide individuals with enough information and motivation to help them understand the factors that promote and/or threaten health so that they may have a better opportunity to make informed choices in their lives (Levant, 1986). In addition, psychoeducation provides the support, as well as the technical assistance necessary, to help individuals carry out their choices. The following subsections describe how to assess clients' needs and various psychoeducation techniques and materials.

Assessing Clients' Needs.   The most challenging task in the psychoeducation process is to identify what the client actually needs to do or to know. A structured approach can help health counselors analyze the presenting problem or risk in terms of behavioral causes and determine the educational or psychoeducational technique most appropriate for the treatment goals and desired outcomes. This type of assessment leads to the articulation of *educational objectives* based on the individual's behaviors, or absence of behaviors, that influence or cause a particular health problem. If the individual's health-related behavior is appropriate, reinforcement may be the only client-education intervention required. However, if some deficiency is obvious, it will be necessary to identify that behavior and the appropriate actions that may help to resolve it.

Establishing the cause of the performance deficit is most important. Is it a knowledge gap, a skills deficiency, an emotional factor, a social or environmental variable, or some combination of these? Assessment of an individual's knowledge and skills regarding a particular positive health behavior or lifestyle prescription is essential. Knowledge about family or a significant other can also be relevant to the individual's psychoeducation. Attitudes, beliefs, or emotions can also be predisposing factors that interfere with one's appropriate health behavior. An individual may be so influenced by religious or cultural doctrine or so preoccupied with peripheral concerns, such as attaining a perfect physique, that noncompliance is inevitable. In addition, health counselors should assess social and environmental constraints that may influence health behavior. It is not possible to create ideal environments for clients or to dictate what they should do, but counselors can help clients recognize mitigating factors, weigh the pros and cons for change, identify alternative options, and learn to gain more self-control over their personal environment and their lives.

Psychoeducation Techniques and Materials.   Learning facts and skills is a prerequisite to clients' successful involvement in the maintenance of good health. The following are some basic educational principles for transferring information and teaching new skills.

1. Psychoeducation cannot accomplish more than behavioral change.
2. A combination of strategies is required for all learning.
3. Clients cannot be taught in isolation from family, friends, peers, and/or employers.
4. Audiovisual and printed materials cannot substitute for personal instruction.
5. Psychoeducation begins where the client is now, relates new information to previous knowledge, and adapts available aids to individual needs.
6. Psychoeducation encompasses the KISS (keep it simple and short) principle. Client education should be specific, brief, and direct, avoiding overkill.
7. Clients should be encouraged to write down critical or complex information and then repeat it.
8. Clients should be encouraged to practice skills in simulated settings and to implement them in real-life situations.
9. Effective psychoeducation recognizes that follow-up is essential.

Counseling and psychological support of clients is essential in the psychoeducational process. Social support, family sessions, self-care instructions, and ongoing reassurance are common interventions used by counselors in the course of psychoeducation.

Self-help organizations are another form of psychoeducation. Individuals with a particular condition or problem can be referred to any number of groups that share information and provide mutual support. The most common self-help groups are based on the 12-step model—AA, ACOA, Overeaters Anonymous, Procrastinators Anonymous, and Smokers Anonymous—to name a few. In addition, a number of self-help groups are relevant to health behaviors that are not based on a 12-step program; examples are TOPS (Take Off Pounds Sensibly) and cardiac and cancer support groups. The community bulletin-board section of most metropolitan-area newspapers lists the various support groups available locally. A similar and extended list is usually available in the community resource directory for particular areas and are available to most health-care providers.

The most common type of psychoeducation material is the handout. It is usually a simple one- to two-page information sheet that is either commercially available, or developed by the health counselor himself or herself or adapted from any number of sources. The Professional Resource Press annual publication *Innovations in Clinical Practice* has a Client Handouts section that can be copied and made available to clients; for example, one selection is "Insomnia: Sleeping Tips from A to Zzzz."

Newsletters and magazines that focus specifically on health and client education are becoming more available. Health newsletters published by several university health departments are offered to the general public on a subscription basis. The Harvard Medical School health letter and the *Harvard Mental Health Letter* are two examples. Tufts University and the University of California at Berkeley offer similar newsletters on the topic of nutrition. The *Medical Self-Care* magazine, published quarterly, is an excellent background resource for both health counselors and clients.

An abundance of printed materials useful in psychoeducation is available from any number of sources, including government agencies and departments, voluntary community agencies, pharmaceutical firms, and insurance companies. For instance, the American Lung Association offers a considerable amount of audiovisual and printed materials on smoking cessation. In addition, a number of companies specialize in health education materials; Trainex and Professional Counseling Aids, Inc., sell or rent a variety of elaborately packaged learning systems. These, and other such firms, have resource catalogs of materials available. One of the most comprehensive listings of psychoeducational materials is *The Guide to Health Information Resources in Print* (available from Health Information Library, PAS Publishing Company, Daly City, CA 94015).

Accounting for Social Systems' Factors

As previously stated, a knowledge of health-promotion principles does not translate to health-behavior changes—changes require specific health counseling interventions and strategies. One more factor needs to be added to the equation: social systems' influences. As the remaining chapters of this book show, the influence of peers, families, spouses, and subcultures cannot be ignored when assessing and intervening in any of the areas of lifestyle or health-behavior change. For instance, in weight-control programs, the health counselor quickly becomes aware of how the obese person's spouse can sabotage the best-conceived treatment interventions if that spouse's influence and collaboration with treatment have not been considered (Brownell & Foreyt, 1985). Similarly, Allen (1981) argues that the counselor's failure to account for the impact of subcultural norms can, for all practical purposes, sabotage a treatment plan. In short, systems' factors play a significant role not only in assessment and intervention but also, as the next chapters repeatedly demonstrate, in the reduction of relapse and the enhancement of treatment adherence.

MULTICULTURAL STRATEGY IN HEALTH COUNSELING

The previous chapter notes the changing demographics of the population and the role of incorporating a multicultural perspective and strategy into counseling practice. Race, culture, ethnicity, gender, social class, and other factors have been increasingly recognized as important variables in counseling, mental health services, and intervention efforts (Jackson, 1995; Sue, Arrodondo, & McDavis, 1992). The increased awareness of cultural issues and their impact on the well-being of clients has led clinicians and researchers to better understand how cultural factors influence clinical practice. This attention to multiple cultures has elevated awareness of the role of cultural and contextual factors in counseling and has generated ideas about counselors' responsibility to attend competently to the culture and context in which clients live and operate (Pope-Davis, Reynolds, Dings, & Nielson, 1995). To ensure the integration of multicultural factors and the promotion of multicultural competence, it is necessary for mental health professionals to make a lifelong commitment to developing cultural expertise and culture-centered practice (Arrodondo, 1999).

Because cultural factors are present in the four phases—engagement and relationship, assessment, intervention, and maintenance and relapse prevention—of health counseling, it is essential that a multicultural strategy be incorporated into the process of tailoring counseling to the needs of clients. Such a strategy needs to be reflected in each phase of health counseling.

Engagement and Relationship

Counselors recognize the importance of establishing rapport and acceptable working conditions with clients. Normally, this is done automatically without thinking about being engaged in a "cross-cultural" relationship. The difference, however, is that counselors need to specifically think about the cultural factors present in counseling relationships when working in interethnic and intercultural situations as opposed to situations when these factors are not clearly present (Wohl, 2000). Many counselors adapt their communication, including vocabulary, eye contact, language level, and style of relating in order to better connect with clients. Whereas the intention in this type of adaptation is to provide a warm and welcoming environment, some clients may be surprised to encounter rapport-building behavior and an egalitarian relationship from someone viewed as an "authority." Literature notes (Atkinson & Lowe, 1995; Root, 1998) that Asian Americans tend to expect a more direct, forceful, and authoritative manner and a less personal demeanor in their counselors, whereas Latino clients are said to expect an authoritative approach blended with more personal intimacy. When cultural differences between a counselor and a client are evident, counselors might want to explore how the differences may become noticeable within the therapeutic relationship and also begin to create an open dialogue in which culture issues can be discussed.

Assessment

In the assessment phase of health counseling, counselors can begin to assess a client's cultural orientation. Because this phase is focused on gathering information about a client, the counselor may want to include culture-related questions to assess cultural background and his or her worldview. It has previously been noted that the health counseling assessment phase is often brief when compared to that phase in formal psychotherapy. Therefore, health counselors are encouraged to spend time exploring a client's level of acculturation, worldview, family background, and expectations about health counseling as opposed to a more lengthy assessment about cultural orientation.

Comprehensive assessment entails viewing the client as a unique individual, as a social unit within a family, and as a member of a cultural group (Ponterotto & Casas, 1991). At the minimum, a cultural assessment should include an understanding of a client's worldview. A person's worldview influences one's understanding of the traditional Western counseling process and its interventions, one's willingness to see a counselor, one's level of psychological mindedness, one's comfort with family- and self-disclosure, and one's expectations for the counseling relationship. Clearly, a worldview assessment should be a key aspect of any client assessment and treatment planning (Grieger & Ponterotto, 1995).

The brief cultural assessment can also include exploring how a client's religious and spiritual background, sexual orientation, and gender role contribute to both one's identity and his or her presenting concern. In exploring a common factors view to multicultural counseling, Fischer, Jome, and Atkinson (1998) note that a more successful counseling outcome occurs when the client feels that the counselor understands the reason for the symptoms and provides a process of healing (intervention plan or goal) that makes sense to him or her. Therefore during the assessment process, a counselor should work to understand one's cultural context and then look to convey this understanding back to the client.

Intervention

At the intervention level, cultural factors should be considered when tailoring interventions. Based on knowledge gained from the therapeutic relationship and the assessment process, counselors need to tailor interventions that are congruent with cultural beliefs and values. This can mean being open to folk remedies or indigenous interventions that operate within a client's specific worldview (Koss-Chioino, 2000). Another aspect of multicultural health counseling is being open to nontraditional modes of therapy. As previously mentioned, when families can be directly involved in individual or group sessions, they should be encouraged to participate. The therapeutic scope may also be broadened to include some members of the extended family and/or members of a client's cultural community, or to conduct interventions within a religious group. The goal of effective multicultural counseling is to intervene in a manner that takes a client's worldview into account; to reach this goal a health counselor may need to shift his or her expectations about treatment to include the client's vision.

Maintenance and Relapse Prevention

This stage is no different than the three phases of treatment in that multicultural factors and sensitivity is crucial to ensure client success. Maintenance has previously been described as encompassing relapse prevention in conjunction with the process of empowering clients to assume more responsibility for new health behaviors. Critical to success in this phase is keeping clients engaged in maintaining behavioral change. Paniagua (1998) notes that attrition from therapy is a core concern when working with clients from culturally diverse groups. Common strategies to keep clients involved in the therapeutic process, such as follow-up phone calls and letters, may not be successful with all populations. Paniagua outlines several culturally specific guidelines to prevent attrition of African American, Native American, Asian American, and Latino clients.

General maintenance and relapse-prevention guidelines include exploring a client's further expectations about how to maintain change without continued direct clinical attention; looking to incorporate family and community members into the maintenance process, which may not be appropriate for all clients because issues of shame and humiliation may preclude their inclusion; and providing clear explanations for the reasons for the reduction of length and frequency of clinical contacts to avoid a perception of lack of interest in working with a particular cultural group. By maintaining a culturally sensitive and tailored intervention approach from initial engagement to treatment maintenance, all clients can come to believe that the therapeutic process is focused on their concerns, with inclusion of their specific, salient cultural factors.

CONCLUDING NOTE

This chapter has emphasized several counseling strategies and skills useful in the practice of health counseling. These and other strategies and skills will be described and illustrated in Part II of this book.

REFERENCES

Allen, R. (1981). *Lifegain*. New York: Appleton-Century-Crofts.

Annis, H. (1986). Relapse model for treatment of alcoholics. In W. Miller & N. Heather (Eds.), *Treating addictive behaviors* (pp. 407–433). New York: Plenum.

Atkinson, D. R., & Lowe, S. M. (1995). The role of ethnicity, cultural knowledge, and conventional techniques in counseling and psychotherapy. In J. G. Ponterotto, J. M. Casas, L. M. Suzuki, & C. M. Alexander (Eds.), *Handbook of multicultural counseling* (pp. 387–414). Thousand Oaks, CA: Sage.

Arrodondo, P. (1999). Multicultural counseling competencies as tools to address oppression and racism. *Journal of Counseling and Development, 77,* 102–108.

Backeland, F., & Lundwall, L. (1975). Dropping out of treatment: A critical review. *Psychological Bulletin, 82,* 738–783.

Bandura, A. (1997) *Self-efficacy.* New York: Freeman.

Benson, H. (1996). *Timeless healing: The power and biology of belief.* New York: Scribner.

Blackwell, B. (1973). Drug therapy: Patient compliance. *New England Journal of Medicine, 289,* 249–252.

Blackwell, B. (1982a). Treatment adherence. *British Journal of Psychiatry, 129,* 513–531.

Blackwell, B. (1982b). Treatment compliance. In J. Greist, J. Jefferson, & R. Spitzer (Eds.), *Treatment of mental disorders.* New York: Oxford University Press.

Brownell, K. (1984). The psychology and physiology of obesity: Implications for screening and treatment. *Journal of American Dietetics Association, 84,* 406–414.

Brownell, K. D., & Foreyt, J. P. (1985). Obesity. In D. Barlow (Ed.), *Clinical handbook of psychological disorders.* New York: Guilford.

Cormier, W., & Cormier, L. S. (1979). *Interviewing strategies for helpers: A guide to assessment, treatment and evaluation.* Pacific Grove, CA: Brooks/Cole

Cormier, W., Cormier L. S., & Weiser, R. (1984). *Interviewing and helping skills for health professionals.* Boston: Jones and Bartlett.

Cox, M. H. (1984). Fitness and lifestyle programs for business and industry: Problems in recruitment and retention. *Journal of Cardiac Rehabilitation, 4,* 136–142.

Daley, D. C. (1989). Relapse prevention: *Treatment alternatives and counseling aids.* Blaze Ridge Summit, PA: TAB Books.

Daley, D. (1987). Relapse prevention with substance abusers: Clinical issues and myths. *Social Work, 45*(2), 38–42.

DiMatteo, M., Taranta, A., Friedman, H., & Prince, L. M. (1980). Predicting satisfaction from physicians' nonverbal communication skills. *Medical Care, 18,* 376.

Dinkmeyer, D., & Sperry, L. (2000). *Counseling and psychotherapy: An integrated, individual psychology approach,* 3rd ed. Columbus, OH: Merrill/Prentice-Hall.

Dishman, R., Ickles, W., & Morgan, W. (1980). Self-motivation and adherence to habitual physical activity. *Journal of Applied Social Psychology, 10,* 115–132.

Doherty, W., & Baird, M. (1983). *Family therapy and family medicine.* New York: Guilford.

Duncan, B., Solovey, A. & Rusk G. (1992). *Changing the rules: A client-directed approach to therapy.* New York: Guilford.

Egan, G. (1986). The skilled helper: A model, for systematic helping and interpersonal relating. Pacific Grove, CA: Brooks/Cole.

Engel, G. (1977). The need for a new medical model: A challenge to biomedical science. *Science, 196,* 129–136.

Fennel, P. (2001). *The chronic illness workbook.* Oakland, CA: New Harbinger.

Fischer, A. R., Jome, L. M., & Atkinson, D. R. (1998). Reconceptualizing multicultural counseling: Universal health conditions in a culturally specific context. *The Counseling Psychologist, 26,* 525–588.

Frank, J., & Frank, J. (1993) Persuasion and healing: A comparative study of psychotherapy (3rd ed.). Baltimore: Johns Hopkins Press.

Frank, J. D. (1984). Therapeutic components of all psychotherapies. In J. M. Myers (Ed.), *Cures by psychotherapy. What affects change?* New York: Praeger.

Garrity, T. (1982). Medical compliance and the clinician–patient relationship: A review. *Social Science and Medicine, 15,* 215–222.

Goldstein, A. P. (1973). *Structured learning therapy.* New York: Academic.

Goodheart, C., & Lansing, M. (1997). *Treating people with chronic disease: A psychological guide.* Washington, DC: American Psychological Association Books.

Grieger, I., & Ponterotto, J. G. (1995). A framework for assessment in multicultural counseling. In J. G. Ponterotto, J. M. Casas, L. M. Suzuki, & C. M. Alexander (Eds.), *Handbook of multicultural counseling* (pp. 357–374). Thousand Oaks, CA: Sage.

Harrington, A. (Ed.). (1997). *The placebo effect: An interdisciplinary investigation.* Cambridge: Harvard University Press.

Jackson, M. (1995). Multicultural counseling: Historical perspectives. In J. G. Ponterotto, J. M. Casas, L. M. Suzuki, & C. M. Alexander (Eds.), *Handbook of multicultural counseling* (pp. 3–16). Thousand Oaks, CA: Sage.

Kirscht, J., & Rosenstock, I. (1979). Patient problems in following recommendations of health experts. In G. Stone, F. Cohen, & N. Adler (Eds.), *Health psychology: A handbook.* San Francisco: Jossey-Bass.

Koss-Chioino, J. D. (2000). Traditional and folk approaches among ethnic minorities. In J. F. Aponte & J. Wohl (Eds.), *Psychological intervention and cultural diversity* (pp. 149–166). Boston: Allyn & Bacon.

Lambert, M. (1992). Implication of psychotherapy outcome research for eclectic psychotherapy. In J. Norcross (Ed.), *Handbook of eclectic psychotherapy* (pp. 436–462). New York: Brunner/Mazel.

Levant, R. (1986). *Psychoeducational approaches to family therapy and family counseling.* New York: Springer.

Marlatt, G., & Gordon, J. (1985). *Relapse prevention: A self-control strategy for the maintenance of behavior change.* New York: Guilford.

Mathews, D., & Clark, C. (1998). *The faith factor.* New York: Viking.

Miller, S., Duncan, B., & Hubble, M. (1997). *Escape from babel: Toward a unifying language for psychotherapy practice.* New York: Norton.

Orlinsky, D., Grawe, K., & Parks, B. (1994). Process and outcome in psychotherapy. In A. Bergin, & S. Garfield (Eds.), *Handbook of psychotherapy and behavior change* (4th ed., pp. 270–376). New York: Wiley.

Paniagua, F. A. (1998). *Assessing and treating culturally diverse clients: A practical guide* (2nd ed.). Thousand Oaks, CA: Sage.

Pope-Davis, D. B., Reynolds, A. L., Dings J. G., & Nielson, D. (1995). Examining multicultural counseling competencies of graduate students in psychology. *Professional Psychology: Research and Practice, 26,* 322–329.

Riccardi, V., & Kurtz, S. (1983). *Communication and counseling and health care.* Springfield, IL: Charles C Thomas.

Rogers, C. (1951) *Client-centered therapy.* Boston: Houghton Mifflin.

Root, M. P. P. (1998). Facilitating psychotherapy with Asian American clients. In D. R. Atkinson, G. Morten, & D. W. Sue (Eds.), *Counseling American minorities* (5th ed., pp. 214–234). New York: McGraw-Hill.

Sachs, M. (1982). Compliance and addiction to exercise. In R. Cantu (Ed.), *The exercising adult.* Lexington, MA: Collamore Press.

Sackett, D., & Haynes, R. (Eds.). (1976). *Compliance with therapeutic regimens.* Baltimore: Johns Hopkins University Press.

Snyder, C., Irving, L., & Anderson, J. (1991). Hope and health. In C. Snyder, & D. Forsyth (Eds.), *Handbook of social and clinical psychology.* New York: Pergamon.

Sperry, L. (1986). The ingredients of effective health counseling: Health beliefs, compliance and relapse prevention. *Individual Psychology, 42,* 279–287.

Sperry, L. (1987). ERIC: A cognitive map for guiding brief therapy and health care counseling. *Individual Psychology, 43*(2), 237–241.

Sperry, L. (1988). Biopsychosocial therapy: An integrative approach for tailoring treatment. *Individual Psychology, 44*(2), 225–235.

Sperry, L. (2001). Biopsychosocial therapy with individuals and couples. In L. Sperry (Ed.), *Integrative and biopsychosocial therapy: Maximizing treatment outcomes with individuals and couples* (pp. 67–99). Alexandria, VA: American Counseling Association.

Sperry, L., Brill, P., Howard, K., & Grissom, G. (1996). *Treatment outcomes in psychotherapy and psychiatric interventions.* New York: Brunner/Mazel.

Sperry, L., Carlson, J., & Kjos, D. (2003). *Becoming an effective therapist.* Boston: Allyn & Bacon.

Squyres, W. (1980). *Patient education: An inquiry into the state of the art.* St. Louis: Mosby.

Strupp, H. (1995). The psychotherapist's skills revisited. *Clinical Psychology, 2,* 70–74.

Sue, D. W., Arrodondo, P., & McDavis, R. J. (1992). Multicultural counseling competencies and standards: A call to the profession. *Journal of Counseling and Development, 70,* 477–486.

Tkachuk, G. A., & Martin, G. L. (1999). Exercise therapy for patients with psychiatric disorders: Research and clinical implications. *Professional Psychology: Research and Practice, 30,* 275–282.

Ward, A., & Morgan, W. (1984). Adherence patterns and health: Men and women enrolled in an adult exercise program. *Journal of Cardiac Rehabilitation, 4,* 43–159.

Williams, R. (1956). *Biological individuality.* New York: Wiley.

Wohl, J. (2000). Psychotherapy and cultural diversity. In J. F. Aponte, & J. Wohl (Eds.), *Psychological intervention and cultural diversity* (pp. 75–91). Boston: Allyn & Bacon.

Zackon, F., McAuliffe, W., & Chien, J. (1985). *Addict aftercare: Recovery training and self-help,* DHHS Pub. No. (Adm) 85-1341. Rockville, MD: National Institute on Drug Abuse.

PART **II**

HEALTH COUNSELING
IN ACTION

As envisioned in this book, health counseling is an integrated approach. It combines health information, psychotherapeutic interventions, and client skill-building strategies with environmental interventions. Such an integrated approach is helpful for dealing with a variety of health-related issues. The chapters in Part II focus on specific health-related problems or behaviors—chapter 4 on weight control, chapter 5 on smoking cessation, chapter 6 on substance abuse, chapter 7 on exercise, chapter 8 on sleep, chapter 9 on sexual health, chapter 10 on chronic pain, and chapter 11 on chronic disease and other illness-related conditions. Each chapter surveys the theoretical and research literature related to its topic and also provides clinical input on relationship development, assessment, intervention, treatment maintenance, and prevention. Each chapter also includes case materials and available health counseling resources.

CHAPTER FOUR

WEIGHT CONTROL

*Clogged with yesterday's excess, the body drags the mind down
with it, and fastens to the ground this fragment of divine spirit.*

—Horace

Obesity has been identified by the World Health Organization (1998) as one of the major chronic diseases. Obesity increases the risk for several chronic illnesses, such as Type 2 diabetes, hypertension, and cardiovascular disease, as well as reducing mortality (i.e., life expectancy). The estimated annual U.S. death rate attributed to obesity in 1998 was 325,000, which is slightly less than the mortality attributed to smoking—400,000 per year (Field, Barnoya, & Colditz, 2002). Obesity usually is defined by an indirect measure of body fat—the body mass index (BMI), which can be calculated by the formula: (weight in kg)/(height in meters)^2. Operationally, the World Health Organization defines overweight as a BMI of 25.0 to 29.9 and obesity as a BMI greater than 30 (Noëël, Pugh, & Crawford, 2002).

The prevalence of those who are overweight and obese among U.S. adults is increasing. While 55 percent of all adults were found to be either overweight or obese in 1994, 5 years later that prevalence had increased to 61 percent. This translates to approximately 60 million adults who are overweight and approximately 26 percent who are obese (Field, Barnoya & Colditz, 2002). The annual cost of obesity to the U.S. health-care system is estimated to be close to $100 billion, which represents between 5 to 10 percent of the country's health-care budget (Wolf & Colditz, 1996). Americans spend more than $20 billion per year on commercial weight-loss treatments, and the increasing level of media attention to crash diets, weight-loss clinics, and exercise programs and equipment suggests that this figure can only be on the increase. Interestingly, the massive investment in weight-reducing treatment has failed to produce any decrease in the frequency of obesity, which has actually risen over the past 40 years.

A review of the literature confirms the perception of the negative stereotype of obesity, which ranges from criticism and public ridicule accorded to obese children to active prejudice, particularly against obese females in occupational settings. Obese individuals can be expected to be teased and taunted, treated as less intelligent than they are, and/or rejected from training or jobs in favor of less-qualified but slimmer individuals. At a personal level, excess weight is associated with low self-esteem and low body image satisfaction. Embarrassment about body shape can make overweight individuals reluctant to engage in sexual relationships or to take part in activities in which the body shape is exposed, taking a further toll on physical and emotional well-being (Wadden et al., 2002).

This chapter provides an overview of both the theoretical and the clinical information on weight control. It begins by examining obesity in terms of etiology, theories, and classifications. As in other chapters, biopsychosocial factors are emphasized, particularly as they relate to weight gain and weight loss. Various approaches to the assessment and treatment of obesity are then reviewed with an emphasis on a comprehensive, biopsychosocial view of the process of change. The discussions include two different treatment protocols that health counselors have found useful when working with clients who have weight-control issues. Further, because relapse prevention is such a critical weight-management issue, there is an extended discussion about it, including primary prevention measures. Finally, the chapter concludes with two detailed cases and an extended Resources section.

To begin, it is important to define and clarify two terms used in this chapter—obesity and being overweight are not synonymous terms. *Obesity* specifically refers to excess body fat, whereas *overweight* refers to weighing more than is standard for height and age. However, highly active individuals, such as conditioned athletes who have substantial muscle mass, may weigh slightly more than the standard for their height despite low body fat. "Thus, people may be overweight, but not over-fat" (Field, Barnoya, & Colditz, 2002, p. 3).

A BIOPSYCHOSOCIAL APPROACH

Causes of Obesity

Obesity is understood to result "from a chronic imbalance between energy intake and energy expenditure" (Tataranni & Ravussin, 2002, p. 42). Three factors have been shown to contribute to the overweight and obesity states: individual, biological, and environmental factors (Horgen & Brownell, 2002). Until recently, the individual has been the primary focus of intervention efforts. In this discussion, *individual* refers to factors such as food preferences, eating habits, and motivation to lose weight; *biology* refers to familial and genetic factors; and *environment* refers to influences such as advertising, cultural norms about exercise and physical activity, and the availability of inexpensive, convenience foods high in fats and calories. Since the cause of obesity is multiply determined, and the focus on the individual has not been particularly effective, an increasing number of clinicians, researchers, and policymakers are proposing that interventions should begin to focus more on biological and environmental factors.

Recent research suggests that approximately 67 percent of the variability in BMI can be attributed to genetic factors while the other 33 percent is attributed to environmental factors. It appears that a genetic predisposition to obesity is related to energy metabolism, meaning that overeating, a low metabolic rate, a low fat-oxidation rate, and impairment of sympathetic nervous system activity characterize humans' susceptibility to weight gain.

Thus, it may well be that "obesity results from normal physiological variability within a pathoenvironment. The corollary of this is that the pathology does not lie within the individual, but within the environment" (Tataranni & Ravussin, 2002, pp. 61–62).

In the past few years, more researchers are pointing to environmental factors as the primary cause of obesity. For instance, Horgen and Brownell (2002) contend that while biology may explain why some individuals become obese, biology cannot explain it any more than understanding how "biological vulnerabilities in individuals explain why there is so much lung cancer. There is so much lung cancer primarily because of tobacco, and there is so much obesity because of a dangerous food and physical activity environment" (p. 97).

In biopsychosocial terms, *bio* refers to biology and genetics, *psycho* refers to the individual, and *social* refers to the environment. At the present time, social or environment appears to be the most prominent overweight and obesity causative factor.

An Obesity Classification Scheme

Classification systems arose from the observation that obese clients differ in their response to treatment. The World Health Organization (1998) and others have proposed classifications based on the body mass index (see Table 4.1).

Theories of Obesity

During the 1980s, it was in vogue to propose various physiological and psychological theories to explain the phenomenon of obesity, and the first edition of this book did describe the set-point, fat-cell, and weight-cycling, or yo-yo, theories of obesity. Today, researchers and clinicians seem to focus less on such theoretical explanations and more on biological; psychological; and social, familial, and cultural factors related to being overweight or obese.

BIOLOGICAL FACTORS

The Buckmaster and Brownell (1989) study indicates that there are five factors involved in weight control: (1) exercising (2) nutrition training, (3) changing the act of eating, (4) cognitive retraining, and (5) developing support systems. From a biopsychosocial perspective,

TABLE 4.1   Classification of Overweight and Obesity

DESCRIPTION	BMI	OBESITY CLASSIFICATION
Underweight	< 18.5	
Normal	18.5–24.9	
Overweight	25.0–29.9	
Obesity	30.0–34.9	I
	35.0–39.9	II
Extreme obesity	≥ 40.0	III

Source: Adapted from World Health Organization (1998).

all five are integral in understanding the change process. Nutrition training and exercise are clearly biological factors and are discussed in detail next. Then, another factor, biological individuality, is described.

Exercise

Exercise appears to be the single most important behavior for long-term weight control in obese individuals (Wadden et al., 1997). Even though it is not the most efficient method of losing weight, exercise is crucial for maintaining weight loss. Furthermore, regular exercise and cardiorespiratory fitness have significant health benefits that far exceed weight loss and maintenance. Exercise reduces the risk for several chronic diseases, most notably cardio-vascular disease and Type 2 diabetes, and it also delays mortality in overweight and obese individuals (Blair & Leermakers, 2002). In addition to physiological benefits, there are considerable psychological benefits to regular exercise.

Expert panels and commissions recently reached a consensus on a recommendation for physical activity for adults. "All sedentary adults should accumulate at least 30 minutes of at least moderate-intensity physical activity over the course of most, preferably all, days of the week" (Blair & Leermakers, 2002, p. 288). "Moderate intensity" is variously defined as moderate to brisk walking such that three walks of 10 minutes each week will meet the consensus recommendation. A fuller discussion of this and other matters related to exercise can be found in chapter 7 of this book.

Nutrition

Because improper nutrition can lead to loss of lean body tissue, as well as to other physical problems, nutrition is important for optimal weight reduction and maintenance. Generally speaking, many weight-management groups do not forbid particular foods because mandated abstinence only seems to enhance the desire and craving for certain foods. Also, most programs tailor diets to incorporate clients' food preferences. Not to do so only encourages the client to return to old eating patterns and thus to regain any weight lost on a prescribed diet. Achieving a positive energy balance between intake and expenditure and an appropriate balance among protein, carbohydrates, and fats tailored to clients' needs is important (Tataranni & Rauvussin, 2002).

Biological Individuality

There is a growing awareness today that just as there are individual differences in a person's emotional makeup and identity there also are individual differences in a person's biological and biochemical needs and processes. Although scientists have long recognized that unique personality differences among individuals exist, they have been slow to acknowledge and accept that there also are unique biological differences. Take the "food pyramid," which all students are being taught is the framework for a healthy and balanced diet for everyone; such a "one-size-fits-all" health prescription probably should be called the "myth of uniformity." Among other noted scientists, Roger Williams, Ph.D. has challenged the pyramid myth with research studies that have convincingly shown that there are wide structural and biochemical variations among individuals of the same age, gender, and body size. He was convinced that every individual has distinct biological needs programmed into his or her unique genetic makeup. Williams (1956) coined the term "biochemical individuality" to describe this biological uniqueness—biological individuality—phenomenon.

What are the implications of biological individuality for weight control? The main implication is that there can be no uniform, one-size-fits-all, diet plan or weight-control regimen that will be effective for everyone. It also means that any weight-control prescription must be tailored to the individual's unique biological needs, as well as expectations.

PSYCHOLOGICAL FACTORS

Research and clinical practice has pointed to a number of psychological factors involved in weight gain and control. This section briefly discusses them beginning with the psychological characteristics of those who are overweight and obese. It continues with discussions about modifying eating behavior, the cognitive and psychodynamic aspects of obesity, and how Adlerian psychology views obesity.

Psychological Characteristics

The majority of overweight and obese individuals appear to have normal psychological functioning despite their daily exposure to a culture that glorifies thinness and practices weight-related prejudices and discrimination (Wadden, Womble, Stunkard, & Anderson, 2002). In a clinical setting, about 10 to 20 percent can be expected to suffer from clinical symptoms of depression, negative body image, or some impairment in health-related quality of life. These will most likely be experienced by women, particularly those with the following risk factors: extreme obesity, (i.e., BMI $\geq$ 40), higher socioeconomic status, or binge-eating disorder.

Modification of Eating Behavior

Traditional behavioral techniques were used in early behavioral weight-control programs to minimize excessive eating (Ferster, Nurnberger, & Levitt, 1962). Such techniques were self-monitoring, stimulus control, preplanning, slower eating, and so on. For example, in self-monitoring, the client was asked to keep a daily record of calories consumed; the records were then checked by the health counselor to assess their accuracy and to detect problem areas. Stimulus-control techniques often included always sitting in the same place when eating; not engaging in other activities, such as reading or watching television, while eating; eating from a smaller plate; or storing food out of site. Preplanning was another commonly used technique; clients were helped to anticipate the what, when, and where of meals. For instance, if the client decided in advance to eat broiled chicken and vegetables at home at 5:30 P.M. and had the proper ingredients available, the likelihood of eating other foods was decreased. Preplanning also reduced the chance of impulsive eating. Slowing the act of eating allowed the client to experience satiety, or a sense of fullness, before overeating.

The purpose of these techniques was to help clients develop an awareness of their eating habits, as well as to learn how the structure of their environment can minimize eating cues that might lead to excessive eating. Unfortunately, the early applications of behavioral techniques were not particularly effective and have been mockingly oversimplified as, "Put your fork down and chew each mouthful twenty times."

Today the behavioral or, more correctly, cognitive-behavioral, approach deals with all behaviors that affect weight loss, weight gain, and weight maintenance. The same principles that could be applied to eating—shaping, goal setting, self-monitoring for feedback, reinforcement, stimulus control—can be used for changing exercise patterns, food selection, and self-defeating thoughts and for engendering social support from others in the clients' environment.

Cognitive and Psychodynamic Aspects

The cognitive component of weight control includes setting goals, restructuring dysfunctional beliefs about eating, improving self-image, coping with mistakes, and developing motivation. Emphasis is placed on clients' attitudes toward treatment, especially in the later stages when relapse prevention is of particular concern. The cognitive component in weight-control programs seeks to emphasize primarily positive attitudes and to enhance adherence to the exercise, lifestyle, and nutritional parts of the program (Wadden & Osei, 2002).

Although there has been only limited interest in obesity by psychoanalytic and psychodynamic therapists, there are a few contributions from this orientation that a health counselor may do well to heed. An early concept that emerged from psychoanalytic theory was the oral character structure. Conflicts over the satisfaction of libidinal and aggressive needs, met through sucking or biting, were believed to be related to obesity. Hilde Bruch's (1973) ongoing experience with obese individuals offers an important perspective on motivation for weight loss. Bruch divided her obese patients into three groups: those without significant psychological problems; those whose obesity was "interwoven with their whole personality development," which she called developmental obesity; and those who became obese as a reaction to some traumatic event, called *reactive obesity*.

Bruch describes the reactive form of obesity as characteristic of relatively psychologically mature individuals who eat more when they are worried, tense, or anxious. Reactive obesity usually develops after the death of a family member, separation from home, loss of a love object, or other situation involving the fear of abandonment. These individuals have difficulty coping with their aggressive feelings and tend to become depressed. They overeat in response to their feelings of aggression and other undesirable emotions.

Bruch found that individuals who were developmentally obese suffered from disturbances in psychological functions. Developmental obesity is often evident by late childhood or early adolescence. Rather than developing a positive image of their bodies, obese adolescents tend to have serious adjustment problems, whereby inactivity and overeating become integral parts of their personal development. They are not fully aware of themselves as separate from the important figures in their environment and feel a lack of control over their sensations and actions. In addition, they fail to achieve a sense of ownership of their bodies or a sense of themselves as active participants in the outcomes of their lives. Thus, their initiative and autonomy appear poorly developed.

For the developmentally obese individual, commitment to a sustained, systematic, but gradual weight-loss program is very difficult because of their unrealistic expectations for quick, painless cures. In short, Bruch believes that, in contrast to reactively obese patients, developmentally obese patients seldom have the motivation to commit themselves to a serious weight-management program.

The Adlerian View of Obesity

Closely related to the psychodynamic approach, as well as to the cognitive approach, to obesity is the view of Adlerian psychology. In the Adlerian view, individuals with obesity or other eating disorders develop mistaken convictions or cognitions about themselves, other people, and life. Obesity is understood as the purposeful maintenance of body weight through overeating. It is viewed as a lifestyle that protects, excuses, and silently communicates dependency and fear of dependency, or independence and fear of independence. Nearly always, obesity serves a family function: The unconscious goal of the obese person is to focus attention away from a parental or family problem and onto themselves. The obese individual focuses on food rather than issues, weight rather than judgment, and unreality rather than decision. The eating disorder then comes to symbolize control issues, denial, avoidance, excesses, and emptiness of the family (Casper & Zachery, 1984).

SOCIAL, FAMILIAL, AND SOCIOCULTURAL FACTORS

Social factors play an important role in both the etiology and the treatment of obesity. Among the most influential social factors are social-support systems and cultural values. Research shows that social support can decrease attrition or early termination from treatment programs, increase weight loss, and improve weight-loss maintenance (Wadden & Phelan, 2002). Family and spouse interactions and spousal involvement in obesity programs have generated much research interest in this field.

Familial Factors

Spousal interaction factors can highly influence whether an individual will succeed in treatment. A client's family network can greatly help or hinder progress. For instance, a spouse can act as the "gatekeeper" of food that enters the house, overtly or covertly encourage or discourage weight loss, and invariably changes the homeostasis in the marital relationship and in sexual intimacy.

The Stuart and Jacobson (1987) study found that being overweight could serve four purposes in a marriage. First, being overweight served to allay a woman's fears of becoming too sexually attractive or even promiscuous. Second, weight gain served to diminish a husband's sexual interest and to inhibit the woman's own sexual desire; the end result was that consciously or not, excess weight served as a means of avoiding intimacy. Third, weight gain served to control anger and to neutralize the husband's efforts to overcontrol his wife; these women internalized anger by "swallowing" it. Some even gained weight to rebel against their husband's insistence that they become thin. Thus, the women's bodies became the battleground in a power struggle that neither they nor their husbands could win. Finally, weight gain was used to hide a woman's fear that she would be a failure, or a success, in life. As such, weight became a convenient scapegoat for insecurity and other problems in the women's lives. In short, many women want to be thin, but they need to overeat to nourish their empty lives, to soften the threat of failure or success, and to shield themselves against the demands for sex or against the control of their husbands. Unfortunately, these purposes serve to confirm the role of the wife as a victim.

Particularly surprising were the Stuart and Jacobson findings about the husband's view of his overweight wife. Insecure husbands often blocked and sabotaged their wives' efforts to lose weight. Using both survey data and their clinical observations, these researchers note a number of reasons why a husband preferred that his wife remain over-weight. The husbands in the study were unwilling to change their comfortable routines, to tackle their own weight problems, or to deal with their own addictive behavior such as drinking or gambling. Some used their wives' weight to divert attention from marital or sex-ual problems in the relationship. Furthermore, some men feared that their wives would become unfaithful or leave them if they lost too much weight. Finally, Stuart and Jacobson (1987) found that approximately half of the women wanted their husbands' positive collab-oration and support in losing weight, and the other half did not. The researchers' experience as marital therapists confirmed that when a woman wants and expects her husband to col-laborate in her weight-loss program, she will more likely than not lose weight and maintain the weight loss.

Sociocultural Factors

An important social factor related to eating patterns and weight control is the influence of one's cultural background and identity. Eating patterns and ideals about weight clearly have cultural roots. Biological and psychological factors about weight and weight control exist with a cultural context that influences how people view their bodies, nutrition, and an appropriate means to control weight. Even the idea of "controlling weight" clearly rests within a cultural context of beauty, health, and well-being. Eating habits and patterns are based on cultural norms and provide a sense of belonging, affirm cultural and social identi-ties, are kept with pride, and cannot be easily altered. One's cultural identity is often the main determinant of what and when one eats, and to a lesser extent, how much one eats. Food habits and preferences are among the last characteristics of a culture to be lost during immigration and through the process of acculturation (Marks et al., 2000).

ASSESSMENTS FOR WEIGHT-CONTROL TREATMENT

This section describes assessment in terms of biological, psychological, and social-support system evaluation. Assessment in the area of weight control is usually carried out in stages. Often, an initial screening is done to collect basic background information, frequently col-lected on paper-and-pencil forms and inventories. The first in-person interview then focuses on the assessment of the client's general psychological state and motivation for treatment.

Finally, a self-monitoring phase is generally needed to record eating and activity pattern details; typically the client completes the forms between sessions.

Biological Assessment

The client's biological assessment includes at least three dimensions—weight and weight-loss histories, assessment of fatness, and assessment of fitness and exercise behavior—and a medical evaluation.

Weight History.   A history of one's weight is an important part of the assessment process. Gathering information begins by asking when the client first became significantly overweight. Childhood onset of obesity generally is associated with greater body weight as an adult and with an excess of fat cells. On the other hand, weight gain in an adult who was previously at a normal weight is generally not associated with an increase in fat-cell numbers. Therefore, the prognosis for returning to an ideal body weight is more favorable for people with adulthood-onset than for those with childhood-onset obesity. This is not to say that individuals who have been severely overweight since childhood cannot lose significant amounts of weight; however, they are likely to fall far short of reaching ideal weight and to have greater difficulty maintaining the weight loss (Wadden & Phelan, 2002).

Next, the inquiry is directed at any family history of obesity. If neither parent is obese, the likelihood of one of the children becoming obese is relatively small; if one parent is obese, the likelihood rises to 40 percent; and if both parents are overweight, the probability jumps to 80 percent.

Weight-Loss History.   An inquiry into prior efforts to lose weight is essential. The number and type of programs or diets tried, and the short- and long-term results should be elicited either by interview or an inventory such as the WALI (see Eating Patterns section that follows). This inquiry may or may not indicate the presence of weight cycling (i.e., weight is quickly regained after weight loss). Weight cycling is a marker of the set-point theory of weight management. Some studies have found that most individuals have not lost and regained hundreds of pounds, despite frequent anecdotal reports (Wadden & Phelan, 2002).

Assessment of Fatness.   Today, calculating the client's BMI is an essential and relatively easy part of assessment. An accurate recording of the patients weight and height is made, preferably using a balance with a beam rather than a spring scale (Wadden & Phelan, 2002).

Assessment of Fitness and Exercise Behavior.   It is useful to make some estimate of fitness both to plan an appropriate exercise program and to provide a baseline against which to assess change (Blair & Leermakers, 2002). Fitness can be determined easily using the step test, in which the patient is asked to step up and down a 13-inch-high step at a rate of about 80 steps per minute. Pulse rate is recorded both immediately after finishing the exercise and then again after a recovery period. These results are then used to classify the initial fitness level and can be repeated after implementing a treatment program (Katch & McArdle, 1983).

Medical Evaluation.   Moderately and severely overweight individuals should be referred for a thorough medical evaluation before undertaking a weight-reduction program. Furthermore, the health counselor should fully apprise the physician of the details of the proposed program for the client. Often, clients take medications or have a history of illness that may contraindicate the use of some weight-reduction approaches such as a very low carbohydrate diet (VLCD) or surgery. In addition, clients need to be medically monitored during their diet to assess changes or complications in indicators such as cholesterol level, blood glucose level, blood pressure, and electrolytes. It is also advisable for even mildly obese individuals to consult with their physician before dieting, even though there are fewer risks of complications. As with the most severely overweight individuals, it is useful to track changes in blood pressure, cholesterol, and other health measures. Finally, the medical evaluation should rule out any contraindication to weight loss such as pregnancy or terminal illness (Aronne, 2002).

Psychological Assessment

Whereas the biological assessment focuses on the effects of food on the body, a psychological assessment focuses more on what, how, and why a person eats particular types and amounts of foods. This section describes a number of methods for assessing these concerns. It begins by describing two eating disorders, which are important for clinicians and health counselors to recognize, and then discusses eating patterns and some procedures and evaluation instruments.

Eating Disorders.   There are two eating disorders that involve overeating. Not to be confused with bulimia, which involves purging, the *binge-eating disorder* is when one engages in overeating episodes in which there is a total lack of control over amounts eaten. Currently, binge eating is only a proposed diagnosis in *DSM-IV. Night-eating syndrome,* on the other hand, has yet to receive much recognition in the professional community. Stunkard (2002) proposes diagnostic criteria for this disorder. He indicates that this syndrome is characterized by the triad of morning anorexia (i.e., little desire for food in the morning); evening hyperhagia (i.e., eating more than 50% of one's total daily caloric intake in snacks after the evening meal); and insomnia, wherein the individual awakens in the night and typically consumes highly caloric snacks.

Eating Patterns.   An assessment of the client's eating patterns and food intake is useful in planning and monitoring treatment. Three sections of the Weight and Lifestyle Inventory (WALI) are quite useful in eliciting this information. Sections H and J permit useful ratings of Eating Patterns; Section I, Food Intake Recall, is a short and clinically useful measure of food intake for a typical weekday and a typical weekend day (Wadden & Phelan, 2002). The WALI is thought to be the most valuable of all available weight assessment devices and using it is highly recommended.

A Biopyschosocial Approach.   A very promising and comprehensive evaluation procedure in the assessment of obese individuals prior to treatment has been developed and described by Wadden and Phelan (2002). The purpose of the evaluation is to obtain a biopsychosocial understanding of the factors contributing to clients' obesity, and to examine their goals and expectations for weight reduction. It is organized around five factors: biological, environmental, social, psychological, and the timing of the present weight-loss effort (i.e., why the individual decided to lose weight now, and whether this is a favorable time to lose weight). The evaluation consists of an interview and self-report data. Prior to the interview, clients are asked to complete Beck's Depression Inventory-II and the WALI. The highly regarded WALI questionnaire typically takes a client an hour and a half to complete; it is included in an appendix to the Wadden and Phelan paper (2002).

Social-Support System Assessment

Because social factors appear to play a significant role in the etiology and treatment of obesity, it is important to assess their impact (Wadden & Phelan, 2002). Earlier discussions covered family, social, and cultural factors that affect not only the process of weight gain and loss but, more important, weight maintenance. Therefore, it is essential for the health counselor or clinician to assess the partner's expectations and feelings about the client's desire to lose weight. In addition, one should inquire as to the partner's degree of encouragement and cooperation, as well as any overt or covert indications of sabotage of the client's weight-control program. The following are useful interview questions: What did your partner do that helped you lose weight? What did your partner do that hindered your efforts to lose weight? Does your partner want you to lose weight? Has your partner expressed an interest in helping with your plan to lose weight?

Dietary health behaviors are culturally influenced in that food choices, methods of cooking, and traditions associated with diet all reflect cultural values. Therefore, it is important to have adequate knowledge and respect for a client's community, culture, and language when developing weight-control and dietary-based interventions. During the assessment phase of treatment, evaluating the client's cultural orientation and worldview should accompany biological and psychological inquiries. Cultural assessment is critical in expanding the professional's knowledge base about a client and in developing culturally sensitive and meaningful interventions (Ibrahim, Roysircar-Sodowsky, & Ohnishi, 2001). Rozin (1996) suggests that sociocultural factors are so important in determining food choices and dietary attitudes that if you can only ask one question during an assessment, the question should be, "What is your culture or ethnic group?" (p. 235).

TREATMENT ISSUES AND STRATEGIES

Following a detailed assessment, and before a client begins a specific program, the clinician or health counselor would do well to review a number of treatment considerations; be aware of treatment modality issues; and understand biological, psychological, cognitive-behavioral, and social interventions.

General Treatment Considerations

The general treatment issues to review include possible contraindications, the appropriateness of client expectations, and cultural considerations.

Contraindications to Weight Reduction. There are some weight-reduction contraindications. Pregnancy and terminal illness are absolute contraindications. A history of eating disorders, particularly involving purging by vomiting or laxative abuse, is a relative contraindication and referral to a specialist in eating disorders is indicated (Aronne, 2002). Clients who harbor an obsessive concern about their weight should not be accepted automatically for weight-control treatment. Weight reduction still may be indicated, but only after the obsession with weight has been dealt with in therapy. Often, these individuals are only mildly overweight, if at all; have a history of continuous dieting; have negative body images; and report thinking about their weight constantly.

Realistic Client Expectations. Expert panels and governmental guidelines recommend that obese persons seek modest or "reasonable" weight loss (i.e., about 10%) rather than striving to achieve their "ideal" weights. Even a modest 10 percent sustained weight loss can have significant benefits to one's physical health and well-being (Field, Barnoya, & Colditz, 2002). However, little is known about how obese individuals view reasonable weight loss. Researchers assessed the goals, expectations, and evaluations of various outcomes before, during, and after 48 weeks of obesity treatment. Before treatment, 60 obese women defined their "goal weight," as well as their "dream weight," "happy weight," "acceptable weight," and "disappointed weight." After treatment and a 16-kg weight loss, 47 percent of these women did not achieve even what they considered the "disappointed weight." Interestingly, the "goal weight" they reported was nearly 3 times the amount of their actual weight losses. These data illustrate the dramatic disparity between individuals' expectations and professional recommendations and the need to help obese individuals accept more modest weight-loss outcomes (Foster et al., 1997). It behooves the health counselor or clinician to elicit clients' expectations and to use health education and therapeutic processing strategies to modify such expectations to more realistic levels.

There also may be some individuals who are quite overweight but should be encouraged to accept their condition rather than to suffer through the rigors of a weight-control program. Acceptance rather than weight reduction can be a wise course to follow, particularly for those clients who have repeatedly tried and failed to follow the best available treatment programs. A more humane and ethical course of treatment may be to focus on helping them accept their body size. Focusing on acceptance is sometimes better than continuing to fail at diets; using financial resources that could be better spent; and incurring the negative reactions of disappointed family members, friends, and fellow employees (Brownell & Foreyt, 1985).

A final concern regarding who should be treated involves the "new" weight client; "new" refers to the individual who has never sought professional help for weight loss. Since many obese people lose weight on their own and maintain that weight loss for years, some counselors believe that those individuals who have never sought treatment should first try to lose weight on their own. Accordingly, these clients can be counseled to choose a good, well-balanced diet and to gradually increase their activity level; telling them that they may be successful by themselves could help too. If they are not able to lose much weight or to maintain any weight loss, then such individuals may be candidates for formal, professional treatment.

Cultural Considerations. The specific content of an intervention can vary across ethnic groups. For example, when working with the Mexican American community, an intervention may target reducing the use of lard in food preparation, whereas in the African American community the target may be focused on lowering sodium consumption (Wilson, Nicholson, & Krishnamoorthy, 1997). In addition, the specific components of any weight-control intervention will vary across ethnic groups (e.g., use of community leaders, inclusion of culturally specific interventions, target behaviors). In terms of tailoring weight-control interventions, cultural influences in the environment may be particularly relevant. Many weight-management programs, drawing on the influence of White culture, focus on the individual and individual-based interventions. However, some ethnic groups' members may exude greater influence from their family and community, therefore multileveled weight-control interventions focused on clients' social-support system may be more successful.

Treatment Modality Issues

Two modality issues need to be considered by the counselor before initiating specific interventions: individual versus group treatment and self-help versus commercial groups.

Individual versus Group Treatment.   The issue of individual versus group treatment for obese individuals has received relatively little attention in the scientific literature, despite its obvious importance. Each approach has different social affects on most clients, such that the same treatment may benefit a person in one setting and be ineffective for another (Brownell & Foreyt, 1985).

A study by Kingsley and Wilson (1977) compared group versus individual treatment of trained counselors and found that, although the two approaches did not differ at the end of the formal treatment, the group approach was superior during the follow-up period. Generally speaking, group treatment is cost-effective as well as effective in providing peer support and encouragement, which is different in nature from that provided by the counselor–client relationship. Clients often feel more at ease discussing their problems among others with similar concerns and may accept advice better from a fellow group member than from a professional. Finally, clients in a group often generate creative solutions to specific problems that may not arise in individual treatment.

In some circumstances, individual sessions may be more appropriate for a particular client. This is definitely true when a client has emotional difficulties that are not appropriate for a group or that may require more attention than group members can provide. Some clients may not be able to profit much from the group process because of their shyness and reluctance to talk openly. Others may be too suspicious and guarded or may be unwilling to disclose personal information, particularly their weight status. Finally, there are those clients who easily create negative group contagion, which can be destructive to the group process. For the benefit of other members, these clients should be seen individually. Clients with borderline and/or antisocial issues may be appropriate for severe personality-disorder groups (Linehan, 1987), but they tend to do poorly in task-oriented situations such as weight-control groups.

Individual treatment and group treatment are not mutually exclusive. Some clients do well in groups if they receive periodic individual sessions; others can do well in groups but may require individual treatment during a crisis period. Then, there are those clients who need individual treatment to start the behavior change process but can then make the transition into group treatment. Counselors experienced in both individual and group treatment can usually make this determination at the outset. Finally, some health counselors have experimented with a combination of individual treatment and an adjunctive self-help group treatment, such as Overeaters Anonymous (OA). In any event, a careful and comprehensive assessment of a client's needs and status should govern the decision about individual versus group treatment.

Self-Help versus Commercial Groups.   Health counselors trained at an obesity clinic that operates within a university department of psychology or a medical school know that their clinics often provide treatment that is free or for a nominal fee. Subsequently, many counselors are wary of commercial weight-control programs because of the high fees they charge; others may be wary of self-help groups, but for different reasons. Often this distrust results from a lack of knowledge about these groups, the absence of published research on their treatment outcomes, a disdain for profit enterprises for group treatment, or the etiological bias of certain self-help groups. Inasmuch as the vast majority of dieters seek out treatment from self-help and commercial programs, these groups are an important part of treating obesity from a public health perspective, and they can be a valuable resource for the health counselor.

A detailed overview of such groups is beyond the scope of this book; however, reviews of the outcome literature by Colletti and Brownell (1982) and by Stuart and Mitchell (1980) show that the major shortcomings of these groups is attrition. Approximately 50 to 80 percent of participants drop out of the programs within 6 weeks; for example, the average individual who joins Weight Watchers has joined 3 times before. For those who remain in a program, weight losses are usually only moderate. The high attrition rate can be viewed as an indictment of these groups self-help approaches. Yet, since some of the groups are offered at no cost or at low cost, minimally motivated clients may join and then drop out.

The therapeutic issue is to decide which client can profit from which approach. This requires that the health counselor become acquainted with details of the various programs by calling or visiting them and/or by obtaining information from clients who have participated in the various groups. Several factors distinguish them both in their procedures and in the way in which each one views obesity; for instance, OA is modeled after Alcoholics Anonymous (AA). The participants are referred to as compulsive overeaters, and they are encouraged to call on a higher power for strength and to rely on a sponsor to help them cope in times of crisis. On the other hand, Take Off Pounds Sensibly (TOPS) has no spiritual overtones and stresses a buddy system, gentle competition, and group support. Not surprisingly, middle-class, gregarious women find TOPS both attractive and helpful. Weight Watchers uses specific diets, markets, and food products and relies on regular weigh-ins for motivation.

Assuming that the health counselor and the client jointly determine that a self-help or commercial group would be appropriate, the challenge is to match the client to the best possible group. This can be done by discussing the details of the different approaches with the client and encouraging him or her to speak to others who have been in the program. Finally, it should be noted that clients also can benefit from joining a self-help group after a course of individual or clinic treatment (Womble, Wang, & Wadden, 2002).

Biological Interventions

Four types of biological interventions are commonly available for weight control: exercise, nutritional prescription, gastric bypass surgery, and diet plans.

Exercise.   At one time it was assumed that a formal exercise program (e.g., running, aerobics, swimming, cycling, and/or taking part in regular sporting event was a necessary and integral part of a weight-control program. The recent consensus recommendation of 30 minutes per day of any physical exertion has changed the way exercise is now incorporated into weight-loss programs (Blair & Leermakers, 2002).

Nutritional Prescription.   Since obese clients typically derive more than 40 percent of their calories from fat, most nutritionists recommend a diet that derives no more than 30 percent of one's calories from fat, 12 percent from protein, and 58 percent from carbohydrates (Buckmaster & Brownell, 1989).

Health counselors and weight-control programs are divided on the issue of prescribing specific diets. Some routinely refer their clients to a registered dietician for a diet prescription. Others believe that prescribing a diet sets the stage for abandoning the program when the inevitable dietary transgression or relapse occurs. Instead, these counselors ask female clients to limit their calories to 1,200 per day and male clients to limit themselves to 1,500 calories per day. Caloric intake should be adjusted to reflect the individual's energy expenditure, but the specifics of the diet—within the boundaries of good nutrition—are left to clients. Such nutritional changes are subsequently woven into individuals' entire lifestyle.

A weight-control program that incorporates a 1,200- to 1,500-calorie diet with a behavioral-modification component should produce an average weight loss of 11 pounds in 10 to 12 weeks; a 25-pound weight loss should be realized after 25 weeks of treatment (Wilson & Brownell, 1980). For the mildly obese patient, these results are more than sufficient. However, for the moderately obese person who needs to lose 60 to 100 pounds, or for the morbidly obese individual who needs to lose 100 or more pounds, such a treatment program is not appropriate. These people are likely to require more aggressive treatment based on a very-low-calorie diet (VLCD). Such diets provide 300 to 600 calories per day and produce an average weight loss of 2 to 3 pounds per week. VLCDs are designed to produce the same large weight losses as fasting but to reduce the loss of lean body mass, by providing dietary protein, common in starvation diets.

To date, VLCDs take two forms. The protein-sparing, modified-fast (PSMF) diet, which was developed in 1978 by Dr. Blackburn and his colleagues, provides the client with the equivalent of 70 to 100 grams of protein per day. This protein is obtained from lean meat, fish, and fowl. The PSMF diet prohibits carbohydrates, and fat is restricted to only that present in the protein source. The other type of VLCD relies on a milk- or egg-based protein formula to serve as a liquid diet. These commercially prepared diets provide a daily ration of approximately 35 to 70 grams of protein, 30 to 45 grams of carbohydrates, and about 2 grams of fat. Optifast and Medifast are two medically supervised liquid-protein diets; Ultra Slim-Fast is a similar over-the-counter preparation. The PSMF is supplemented by vitamins and minerals, particularly potassium, calcium, and sodium. Both approaches produce similar weight losses, but some studies have shown that patients prefer the PSMF diet over the liquid-protein diet (Wadden, Stunkard, Brownell, & Dey, 1984).

Gastric Bypass Surgery.   There continues to be an option for the extremely obese (i.e., those with a BMI of ≥ 40.0 who have not responded to other less-invasive interventions. The results of this surgery can be very dramatic. Clients not only eat less but are also likely to experience a change in food preference. They eat smaller amounts of high-density fats, high-density carbohydrates, high-calorie beverages, and high-fat meats. In addition, the postoperative course for clients who have had gastric surgery is more benign psychologically than is dieting. Morbidly obese clients who have a grossly negative body image report more positive evaluations of the body several months after the surgery, even though they are still somewhat obese. Clients have exhibited increased mobility, stamina, assertiveness, and self-confidence and tend to be less self-conscious and withdrawn in social situations. They also begin to explore social and occupational activities formally inaccessible to them (Aronne, 2002).

Popular Diet Plans.   Most weight reduction is not supervised by a clinician or health counselor, meaning that individuals choose a commonly available diet plan, often described in best-selling books or on Web sites. Melanson and Dwyer (2002) compare the advantages and disadvantages of various popular reducing diets: high protein, low protein, high fat, low carbohydrate, and high carbohydrate. They also review various powdered-diet formulas, meal replacement products, meal replacement bars, and prepared low-calorie meals. All are evaluated in terms of the seven criteria, the so-called seven Cs: calories, composition, cost, consumer friendliness, coping with coexisting health risks, components of sound weight management, and continuation of provisions for long-term maintenance (Melanson & Dwyer, 2002). Unfortunately, while these criteria may be evidence-based, they make no provision for individual differences (e.g., a high-protein diet may be quite appropriate for one individual with a certain metabolism but inappropriate for someone with a different metabolism).

Psychological Interventions

The best weight-control programs are multimodal and tailored to the needs of the individual client or group. A behavioral or cognitive-behavioral component is an essential part of all multimodal programs. The main behavioral components are self-monitoring, stimulus control, response prevention, and cognitive restructuring.

Self-Monitoring.   As an integral part of the weight-control program, self-monitoring provides the basis for frequent discussions during treatment sessions. Once treatment has begun, self-monitoring becomes a long-term necessity, requiring that the health counselor set the expectations as well as follow up on clients' compliance with self-monitoring assignments. For example, eating diary sheets should be collected regularly and the data should be recorded on a weight chart and compliance record so that clients can see a tangible record of change. The importance of accuracy and truthfulness on the diary sheets should also be stressed from time to time, since clients may be tempted to omit certain details; these problems can be minimized if the treatment program is presented as a collaborative endeavor.

Eating behavior is affected by numerous environmental cues, which obviously vary; however, they include being offered food, being in a place where eating takes place, shopping for food, engaging in activities commonly associated with eating, and being given presents with a variety of foods. A good eating diary should reveal these environmental cues. There are two behavioral approaches for dealing with them: (1) either the environment is modified so that exposure to the situation that cues eating is limited—stimulus control—or (2) systematic, unreinforced exposure is offered so that the association is broken—response prevention (Wadden et al., 1984).

Stimulus Control.   Stimulus control is appropriate for situations in which environmental modification is practical and possible. Changes could include persuading family members not to buy food for or offer food to the client, confining eating to only one room in the house, and increasing the length of meals by putting down utensils after each mouthful or following the slower eating pace of a family member. Once environmental cues are isolated and stimulus-control methods are begun, the new behaviors must be monitored and systematically reinforced so that they are maintained (Stuart, 1980).

Many aspects of the meal structure itself also may be modified to contribute to a lower food intake. Palatability of food is one important determinant of food intake. Since people eat more of foods they like, clients should be counseled to avoid highly preferred food at times when their self-control may be low. Variety is another critical feature. People tend to eat more when provided with a wide variety of food. Accordingly, limiting the number of different tastes and textures in a meal can help to limit intake.

Response Prevention.   The essence of response prevention is that a behavior should be possible but not performed; in other words, food should be available but not eaten. Clients are often disturbed by occasions when they eat even though they are not hungry, particularly when there is a compulsive quality to their eating behavior. Clients need to be told that eating in the absence of hunger, also called nonregulatory eating, is common and is not necessarily a sign of ineffective willpower or lack of control. On the other hand, a reduction of food intake does require an increase in self-control, which can be increased through exposure (i.e., response-prevention training). During counseling sessions, clients can be exposed to the cue conditions either in vivo or by an imaginal exposure regimen. The latter regimen might include looking at advertisements of foods or evoking emotion-arousing images. Between sessions, homework can be assigned in which the clients practice response prevention by going into food stores or bakeries and not buying anything (Wardle, 1989).

Cognitive Restructuring.   Because cognition plays an important role in mediating behavior change, particularly in response to transgressions, such as food binging, cognitive-restructuring techniques have an important place in weight-control treatment. Negative thoughts about the difficulty of dieting, the unfairness of some people being naturally thin, and so on have the potential to both induce a negative mood and increase noncompliance with treatment. After a minor transgression, negative thoughts (e.g., "Now that I have ruined my diet for the day, I might as well abandon the whole thing") often trigger binge eating.

The usual techniques of cognitive therapy (Beck, 1976) can be used to develop alternative and more adaptive thoughts to substitute for the negative ones. Cognitive restructuring begins by helping clients discover their predictable negative self-talk and develop arguments against them. Health counselors will readily learn that obese clients are easily discouraged by self-talk such as "It takes too long to lose weight" and "I find myself obsessed by thoughts of food." The counselor must coach clients to interrupt such thoughts and to replace them with more optimistic ones such as: "A pound a week adds up over time"; "If I can just cut down on snacks, I will be ahead of the game"; and "I can replace thoughts of food with images of places I like to be and people I really like being with." If the eating diary sheets require that clients list the negative self-talk they engage in while eating, the counselor can then help them dispute the negative thoughts, restructure them, and replace them with more positive thoughts and self-affirmations (Brownell & Foreyt, 1985).

Cognitive-Behavioral Interventions   Behavior therapy has become a mainstay of treatment for overweight individuals and for those with mild to moderate levels of obesity. Increasingly, there are indications that including a cognitive component within such therapy may increase its clinical utility and value. While there are already some cognitive-behavior therapy approaches for the treatment of eating disorders, it is only recently that a cognitive-behavioral treatment of obesity has been described (Cooper & Fairburn, 2002). This approach is administered on an individualized, one-to-one basis over a period of 11 months. It is organized as a series of 11 treatment modules with specific targets: barriers to weight loss, body image, physical activity, personal weight maintenance plan, and so on.

Social Interventions

Richard Stuart (1984) coined the term *indirection* as an alternative to the directive approach taken in most health counseling programs. Because he believes that most lifestyle problems are integrally related to the context in which they occur, he initiates treatment efforts within the marital/partner relationship. The first stage of treatment, then, is to modify that relationship. Only then can the second stage of intervention, which focuses on the issue of weight control, be realized.

Brownell and Foreyt (1985) believe that it is important to involve the partner in weight-control treatment, even though it is not always possible to elicit his or her cooperation. They suggest approaching him or her as an ally in aiding the client's progress and treatment. A phone call from the counselor can convey that he or she is important to the client and that the counselor would benefit from the perspective of the person who knows the client best. This approach must be explained to the client so that the partner is receiving consistent messages. Once the other person is involved, both the client and he or she can be trained in specific ways to deal more effectively with each other around the weight-control issue.

AN INTEGRATIVE INTERVENTION APPROACH

The basic conviction presented here is that health counseling prescriptions for weight control should be tailored to the unique needs and expectations of individual clients. It is becoming more evident that optimal weight control involves more than nutrition and exercise; the other key factors include psychological and spiritual well-being and, particularly, the capacity to effectively manage stress. As noted previously, stress and other psychological factors often function as triggering and/or sustaining factors in weight gain, so it is reasonable to include the stress factor. Presumably, an optimal weight-control intervention would involve and integrate nutritional, exercise, and stress-management factors for the purpose of controlling and maintaining clients' weight, as well as optimizing their energy and endurance, while reducing stress.

Interestingly, in the past few years, there has been a growing awareness among more and more health counselors, consultants, and researchers that there are discernable individual differences in not only energy patterns (i.e., nutrition and exercise patterns), but also in one's stress-response pattern. Just as there is no uniform energy pattern, there is no single response pattern to deal with stress. This means that one-size-fits-all nutrition and exercise programs, as well as one-size-fits-all stress-management programs, are highly suspect.

This section offers an integrative perspective and framework for developing and tailoring interventions for weight control that endeavor to optimize energy and endurance, and also reduce stress. This framework has been adapted from various integrative weight-control approaches (Abravanel, 1999; Baum, 2000; Wolcott, 2000) and emphasizes four different nutrition, exercise, and stress-reduction topologies and strategies. The case example that follows the descriptions summarizes one health counselor's evaluation and treatment of a client who ncceded a stress-management and weight-reduction program.

Typologies and Strategies

The three-dimensional typology described next emphasizes how nutrition, exercise, and stress-reduction strategies can be used to optimize client well-being. Over the years, experience shows that this typology and the related intervention strategies have been quite useful and effective in health counseling and consultation work with executives. It has been clinically useful in assessing executives' "other" individual differences—not usually assessed or monitored by common psychological instruments and categories—particularly the subtle biological dimensions of executive functioning. Furthermore, this typology has been invaluable in tailoring the advice and counsel that can be provided.

In the following pages each of the four types is discussed in terms of their characteristic energy pattern, body shape, personality pattern, and stress response (based on Abravanell, 1999). Then custom-tailored nutrition, exercise, and stress-reduction strategies to optimize energy are presented. Clinical research suggests that one of these four—Types 1, 2, 3, and 4—accurately characterizes about 75 percent of adults, while the remaining 25 percent of adults are a combination of two of the types.

Type 1. Individuals who can be characterized as Type 1 are hard-working, steady individuals with tremendous perseverance. Not surprisingly, their energy level remains high throughout the day, while decreasing somewhat in the evenings. In terms of disposition, they tend to be friendly, open, and practical. Others enjoy being around them. Characteristically, they value stable relationships, particularly with their family and significant other although some have difficulty with intimacy; nevertheless, they tend to have a number of social friends. At work, Type 1 individuals are likely to cultivate friendly but competitive relationships. They are typically not easily angered but when they are they often remain upset for quite a while; talking about an issue can help them resolve it. Type 1 individuals seem to have cast-iron stomachs in that they can eat and drink just about anything, and they seem to need less sleep than the other types.

Balanced male Type 1s appear to be strong and sturdy with a muscular appearance; balanced females also appear strong and sturdy but their strength derives from strong bones more than muscles. Their personalities reflect this power and warmth (i.e., their liveliness and strength). Balanced Type 1s can and do learn to relax and enjoy. When unbalanced, both men and women typically put on weight such that they appear sturdy and heavy-looking, particularly in the front of the body—commonly referred to as a potbelly. Their main food craving is for greasy, salty food such as a cheeseburger.

Type 1 individuals prefer situations that are relatively predictable, controllable, and nonemotional. Accordingly, they tend to be single-minded in their efforts and capable of dealing with detail and repetition. Typically, they experience stress in situations and circumstances that involve changes in their daily routines. To the extent that things are unpredictable and unable to be controlled, they are likely to become distressed. Since children and adolescents tend to act unpredictably, Type 1 individuals often favor their jobs over home situations because of their difficulty relating to this source of lack of control. Similarly, because the expression of emotions can be unexpected and uncontrollable, these individuals avoid situations in which emotionality is likely. Not surprisingly, they are often workaholics with a commitment to their job life that seems stronger, and to them safer, than a commitment to their family. Even vacations, when circumstances and events cannot be adequately anticipated and controlled, tend be a source of considerable stress for Type 1 people. Alcohol and drugs may be used to "dull the edges" of unpredictability in their social lives.

Optimal Nutrition Strategy.   For Type 1 individuals, the optimal nutrition strategy for achieving balance includes the following: plentiful amounts of low or nonfat dairy foods (e.g., yogurt, cottage cheese, string cheese, skim milk), fruits, vegetables, whole grains, and legumes; moderate amounts of fish, poultry, eggs, coffee or tea, vegetable oils, and light desserts; and rarely any salty foods, aged cheeses, red meat, shellfish, butter, and alcohol. In short, the nutrition strategy should be to eliminate craved foods (e.g., spicy and salty ones) and to emphasize poultry, fruits, vegetables, and light dairy foods.

Optimal Exercise Strategy.   Because of their unique metabolism, Type 1 individuals are already strong and muscular and have considerable stamina and endurance. However, they should improve cardiovascular conditioning, flexibility, and eye–hand coordination. Accordingly, the primary focus of this exercise strategy is on cardiovascular activities with only a limited focus of strength training. Exercises that involve both conditioning and eye–hand coordination include squash, handball, and tennis. Regular jogging, walking, or swimming increases cardiovascular conditioning. Yoga or a simple stretching routine increases flexibility. Abravanel (1999) notes that some Type 1s engage in compulsive weight lifting on a daily basis because they crave the spaced-out feeling associated with pumping iron. Not surprisingly, this can become quite addicting and further unbalance their metabolism. Thus, health counselors recommend once-a-week strength training using light weights as an exercise strategy, but regular lifting of heavy weights and Nautilus workouts should be avoided.

Optimal Stress-Reduction Strategy.   Following the Type 1 nutrition and exercise strategies should considerably improve the individual's capacity for flexibility and creativity in stressful situations. In addition, it is essential that these individuals set aside some time every day to just "be"—to "smell the roses" or just plain relax. Spending just 15 to 20 minutes a day shifting their thoughts away from productivity—tasks, problems, and deadlines—and mentally vegetating, can trigger the relaxation response. If applicable, Type 1 individuals may need counseling to control their alcohol and nicotine usage; often, they have used alcohol, nicotine, and other drugs as stress reducers. But, given their unique metabolism and the continuous high stress load they live with, alcohol not only jeopardizes the Type 1 individual's general health but increases their vulnerability to substance addiction.

Since positive social support, particularly close, interpersonal relationships, are an important stress buffer, Type 1s need to focus more on listening and be available to those who could provide this buffering during stressful, difficult times. Unfortunately, Type 1s tend to discount the importance of their significant other, family, coworkers, and subordinates, viewing such relationships as uninteresting and unimportant to their high-priority goals. Thus, they spend little quality time cultivating relationships, even though enhancing them could be mutually beneficial.

Type 2.   Individuals who can be characterized as the Type 2s usually experience bursts of energy but seldom maintain a high energy level for long. Rather, their energy pattern noticeably varies from high to low throughout the day. When attempting to keep it high, they are likely to resort to easily available stimulants (e.g., caffeine, sugar, and nicotine) in an almost addictive fashion when their energy starts to fade. In terms of disposition, they are lively and changeable, even temperamental. Type 2s easily experience impatience and angry feelings and become depressed when their efforts are thwarted; resting is a good antidote for resolving these feelings. They value variety and stimulation in relationships, so tend to have a large number of friends. At work, they can be quite comfortable working alone for awhile, but at other times, they prefer to work with others. They are energetic, with little apparent need for rest.

Balanced Type 2 individuals have the uncanny ability to eat almost endlessly without gaining weight. As a result, they tend to be slender and streamlined in appearance with a good balance of weight and strength above and below the waist. When unbalanced, they can gain weight quickly, noticeably a roll or tire around the midsection, usually referred to as "love handles." Their main food craving is for sweets and starches such as a candy bar, cookie, or sweet roll.

On the other hand, Type 2 individuals prefer novel and challenging situations, and experience those that involve repetition, detail, lack of change or stimulation, and continuing demands as stressful. Far from being stress-producing, unpredictability is perceived as a stimulant. They become energized and creative when beginning projects but find it difficult to focus and experience considerable stress when they must deal with deadlines, minutiae, and pressure to complete something. However, they are likely to experience pain, even relatively minor pain (e.g., a cut, an injection), as stressful. In interpersonal relationships Type 2 individuals are overly sensitive to rejection. Interestingly, of all the stress types, hypochondriacal concerns and complaints (i.e., unrealistic fear of illness) are a common stress response for them.

Optimal Nutrition Strategy.   For Type 2 individuals, the optimal nutrition strategy for achieving balance includes the following: plentiful amounts of eggs, poultry, fish and shellfish, and fresh vegetables; moderate amounts of red meats, legumes, whole grains, butter, and fruit; and rarely any refined grains, caffeine, and sugar. In short, the strategy is to eliminate craved foods (e.g., sweets, starches, and caffeine) and to emphasize eggs, poultry, fish, and vegetables.

Optimal Exercise Strategy.   Because Type 2s cannot naturally sustain high energy levels for long periods of time, they primarily need exercises to develop stamina and endurance. Thus, the main focus should be on strength training with a secondary focus on cardiovascular conditioning. A complete set of strength exercises (e.g., Nautilus or free weights) 3 times a week, along with a light cardiovascular workout up to 4 times a week, is recommended. Type 2 individuals do well with a personal trainer who can tailor and monitor a specific strength-training program to increase muscle mass. Walking may be sufficient for maintaining cardiovascular fitness; however, exercises that require intermittent rather than sustained effort, such as tennis, are not particularly useful for these individuals.

Optimal Stress-Reduction Strategy.   Following the Type 2 nutrition and exercise strategies should considerably improve these individuals' capacity for endurance, steadiness, and personal power. It is important to look carefully at their work situation because it may be the source of considerable stress for them. A good-fit job for these individuals is one that primarily allows them to conceptualize, develop support for, and initiate projects; performing these functions tends to energize Type 2s. On the other hand, jobs that demand attention to detail, follow-through, deadlines, and tedium are poor fits because they devitalize and enervate these individuals. If these poor-fit job functions cannot be modified to better accommodate Type 2 individuals' style, changing to a better-fit job may considerably reduce stress. Type 2s often find themselves in overstimulating environments (e.g., ones with constantly ringing phones, lots of foot traffic, buzzing office machines), or ones with the ongoing pressure of deadlines. Modifying such an overstimulating environment to one that is more relaxing can significantly reduce stress.

Irrespective of their job, these individuals tend to ignore their need for rest and sleep; Type 2 individuals must be counseled to take periodic rest breaks throughout the day and to get a minimum of 7 to 8 hours of sleep a night. Finally, another major source of stress for these individuals is that they want to do everything at once rather than to pace themselves. Taking one day at a time, doing one thing at a time, and alternating activity with periods of rest can be a powerful stress reducer for Type 2s.

Type 3.   Individuals who can be characterized as Type 3s exhibit an energy pattern that is noticeably high in the morning compared to the rest of the day and are likely to think of themselves as morning persons. In terms of disposition, they are likely to be considered by others as detached, idealistic, and intellectual. When frustrated, they are likely to feel hurt but have a difficult time communicating their concerns and feelings. Type 3 individuals are typically slow to anger and quick to get over it after they have had a chance to think about the precipatating incident. They value companionship and, though they may have only a few close friends, these relationships are intense and meaningful. At work, they can be pleasant but do not easily share personal information with others because they often keep their professional and personal lives separate.

Balanced Type 3s are likely to maintain a youthful appearance far longer than other types. Since they are naturally comfortable in their heads, ideal development for them involves an integration of mind and body. To the extent they achieve this integration, Type 3s are lively and intelligent individuals in vibrant health. They can seem somewhat undeveloped and childlike in their appearance, more like a boy or girl than a man or woman. When unbalanced, these individuals may put on weight in such a way that they appear to be uniformly heavy all over. Medically, this fat pattern is referred to as diffuse subcutaneous fat, which is commonly called "baby fat." Their main food craving is for dairy products such as a milk shake, yogurt, or slice of cheese.

Type 3 individuals prefer situations that draw on their capacity for reasoning and judgment. Rather than being experienced as stressful, intellectual challenges—even unexpected mental challenges and demands, which require careful analysis and problem solving—are energizing for them. While these individuals tend to live in their heads and are confident in their mental abilities, they tend to doubt their ability to deal with situations that do not require mental prowess. So, Type 3s experience these situations as stressful and attempt to avoid them as much as possible. Accordingly, the prospect of being physically ill or injured and requiring medical care, of meeting with others socially for a meal, or of dealing with emotions and conflicts that cannot be reasoned away in interpersonal relationships can be quite stressful for them. As a result, they dislike seeking medical care and avoid conflictual situations; when they cannot sidestep conflicts, they give in easily. Furthermore, sexual concerns and difficulties can be a major stressor for Type 3 individuals. It is not that they cannot enjoy sex with the right partner, it is rather that demands or perceived demands for sexual performance, or even talking about sexual issues, tend to be anxiety-provoking for them.

Optimal Nutrition Strategy.   For Type 3 individuals, the optimal nutrition strategy for achieving balance includes the following: plentiful amounts of beef, lamb, pork, and organ meats like liver, eggs and poultry, and fresh vegetables; moderate amounts of fruits, legumes, whole grains, and yogurts; and rarely any sugar, caffeine, and dairy products other than yogurt. In short, the basic strategy is to eliminate craved foods (e.g., dairy products) and to emphasize beef, organ meats, and vegetables.

Optimal Exercise Strategy.   This type is characterized by an imbalance between mind and body. Accordingly, an optimal exercise strategy is a program that focuses on mind–body integration and combines strength training and cardiovascular conditioning. This means that exercise that is done compulsively or to the point of exhaustion is counterproductive. On the other hand, four days a week of cardiovascular conditioning routines (e.g., t'ai chi, karate, jazz dance, complex aerobic routines, kick boxing) require mental involvement and foster mind–body integration. Strength exercises using weights or Nautilus equipment three times a week is recommended. The Type 3 individual is overrepresented among diehard joggers and long-distance runners; many report that they jog or run because of the spacey feeling known as the "runner's high." Needless to say, this form of exercise further unbalances their metabolism. Thus, jogging and running exercise is to be avoided. Similarly, repetitive exercises (e.g., calisthenics), which can trigger obsessive rumination, also should be avoided.

Optimal Stress-Reduction Strategy.   Following the Type 3 nutrition and exercise strategies should considerably improve the individual's capacity to stimulate body awareness and achieve a better mind–body integration. Because they have never really become "in-tune" with their bodies, eating and mealtimes can be particularly stressful for Type 3 individuals. A key strategy is to specify ways to destress the process and to begin to understand the physical pleasure of eating. For example, these individuals are coached to create an atmosphere of relaxation associated with mealtimes; they are told to first think about what they might want to eat—besides their craved foods—then prepare the food or order it, and finally to taste and enjoy it. Also, by applying a similar strategy to self-care, Type 3s can increase their comfort level with their bodies; while this may be difficult initially, with practice it becomes much easier. Finally, because they tend to avoid emotional situations and conflicts, these individuals need to learn to remain physically and emotionally"in the situation." They discover that compromise is an alternative to avoidance and giving in, and, with time, that they can handle conflicts with minimal stress.

Type 4.   Unlike the other metabolic or energy types, Type 4 is recognized exclusively in women. Their energy pattern is noticeably good in the mornings but may be better in the evenings. In terms of disposition, they tend to come across as warm, sensuous, and comfortable. They may be quick-tempered but can be easily distracted from their anger by apologies or flattery. In terms of relationships, they seem to need close and warm relationships to feel good about themselves. They value nurturing relationships and typically are friendly team players with coworkers on the job or in community projects.

Balanced Type 4 individuals are typically pleasant, energetic, and loving. Physically, they tend to be smaller above the waist than below, and the lower body is likely to be more well developed and stronger than the upper body. When unbalanced, these women tend to put on weight such that they appear disproportionately heavier below the waist and tend to carry that weight on their outer thighs and rear. Their main food craving is for rich and spicy food, and also salty foods such as tacos, barbecued ribs, and cashews.

These individuals tend to prefer situations that require patience, persistence, and responsivity. Type 4s easily form intimate, emotional relationships with others and are energized by engaging in worthwhile activities even when they involve tedium, boredom, or a lack of stimulation. Not surprisingly, they gravitate toward the helping professions (e.g., teaching, counseling, nursing, and other forms of pastoral ministry). Type 4s tend to experience interruptions, disorderliness, and changes in routine as stressful. Furthermore, the expectation that they should act competitively, particularly in situations involving peers and coworkers, can be very distressing. Similarly, situations that require them to respond or act assertively can be very stressful for them. Finally, these women are likely to avoid situations that require risk-taking.

Optimal Nutrition Strategy.   For Type 4 individuals, the optimal nutrition strategy for achieving balance includes the following: plentiful amounts of fruits, vegetables, whole grains, and light dairy foods (e.g., yogurt, cottage cheese, and skim milk); moderate amounts of whole grains, poultry, fish, eggs, and light desserts; occasionally red meat, cream, butter, rich desserts, and caffeine; and rarely any spices and spicy foods. In short, the strategy is to eliminate craved foods (e.g., spicy and salty foods) and to emphasize fruits, fresh vegetables, whole grains, and light dairy.

Optimal Exercise Strategy.   This type requires better coordination between the upper and lower body as well as eye–hand coordination. Accordingly, the optimal exercise strategy for Type 4 individuals is a program that focuses primarily on moderate amounts of cardiovascular conditioning and full-body strength training emphasizing the upper body; secondarily, it should focus on eye–hand coordination and mind–body integration. The recommendation is for 4 days a week of cardiovascular conditioning routines, such as complex aerobic routines, jazz dance, or t'ai chi, to promote coordination and mind–body integration. In addition, walking is recommended. Upper-body strength routines should be done 3 times a week, in addition to lower-body strength routines twice a week. A personal trainer can tailor and monitor strength training to emphasize upper-body muscle development. Since bicycling, roller skating or roller blading, and horseback riding primarily exercise the lower body, these should be avoided.

Optimal Stress-Reduction Strategy.   Following the Type 4 nutrition and exercise strategies should considerably improve these individuals' capacity to handle risky, challenging, or unexpected demands. Feeling in more control of their lives, learning to become more assertive as well as more comfortable in competitive situations will significantly reduce stress for these individuals. Making minor changes in their work or home environment, such as rearranging furniture or changing décor, helps them to feel more in charge of their lives; presumably, with time and effort, this can generalize to other areas. It is also important for them to reduce routine in their lives and to slowly but surely take small risks. Finally, because of their high need to nurture and to be nurtured, Type 4 women find it very stressful when they do not receive the kind of caring they expect. They assume that others should be able to read their minds and respond to their need for love and attention; not being loved back is very stressful for them. Consequently, Type 4s need to learn to ask for what they need from others.

Case Example

Quentin L. was referred by his primary care physician for health counseling for stress reduction and weight management. Over a period of four months, Quentin had been given a diet plan and pep talk by the physician, followed by weekly diet and stress-management "counseling" sessions with the clinic's nurse practitioner. Because these efforts had made little difference, a referral was made to a therapist who specialized in health-promotion counseling.

Quentin owns a software consulting company and manages three programmers and one systems engineer. He is deeply committed to his family and community and has been coaching softball for preteens at the community center for 2 years. He is 38, has been married for 13 years, and has an 11-year-old son and a 9-year-old daughter. For the past year he has not had the energy and stamina that has marked his life previously. He says his job is stressful, but not any more so than it has been for several years. In addition to his declining energy level, and occasional moodiness and irritability, last year he was sick 11 days for various illnesses. During previous years he took no more than 1 or 2 sick days. Because he is the boss, he coordinates his employees' work, so missed days means lower productivity for his company. Being away from work has only increased Quentin's stress level to which he responds by eating and then gaining weight.

The initial health evaluation assessed the client's energy pattern, stress-response pattern, body type, and weight gain, as well as personality and relational patterns as primarily Type 2. With some focused questioning, the therapist learned that Quentin's diet consisted mostly of complex carbohydrates, no red meat, and only occasional fish and chicken. Quentin said he was embarrassed to admit that his craved snack foods include chocolate-covered nuts, donuts, and chocolate chip cookies, but added that he also snacks on apples, grapes, and bananas. Except for an occasional glass of wine, he used no other alcohol or recreational drugs. He took a number of vitamins, some minerals and herbs but no prescription medicines.

Quentin indicated that the nurse practitioner had him start a high-carbohydrate, low-fat diet. He agreed to it because his wife had used such a diet to return to her ideal weight for the first time since the birth of their son. Quentin noted that it was ironic that while she had lost weight on this diet, he had actually gained an additional 20 pounds despite his 4 hours of exercise a week! He had been jogging for 18 years, even though his knee joints were becoming increasingly painful and arthritic. Quentin made it clear that he was not interested in taking prescription medicine for either stress or weight loss; however, he agreed to have a medical evaluation.

Before they met again, the therapist referred Quentin for a comprehensive health evaluation; this included extensive lab testing and, given a family history of heart disease, a cardiac stress test. It had been more than 2 years since his last complete physical examination. The report of the evaluation indicated that Quentin was approximately 28 pounds above an optimal weight for someone his age and level of conditioning. His cardiac stress test was in the normal range, and he exhibited a level of exercise conditioning usually seen in amateur athletes. He was noted to have chronic sinusitis and mild-to-moderate levels of osteoarthritis in both knees and the right hip.

Two treatment recommendations were provided. To reduce sinus symptoms, he should reduce sugar and eliminate dairy products from his diet. In addition, a trial glucosamine sulfate, an extraordinarily effective natural remedy, was suggested for 12 weeks for his knees and hip; if the trial was not successful, a referral to a joint specialist would be made. The diagnosis of insulin-dependence, which the examining physician said was the first stage of adult-onset or type II diabetes, was also given along with the recommendation for an initial trial of either weight loss or medication. Overall, the physician assessed Quentin's health status as being average to above average for an individual of his age and gender.

Quentin met with the therapist 2 weeks later to review the medical evaluation and continue the health assessment. An important focus of that session was on assessing strengths and motivation for change as well as establishing an intervention plan. Quentin reported that he stopped smoking when he was hospitalized for pnuemonia 4 years ago. Although he had smoked 2 packs a day for 16 years, he responded well to nicotine gum and a short behavioral counseling regimen. His current readiness for change was assessed as at the decision level. In short, Quentin appeared to be a good candidate for health counseling given that he had target symptoms, was reasonably motivated in terms of readiness for change, and had been previously successful in making a major behavior change.

The therapist suggested a 12-session, 45-minutes a week, course of counseling over a 6-month period. Sessions would be for 5 weeks, followed by biweekly, then monthly counseling. Two health-promotion target goals were proposed: stress reduction and weight loss and maintenance—to remain within 15 percent of his ideal weigh. Three intervention strategies would be involved: an individualized diet plan, an individualized stress-management plan, and an individualized exercise program. A contract was made in which Quentin agreed to the goals and made the personal and time commitment to the intervention strategies.

The next session focused on increasing his readiness for change and identifying reasons why recent weight-loss and stress-reduction efforts with the nurse practitioner had failed. Not surprisingly, Quentin noted his discouragement at gaining weight on the diet prescribed by the nurse practitioner and the increase in his cravings for sweets. The therapist described the concept of biological individuality and the difference between one-size-fits-all health programs and individualized diet, exercise, and stress-management prescriptions.

A profile of Quentin's health concerns, health status, health behaviors, personality patterns, and body type was shared with him. The therapist noted that Quentin's energy level was inconsistent throughout the day, that he craved sweet and starchy food; that he was creative, impatient, irritable, and easily angered; and that he appeared to be carrying most of his weight around his waist and hips (i.e., love handles). Psychosocially, he had a variety of friends and colleagues and was most attracted to individuals who were original thinkers and stimulating conversationalists; and Quentin seemed energized and exhilarated when initiating new projects but the most stressed when finishing projects and engaging in work that was repetitive, detailed, and tedious. The process of describing and explaining Quentin's unique dietary needs and his stress pattern, a key strategy in motivational counseling, fostered his shift from the decision to the action level of readiness.

They talked about the health patterns that Quentin exhibited and about ways to optimize his diet in order to both reduce his food cravings and lose weight. It appeared that the high-carbohydrate diet that he had been on was a poor match for him. The nutritional strategy that better matched him was a higher protein one that would emphasize eggs, poultry, fish, with some complex carbohydrates but limited nonstarchy vegetables.

It appeared that Quentin's exercise plan needed some fine-tuning. A more optimal exercise strategy would emphasize strength training with some aerobic conditioning. He expressed interest in working with a personal trainer who could design and monitor a strength-training program for him. It is interesting to note that, given his joint pain and damage, the trainer urged Quentin to replace jogging with lap swimming.

Another key part of the recommended changes involved stress reduction and management. It was noted that Quentin was overly stressed by job functions that required extensive involvement in detail-oriented oversight of consulting projects. The therapist asked whether it would be possible to delegate much of this activity to one of his employees. While it was not one of his stated job functions, Quentin had believed he needed to show his employees his personal commitment to the projects. However, it had become clear recently that he was a "big picture" person rather than a "detail" person. He agreed that such delegation might reduce his stress considerably. It was mutually agreed to try these recommendations for 4 months and then evaluate the outcomes.

A major focus of the fourth session was job-related stress. There was considerable discussion about the origins and impact of his need to control and micromanage. While Quentin realized that it would be uncomfortable changing his management style, he also realized that it was a major source of stress in his life. Limiting his monitoring and oversight of consulting projects to a weekly rather than a daily responsibility was a strategic part of his stress-reduction prescription.

During their seventh session, Quentin indicated that he was feeling considerably better. He felt less pressured and irritable since he had delegated many onsite management responsibilities to his foreman. Now he was simply monitoring progress at the various construction sites on a weekly basis. Using his creativity to conceptualize and plan new projects was not only immensely gratifying for him, but also more energizing and less stressful. Furthermore, being on the new diet plan seemed to be working. He was now within 5 pounds of his ideal weight, and his sinus and joint symptoms had lessened considerably. His physician indicated that his lab tests revealed no indication of diabetes or insulin resistance.

At 6 months Quentin continued to do well. For the first time since he had played soccer in college, he was at his ideal weight. He enjoyed lap swimming and the strength-training workouts with his trainer. He was able to exercise without joint pain and having no dairy products in his diet had nearly eliminated sinus congestion. He was pleased to report that he had taken only 1 sick day during the past 6 months.

■ ■ ■ ■ ■

RELAPSE PREVENTION

The issue of maintaining weight loss following therapy for obesity has received limited attention in the past. Recently, however, a number of maintenance strategies have been proposed, including extended treatment, relapse-prevention training, monetary incentives, telephone prompts, peer support, and exercise regimes. Initial reports suggest that extended treatment in the form of weekly or biweekly behavior-oriented sessions improves the maintenance of treatment effects for as long as one year following initial therapy (Perri & Corsica, 2002). When obesity is viewed as a chronic condition requiring long-term and perhaps even lifelong care, ongoing, periodic treatment will be accepted more easily as the norm for obesity treatment, just as it is for hypertension, diabetes, and osteoarthritis.

Keeping clients involved in treatment is a key consideration. The attrition in behavioral and cognitive-behavioral-based weight-control programs is far lower than in other kinds of treatment programs, with dropout rates averaging 13.5 percent (Wilson & Brownell, 1980). Because relapse and noncompliance with treatment are such major issues in weight-control treatment, the health counselor is encouraged to become an expert in relapse prevention. Whether in the formal course of a weight-control program or in its maintenance phase, clients will inevitably lapse or slip. Clients will eat foods that they think they should have avoided, want to give up dieting at some point, or gain weight. Most dieters initial relapses are the result of two high-risk factors: 50 percent of clients who slip do so when experiencing negative emotions such as anxiety, boredom, and depression; the other 50 percent of clients who slip do so in interpersonal situations—often positive events, such as parties, when one's guard is down and the social pressure to eat is high. In many cases, the relapse or slip itself is much less important than the thoughts and feelings that it engenders. Invariably, clients believe that one relapse is a signal that more relapses will occur. This weakens restraint and increases the likelihood of further eating, which in turn weakens restraint even more, and the pattern continues.

Relapse prevention must be a component of any weight-control program. The client is helped to prevent relapses by identifying high-risk situations, by developing coping skills for such situations, by practicing coping with potential relapses, by developing cognitive coping strategies to be used immediately after a relapse, and by developing a more balanced lifestyle (Marlatt & Gordon, 1985). The health counselor needs to work with the client both to restructure the environment through stimulus-control techniques and to restructure the client's thoughts through cognitive-restructuring techniques. The client should learn how to anticipate troublesome negative thoughts or self-statements and learn to counter them with more positive ones. There are dozens of countering statements, which must be matched to the client's needs. The key is to have a client prepare for relapses by rehearsing the negative statements and their positive counterstatements (Brownell & Foreyt, 1985).

Several studies have tested relapse-prevention methods with obese clients. Rosenthall and Marx (1979) studied the Marlatt and Gordon model of relapse prevention by identifying high-risk relapse situations. They found that situations involving the inability either to deal with depression, anger, or boredom or to cope with positive social events (e.g., celebrations or parties) were frequently involved in relapse episodes. In addition, Rosenthall and Marks designed a relapse-prevention program to teach obese clients to analyze high-risk situations and to use global problem-solving strategies to avoid relapse. Although the obese clients who received this training did not differ significantly at the end of treatment from those who received no training, they did maintain their weight losses much better. Those who learned relapse-prevention techniques used more external attributions; in fact, they felt less guilty following a relapse and were less influenced by their "lack of willpower" than were those who did not receive relapse-prevention training. Perri and his associates (Perri et al., 1984) studied relapse-prevention techniques used in conjunction with posttreatment contact with the counselor. These researchers found that the relapse-prevention program boosted long-term results only when teamed with continuing therapist contact.

Morton (1988) notes that, in addition to the relapse-prevention training system developed by Marlatt and Gordon, there are a number of other strategies that ensure weight maintenance. The first of these is exercise. Exercise may prevent relapse because it can serve as a positive replacement for a problem behavior, it can positively influence the client's self-concept, and it can remove the client to a safe setting. In addition, exercise becomes a constructive means for managing stress and other negative emotions while enabling the person to metabolize a greater number of calories than would otherwise be possible. A second strategy for weight-loss maintenance is continued self-monitoring. Stuart (1980) found that those who maintain their weight more successfully continue many of the techniques they used to reach their weight goal, particularly self-monitoring. Another strategy is posttreatment support. As noted before, continuing therapist contact has a role in successful weight maintenance. Finally, positive support from significant others in the client's life has also been shown to foster long-term weight management.

CASE EXAMPLES

The following two case examples illustrate many of the points made throughout this chapter. The first one involves a group format for weight control, and the second case illustrates the individual weight-control counseling format.

Case 1

Mary Z. is a 42-year-old, married female who is employed as an insurance underwriter. She applied for treatment at the University Weight Management Clinic in late November, but requested that her treatment not begin until after the Christmas holiday so that she "could have one last food fling and really enjoy it." Holidays were difficult times for her, as she anticipated being embarrassed around her average-weight relatives whom she saw only once or twice a year.

Mary reported being overweight as a child, as was her mother, and having been on numerous diets since the age of 14. On these diets, she alternately lost and then gained back the weight "at least 15 to 20 times." She noted that while she was dieting as an adult, she seemed to add a few more pounds above her baseline after each attempt at weight control. She had joined TOPS but, after three months, had left the program and gained back all the weight plus five pounds more. She had begun various exercise classes at local health clubs but found she was often the heaviest one in the class and would eventually drop out with the justification that "my arthritis started to act up anyway." The reason for seeking weight-loss treatment at this time was that she wanted to lose sufficient weight to look presentable at her daughter's wedding, which was scheduled for the following summer.

During the treatment screening phase, it became clear that Mary had a history of success at lifestyle change, having stopped smoking on her own 2 years earlier. This success "neutralized" some of her external motivation to lose weight to please her daughter and the wedding guests.

As part of the screening, Mary was asked to keep a food diary and self-monitoring records and to lose 1 pound per week for 2 weeks, as a condition for acceptance into the program. She lost 3 pounds during that time, but only kept records for 8 of the 14 days. She was offered group treatment with six other moderately obese individuals. The group was to meet for 20 sessions, and she was to begin on a PSMF diet within a cognitive-behavioral format. She verbalized some skepticism about the program's goals, which she thought represented too little weight loss over too long a period of time; she wanted to be prescribed a much-publicized appetite suppressant. As do many weight clients, Mary had applied magical attributions to weight-loss plans. Because her physician had previously discouraged the use of prescription appetite suppressants, the health counselor confirmed this advice, but only after exploring Mary's beliefs and magical expectations for an instant, dramatic change in her body image. Both Mary and the counselor jointly agreed to a target goal of a 35- to 40-pound weight loss over the course of the 20 weeks.

Mary had little difficulty adhering to the total lifestyle-change program, which included the diet, prescribed exercise, stimulus control, response prevention, and challenges to her dysfunctional self-talk. Initially, she took the role of devil's advocate in the group, questioning the intentions and behaviors of other members. Yet, after others confronted her on this, she ceased the role behavior. Since the group planned and scheduled food relapses and focused on relapse-prevention skills, Mary reported only two minor, unplanned relapses during the 20 weeks.

After the fourth group session, the counselor met with Mary and her husband whose resistance to her weight loss was the focus of three individual sessions. As he became convinced that she would not leave him when she became more slim and attractive, he started to be more of an ally in the treatment process.

By the sixteenth session, Mary had lost 41 pounds, at which time she was switched to a regular 1,500-calorie diet. In the following weeks, she regained a few pounds but had lost them by the time of her daughter's wedding, and she has remained at that weight for approximately 12 months. Posttreatment follow-up sessions were scheduled for the group every 4 weeks for the first 3 months, and then at 2-month intervals over the next year.

■ ■ ■ ■ ■

Case 2

The case of Eleanor S. was introduced in chapter 2. As you'll recall, Eleanor was 50 pounds over her ideal weight and was referred for health counseling as an adjunct to a prescribed 1,200-calorie diet, which was being monitored by her family physician.

A weight-loss plan was negotiated between the health counselor and Eleanor, in which she would meet for 20 weekly sessions for individual counseling and then for follow-up sessions at 6-month intervals for the next 2 years. Her goal was to lose 45 pounds over the 20 sessions—approximately 2 to 3 pounds per week—and to commit to a graduated exercise program, along with a behavioral and cognitive-restructuring plan that included at least three conjoint sessions with Mr. S. Because she would continue to be monitored medically by her physician, Eleanor signed a consent form so that her counselor and physician could consult regularly about her progress.

At the behavioral level, Eleanor was quick to learn. She applied a number of methods for changing her eating behaviors, and she learned and practiced some relapse-prevention skills. Because lack of assertiveness was defined as a major issue, especially, within the marriage, skill training was done during the third session. Environmental and stimulus-control measures were stressed from the beginning. Eleanor agreed that she must avoid situations in which she would be "forced" by social convention to overeat, such as Sunday meals with her overeating relatives. She partially solved this problem by scheduling social activities with her children during that time and by inviting her relatives to her house for a light dinner that she prepared. She and a friend joined a beginner's aerobics class at a local YWCA.

At the cognitive level, Eleanor worked with the counselor to change and to restructure some of her personality-style convictions and health beliefs in a more socially useful direction. The counselor reframed her occasional relapses as slips rather than as failures.

At the social-support level, conjoint marital sessions were helpful in reducing Mr. S's fears about Eleanor leaving him should she slim down. And, after some communication training, he became more sensitive to her needs to assert independence. He also supported her when both sets of parents were upset about the change in their Sunday schedules. By the fifth session, Mr. S. agreed to go on the same diet plan as his wife, which helped her in complying with the program. Eleanor's friend was of inestimable value in helping her stick to the weight-loss plan and maintenance on the job and helped her with menu planning.

At the physiological level, Eleanor continued to be monitored weekly by her physician, who conferred regularly with the counselor. By the twentieth session, Eleanor had shed 55 pounds and 12 months later was within 8 pounds of her ideal weight.

■ ■ ■ ■ ■

PREVENTIVE MEASURES

The majority of preventive efforts to date have focused primarily on educational strategies with limited and mixed results. Efforts with higher impact will involve public health policy changes such as controlling food advertising during television shows for children, taxes on high-fat foods, federal funding to restore daily exercise and activity programs in schools, and/or price support for healthy food and activity choices.

Several promising areas in the primary prevention of obesity include interventions with children and adults, mass media campaigns to promote healthy eating, and microenvironmental interventions particularly with cafeterias and vending machine companies (Schmitz & Jeffrey, 2002). Because of the limited success of interventions focused on the individual, Horgen and Brownell (2002) advocate shifting the focus to the environment, specifically toward prevention and public policy efforts.

Since helping clients achieve and maintain a healthy weight is the most difficult and perplexing challenge for health-promotion counselors, there is much to be said for primary prevention regarding nutrition and weight control. Streigel-Moore, and Rodin (1985) provide an extensive review of the research on prevention of obesity. In their report, they emphasize primary prevention strategies that can be implemented throughout the course of human development and provide specific recommendations for prenatal health care and maternal nutrition during pregnancy, infancy, childhood, and adolescence. Their review of this research suggests that the best place to start the prevention of obesity is with the pregnant women. In their recommendations for prevention with adolescents, they note that considerable efforts should be directed toward helping them accept the normal physical changes that accompany this stage of development. These authors believe that adolescents must be thoroughly apprised of the ill effects of crash dieting to control body weight.

Streigel-Moore and Rodin advocate that communities implement preventive efforts aimed at reducing the effects of the social pressure for thinness. For example, a wider range in what is considered the female beauty ideal is needed, and the mass media can have a critical role in this change. They note that the sociocultural pressure to maintain a sylphlike body motivates thousands of girls to follow unhealthy diets that upset their biological balance and contribute to later obesity. Finally, these authors acknowledge the consequences of the extraordinary emphasis placed on weight by Western culture, which they believe is at the root of the enormous increase in eating disorders among the groups most affected by this weight obsession—women, dancers, wrestlers, jockeys, and gymnasts.

There are a number of reasons for targeting obesity-prevention measures in the early years of life. First of all, obesity in childhood is likely to continue into adulthood; whereas only 14 percent of obese infants become obese adults, 70 percent of obese 10- to 13-year-olds do. Few normal-weight children become obese adults. A second reason is that those children who are in the most need of preventive interventions are not likely to receive them at an early age. Efforts to help children control their weight need to focus on both diet and physical activity.

Therefore, health and physical education programs in schools can provide excellent opportunities to promote healthful eating and exercise habits in all schoolchildren. Streigel-Moore and Rodin (1985) note that primary preventive measures, such as receiving instruction on healthful diets, result in children's bringing healthier lunches to school and throwing fewer healthy foods away. Secondary preventive measures include identifying children who are at high risk of becoming obese on the basis of family history or because they are currently overweight. These children can then be given special attention and training in dietary and exercise behavior. Finally, since parents provide access to most of the food that children eat, primary preventive interventions should be directed at ways that parents can help their children keep from becoming overly fat. Recommendations include encouraging regular physical activity and discouraging excessive TV watching; having fewer high-cholesterol and sugary foods in the home; using fruit, nuts, and other healthful foods as regular desserts, reserving rich, less healthful ones for special occasions; ensuring that children eat a healthful breakfast each day; eliminating high-calorie snacks at night; and monitoring children's weight on a regular basis by comparing it against the chart of desirable weight.

In short, childhood is probably the ideal time to establish exercise and dietary habits to prevent people from becoming obese. Parents, schools, the mass media, and community agencies can and should play important roles in helping with this so that weight control does not become a major issue during adulthood.

CONCLUDING NOTE

This chapter presented a biopsychosocial view of normal weight and obesity. It reviewed the etiology and theories of obesity, as well as a classification scheme for types of obesity, in addition to the five principal weight-control factors: exercise, nutrition information, behavioral aspects of eating styles, cognitive aspects of weight control, and partner and other social support factors. The chapter described a comprehensive approach to the biopsychosocial assessment of weight problems and offered a number of general treatment guidelines and specific interventions for both individual and group treatment of obesity. In addition, it outlined clinically useful treatment protocols and presented two case histories that illustrate weight control in both the individual and the group format. Finally, the stress here has been on the need for health counselors to emphasize relapse-prevention strategies within and during the course of treatment; the list of primary and secondary prevention measures that can be employed in helping individuals control their weight should be very useful to them. The chapter concludes with an annotated list of weight-control resources.

R E S O U R C E S

Organizations

Overeaters Anonymous (OA) and Take Off Pound Sensibly (TOPS) have been described earlier in the chapter. Meetings of these two organizations take place in most cities. Consult the phone directory or their Web sites for the nearest meeting place or contact person.

- OA (*www.overeatersanonymous.org*)—Provides services and support groups for individuals

with obesity and other eating disorders; includes their newsletter and meeting schedule for local areas.

- TOPS (*www.tops.org*)—Provides information on a safe weight-loss program for dieting and weight control; includes addresses and phone numbers for programs in various localities.

Professional References

- Wadden, T., & Stunkard, A. (Eds.). (2002). *Handbook of obesity treatment.* New York: Guilford.   This is currently the best available single source of information on the assessment and treatment of those who are overweight and obese. The clear and easy-to-read chapters are written by noted experts in the field.
- Fairburn, C., & Brownell, K. (Eds.). (2001). *Eating disorders and obesity* (2nd ed.). New York: Guilford.   This handbook presents virtually all that is currently known about eating disorders and obesity in a single volume. It provides extensive coverage of all eating disorders, including binge eating, and is a useful companion volume to the Wadden and Stunkard text just noted.
- Fairburn, C., & Wilson, T. (Eds.). (1995). *Binge eating: Nature, assessment and treatment.*   This book provides comprehensive coverage of assessment and treatment. It includes the complete Eating Disorder Examination form, the gold standard for assessing eating disorders during health counseling and clinical interviews.

REFERENCES

Abravanel, E. (1999). *Body type diet and lifetime nutrition plan* (rev. ed.). New York: Bantam.

Baum, K. (2000). *Metabolize: The personalized program for weight loss.* New York: Putnam.

Beck, A. (1976). *Cognitive therapy and the emotional disorders.* New York: International Universities Press.

Blackburn, G. (1978). The liquid protein controversy: A closer look at the facts. *Obesity and Bariatric Medicine, 7,* 25–30.

Blair, S., & Leermakers, E. (2002). Exercise and weight management. In T. Wadden & A. J. Stunkard (Eds.). *Handbook of obesity treatment* (pp. 283–300). New York: Guilford.

Brownell, K. D., & Foreyt, J. P. (1985). Obesity. In D. Barlow (Ed.), *Clinical handbook of psychological disorders.* New York: Guilford.

Bruch, H. (1973). *Eating disorders.* New York: Basic Books.

Buckmaster, L., & Brownell, K. D. (1989). Behavior modification: The state of the art. In R. Frankle & M. Yang (Eds.), *Obesity and weight control.* Rockville, MD: Aspen.

Colletti, G. & Brownell, K. D. (1982). The physical and emotional benefits of social supports: Applications to obesity, smoking and alcoholism. In M. Herson, R. Eisler, & P. Miller (Eds.), *Progress in behavior modification.* New York: Academic.

Cooper, Z. & Fairburn, C. (2002). Cognitive-behavioral treatment of obesity. In T. Wadden & A. J. Stunkard (Eds.). *Handbook of obesity treatment* (pp. 465–479). New York: Guilford.

Ferster, C. B., Nurnberger, J., & Levitt, E. (1962). The control of eating. *Journal of Mathematics, 1,* 87–109.

Field, A., Barnoya, J., & Colditz, G. (2002). Epidemiology and health economic consequences of obesity. In T. Wadden & A. Stunkard (Eds.), *Handbook of obesity treatment* (pp. 3–18). New York: Guilford.

Foster, G., Wadden, T., Vogt, R., & Brewer, G. (1997). What is a reasonable weight loss?: Patients' expectations and evaluations of obesity treatment outcomes. *Journal of Consulting and Clinical Psychology, 65*(1), 79–85.

Horgen, K. & Brownell, K. (2002). Confronting the toxic environment: Environmental public health actions in a world crisis. In T. Wadden & A. J. Stunkard (Eds.). *Handbook of obesity treatment* (pp. 95–106). New York: Guilford.

Ibrahim, F. A., Roysircar-Sodowsky, G., & Ohnishi, H. (2001). Worldview: recent developments and needed directions. In J. G. Ponterotto, J. M. Casas, L. A. Suzuki, & C. M. Alexander (Eds.), *Handbook of multicultural counseling* (2nd ed. pp. 425–456). Thousand Oaks, CA: Sage.

Katch, F., & McArdle, W. (1983). *Nutrition, weight control and exercise.* Philadelphia: Lea & Febiger.

Kingsley, R., & Wilson, G. (1977). Behavior therapy for obesity: A comparative investigation of long-term efficacy. *Journal of Consulting and Clinical Psychology, 53,* 43–48.

Linehan, M. (1987). Dialectical behavior therapy in groups: Treating borderline personality disorders and suicidal behavior. In C. Brady (Ed.), *Women's therapy groups.* New York: Springer.

Marks, D., Murray, M., Evans, B., & Willig, C. (2000). *Health psychology: Theory, research, and practice.* London: Sage.

Marlatt, G., & Gordon, J. (Eds.). (1985). *Relapse prevention: Maintenance strategies in the treatment of addictive behaviors.* New York: Guilford.

Melanson, K., & Dwyer, J. (2002). Popular diets for treatment of overweight and obesity. In T. Wadden & A. J. Stunkard (Eds.), *Handbook of obesity treatment* (pp. 249–282). New York: Guilford.

Morton, C. J. (1988). Weight loss maintenance and relapse prevention. In R. Frankle & M. Yong (Eds.), *Obesity and weight control.* Rockville, MD: Aspen.

Noëël, P., Pugh, J., & Crawford, A. (2002). Management of overweight and obese adults. *British Medical Journal, 325,* 757–761.

Perri, M., & Corsica, J. (2002). Improving the maintenance of weight loss in behavioral treatment of obesity. In T. Wadden & A. J. Stunkard (Eds.), *Handbook of obesity treatment* (pp. 357–381). New York: Guilford.

Perri, M., Shapiro, R., Ludwig, W., et al. (1984). Maintenance strategies for the treatment of obesity. An evaluation of relapse-prevention training and posttreatment contact by mail and phone. *Journal of Clinical and Consulting Psychology, 52,* 404–413.

Rosenthall, B., & Marx, R. (1979, December). *A comparison of standard behavioral and relapse prevention weight reduction programs.* Paper presented at the Association for Advancement of Behavior Therapy convention, San Francisco.

Rozin, P. (1996). Sociocultural influences on human food selection. In E. Capaldi (Ed.), *Why we eat what we eat: The psychology of eating* (pp. 233–263). Washington, DC: American Psychological Association.

Schmitz, K., & Jeffrey, R. (2002). Prevention of obesity. In T. Wadden & A. J. Stunkard (Eds.), *Handbook of obesity treatment* (pp. 556–593). New York: Guilford.

Streigel-Moore, R., & Rodin, J. (1985). Prevention of obesity. In J. Rosen & L. Solomon (Eds.), *Prevention in health psychology.* Hanover, VT: University Press of New England.

Stuart, R. (1980). Weight loss and beyond: Are they taking it off and keeping it off? In P. Davidson & S. Davidson (Eds.), *Behavioral medicine: Changing health lifestyles.* New York: Brunnel/Mazel.

Stuart, R. (1984, October). *Indirection and promoting health behaviors.* The 1984 Polachek Lecture. Milwaukee: Mount Sinai Medical Center.

Stuart, R., & Jacobson, B. (1987). *Sex, weight and marriage.* New York: Norton.

Stuart, R., & Mitchell, C. (1980). Self-help groups in the control of body weight. In A. J. Stunkard (Ed.), *Obesity.* Philadelphia: Saunders.

Stunkard, A. (2002). Binge-eating disorder and night-eating syndrome. In T. Wadden & A. Stunkard (Eds.), *Handbook of obesity treatment* (pp. 107–121). New York: Guilford.

Tataranni, P. & Ravussin, E. (2002). Energy metabolism and obesity. In T. Wadden & A. J. Stunkard (Eds.), *Handbook of obesity treatment* (pp. 42–72). New York: Guilford.

Wadden, T., & Osei, S. (2002). The treatment of obesity: An overview. In T. Wadden & A. J. Stunkard (Eds.), *Handbook of obesity treatment* (pp. 229–248). New York: Guilford.

Wadden, T., & Phelan, S. (2002). Behavioral assessment of the obese patient. In T. Wadden & A. J. Stunkard (Eds.), *Handbook of obesity treatment* (pp. 186–227). New York: Guilford.

Wadden, T., Stunkard, A., Brownell, K. D., & Dey, S. (1984). The treatment of moderate obesity by behavior modification and very low-calorie diets. *Journal of Consulting and Clinical Psychology, 52,* 692–694.

Wadden, T., Vogt, R., Andersen, R., et al. (1997). Exercise in the treatment of obesity: Effects of four interventions on body composition, resting energy expenditure, appetite, and mood. *Journal of Consulting and Clinical Psychology, 65*(2), 269–277.

Wadden, T., Womble, L., Stunkard, A. J., & Anderson, D. (2002). Psychosocial consequences of obesity and weight loss. In T. Wadden & A. J. Stunkard (Eds.), *Handbook of obesity treatment* (pp. 144–171). New York: Guilford.

Wardle, J. (1989). The managment of obesity. In S. Pearce & J. Wardle (Eds.), *The practice of behavioral medicine.* Oxford: British Psychological Society, Oxford University Press.

Wilson, G., & Brownell, K. D. (1980). Behavior therapy for adults. An evaluation of treatment outcomes. *Advances in Behavior Research and Therapy, 3,* 49–86.

Wilson, D., Nicholson, S. & Krishnamoorthy, J. (1997). The role of diet in minority adolescent health promotion. In D. Wilson, J. Rodriguez, & W. Taylor (Eds.), *Health-promoting and health-compromising behaviors among minority adolescents* (pp. 129–152). Washington, DC: American Psychological Association.

Wolcott. W. (2000). *The metabolic typing diet.* New York: Doubleday.

Wolf, A., & Colditz, G. (1996). Social and economic effects of body weight in the United States. *American Journal of Clinical Nutrition, 63* (Supp. 3), 466s-469s.

Womble, L., Wang, S., & Wadden, T. (2002). Commerical and self-help weight loss programs. In T. Wadden & A. Stunkard (Eds.), *Handbook of obesity treatment* (pp. 395–415). New York: Guilford.

World Health Organization (1998). *Obesity: Preventing and managing the global epidemic.* Publication No. WHO/NUT/NCD/98.1. Geneva: Author.

CHAPTER FIVE

SMOKING CESSATION

To cease smoking is the easiest thing I ever did:
I ought to know because I've done it a thousand times.
—Mark Twain

Cigarette smoking is a major public health problem despite decreases in the number of people who smoke over the past two decades, and it remains the largest preventable cause of illness and premature death (Breslau et al., 2001; Spring, Pingitore, & McChargue, 2003). Current estimates suggest that about 30 percent of the U.S. population smokes, with the age range of 30 to 44 being disproportionately represented (Disco, Moorman, & Noble, 2001). Additionally, a large number of children and adolescents begin smoking each year. It is interesting that most smokers report wanting to stop and having tried to do so unsuccessfully, with only approximately 25 percent experiencing lasting success.

Tobacco is probably the most dangerous substance commonly consumed by humans, and inhaling its burned by-products is an added health risk. A one-pack-a-day smoker inhales about 400 "doses" a day, or 150,000 doses per year. More than 300 known poisons are in the tobacco and smoke, including substances such as nicotine, arsenic, cyanide, carbon monoxide, phenol, and formaldehyde. Smoking shortens a two-pack-a-day smoker's life expectancy by 8 years, and even light smokers—those who smoke 1 to 9 cigarettes per day—shorten their life expectancy by approximately 4 years. Smokers have a 22 percent higher rate of sickness and loss of on-the-job time and take 10 percent longer to recover from illnesses than do nonsmokers (Spence, 1987). This list of the diseases or conditions related to smoking resembles a medical encyclopedia: alcohol interaction, allergies, arterial sclerosis, bladder cancer, bronchitis, burns, cardiomyopathy, cavities, cerebral profusion deficiencies, child abuse, circulatory deficiencies, drug interferences, emphysema, cancer of the esophagus, fetal smoking syndrome, gingivitis, halitosis, headaches, heart attack, hypertension, infertility (male and female), influenza, kidney cancer, cancer of the larynx, leukoplakia, lung cancer, menopause complications, oral cancer, osteoporosis, pancreatic cancer, PNIS, radioactivity reactions, strokes, ulcers, and wrinkles.

Traditional medical approaches have been relatively ineffective in dealing with this health problem. For example, medical and surgical interventions for lung cancer are still mostly ineffective yet, in theory, these smoking-related deaths and problems are 100 percent preventable.

Statements by the U.S. Surgeon General have underlined four general points: (1) smoking has adverse effects on several aspects of health, (2) secondary smoke affects the health of the nonsmoker, (3) nicotine meets the addiction criteria in a way similar to that of other addictive behaviors, and (4) major and immediate health benefits are achieved by quitting smoking.

Researchers have traditionally focused on the physiological components of addiction rather than on its psychological or social aspects. When smoking is viewed as a total process, researchers begin to examine clients' participation in the process and its impact on society. Through this altered way of viewing smoking, a range of psychological, biological, and social interventions have been developed. In the research, as well as in this chapter, procedures are presented as separate approaches; however, in clinical practice, most procedures are used in combination.

STAGES OF SMOKING

Smoking is a behavior that develops in a series of stages: preparation, initiation, and habituation. If this developmental progression is followed further, individuals may either quit and remain abstinent or quit unsuccessfully and relapse. Different variables—biological, psychological, and social—are important at different stages of the smoking process.

The preparation for smoking begins very early. By observing smokers, the young child is provided with information about the nature of smoking, its functions, and its acceptability. Thus, a more or less appealing, positive image is created early in the smoking process. Social pressure from peers is one of the prime initiators of experimentation. Smoking by family, members, and other important models may further promote experimentation. Smoking in adolescence is commonly conceptualized as progressing through a sequence of developmental stages that are characterized by different stages of smoking frequency and intensity. The basic definitions of these stages of adolescent smoking have been summarized as preparation, initial trying, experimentation, regular use, and addictive use (Flay, 1993). The preparation stage involves formation of beliefs and attitudes about smoking prior to ever trying a cigarette. Initial trying refers to experimentation with the first few cigarettes. Experimentation is characterized by irregular use of cigarettes, with a gradual increase in the frequency of smoking in various situations. Regular use refers to smoking on a regular, although still infrequent, basis, such as every weekend or weekdays before or after school. Addictive use refers to adolescent smoking that occurs on a regular basis and is driven by cravings for nicotine, regular daily smoking, and experience of withdrawal symptoms (Colby et al., 2000).

Snyder (1989) outlined five stages of smoking for adolescents and adults alike. These stages have been summarized as preparation, initiation, habitual, stopping, and resuming. The preparation stage incorporates psychological factors before the onset of smoking and involves modeling by significant others in regards to the function and desirability of smoking. The initiation stage includes psychosocial factors that lead to experimentation. This could include peer pressure, availability of tobacco, curiosity, and attitudes related to positive images of smoking. The habitual stage includes psychosocial and biological factors that lead up to the maintenance of smoking. This could include a desire to regulate nicotine and control emotions, and cues in the environment that encourage smoking. The stopping stage includes psychosocial cues that lead to attempts to quit smoking. This could include health concerns, setting positive examples for others, social and environmental support for quitting, and ideas about self-control. The resuming stage includes psychosocial and biological factors that lead back to smoking behavior. This could include withdrawal symptoms, increased stress and other negative effects, and social pressure from peers.

After beginning smoking, it takes 2 to 3 years of continued use or practice to fully establish the habit. There is a gradual increase in the number of cigarettes smoked; more situations, activities, and experiences cue smoking, and more reinforcers accrue to the behavior until the person becomes a habitual smoker. Once it is a well-established habit, smoking becomes part of the daily routine. Smoking is evoked and reinforced by a wide variety of stimuli. At a biological level, nicotine is very addictive. With continued use, the smoker's body expects a certain level of nicotine and cues the individual to smoke if actual levels fall below those expected. Nicotine withdrawal symptoms are painful, and smoking is reinforced by a reduction in such symptoms. Smoking may be further reinforced by the stimulating and alerting effects of nicotine.

SMOKING MAINTENANCE

Smoking can play a central role in the regulation of emotions. The experience of unpleasant emotions, such as anxiety, anger, boredom, and depression, may cue smoking. A consequent relaxation or reduction of these emotions then reinforces the smoking response. Smokers also report cravings for other tobacco products. These cravings may be cognitive correlates of low nicotine levels or of affective arousal, or they may be correlates of the positive consequences associated with smoking, including taste, relaxation, and stimulation. Cravings can also be triggered by external stimuli, such as seeing others smoke, or by other behaviors, such as drinking a cup of coffee. Finally, a smoker may engage in self-reinforcement, such as seeing oneself as more adult or as having more machismo.

The social and physical environments, along with the smoker's own behavior developed through past associative learning, constantly bombard the habitual user with cues to smoke. Seeing others smoke, receiving invitations to smoke, seeing a pack of cigarettes, drinking coffee, finishing a meal, and watching TV are all capable of evoking tobacco use. That use may in turn be reinforced by social approval, peer affiliation, and the oral, manual, and respiratory actions involved in smoking.

Health counselors understand how behavior plays a central role in health and illness. Health-impairing habits and lifestyles are important risk factors for chronic disease and death, whereas health-promoting habits and lifestyles enhance biological and psychosocial functioning.

Maladaptive and adaptive health behaviors are acquired and maintained by the same processes. Their acquisition and shaping are a function of maturation and learning. Once established, their performance is evoked and maintained by the biological, cognitive-affective, social, environmental, and behavioral cues and consequences that define an individual's daily experiences. Initiating modification of healthy behaviors is therefore a complicated intervention that involves a collaborative, mutually active client–health provider relationship and the utilization of cognitive, behavioral, environmental, and biological change strategies.

REVIEW OF THE LITERATURE

Since 1968, the U.S. Department of Health and Human Services has issued an annual annotated bibliography of all published research studies on the topic of smoking and health. Each year, there are several thousand published research studies from around the world. Publications are divided into 16 different sections, including topics such as pharmacology and toxology, mortality and morbidity, neoplastic diseases, cardiovascular diseases, pregnancy and infant health, behavioral and psychological aspects, smoking prevention and intervention, smoking-cessation methods, tobacco product additives, tobacco manufacturing and processing, tobacco economics, and legislation about various smoking-related issues.

Because of the magnitude of the literature in this area, this section is limited to highlights of the social, psychological, and biological literature. Basically, three theoretical models for understanding smoking behavior have been developed: a psychosocial, a psychological, and a biological or pharmacological one.

The *psychosocial model* views smoking behavior as a means of coping with stress and with stressful life events. Successful coping serves as the reinforcer for smoking behavior. Laboratory studies tend to support the hypothesis that smoking facilitates coping. Smoking has been found to reduce fluctuations or changes in mood during stress and to serve as a successful means for enduring a stressor, such as an electric shock. When compared to nonsmokers, people who smoke more than one pack of cigarettes per day have been found to have a lower tolerance for stress if they are not permitted to smoke and a greater tolerance for stress if they can smoke. Thus, people under high stress may have unusual difficulty in trying to quit smoking.

Another aspect of the psychosocial model is the concept of psychosocial assets— those personal attributes that may provide special strength in developing more satisfactory long-term coping mechanisms. Included in the concept of psychosocial assets are attributes such as self-efficacy (Bandura, 1977), internal locus of control (self-control), and a strong social-support network. These personal assets may make it easier for a person under high stress to quit smoking.

The *psychological model* focuses on needs, drives, and emotions. This model views smoking behavior as serving to minimize negative emotions such as distress, anger, fear, and shame; smoking is reinforcing and persistent because it is successful in warding off these feelings (Tomkins, 1966). This model has been elaborated and evaluated, and there is considerable evidence that an association exists between the amount of smoking and the extent to which cigarettes are used to ward off negative emotions. In addition, heavy smokers have been found to manifest more psychological disturbances than do light smokers.

The *pharmacological/biological model* seeks the cigarette's specific chemical agent on which a smoker can become dependent or addicted. The most likely agent appears to be nicotine, and a number of studies support this hypothesis. Studies show that people smoke more when the amount of nicotine in their cigarettes is reduced and that smoking is decreased when nicotine is provided in other ways, such as in nicotine gum, which is often part of a comprehensive smoking-cessation program.

In reviewing the large number of studies that have sought to evaluate the various smoking-cessation programs, psychologists have noted five methodological problems that they keep encountering. These problems are: (1) difficulties in verifying self-reports of smoking behavior, (2) lack of control groups in evaluating smoking-cessation programs, (3) difficulties in classifying levels of previous smoking and/or levels of smoking reduction, (4) lack of agreement regarding optimal length of follow-up, and (5) differences in the methods used to determine outcomes of smoking-cessation programs.

There does not appear to be agreement about how to classify smoking behavior and decreases in smoking, therefore it is impossible to compare and contrast the different outcomes of smoking-control programs. When studying smoking behavior, most researchers assess the number of cigarettes smoked per day. It is clear, however, that one also needs to take into account factors such as how long people have smoked, how many puffs they take per cigarette, and how much they inhale when they smoke. To assess the degree of smoking reduction obtained, each study seems to use its own criteria: no cigarettes smoked in the previous week, no more than six cigarettes smoked in any given week, and so on.

Psychosocial Model

The social perspective involves understanding both how social and cultural forces affect the creation of smoking behavior and how such influences can be used to prevent smoking and to help people stop smoking once they've started. When dealing with a global problem that affects millions of people, taking a social perspective is often more useful than dealing with one smoker at a time. It is important to realize how changes in public policy could be the most effective route to smoking cessation for many. For example, high prices for or lack of access to cigarettes could well have a far greater impact on the smoking habit than could the results of any psychological research into smoking motivators or cessation methods. In a sense, the researchers could themselves be accused of helping to sustain the habit, since the focus of their concern is typically on the nature of the smoker rather than on the larger social and economic structures that support the tobacco industry. Tobacco companies are multinational, multiproduct corporations that benefit society through a wide range of diversified manufacturing and commercial enterprises, including providing employment and stimulating local economies. They also have considerable power to act as pressure groups to influence government policy as well as potential customers. Tobacco companies' advertising budgets far exceed the funds allocated by health-promotion organizations for their ads. Even when traditional advertising routes are closed, tobacco companies willingly sponsor sports events and the arts and fund various basic research.

There is considerable evidence that some social groups consistently smoke more than others. Research indicates that men smoke more than women and that both men and women in the 30- to 44-age group smoke more than those in any other group. However, the rate at which adolescent and young women begin smoking is higher compared to men. Certain ethnic groups, such as African Americans, tend to smoke more than Whites, regardless of gender. People with less education smoke more than those with more education, and blue-collar workers smoke more than white-collar workers. Divorced and separated people tend to smoke far more than people who have intact marriages. Only a social perspective can help us to understand and to focus intervention programs on the differences between groups.

Two major social influences on the establishment of smoking behavior have been noted: the influence of others and the influence of media advertising. During adolescence, when most individuals start smoking, behavior plays a symbolic role in the three great issues that teenagers face: the deemphasis of parental influence, the establishment of bonds with peers, and the establishment of an independent self-identity. Teenagers who have parents, older siblings, and friends who smoke are more likely to smoke themselves. In fact, those who have two parents who smoke are twice as likely to smoke as those who have no parents who smoke. Smoking is thought of by adolescents as adult behavior that is normally off-limits to children. Thus, by smoking, teenagers are showing signs of emerging adulthood and are probably defying their parents as well. On the other hand, fewer adolescents smoke now than did a few years ago, partly because of an increased concern with health and partly because smoking does not have the peer approval that it once had. However, smoking among teens is still an area of concern.

Increasing evidence in the 1990s suggested that the prevalence of smoking was higher among students from low socioeconomic status backgrounds and among White students when compared to African American and Latino students (Kann et al., 1993). The 1997 Youth Risk Behavior Survey conducted by the Centers for Disease Control and Prevention (CDC) showed greater numbers of high school students who reported that they had smoked in the last 30 days—an increase of nearly one third from 28 percent in 1991 to 36 percent in 1997. The rate of African American students who reported smoking in the last 30 days showed an increase of 80 percent from 1991 to 1997 (CDC, 1998).

Like adults, adolescents smoke to meet some emotional needs. Weinrich and colleagues (1996) found that adolescents are more likely to smoke to control stress if they have less social support. Their research showed that adolescents who smoke have fewer anger-coping skills and are more likely to manifest somatic complaints in response to anxiety compared with adolescents who do not smoke. However, African American adolescents smoke less in response to stress than their White counterparts. Evidence suggests that these adolescents, in particular African American girls, smoke to augment their self-esteem (Crump, Lillie-Blanton, & Anthony, 1997). Yet African American females are less likely than their White counterparts to use smoking to control weight (Camp, Klesges, & Relyea, 1993). Whereas one would assume that it might be easier for adolescents to quit smoking due to shorter longevity of smoking behavior, few adolescents succeed in stopping smoking (Stanton, 1995). The younger boys or girls are when they start smoking, the less likely they are to succeed at quitting (Breslau & Peterson, 1996) and the deeper is their addiction (Stanton, 1995).

Today, U.S. society—including the mass media—continues to encourage smoking, although there is considerable evidence that societal values are changing and that cigarette advertising is having a less persuasive impact on smoking behavior. Educational efforts have been fairly successful in discouraging smoking. Further advances will need to include the social perspective—that is, the examination of the context within which smoking occurs. Scientists who emphasize the importance of a social perspective in considering smoking cessation stress four general points (Bloom, 1988):

1. Efforts to inform the public about the dangerous effects of smoking on health will probably need to continue indefinitely.
2. In terms of its prevalence, smoking must be presented for what it is—an atypical behavior of a minority of the population. The increasing constraints on smoking behavior and the increasing attention being accorded to the rights of nonsmokers help to keep smoking in its proper demographic perspective.
3. Constant attention needs to be devoted to the influence that public policy and public policymakers have for counteracting the tobacco industry's efforts to encourage smoking.
4. In spite of their high cost and the enormous effort involved in producing and getting them shown, antismoking advertisements must be revived, maintained, and increased.

Perhaps the best antismoking advertisement is the nonsmoker, and as the number and proportion of nonsmokers continue to increase, smoking will be increasingly seen as deviant and unacceptable. It is thought that it will become more and more unattractive and difficult to smoke when a larger and larger proportion of the population think of smoking not only as unhealthy and unpleasant but also as stupid (Martin & Lambrecht, 1998).

The list of antismoking strategies is remarkably long, and many of them can be used in combination. In addition to prohibiting smoking in general (a strategy that few, if any, people believe will be effective), other strategies that have been suggested (e.g., Bloom, 1988) include the following:

1. Restricting where people can smoke (and, in some cases, who can smoke)
2. Identifying and reducing hazardous substances in cigarettes
3. Restricting advertising of tobacco products even more
4. Increasing knowledge of the harmful effects of smoking, particularly among preadolescents and pregnant women, through health education efforts
5. Incorporating information about the dangers of smoking into the public school curriculum
6. Expanding the availability of smoking-cessation programs for people who want to quit smoking
7. Increasing taxation of tobacco products
8. Finding other uses for tobacco, such as in animal feed or in the manufacture of pesticides and medicinal products, to alleviate the industry's loss of income
9. Retraining tobacco farmers for other ways of earning a living

Smoking is an integral part of common social situations. Bars and parties are the most frequently encountered places, and they are doubly troubling. They provide potent smoking cues, and the disinhibitory effects of alcohol can easily overcome any smoker's resolve. Counselors often warn clients about these effects and suggest that they avoid such social situations immediately after quitting.

The importance of interpersonal relationships in facilitating, as well as impeding a smoker's abstinence from cigarettes, is well documented in the research literature (Lichtenstein & Glasgow, 1992), but the mechanism by which this influence is exerted is not clear. Perceived support of others helps the smoker maintain abstinence. Several researchers (Gulliver et al., 1995; Ginsberg, Hall, & Rosinski, 1991; McIntyre, Mermelstein, & Lichtenstein, 1982) suggest that partner behaviors can be categorized as either helpful or detrimental. These investigators acknowledge that the exact form that helping takes depends in part on the couple. However, research has shown that helpful behaviors include providing rewards, giving compliments for the decision to quit as well as for the actual quitting, expressing both interest in being involved and confidence in the partner, and not smoking in the quitter's presence. Detrimental behaviors include nagging, shunning, and policing. Further, research suggests that interventions to enhance partner support showed the most promise for clinical practice when implemented with live-in, married, and equivalent-to-married partners. Such interventions should focus on enhancing supportive behaviors, while minimizing behaviors critical of smoking (Park et al., 2004).

Psychological Model

Psychologists have emphasized the role that specific knowledge of the health consequences of smoking, beliefs about personal susceptibility, attitudes toward smoking, and expectations of the benefits of quitting play, both in the decision to quit smoking and in the long-term success or failure of that decision. Most smoking intervention programs focus on the participants' attitudes and beliefs as well as on their behavior during smoking and during the quitting process. For example, a review of the health consequences of smoking is often used as a motivational boost for quitting. Programs also can emphasize clients' self-defeating thoughts, particularly when the focus is on the maintenance of treatment gains or on relapse prevention.

One particular set of cognitions has been given a good deal of attention in the literature on smoking: the concept of perceived self-efficacy (Bandura, 1977) appears to be a very useful tool in the cessation process. Self-efficacy is defined as an individual's belief in his or her ability to perform and stick to a given behavior. Information from past behaviors, modeling, affective states, and instruction all combine to produce a performance expectation that predicts future behavior. It is likely that these self-efficacy expectations are better predictors of behavior than are previous behaviors alone. These self-efficacy beliefs often reflect an individual's perceived ability to refrain from smoking in various situations or for designated periods of time. Just as personality factors are likely to affect one's ability to refrain from smoking, self-efficacy factors further underlie the origins of smoking behavior. Research (Larimar, Palmer, & Marlatt, 1999) has shown that certain personality factors, such as the lack of ability to delay gratification, predispose individuals to substance abuse, including smoking. When predisposing factors are paired with certain situational factors, such as the availability of substances and positive reinforcing stimuli, a common response is substance use.

There appear to be at least three stages in the process of quitting smoking: preparing to quit, quitting itself, and maintaining cessation. Researchers have demonstrated that individuals who want to quit smoking tend to use different types of coping strategies at different stages of the quitting process. For example, during the course of a cessation program, especially after initially quitting, ambivalence about nonsmoking and rationalizations for resuming smoking may become critical concerns. As clients strive to maintain their newly achieved nonsmoking status, they are often beset with thoughts that can undermine their efforts. Clinicians and health counselors have found that the measurement of such thoughts or rationalizations can provide a useful stimulus for treatment planning and coping. Danaher and Lichtenstein (1978) have outlined the following potentially self-defeating thoughts or rationalizations.

- Nostalgia—"I sure did like to smoke with coffee after dinner. I wonder how a cigarette would taste now."
- Testing—"I wonder if I could smoke just one cigarette, and then not have any more."
- Crisis—"I could handle the situation much better if I only had a cigarette." Or alternatively, "I've been under such pressure that I deserve a cigarette."
- Avoiding unwanted side effects—"Quitting smoking is causing me to become overweight."
- Self-doubts—"I'm still getting strong urges to smoke. I must be one of those addicted people."

Labeling such rationalizations helps clients recognize how they can undermine their efforts to quit smoking. Clients can then be trained and encouraged to combat or rebut self-defeating thoughts.

Biological Model

A number of theorists in the late 1970s conceptualized smoking as primarily an escape/avoidance response to the aversive consequences of nicotine withdrawal (Schachter, 1978). This formulation is essentially an addiction model, which states that a minimal amount of nicotine must be provided because withdrawal symptoms will occur. Nicotine withdrawal symptoms, however, have been somewhat difficult to document and generally have been found to vary from smoker to smoker, as well as from environment to environment. Several investigators have observed that smokers are able to undergo extended periods of deprivation under certain conditions without experiencing much discomfort (Piasecki et al., 2000). Only recently have investigators agreed that there is a physiological addiction to nicotine.

Although addiction is clearly a factor in the maintenance of smoking, the theories seem inadequate to provide a comprehensive explanation or to account satisfactorily for the difficulties most smokers experience in quitting. Researchers, however, indicate that stimuli independent of the nicotine-addiction cycle (i.e., unrelated to the time since the last cigarette) reliably increase the probability of smoking. Such stimuli include the end of a meal, the consumption of coffee, feeling upset or unhappy, and cognitive and intellectual pressures. Consistent with these observations are reports that many cigarettes are smoked because the smoker perceives improvement in performance, enhancement of pleasure or relaxation, and relief of anxiety (Pomerleau, Pomerleau, & Namenek, 1998). Thus, with the exception of the first cigarette of the day or after an extended period of deprivation, many cigarettes smoked have no clear connection with nicotine deprivation or time since the last cigarette.

Schachter, a prominent proponent of the addiction model, attempted to resolve this apparent difficulty. He and his colleagues demonstrated that smokers have more cigarettes when anxious or when subjected to painful stimulation. Their research also found that these stressors decreased urinary pH, which led them to hypothesize that acidification of the urine by stress caused nicotine withdrawal. From these and related studies, Schachter (1978) concluded that the principal consequence of smoking is simply relief from the painful and anxiety-provoking state of nicotine withdrawal.

There is now considerable evidence to suggest that the tenacity of the cigarette-smoking habit is based on different reinforcing effects that are appropriate to a variety of circumstances (Pomerleau, Pomerleau, & Namenek, 1998). In fact, most behavioral strategies for treating smoking have been based on the assumption that both escape from withdrawal and disruption of other reinforcing consequences of smoking must occur in order to break the habit. This perspective is derived from behavior-modification theory and ultimately from operant-conditioning concepts that emphasize the contribution of antecedent and consequent environmental stimuli in determining behavior. Implicitly or explicitly, however, these formulations ascribe the rewarding aspects of smoking to conditioning and have little to say about the biological basis for the reinforcement of smoking or for the mediation of environment–behavior interactions.

What is called for at this time is an integrative formulation of smoking that takes into account the complexity of the pharmacological actions of nicotine and the contributions of social, psychological, and biological factors.

Ney and Gale (1989) outlined some of the consequences of smoking and not smoking in habitual smokers. For habitual smokers, smoking can lead to improved memory, the ability to concentrate and tune out irrelevant stimuli, more alertness and arousal, the facilitation of pleasure, decreased appetite, and less tension. The consequences of not smoking for habitual smokers can lead to a craving for cigarettes, increased anxiety and tension, increases in body weight, irritability, dullness or anhedonia, some memory impairment, and difficulties concentrating. The congruence of these consequences with the psychological effects of the endogenous neuroregulators known to be stimulated by nicotine is striking. This highlights why quitting can be so difficult and why smokers maintain their habits.

In addition, the number of affective states or performance demands that might cue smoking, independent of nicotine withdrawal, is potentially very large and provides a plausible explanation for the thorough interweaving of the smoking habit into the fabric of daily life. The fact that nicotine does not produce dramatic intoxication or withdrawal may even add to its reinforcing value in that the benefits of smoking may be achieved without disrupting ongoing activities.

The withdrawal symptoms that occur immediately after cessation of drug use are collectively called *acute withdrawal syndrome*. It is not clear whether there is a specific acute syndrome that can be ascribed to tobacco dependency. Most smokers report some symptoms when not smoking, but the nature of them varies greatly from smoker to smoker. Generally, symptoms are most acute during the first 7 to 10 days of quitting. The most common complaints are heightened anxiety, irritability, inability to concentrate, fatigue, increased mucus production, and headache. Occasionally, smokers report mouth sores and mild gastrointestinal upset. A nearly universal symptom is tobacco craving. At first, the ex-smoker may experience constant withdrawal symptoms but, with the exception of craving, most symptoms usually subside after the first week or so.

Counselors may find it helpful to have the client rank the intensity of the tobacco craving on a scale from 1 to 10, with 1 being nonexistent and 10 being severe. Most clients find that they are able to get some control over the cravings and are able to see some moderate changes.

From a physiological perspective, the occurrence of such symptoms is puzzling. Nicotine has a half-life of 2 to 3 hours. Its most active metabolite, cotinine, has a half-life of 18 to 20 hours. Therefore, the symptoms continue to occur long after nicotine and its major active metabolite are cleared from the body. Similar phenomena have been described with opiates. Theorists suggest that chronic withdrawal symptoms are classically conditioned reactions to internal and environmental stimuli associated either with smoking or with changes in level of nicotine in the blood. For example, within minutes after smoking, the blood's nicotine level peaks and then begins to fall. The decrease in the level of nicotine in the blood may result in mild withdrawal symptoms, which become conditioned to the environment in which they occur (Caraballo, Giovino, & Pechaek, 2001).

From the preceding review of the literature, it is obvious that the interactions among the biological, psychological, and social factors are numerous. The next section focuses on assessing how these factors are associated with people who are looking for relief from their smoking habit.

ASSESSMENT

Assessment is an ongoing process tied to the course of treatment. Some assessments occur prior to or early in treatment, whereas others are possible only once smoking has been stopped, and still others are most relevant during long-term follow-up. Generally, assessment begins with a smoking history that leads up to the current cessation attempt. Self-reports of smoking patterns and motives are best when obtained early in treatment, because responses change as treatment proceeds. Assessment then progresses to a more detailed evaluation of the client's current smoking behavior. Self-reports and self-monitoring are used to measure the amount and distribution of smoking. This type of information can help provide the counselor with a client's self-reported baseline of smoking behavior.

Assessment procedures vary in their clinical utility. Many valid assessments yield information that is primarily of prognostic value—that is, predicting the client's probability of success. Although this data may be intellectually interesting, it is of little clinical value because it provides little information for action. Knowing that a particular person is a poor risk for treatment is of little use unless the information provided suggests actions that could improve the outcome. To be clinically useful, an assessment should have immediate implications for the conduct of treatment; that is, it is the most valuable when it can be linked to a set of procedures to be differentially applied—each dependent on the results of the assessment.

In addition, assessment often increases clients' motivational level by changing their way of thinking; for example, it may help clients if they list the benefits that they plan to receive from quitting. A handout sheet, with the following list, can be provided; then ask: "Does your list include these?"

- Overall improved health
- Lower pulse rate
- Easier breathing
- No more smoker's cough
- No more angina chest pain
- Improved taste and smell
- Cleaner, fresher-smelling clothes
- More energy
- Less tension
- Less need for sleep
- More refreshing sleep
- Increased physical endurance level
- Monetary savings
- Pride of accomplishment
- Improved self-confidence and self-esteem
- Personal satisfaction of a job well done

Clients should be told to carry this list with them at all times and to agree to look at it before putting another cigarette in their mouths.

A variation of this technique comes from Judy Perlmutter (1986). In her strategy, clients are asked to go through a list of smoking consequences and quitting benefits and to check off the items that apply to them. The questionnaire focuses on the emotional, health, social, and financial consequences of smoking and the benefits of quitting. During this process of assessment, those who use this strategy are learning those consequences and benefits. Clients understand what they're willing to give up as well as the benefits and pay-offs that they expect to obtain once they've quit. This helps them recognize that they are not just stopping, quitting, or losing something, but rather are gaining and benefiting from not smoking.

Lederman and Scheiderman (1986) have developed a smoker's self-assessment profile that helps smokers understand what motivates them to smoke. The simple, 18-item questionnaire provides a useful way of categorizing smoking motivation. The six motivational categories are: (1) stimulation by nicotine, (2) handling or touching things, (3) pleasure/accentuation of pleasure, (4) tension reduction/relaxation, (5) psychological dependency, and (6) habit.

Additionally, during the assessment phase it is helpful to develop a profile of the client's current level of physical and psychological stress and to identify what coping skills he or she has or needs to attain to cope effectively with such stress and to meet his or her goal (Donovan & Marlatt, 1988; Davis & Glaros, 1986; Shiffman; 1985). The level of stress in a smoker's life influences the treatment process. Lower levels of stress can be a motivational factor that stimulates clients to seek change, whereas clients who experience high levels of stress are less likely to see themselves as capable of effecting a change until some tension is reduced. Clinical instruments are available to assess the client's current level of stress and anxiety; however, generally it useful just to ask a simple question: "On a scale of 1 to 100, with 1 being low and 100 being high, what would you estimate is your current level of stress?" This simple question can help the client assess present stress, predict the likelihood that this stress is going to change in the future, and better understand whether this is the best time to be considering smoking cessation.

Donovan and Marlatt (1988) feel that social contagion (i.e., external cues) is an important factor in the assessment phase of the treatment process. By determining the external cues that have an impact on the client, the counselor can help identify possible pitfalls in the cessation program. Once external cues and situations that increase the likelihood of smoking have been identified, the client can consciously choose to develop preventive self-adaptive responses to modify the environment or to cope more effectively with such situations. It is important for the client to realize that external cues change and often require revision throughout the cessation process. Although it is desirable to continue to monitor changes, experience shows that noncompliance with instructions to monitor oneself is a common difficulty. Rather than develop a power conflict with the client regarding self-monitoring, it is helpful for counselors to shift the focus, keep the client busy with other activities (e.g., exercise and diet), and repeat positive affirmations.

During the assessment process, it is also important to help the client understand and develop his or her coping skills—that is, how to take direct action to prevent or to resist temptation. According to Shiffman (1985), coping is easily assessed through self-reports. Clients can be asked open-ended questions about what they have been doing or saying to themselves to prevent, to resist, or to recover from temptation. This process not only assesses coping strategies but also helps educate clients about other possibilities. The Coping with Temptation Inventory (CWTI) is organized by categories of responses with specific examples for each type of response. The questionnaire highlights both behavioral and cognitive coping responses, and it provides many helpful suggestions derived from ex-smokers' reports about coping strategies.

Because they are diverse, when coping strategies are assessed both cognitive and behavioral aspects should be examined. Many clients will favor either a cognitive or a behavioral approach and will use it almost exclusively. Helping clients determine their dominant coping orientation is helpful because it can be employed throughout the smoking-cessation process, especially during relapse prevention (Donovan & Marlatt, 1988). Through the assessment process, counselors can help them develop a repertoire of coping strategies—possible responses to what clients perceive to be difficult or challenging situations.

INTERVENTIONS

Virtually every procedure imaginable—from talk therapies to behavioral therapies to drug treatments—has been used to beat the smoking habit. Regardless of the strategy, all interventions need to address at least two separate underlying mechanisms: (1) motivation to avoid smoking and (2) coping skills to maintain avoidance. It is also important that successful interventions build on a thorough knowledge of the underlying behavioral, social, and biological mechanisms involved in the development and maintenance of smoking behavior as well as how these mechanisms will interface with interventions. Effective interventions usually involve a combination of approaches, including counseling, pharmacological, and psychoeducation. Counselors need to be familiar with each process and be able to tailor a treatment process to match the client's needs (Beutler & Clarkin, 1990). The recognition that there needs to be an integrated approach to the cessation process is one theme in the literature on this subject (Miller & Heather, 1986). This section describes each of the processes and then provides an integrated case example.

Counseling Approaches

In smoking-cessation programs, two separate counseling goals can be identified: (1) attempts to persuade people to quit smoking and (2) attempts to persuade people who have quit smoking to stick to their decision. Shiffman (1985) views the therapeutic task as one of strengthening clients' motivation to change. This process can be achieved through a series of steps. The first is to educate clients about the risks of smoking behavior; once educated, they become an ally in the cessation process. The actual therapeutic task involves hooking into clients' ambivalent attitudes about quitting and heightening their desire to stop smoking. Shiffman (1985) believes that the motivational resources that clients use originate in the interactive relationship that develops between counselor and client. The counselor can create an atmosphere in which individuals experience the discomfort of cognitive dissonance (Festinger, 1957) between smoking behavior and pro-health values. Once dissonance is experienced, they can move forward from contemplating change to committing to acting.

After the counselor determines that clients have moved into the commitment stage, the next task is to match them with appropriate treatment and adequate supports. Five different smoking-intervention strategies designed to encourage people to quit smoking have been identified in the literature: (1) aversion, (2) self-control, (3) a combination of aversion and self-control, (4) pharmacological approaches, and (5) health education (Bloom, 1988).

Aversion strategies can be grouped into four categories: electric shock, rapid smoking, satiation, and cognitive sensitization. None of these methods has been found to be remarkably effective. Self-control methods include (1) environmental planning, (2) behavioral programming, and (3) cognitive control. Environmental planning involves helping the client change smoking behaviors, either by altering the circumstances in which smoking occurs or by working with smokers to reinforce each other's smoking-cessation efforts. In the case of behavioral programming, the smoker institutes a self-directed system of rewards and punishments to facilitate smoking cessation. In the case of cognitive control, the smoker attempts to limit smoking behavior by changing his or her way of thinking about smoking.

The counselor's real work seems to begin after smoking stops. Research indicates that the majority of relapses occur within the first 3 months following cessation. Clients need to learn cognitive vigilance as a resource to call on during the cessation process. By learning to recognize the thought processes at work, clients can successfully intervene when faulty thinking occurs. Through psychoeducation, they can effectively program new cognitive responses.

Counselors need to have an array of skills to help the client. During the assessment phase of the cessation process, the counselor identifies the client's strengths and develops strategies for how these strengths can best be used. Also, weaknesses and skill deficits need to be assessed and remediations prescribed. In addition to cognitive and behavioral components, some counselors use hypnosis with good results. Crasilneck (1990) reports a cessation rate of 81 percent through the use of hypnotic techniques after a one-year follow-up. His treatment plan utilizes psychoeducation, hypnosis, and reinforcers meted out by the counselor and by mutual-aid groups. Barber (2001) has also produced impressive results—39 of 43 patients achieved abstinence—with hypnosis and a rapid smoking protocol.

Pharmacological Approaches

Pharmacological approaches to smoking cessation are based on the premise that the smoker has become addicted to nicotine. One treatment approach is to provide nicotine to the smoker, mainly in the form of special chewing gum or patches. There is considerable evidence that chewing gum is an effective adjunct in a smoking-cessation program; however, Cooper (2002) found that attendance at a 13-week cognitive-behavioral program was more effective than the use of nicotine gum. Nicotine supplements have been used to lessen the physical symptoms of withdrawal. Gottlieb, Killen, Marlatt, and Taylor (1987) identified the client's expectations as the determinant factor in the effectiveness of nicotine supplements. Their study questions the effectiveness of nicotine supplements and looks at how the client's expectations actually alter the supplements' perceived effects. The West and Shiffman (2001) report contains a review of the literature on the reduction of cigarette withdrawal and craving through the use of various types of oral nicotine. The interventions used included gum, inhalers, lozenges and sublingual tablets. Generally, they found that the results were favorable for the reduction of craving, irritability, and withdrawal.

Other researchers have been experimenting with transdermal clonidine and transdermal nicotine patches. The Food and Drug Administration (FDA) approved several different brands of skin or transdermal nicotine patches in 1992. These adhesive pads—about 2 inches square and available by prescription—release a trickle of nicotine through the skin into the bloodstream, thus satisfying the smoker's craving for nicotine. Studies submitted to the FDA indicate that smokers who used nicotine patches for 8 to 12 weeks were about twice as likely to have quit at the end of that period (i.e., not to have smoked since the second week of the study) as were those who used dummy patches without nicotine. Quitting rates in different studies ranged from 8 to 92 percent for nicotine-patch users, as compared with 3 to 46 percent for those who got dummy patches (Weiss, 1992).

Shiffman and colleagues (2000) compared 16-hour with 24-hour nicotine patches and concluded that smokers who used 24-hour patches experienced longer abstinence rates than those who used the 16-hour variety. The subjects reported better control of cravings throughout the day during a 2-week period of abstinence. Daughton and colleagues' (1999) 4- to 5-year study found that 24-hour patches resulted in higher long-term continuous abstinence compared to lower-dose patches and placebo. Richmond, Kehoe, de Almeida, and Cesar (1997) found that the effectiveness of 24-hour patches doubled when used with a cognitive-behavioral group program.

Unfortunately, quitting smoking is often the easy part. The more difficult problem is not starting again. Etter and colleagues (2002) report, however, that nicotine treatment for smoking reduction has no detectable impact on smoking cessation. Many smokers wonder whether use of the nicotine patch can conquer smoking permanently; so far, research suggests that those who quit with the help of patches relapse at about the same rate as anyone else. The quitting rates for those who use patches seem to be roughly similar to the rates of those who use nicotine gum. The severity of the side effects of both products is comparable: hiccups, sore throat, and jaw aches for gum; minor skin irritation, insomnia, and occasional nightmares for patches. It is important to note that the patches are relatively ineffective unless they are used in conjunction with a smoking-cessation program that includes counseling, relaxation training, hypnosis, or some other form of behavioral therapy. All manufacturers offer forms of psychological support such as toll-free hotlines, day-by-day motivational suggestions, audiotapes, and pamphlets to be given to a friend or spouse/partner that contain hints about how to provide support to the quitter.

Edwards, Murphy, Downs, Ackerman, and Rosenthal (1989) studied the use of antidepressants. In their research, doxepin hydrochloride was identified as an effective agent both in the precessation process and in active quitting. Hall and colleagues (2002) report that sustained-release bupropion hydrochloride and nortriptyline have been shown to be efficacious in the treatment of cigarette smoking. Glover and colleagues (2002) found that bupropion is also just as effective for smokeless tobacco users. Researchers have noticed that, since the symptoms of depression and withdrawal are very similar, treatments for depression are likely to be quite helpful during the withdrawal process. More comprehensive research should help to show how antidepressants and other medications can be used effectively.

Other Treatment Considerations

This section describes two treatment strategies: group versus individual and abrupt versus gradual quitting. There doesn't seem to be any noticeable difference in outcome as a function of which strategy is used.

Group versus Individual Treatment.   Most smoking-cessation treatment is provided in small groups of 5 to 10 people. However, there appears to be no evidence that groups are superior to individual treatment, although many clients who have participated in groups report that the support was central in achieving and maintaining abstinence. Groups are also more cost-effective than individual sessions. However, there are certain pitfalls in group treatment, including the following. First, relapse can sometimes be contagious, especially if those who relapse are vocal or have achieved high informal status in the group. Second, group members sometimes give each other permission to fail. Third, if group members are poorly matched or antagonistic to one another, attendance rates can be poorer than for individual sessions.

Abrupt versus Gradual Quitting.   Abrupt cessation is recommended because it is most congenial with the methods that have been found to be the most helpful. Smokers should set a quit date and stop smoking completely on that day. Many smokers cut down gradually before that day, and some continue to smoke right up until the last moment.

Psychoeducation Approaches

A psychoeducation model for smoking cessation represents an attempt to encourage smokers to stop smoking and to keep from relapsing by using traditional educational approaches, such as curricula that point out the harmful effects of smoking. Marlatt and Gordon (1985) view smoking cessation as one part of the holistic lifestyle approach. In their book, they urge both the client and the counselor to view the smoking behavior as part of the individual's total lifestyle. The program these researchers describe includes four main components.

1. *Learning self-observation skills.* When clients have a clear understanding of the successive steps that led to their smoking behavior, two things happen. First, clients are able to ascertain what stressors, or external cues, precipitate smoking behaviors. By identifying these stressors, clients can then learn which interventions would best alleviate or dissipate their effects, thus enabling them to effectively avoid relapse. The Individuals can also learn to predict what may trigger a potential slip. These self-observation skills are a valuable relapse-prevention tool.

2. *Learning self-efficacy.* As a learned behavior, self-efficacy is an essential feature of a psychoeducational approach. Brod and Hall (1984) list four components of self-efficacy that are necessary for its successful application.

   a. *Past performance*—What past accomplishments can the client recall that would lead to an assumption that this effort will also succeed? When the client remembers past efficacious behaviors, she or he can then begin to visualize success in the cessation process.

   b. *Vicarious experience*—Does the client know someone who has completed a program and successfully quit? If so, the individual can then affirm that his or her goal can be accomplished and can visualize himself or herself as having achieved it.

   c. *Verbal persuasions*—When the individual is able to recall personal past achievements and can see that others have achieved successful cessation, she or he can better put into service the information presented in the psychoeducational process.

   d. *Recognition of internal cues*—Within the context of a greater sense of one's efficacy, the individual can better recognize his or her own physiologic cues and can then respond accordingly. For example, once the client believes that she or he has the capacity to counter a challenge, there is considerably less resistance to identifying negative physiologic reactions from smoking.

3. *Understanding coping strategies.* Another important part of the psychoeducational model is a clear understanding of coping strategies—what they are and how they can be used most effectively. The smoker can also identify which reinforcers are most helpful in situations that call for an immediate coping behavior. One direct way in which the counselor can utilize clients' newly acquired coping skills is to provide an interactive format. When the counselor models his or her belief in clients' ability to successfully reach their goal, clients can then introject the counselor's perception that they can be efficacious in their newly acquired behaviors.

4. *Understanding the cessation process.* Part of the educational process includes clients' development of an understanding of the entire cessation process, including maintenance of the newly acquired behaviors.

In general, recent studies of smoking-cessation programs suggest that their impact is related to (1) the level of motivation to stop smoking, (2) the development of a better sense of physical and psychological well-being, and (3) the achievement of moderation or elimination of the smoking habit. People who have better problem-solving skills and who make greater use of self-reward in controlling their behavior appear to be the most successful with smoking cessation.

PREVENTION APPROACHES

Economic factors, continuing emphasis on the rights of nonsmokers, and the growth of Employee Assistance Programs (EAPs) have contributed to increased interest in workplace smoking-control programs. This section also describes school-based, community-based, physician-based, policy-based, and economy-based smoking-control programs.

The economic factors are apparent. Smokers use significantly more health services, have higher absenteeism rates, and have more accidents at work than do their nonsmoking colleagues. The greatest concentration in workplace programs is to enforce policies that either restrict smoking to certain areas or ban it altogether. Whether these programs actually affect smoking behavior outside of work has yet to be studied. Workplace smoking-control programs usually use one or a combination of the following approaches:

- Company policies that restrict or prohibit smoking
- Economic incentives that encourage smokers to quit or provide rewards for nonsmokers
- Sponsorship of smoking-cessation programs, including educational campaigns, self-help groups, referral to community agencies, and counseling by staff medical personnel

School-Based Smoking-Control Programs

The purpose of school-based programs is to prevent or delay the onset of smoking and to decrease the number of students who smoke. The prevention programs have the following primary goals: (1) to educate the students, and to modify their attitudes, about smoking through traditional health education approaches; (2) to alter social pressure to smoke by increasing their skills to resist peers' influence; (3) to modify the decision-making process of experimental smokers through the development of personal and interpersonal skills; (4) to modify the consequences of smoking; and (5) to stop smoking via behavioral approaches (Elder & Stern, 1986). Even though programs based on the modification of social factors and those based on dissemination of information on the harmful effects of smoking (including the addictive properties of tobacco) both seem to be effective, programs based on the acquisition of skills have been shown to be the most effective.

Community-Based Smoking-Control Programs

Community programs often use varying combinations of mass media, environmental modifications, and group and one-to-one interventions. The mass media programs hope to increase the public's awareness of the smoking problem; increase smokers' desire to make changes in their smoking behaviors; and provide smokers with guidance in quitting, which includes detailed suggestions on how to quit. Many media-based programs depend on public service announcements. Recent trends are to use a much broader array of available media, including special television, news, and radio programs; newspapers; billboards; and educational materials such as pamphlets.

A review of the available literature on smoking indicates that the encouraging effect that smoking advertisements have on smoking behavior is significant and, if it is not countered, advertising is likely to result in continued increases in the number of people who take up smoking and in reinforcement for those who are currently smokers. The literature also indicates that community-based smoking-control programs that utilize the media in combination with other approaches are effective in reducing the prevalence and incident rates of smoking within a community. If the programs are sustained over time, it is likely that the cessation rate will increase and that fewer people will begin smoking.

Physician-Based Smoking-Control Programs

Physicians are in an excellent position to assess a significant portion of smokers in the population, and they are also considered to be credible sources of health information. Physician-based smoking-control programs ideally should include: (1) an office environment that supports the delivery of a nonsmoking message to smoking patients, (2) counseling of patients on quitting strategies, (3) having smoking on patients' problem list, (4) distribution of self-help materials, and (5) involving office staff in some aspect of the program.

Policy-Based Smoking-Control Programs

As mentioned earlier, smoking prevention and control interventions founded on public policy are likely to have the greatest effect because they are population-based and their enforcement is often the responsibility of one or more government agencies. Breslow (1982) identified the following 10 action alternatives that governments could consider as they strive to control the smoking problem: prohibition of cigarettes; restriction of cigarette smoking; reduction in hazardous substances in cigarettes; restriction on advertising of cigarettes; public information, education, and assistance for persons who want to quit smoking; taxation and other economic measures; international cooperation; and research. When policy interventions are combined with specific smoking-prevention and cessation programs, the effect on smoking behavior is significant.

Economy-Based Smoking-Control Programs

Although economic interventions are clearly part of policy-based interventions, they are considered separately because of their popularity and use as a means of influencing smoking behavior (Iverson, 1987). In addition, smoking costs the economy billions of dollars each year in health-related expenses, and job absences—therefore workplace interventions are important.

TREATMENT ADHERENCE, RELAPSE PREVENTION, AND DEALING WITH SLIPS

It is easy for some people to stop smoking, so these people generally do not seek the help of formal treatment programs. The clients of smoking clinics, health counselors, and private practitioners usually are the more physically and psychologically dependent smokers. For these clients, quitting smoking is often a difficult process that involves readjustment in physical, intrapsychic, and social domains. If smokers fail to acknowledge these potential problems when quitting smoking, they will be poorly prepared for the difficulties involved and are at a higher risk for relapse. Relapse can occur because of the following: (1) ex-smokers are not aware that the acute discomfort they are experiencing is time-limited—they fear having to endure it indefinitely; (2) they believe that the problems they are experiencing are uncommon, so relapse because they feel alone and helpless to deal with them; and (3) they do not develop appropriate cognitive and behavioral coping strategies (Hall & Hall, 1987).

The difficulties that occur after quitting smoking are many and varied. It is not possible to predict with any certainty who will experience problems or how difficult the course of quitting will be for a given smoker. Counselors need not discuss all the potential problems with clients who want to quit before treatment begins. However, the client should understand the following points: (1) cigarette smoking is a habit that may have become intertwined in many aspects of his or her life; (2) he or she may have become addicted to nicotine; (3) the client can expect that quitting smoking will be a difficult task that may require readjustment in social, emotional, and physical demands; (4) others with the same problem have succeeded; (5) the difficulties that the client will experience are time-limited; and (6) effective tools are available to help him or her through the quitting period.

Counselors and other health professionals have been effective in helping smokers quit. However, as pointed out earlier, the problem is that most who quit smoking relapse or break their abstinence. The key is not to help an individual to simply quit but, rather, to maintain long-term abstinence. Many of the same factors involved in the cessation phase are involved in the maintenance phase. Social support, for example, can sustain commitment in the face of withdrawal symptoms and assist individuals through potential relapse situations long after cessation is achieved. Mermelstein, Cohen, Lichtenstein, Baer, and Kamarck (1986) conducted research that supported the relationship between perceived level of support—especially from significant others—and long-term maintenance. McGovern (1984) noted that the likelihood of relapse is significantly increased if individuals live with family members who smoke. Additional data indicate that high proportions of smokers in social and occupational networks are associated with less successful outcomes.

In addition, self-reward strategies that are important during the early stages of treatment need to continue in some form later in the maintenance process. Individuals can be encouraged to contract formally for tangible, realistic, and quickly accessible self-rewards. Rewards have the advantage of increasing commitment to abstinence as well as reducing subjective feelings of deprivation. Self-rewards provide individual-achievement recognition without depending on social support. Coping skills, as well as biological/pharmacological agents, are also helpful in preventing relapse.

Marlatt and Gordon (1980) developed the following list of situations that can result in relapse. It is important for the counselor to prepare the client for alternative responses for each of these situations.

1. Eating is a frequent stimulus for smoking and a prominent antecedent of relapse (Shiffman, 1982). Smoking after meals or with coffee is so common that these occasions must be considered high risks for all smokers.

2. Times of stress or upset are frequently associated with smoking and relapse. In these situations, the smoker seems to use cigarettes to blunt unpleasant emotions.
3. Alcohol consumption is strongly associated with smoking. Smokers are almost always drinkers, and laboratory experiments have demonstrated that smoking facilitates drinking.
4. Social situations are common triggers for smoking. In addition to being cued by other smokers, many seem to use smoking to manage feelings of awkwardness in social settings.
5. Boredom is associated with smoking. Smokers who are bored may see it "as something to do" or may seek the stimulating pharmacological action of nicotine. In our clinical experience, boredom is often associated with mild depression.
6. Positive-affect situations are conducive to smoking. Although smoking is more common when one is in the grip of negative emotions, some smokers are especially likely to smoke when they feel good, claiming that smoking accentuates their positive feeling.
7. Food substitution is another function that cigarettes often serve—smokers have a cigarette instead of food. Fear, sometimes justified, of weight gain after quitting can undermine clients' motivation to stay abstinent.

Danaher and Lichtenstein (1978) identified the following common problem thoughts that tend to encourage smoking again: (1) feeling nostalgic about the old pleasures of smoking; (2) keeping cigarettes around to test oneself; (3) believing that a crisis is an acceptable excuse for a cigarette; (4) being sure that not smoking brings about unwanted changes, such as weight gain, that can be ameliorated only by returning to smoking; and (5) believing that one is unable to quit.

Research seems to support the idea that it is important to help the client plan what he or she is going to do. This proactive versus reactive stance will decrease the likelihood of relapse. Very clear, first-line strategies need to be developed to cope with the temptation to smoke, including avoidance, escape, distraction, and delay (Shiffman et al., 1985). Shiffman and colleagues also suggest that clients develop cognitive—imagery, cognitive restructuring, and self-talk—and behavioral—physical activity, relaxation, and other substitute behaviors—coping responses to counter very specific high-risk situations. These suggestions are used later in the case example.

Dealing with Slips

If clients do experience a slip, it is important that they do not fall victim to the so-called abstinence violation effect. In this all too common pattern of self-defeatist thinking, a single slip triggers a period of intense self-castigation, depression, and negativity. Thoughts (e.g., "I'm no good" "I have no willpower" or "I wasn't really cured anyway") lead to a decreased sense of self-control, a drop in self-esteem, and further slips until the person abandons all efforts to quit (Marlatt, 1985).

A slip is basically a two-step process: a smoking-risk situation plus an inadequate coping response. A slip or two on the way to eventual success does not make you a failure. Actually, some psychologists recommend planned slips, or programmed relapse (Marlatt, 1985). The only real failure that clients can experience is giving up their efforts to quit. It is important to teach them that, if they find themselves slipping, they can catch themselves and then take control again. It is important to have clients accept the fact that they have slipped and to allow themselves to return to a nonsmoking state without self-blame. A no-fault approach increases clients' chances of ultimate success. It is helpful to point out to clients that many people who eventually succeed experience many slips on their way to reaching their goal. Slips seldom occur because of physical withdrawal symptoms but, rather, because of anxiety, anger, frustration, or depression. This is one of the reasons that self-hypnosis and relaxation procedures can help clients gain more self-control and therefore minimize the likelihood of relapse.

In summary, health-care counselors tend to know more about how to help people quit smoking than they do about preventing relapse. In the future, it will be important to learn more about smoking relapse and how to prevent it, with specific attention to the variables that contribute to relapse and the mechanisms of relapse. Again, stressing whatever makes the avoidance of relapse possible must be included in the cessation treatment process; plus, specific strategies that individuals can rely on during periods in which they experience the urge to resume addictive behavior need to be developed.

The following case, originally published in Sperry and Carlson (1990), presents a biopsychosocial approach that tailors treatment to the specific individual involved.

Case Example

Jilian is a 42-year-old divorced female with a 25-year history of smoking one and a half packs of cigarettes [per] day. A detailed assessment, which included background information, a smoking history, a health assessment, and lifestyle data, including early recollections (ER), yielded the following profile. The client was a relatively healthy woman with no concurrent medical problems except for chronic neck pain sustained as a result of a car accident about 12 years before her consultation. Her smoking history was quite unique in that the majority of her smoking occurred at only 3 times throughout the day: on arising in the morning, on retiring at night, and while engaged in her livelihood as a portrait artist. Furthermore, her smoking was strictly a solitary activity that gave her a feeling of safety and a sense of satisfaction. Unlike the typical smoker, Jilian would absent herself from social situations to smoke and never smoked in the presence of others. None of her friends smoked, and her decision to quit smoking was primarily for health reasons. She reported that smoking seemed to exacerbate her neck pain. In fact, she noted that she had nearly no neck pain during two previous attempts to quit. She had a family history of heart attacks and stroke among both male and female smokers. Her father had been a three-pack-per-day smoker who had died suddenly at 43 of a heart attack. Her mother was a nonsmoker and did not permit smoking inside the house. Jilian [recalled] that during her parents' marital quarrels, her father would stop fighting abruptly and go outside to smoke. Further inquiry showed that Jilian had learned to "solve" conflicts by "walking out" of a difficult situation and lighting up a cigarette.

Smoking appeared to serve at least two functions for Jilian: first, as a stress reducer and second, as a "trigger" for creative productivity—her painting and artistic efforts. Psychologically, she was an only child and "Daddy's girl." Father was a hard-working and successful businessman with strong perfectionist strivings. He was described as intense, nice, and fun to be around. Mother was described as serious, artistic, and a loner. On the Kern Lifestyle Scale (Kern, 1986), Jilian scored highest on perfectionism and lowest on the need to please. Her early recollections suggested that she was guarded and aloof and cordoned herself off from others following conflicts. It also seemed that she utilized withdrawal as a means of controlling others' feelings, as well as her own. She viewed the world as hostile, unpredictable, and unsatisfying.

It is interesting to note that Jilian's smoking behavior occurred in places and situations in which she was withdrawn from others—such as in her art studio—just as it was a general theme throughout her early recollections. She appeared to use smoking as a socially acceptable way of absenting herself from a social group when she became anxious and uncomfortable. And when it was suggested that perhaps she feared that she might not be able to control herself or others if she was successful in quitting smoking, a recognition reflex was elicited.

On the basis of this information, a treatment program was tailored to her needs. The program consisted of four interventions: education, diet and exercise, behavioral change strategies, and hypnosis. (The reader is referred to Carlson, 1989, for a detailed description of this treatment program. A handout, such as the one in the Appendix at the end of this chapter, provided Jilian with information on smoking cessation.)

It was recommended that Jilian make diet changes to influence the acid–alkaline balance in her body. Nicotine is a very strong alkaline substance, and if Jilian's acidity levels rose, her alkaline levels would need to be changed to maintain a pH, or acid–alkaline balance. (If her acidity levels rose, her alkaline level would drop and she would crave cigarettes.) By making dietary changes, it was possible to minimize changes in the pH balance. This was done by getting her to eat more fruits and vegetables; stay away from meat, eggs, and alcohol; eliminate refined-sugar products; and decrease the use of stimulants. It was further suggested that she increase her intake of juices and water.

On the behavioral level, it was suggested that Jilian practice deep, diaphragmatic breathing and muscle relaxation each hour. A daily exercise program was developed to improve her health, burn off calories, and give her something to occupy her time. She decided that walking and biking would be good for her and that she would rotate these activities on a daily basis. It was further suggested that she make an appointment to get her teeth cleaned in order to get rid of any residual tobacco stain or taste so [that] she would have a fresh, clean mouth. This was to be followed by regular brushing.

She was advised to break up the routines in the places where she smoked and to plan other ways to use her time when rising, retiring, and while engaged in painting. It was further suggested that she plan to keep very busy during the following few weeks and that she increase her daily activity patterns. She should take walks, shower, go to church, bicycle, pray, swim, make love, play tennis, and [also] engage in activities that would keep her hands busy. She was asked to think of times when it was going to be difficult for her not to smoke and to schedule things that she could do instead. Since Jilian used smoking primarily to reduce stress—particularly interpersonal stress—and to induce creativity and productivity, an important behavioral change strategy was to find more effective substitutes for stress reduction and creativity. She recalled that taking a walk through a small horticultural park or looking through a particular art portfolio seemed to have a similar effect of inducing a creative mood. She also decided to join two of her friends for an aerobics class and lunch, thinking that these activities would be interpersonal stress reducers. An assertiveness class was also suggested, as was chewing sugarless gum as a further means of reducing her discomfort when she was with people.

A mainstay of this two-session treatment program was the hypnotic suggestions. These were of two types: positive affirmations and self-hypnosis. Jilian was given a sheet with six affirmations tailored to her underlying motivations. She was asked to write out each of the following affirmations 5 times in the morning and then to repeat them aloud to herself:

> "Taking care of myself physically is important to me. I know I will live a longer and a more satisfying life."
>
> "I have more energy and less pain than I ever had before. I enjoy life and I'm glad to be here."
>
> "I have no habits that control or influence me in any harmful way. I am in control of myself and everything I do. I always do what is best for me, myself, and my future."
>
> "All of my senses are clear and alive. I am more productive and creative than when I was a smoker."
>
> "I give myself permission to relax, feel good, breathe deeply and fully, and enjoy being a healthy nonsmoker at all times and in all circumstances."
>
> "People enjoy being around me, and I like being around others. I have self-confidence and self-respect. I like myself, and it shows!"

The self-hypnosis component began near the end of the first session. Standard breathing, relaxation, and guided-imagery techniques were used, along with directives for smoking cessation. The induction was audiotaped, and Jilian was given a copy of the tape for personal use outside the session. She was told to listen to the tape at least once a day for at least the next 2 weeks, at a time when she could be without interruptions. This was used to reinforce what she had learned during the sessions.

The following is the self-hypnosis script, which was tailored to Jilian's situation.

Hypnosis Script

Begin to become aware of your breathing . . . breathe slowly and deeply . . . breathe freely and easily . . . sit back comfortably in your chair, close your eyes, and let yourself begin to relax . . . feel your muscles relaxing and your mind relaxing . . . sitting quietly and peacefully, more at ease . . . your body is slowing down . . . time is slowing down. . . . There is lots and lots of time . . . lots and lots of time . . . we're in no hurry. . . . You feel more at ease, at peace with your surroundings, at peace with yourself . . . so peaceful, relaxed, calm, and tranquil. . . . As you breathe easily and gently, you feel yourself relaxing more and more . . . calmness is present throughout your body and your mind . . . calmness, peace, and relaxation are spreading throughout every part of your body and your mind as you feel more and more relaxed. . . . You feel as if you're floating along on a soft, soft cloud . . . floating gently and easily . . . so relaxed and calm and comfortable . . . soft, gentle, quiet, peaceful, and restful relaxation. . . . As your mind and your body are relaxing more and more, . . . your thoughts are fading away. . . .

A feeling of well-being now exists, as though all of your cares have been rolled away . . . breathe peacefully and comfortably and imagine your worries, uncomfortable thoughts, and problems being carried away with each breath . . . stop worrying, being anxious, being afraid, being tense, being upset and frustrated. . . . Instead you feel calm, free, at ease, confident, and peaceful. . . . Allow any distractions, whether thoughts or outside noises, to drift away . . . imagine clouds drifting smoothly across the sky, carrying with them all distractions, all worries, all uncomfortable thoughts and problems. . . . Allow stress, tension, worry, and anxiety to float away as clouds with each breath you take . . . allow them to drift easily and effortlessly away . . . feel your pressures disappearing, drifting easily and effortlessly away. . . . Now imagine yourself at the top of a large hill . . . I'm going to count backwards from ten, and I want you to imagine yourself going down the hill . . . as you ease down, you will move further and further into a deeper, more comfortable state. . . . When you reach the bottom, you will find yourself in a special place . . . that's the place, whether it's real or imaginary, where you are peaceful and comfortable . . . whether it's by the sea, on a mountain top, near a brook, in a meadow . . . wherever it is that you are peaceful and comfortable. . . .

Breathe in slowly and deeply as I begin to count: ten, deeper and deeper; nine, eight, feel yourself easing into deeper and deeper relaxation; seven, six, a deeper relaxed state; five, four, breathe in the clean, fresh air as you feel a healthier, happier person; three, two, you are deeper and deeper. . . . Feel yourself fully relaxed as if a cloud of relaxation has covered you; one . . . now imagine yourself deeply relaxed and deeply alive and aware in your special place. . . . Breathe in the clean and fresh air . . . notice the colors, scenery, noises, smells, your good feelings. . . . Imagine them on a canvas now in front of you . . . feel how warm you feel. Warmth has spread throughout your body . . . such a pleasant experience . . . notice how good you feel and how good your body can feel. . . . You can be calm, relaxed, and feel good like this whenever you want . . . whenever you feel tense, you will hear the words "calm and relaxed and peaceful . . . calm and relaxed and peaceful" and they will trigger this good feeling for you. . . . The quality of your life depends on what you do and think . . . smoking is a poison to your physical health and to your creativity . . . therefore, make a private commitment to be healthier and more creative. . . . Smoking is a poison to your body and to your mind . . . therefore make a private commitment to be healthy and more creative . . . raise your finger once you've made this commitment. . . . Each day this commitment becomes stronger . . . every day, in every way, your commitment is stronger and stronger. . . . You don't want to say to yourself when you die that you didn't live your life well, that you wished that you would have quit smoking. . . . When you learned to smoke you had to train your body to really take it in and then want it and then need it . . . feel how it was . . . really experience it. . . . You learned that smoking gave you a way to get away from other people when conflict and bad feelings came up . . . experience that now . . . feel how it was. . . .

Starting today you are going to live your life fully . . . you are going to be comfortable and charming around other people . . . let the beautiful person you are fully emerge. . . . The message now is going through all your mind and all throughout your body, on down into your smoking arm and your smoking hand, programming all of you: no smoking. . . . Your whole system is now programmed . . . you are now a nonsmoker . . . you are now a nonsmoker . . . you are now a nonsmoker . . . you want to live and will choose to live well. . . . When you have the urge to smoke, breathe deeply and say to yourself, "I have a commitment with myself to be a nonsmoker and live well . . . I have a commitment with myself to be a nonsmoker and live well . . . I have a commitment with myself to be a nonsmoker and live well." . . . Let these words go deep . . . deep . . . deep . . . into your unconscious mind . . . so that they will be there when you need them. . . . Breathe in now and breathe out . . . nothing will get in your way. . . . You are free from tension, worry, disruption, and smoking . . . you are free in your life works . . . and you are in control.

■ ■ ■ ■ ■

CONCLUDING NOTE

Smoking cessation is a process, not a discrete event as previously assumed. When the client is aware of the steps involved in the process, she or he can be a more effective agent of change. This awareness also predisposes the client to be more efficacious in the cessation program. Once the client seeks out a cessation program, the counselor makes a thorough assessment of the client's current level of stress and of the coping skills the client has within his or her repertoire. This allows the counselor to understand how to better assist the client.

A number of treatment modalities were examined in this chapter. Counseling, when paired with other interventions, has been an effective treatment option. Psychoeducation plays a very broad part in the cessation process, since one prerequisite for successful cessation is the understanding of the health aspects of the addiction process.

It is important to note that although virtually any smoker can and at some point does quit smoking, the maintenance of cessation is at the heart of success in her or his efforts to stop. Relapse prevention therefore is the essential component in achieving this end. Relapse prevention requires a thorough initial assessment, a solid understanding of the psychoeducational process, and a tailored treatment plan based on the client's initial assessment. A counselor's careful work during the relapse-prevention stage of treatment ensures that the maintenance of cessation has a solid chance.

Another important aspect of relapse prevention is the clients' understanding of their role in the smoking process and their ability to be effective agents of change. Current thinking has shifted away from an acceptance of the smoker as a victim of the habit and toward an understanding of the smoker as capable of learning and incorporating self-management skills. With this new perspective on the cessation process and clients' awareness of and active participation in it, we remain hopeful that future "stop smoking" programs will enjoy a high level of success.

RESOURCES
Organizations

- *Action on Smoking and Health (ASH), 2013 H Street, NW, Washington, DC 20006, (202) 659-4310,* http://ash.org—This is the leading antismoking consumer group in the United States. The organization provides support for antismoking activists and seeks to promote legal changes that will protect the nonsmoker's right to breathe fresh air. ASH also sells buttons and bumperstrips with antismoking messages and a variety of NO SMOKING signs. The ASH newsletter is one of the best available sources of current news on smoking and health and antismoking activism.

- *American Cancer Society (ACS), 4 West 35th Street, New York, NY 10001, (212) 736-3030; (800) ACS-2345*—Local affiliates of the American Cancer Society sponsor a 4-session stop-smoking program called Fresh Start. Sessions last one hour each and extend over a 2-week period; they focus on behavior modification, goal setting, mastering of obstacles, and social support. The ACS also publishes a free handbook for potential quitters, the I Quit Kit, which is available from your local chapter (consult your local directory for the address and phone number) or from their national headquarters at the address above.

- *American Heart Association (AHA), 7272 Greenville Avenue, Dallas, TX 75231, (800) 242-8721;* www.americanheart.org—The AHA offers a wide and varied range of services, which include educational modules, onsite workshops, and the coordination of self-help cessation programs.

- *American Lung Association (ALA), 61 Broadway, New York, NY 10006, (212) 315-8700, (800) 586-4872;* www.lungusa.org—The ALA offers workplace smoking-cessation programs and a family-oriented program that emphasizes prevention, psychoeducation, and cessation. The ALA offers a variety of literature designed to educate the individual as well as to provide a useful adjunct to smoking-cessation programs. The American Lung Association sponsors stop-smoking groups in most cities and also publishes an excellent guide to quitting—Freedom from Smoking for You and Your Family. This book guides readers through a step-by-step, 20-day program that leads to quitting and provides guidelines for remaining a nonsmoker; it is available from your local ALA chapter (consult your local directory for the address and phone number) or from their national headquarters at the address above.

- *Breathe-Free: The Plan to Stop Smoking, Narcotics Education, Inc., 61330 Laurel Street, NW, Washington, DC 20012*—Many local affiliates of the Seventh-Day Adventist Church run a highly recommended program that is usually led by a pastor–physician team. The Breathe-Free plan is based on motivation, lifestyle modification, values clarification, modeling, visualization, affirmation, positive thinking, and self-rewards. There is also an optional nondenominational spiritual component. The plan consists of 8 sessions that take place over 3 weeks, with periodic phone contacts for a year thereafter. Prospective group members are invited to attend the first 2 sessions before making the decision to register

for the remainder of the course. During the third week, a graduation ceremony is held, at which successful quitters receive a BNS (Bachelor of Nonsmoking) degree. MNS (Master of Nonsmoking) degrees are awarded at 6 months, and DNS (Doctor of Nonsmoking) degrees at 12 months.

- *Centers for Disease Control and Prevention (CDC) 4770 Buford Highway, NE, MS-K50 Atlanta, GA 30341-3724, Office of Smoking and Health, Park Building, Room 1-10, 5600 Fisher's Lane, Rockville, MD 20857, (800) CDC-1311;* www.cdc.gov/tobacco—This federal agency offers both scientific and technical information about smoking. With an extensive database of available services and publications that is quite comprehensive, the CDC is an excellent resource center.

- *National Cancer Institute, Smoking, Tobacco and Cancer Program (STCP), 6130 Executive Blvd., Room 4082, Bethesda, MD 20892, (301) 496-8520*—STCP offers various intervention strategies (workplace, self-help, psychoeducation, and one-on-one cessation), as well as preventive efforts.

- *National Clearinghouse on Alcohol and Drug Information (NCADI), 11420 Rockville Pike, Rockville, MD 20852, (301) 770-5800*—This is a resource service for the clinician. This group pioneered behavioral/cognitive research on cessation, and its current focus is on relapse prevention.

- *National Institute on Drug Abuse (NIDA), 6001 Executive Blvd., Room 5213, Bethesda, MD 20892, (301) 443-1124*—This is an excellent resource for materials on cigarette smoking. Titles, editors or authors, and addresses at which to obtain these materials, are given in the Pamphlets section that follows. Descriptions of monograph content in quotation marks are taken from NIDA publications. While supplies last, copies of monographs can be obtained free from the National Clearinghouse for Drug Abuse Information. Copies can also be purchased from the U.S. Government Printing

Office (GPO), Washington, DC, or the National Technical Information Service (NTIS), Deptartment of Commerce, 5285 Port Royal Rd., Springfield, VA 22161; (703) 605-6585.

- *Smokers Anonymous, P.O. Box 25335, West Los Angeles, CA 90025, (212) 474-8997—*

This group provides information on starting your own support group. They will also let you know if there is a Smokers Anonymous group in your area. Write to them at the address here, enclosing a self-addressed stamped envelope.

Books and Reports

- Grabowski, J., & Bell, C. S. (Eds.). (1984). *Measurement in the analysis and treatment of smoking behavior.* GPO Stock No. 017-0240-01181-9, NTIS Publication No. 84-145-184. Washington, DC: GPO—"An attempt to delineate measures for analysis of smoking behavior in research and treatment settings" (NIDA). The chapter by analysis on biochemical verification of abstinence and smoking is excellent.
- Grabowski, J., & Hall, S. M. (Eds.). (1985). *Pharmacological adjuncts in smoking cessation.* NIDA Research Monograph No. 64, DHHS, Washington, DC: GPO—This is a review of smoking treatment and related research issues, using pharmacological adjuncts to smoking treatment. Focus is on nicotine replacement therapy.
- Jarvik, M. E., Cullen, J. W., Gritz, E. R., Vogt, T. M., & West, L. J. (Eds.). (1977). *Research on smoking behavior.* GPO Stock No. 017-024-00694, NTIS Publication No. 276 353/AS. Washington, DC: GPO—"Includes epidemiology, etiology, consequences of use, and approaches to behavioral change" (NIDA). This publication contains useful chapters on smoking and disease (Van Lancker) and sociocultural factors in smoking (Reeder). The treatment section is a bit outdated.
- Krasnegor, N. A. (Ed.). (1979). *Cigarette smoking as a dependence process.* GPO Stock No. 017-024-00895-8, NTIS Publication No. 297 721/AS. Washington, DC: GPO—"Discusses factors involved in the onset, maintenance, and cessation of the cigarette smoking habit" (NIDA). The publication dis-

cusses tobacco use from a psychopharmacologic perspective.

- The Surgeon General's Report—Each year, the Office on Smoking and Health produces a report: *The health consequences of smoking: A report of the Surgeon General,* www.surgeongeneral.gov/library/reports.htm. The content depends on the theme of the report for that year. Topics include the health consequences of smoking for women (1980); health consequences related to changes in cigarette constituents, with emphasis on low-tar, low-nicotine cigarettes (1981); the relationship between cigarette smoking and cancer (1982); and cigarette smoking and cardiovascular disease (1983). The 1980 report is noteworthy for its excellent summary of the etiology, demographics, and descriptive data on smoking in women. It also contains a good review of treatment methods to that time. Sound reviews of treatment outcome can be found in the 1982 and 1983 reports, which are especially good sources for preparing materials on the health consequences of smoking. Topics in recent years include women and smoking (2001), reducing tobacco use (2000), tobacco use among U.S. racial/ethnic minority groups (1998), preventing tobacco use among youth (1994), the health benefits of smoking cessation (1990), and reducing the health consequences of smoking (1989). The Surgeon General's Reports are usually out of print within a year or so of their publication, however, most university libraries should be able to obtain back copies.

Pamphlets

Several government agencies have produced pamphlets that contain information about the effects of smoking and quitting or describe self-management quitting programs. Those published by the ACS, the AHA, and the ALA can be obtained from these organizations' local offices. NIH publications can be ordered from the GPO.

REFERENCES

Bandura, A. (1977). Self-efficacy: Towards a unifying theory of behavioral change. *Psychological Review, 84,* 191–215.

Barber, J. (2001). Freedom from smoking: Integrating hypnotic methods and rapid smoking to facilitate smoking cessation. *International Journal of Clinical and Experimental Hypnosis, 49*(3), 257–266.

Beutler, L. E., & Clarkin, J. F. (1990). *Systematic treatment selection.* New York: Brunner/Mazel.

Bloom, B. L. (1988). Health psychology: A psychosocial perspective. Englewood Cliffs, NJ: Prentice-Hall.

Breslau, N., Johnson, E. L., Hiripi, E., & Kessler, R. (2001). Nicotine dependence in the United States: Prevalence, trends, and smoking persistence. *Archives of General Psychiatry, 58,* 810–816.

Breslau, N., & Peterson, E. L. (1996). Smoking cessation in young adults: Age at initiation of cigarette smoking and other suspected influences. *American Journal of Public Health, 86,* 214–219.

Breslow, L. (1982). Control of cigarette smoking from a public policy perspective. *Annual Review of Public Health, 3,* 129–151.

Brod, M., & Hall, S. M. (1984). Joiners and non-joiners in smoking treatment: A comparison of psychosocial variables. *Addictive Behaviors, 9,* 217–221.

Camp, D. E., Klesges, R. C., & Relyea, G. (1993). The relationship between body weight concerns and adolescent smoking. *Health Psychology, 12,* 34–32.

Caraballo, R. S., Giovino, G. A., & Pechacek, T. F. (2001). Factors associatied with discrepancies between self-reports on cigarette smoking and measured serum cotinine levels among persons aged 17 years or older: Third National Health and Nutrition Examination Survey 1988–1994. *American Journal of Epidemiology, 153*(8), 807–814.

Carlson, J. (1989). Brief therapy for health promotion. *Individual Psychology, 45*(1 & 2), 220–229.

Centers for Disease Control and Prevention (CDC). (1998, April 3). Tobacco use among high school students—United States, 1997. *Morbidity and Mortality Weekly Report, 47*(12), 229–233.

Colby, S. M., Tiffany, S. T., Shiffman, S., & Niaura, R. S. (2000). Are adolescent smokers dependent on nicotine? A review of the evidence. *Drug and Alcohol Dependence, 59* (Suppl. 1), 83–95.

Cooper, T. V. (2002). A placebo-controlled randomized trial of the effects of PPA and nicotine gum on cessation rates and post-cessation weight gain in women. *Dissertation Abstracts International: Section B—The Sciences and Engineering, 63*–5-B.

Crasilneck, H. B. (1990). Hypnotic techniques for smoking control and psychogenic impotence. *American Journal of Clinical Hypnosis, 32,* 147–153.

Crump, R. L., Lillie-Blanton, M., & Anthony, J. C. (1997). The influence of self-esteem on smoking among African-American school children. *Journal of Drug Education, 27,* 277–291.

Danaher, B. G., & Lichtenstein, E. (1978). *Become an ex-smoker.* Engelwood Cliffs, NJ: Prentice-Hall.

Daughton, D. M., Fortmann, S. P., Glover, E. D., Hatsukami, D. K., Heatley, S. A., Lichtenstein, E., et al. (1999). The smoking cessation efficacy of varying doses of nicotine patch delivery systems 4 to 5 years post-quit day. *Preventive Medicine, 28*(2), 113–118.

Davis, J. R., & Glaros, A. G. (1986). Relapse prevention and smoking cessation. *Addictive Behaviors, 11,* 105–114.

Disco, M., Moorman, R., & Noble, S. (2001). Smoking and chewing tobacco cessation. *Drug Topics, 145*(7), 49–56.

Donovan, D. M., & Marlatt, G. A. (1988). *Assessment of addictive behaviors.* New York: Guilford.

Elder J., & Stern, R. (1986). The ABCs of adolescent smoking prevention: An environment and skills model. *Health Education Quarterly, 13*(2), 181–192.

Etter, J-F., Lazlo, E., Zellweger, J-P., Perrot, C., & Perneger, T. V. (2002). Nicotine replacement to reduce cigarette consumption in smokers who are unwilling to quit: A randomized trial. *Journal of Clinical Pharmacology, 22*(5), 487–495.

Festinger, L. (1957). *A theory of cognitive dissonance.* Stanford, CA: Stanford University Press.

Flay, B. R. (1993). Youth tobacco use: Risk patterns and control. In J. Slade & C. T. Orleans (Eds.), *Nicotine* addiction: Principles and management (pp. 653–661). New York: Oxford University Press.

Ginsberg, D., Hall, S. M., & Rosinski, M. (1991). Partner interaction and smoking cessation: A pilot study. Addictive Behaviors, 16(5), 195–202.

Glover, E. D., Glover, P. N., Sullivan, C. R., Cerullo, C. L., & Hobbs, G. (2002). A comparison of sustained-release bupropion and placebo for smokeless tobacco cessation. American Journal of Health Behavior, 26(5), 386–393.

Gottlieb, A. M., Killen, J. D., Marlatt, G. A., & Taylor, C. B. (1987). Psychological and pharmacological influences in cigarette smoking. Journal of Consulting and Clinical Psychology, 55, 606–608.

Gulliver, S. B., Hughes, J. R., Solomon, L. J., & Dey, A. N. (1995). An investigation of self-efficacy, partner support and daily stresses as predictors of relapse to smoking in self-quitters. Addiction, 90(6), 767–772.

Hall, S. M., and Hall, R. G. (1987). Treatment of cigarette smoking. In J. A. Blumenthal & D. C. McKee (Eds.), Applications in behavioral medicine and health psychology. A clinician's sourcebook (pp. 301–323). Sarasota, FL: Professional Resource Exchange.

Hall, S., Humfleet, G. L., Reus, V. I., Munoz, R. F., Ricardo, F., Hartz, D. T., & Maude-Griffin, R. (2002). Psychological intervention and antidepressant treatment in smoking cessation. Archives of General Psychiatry, 59(10), 929–937.

Iverson, D. C. (1987). Smoking control programs: Premises and promises. American Journal of Health Promotion, 1(3), 16–30.

Kann, L., Warren, W., Collins, J. L., Ross, J., Collins, B., & Kolbe, L. J. (1993). Results from the national school-based 1991 Youth Risk Behavior Survey and progress towards achieving health objectives for the nation. Public Health Reports, 106, 47–55.

Kern, R. M. (1986). Lifestyle scale. Coral Springs, FL: CMTI Press.

Larimar, M. E., Palmer, R. S., & Marlatt, G. A. (1999) Relapse prevention: An overview of Marlatt's cognitive-behavioral model. Alcohol Research and Health, 23(2), 151–160.

Lederman, S., & Scheiderman, P. (1986). If you smoke, please try quitting. National City, CA: Learning Process Center, San Diego.

Lichtenstein, E., & Glasgow, R. E. (1992) Smoking cessation: What have we learned over the past decade? Journal of Counseling and Clinical Psychology, 60, 518–527.

Lichtenstein, E., & Mermelstein, R. (1982). Helping your partner quit smoking: A manual for the Oregon Smoking Control Program. Unpublished manu-

script. University of Oregon Psychology Department, Eugene.

Martin, S. & Lambrecht, B. (1998) Trouble on tobacco road. Planning, 64(9), 4–8.

Marlatt, G. A. (1985). Cognitive assessment and intervention procedures for relapse prevention. In G. A. Marlatt & J. R. Gordon (Eds.), Relapse prevention: Maintenance strategies in the treatment of addictive behaviors. New York: Guilford.

Marlatt, G. A., & Gordon J. R. (1980). Determinants of relapse: Implications for the maintenance of behavior change. In P. O. Davidson & S. M. Davidson (Eds.), Behavioral medicine: Changing health lifestyles. New York: Brunner/Mazel.

Marlatt, G. A., & Gordon, J. R. (1985). Relapse prevention: Maintenance strategies in the treatment of addictive behaviors. New York: Guilford.

McGovern, P. (1984). Two statistical analysis procedures applied to multivariate smoking cessation data. Unpublished doctoral dissertation. Iowa State University, Ames.

Mermelstein, R., Cohen, S., Lichtenstein, E., Baer, J. S., & Kamarck, T. (1986). Social support and smoking cessation and maintenance. Journal of Counseling and Clinical Psychology, 54, 447–453.

Miller, W. R., & Heather, N. (1986). Treating addictive behaviors. New York: Guilford.

Ney, T., & Gale, E. (Eds.). (1989). Smoking and human behavior. New York: Wiley.

Park, E., Tudiver, F., Schultz, J. K., & Campbell, T. (2004). Does enhancing partner support and interaction improve smoking cessation? A meta-analysis. Annals of Family Medicine, 2, 170–174.

Perlmutter, J. (1986). Kick it! Stop smoking in five days. Los Angeles: H. P. Books.

Piasecki, T., Niaura, R., Shadel, W., Abrams, D., Goldstein, M., Fiore, M., & Baker, T. (2000). Smoking withdrawal dynamics in unaided quitters. Journal of Abnormal Psychology, 109(1), 74–86.

Pomerleau, O. F., Pomerleau, C. S., & Namenek, R. J. (1998). Early experiences with tobacco among women smokers, ex-smokers, and never-smokers. Addiction, 93(4), 595–599.

Richmond, R. L., Kehoe, L., de Almeida, N., & Cesar, A. (1997). Effectiveness of a 24-hour transdermal nicotine patch in conjunction with a cognitive behavioral program: One year outcome. Addiction, 92(1), 27–31.

Schachter, S. (1978). Pharmacological and psychological determinants of smoking. In R. E. Thornton (Ed.), Smoking behaviour: Physiological and psychological influences. Edinburgh: Churchill Livingstone.

Shiffman, S. (1982). Relapse following smoking cessation: A situational analysis. Journal of Consulting and Clinical Psychology, 50, 71–86.

Shiffman, S. (1985). Behavioral assessment. In G. A. Marlatt & J. R. Gordon (Eds.), *Relapse prevention: Maintenance strategies in the treatment of addictive behaviors.* (pp. 139–187). New York: Guilford.

Shiffman, S., Elash, C. A., Paton, S. M., Gwaltney, C. J., Paty, J. A., Clark, D. B., et al. (2000). Comparative efficacy of 24-hour and 16-hour transdermal nicotine patches for relief of morning craving. *Addiction, 95*(8), 1185–1195.

Shiffman, S., Read, L., Maltese, J., Rapkin, D., & Garvik, M. E. (1985). Preventing relapse in ex-smokers: A self-management approach. In G. A Marlatt & J. R. Gordon (Eds.), *Relapse prevention: Maintenance strategies in the treatment of addictive behaviors* (pp. 472–520). New York: Guilford.

Snyder, J. J. (1989). *Health psychology and behavioral medicine.* Englewood Cliffs, NJ: Prentice-Hall.

Spence, W. R (1987). *The ABCs of smoking.* Waco, TX: Health Edco Inc.

Sperry, L., & Carlson, J. (1990). Hypnosis, tailoring and multimodal treatment. *Individual Psychology, 46*(4), 459–465. (Chapter 5's excerpt copyright © 1990 by The North American Society of Adlerian Psychology and the University of Texas Press.)

Spring, B., Pingitore, R., & McChargue, D. (2003). Reward value of cigarette smoking for comparably heavy smoking in schizophrenic, depressed, and non-patient smokers. *The American Journal of Psychiatry, 160*(2), 316–322.

Stanton, W. R. (1995). DSM-III, tobacco dependence and quitting during late adolescence. *Addictive Behaviors, 20,* 595–603.

Tomkins, S. (1966). Psychological model for smoking behavior. *American Journal of Public Health* (supplement)*, 56,* 17–20.

Weinrich, S., Hardin, S., Valois, R. F., Gleaton, J., Weinrich, M., & Garrison, C. Z. (1996). Psychological correlates of adolescent smoking in response to stress. *American Journal of Health Behavior, 20,* 52–60.

Weiss, R. (1992, April 8). Update on nicotine patches: For some it may help. *New York Times,* p. B9.

West, R., & Shiffman, S. (2001). Effect of oral nicotine dosing forms on cigarette withdrawal symptoms and craving: A systematic review. *Psychopharmacology, 155*(2), 115–122.

APPENDIX

SMOKING-CESSATION PRESCRIPTIONS

1. Physical Dimension (for 2 weeks minimum)

Diet modification:	More sunflower seeds
	More fruits and vegetables
	Less meats, eggs, alcohol
	Less refined-sugar products
	Less stimulant usage
Fluids:	Eight glasses of water or juice each day
Vitamin C (sodium ascorbate):	One 500-mg capsule every 3–4 hrs (i.e., 2,000-mg per day). (*Note:* Do not follow this prescription if you have a problem with sodium intake—for example, cardiovascular disease or edema). An alternative: 100 or 300 mg of Acerola Plus (chewable)
Vitamin B complex:	One high-potency per day
Deep breathing:	Once every hour and as needed
Muscle relaxation:	Once every hour and as needed
Meditative/self-hypnotic exercise:	Once per day and as needed
Walking:	1 to 2 times per day
Vigorous exercise (if medically indicated):	Once per day

2. Behavioral Dimension

- Brush your teeth and use mouthwash at least 3 times per day—after awakening, after every meal, and as the last thing before retiring. Make an appointment to have your teeth cleaned to get rid of any residual tobacco stain and taste.
- Avoid sitting in chairs where you customarily would smoke. Get rid of reminders—ashtrays, lighters, and certainly all cigarettes!
- Change your daily routine, being certain to be busy at those times when you would ordinarily light up. Substitute a healthy activity, such as exercise, relaxation, and so on, for those time periods previously occupied with smoking.
- If necessary, avoid as much as possible the presence of people who smoke, especially those who disapprove of quitting or who are likely to tempt and tease you. Try to increase your time with nonsmokers if possible.
- Increase your daily-activity pattern. Take a lot of walks, showers, go to church, bicycle, pray, swim, make love, play tennis. Engage in activities that keep your hands busy, if necessary.
- Write down at the end of the day (and during the day if you can) about how it was for you today—on your job, at home, at the office or school—and how it was for your

hands, your lungs, and mouth to be breaking the association with cigarettes. Record any "withdrawal side effects" if they occur and how you dealt with them. Watch out for overeating in particular. Record associations that might remind you of smoking.

■ If you feel it would be helpful, set up a program of intermediate rewards (e.g., after 1 week, 3 weeks, 6 weeks, 3 months) and a big reward to be received at the end of 6 months and/or a year.

3. Psychological Dimension

■ Read and reread information about smoking cessation and healthful living daily—at least 15 minutes per day.

■ Estimate the number of cigarettes you have smoked in your life, the amount of money you have spent thus far, and project how many cigarettes you will smoke and how much money you will spend if you live to be 70 years old and continue to smoke at your present rate. Share this information at the next meeting.

■ *Daily* remind yourself of your motives with regard to "giving up" smoking. *Remember, it is your decision.* Take responsibility for yourself! You are not so much quitting but *choosing not to smoke.* Your choice is not out of fear but out of love—love of those who love you and a healthy love of yourself. Your doctor or family is not making you quit. You are the one who has decided not to smoke for your own self-motivated reasons.

■ Also, remember: you are not taking something away from your life (e.g., smoking). Rather, you are *adding something* to your life—a new dimension of self-control. Positive motivation (e.g., an attitude of self-mastery) will be much more effective than negative motivation (e.g., an attitude of self-denial or quitting out of fear of disease).

■ Pick out at least one or two friends or family members whom you feel you can count on to be supportive and encouraging in your decision to quit. Ask them if you can call them if you feel you need support.

■ *Anticipate stress periods* by having stress-reduction strategies ready for implementation at all times. *Do not* undertake any additional stress load during the next few weeks if you don't have to. Do not use stress as an excuse to go back to smoking. That is a game!

■ Remember, each stress period will pass. Wait it out. It will subside. Each time you persist through a stress period, it will leave you stronger so that *you can handle* any future stress periods that may arise. Eventually, stress periods will become farther and farther apart.

■ Focus on the *quality* of your life. Clarify your values and priorities, attitudes, and beliefs. Your decision to not smoke will ideally be made and reinforced in the context of an awareness of self-worth, meaning, and purpose in your life.

■ Choose positive attitudes—not only about freedom from cigarettes but about all aspects of your life. Let yourself experience a sense of vitality and zest in everything you do, think, and say. Do not allow yourself to experience negativity for any prolonged period of time. Generate high amounts of positive energy doing things you enjoy—provided they do not entail any health risk. Increase your enjoyment of life as much as possible. *Your attitude is the most important and the most powerful tool* you have to effectively give up smoking for all time.

CHAPTER SIX

DRUG AND ALCOHOL ABUSE

Reality is a crutch for people who can't cope with drugs.

—Lily Tomlin

Excessive use of alcohol or other drugs can be considered a health-compromising behavior, even when the pattern of use falls short of physical addiction. In today's society, millions of people exhibit problems related to substance use need and deserve assistance, whether or not they are willing to describe themselves as "alcoholics" or "addicts." When a drug or alcohol issue becomes part of the health counseling process, the important questions to be asked involve what effects the substance is having on the person's life and what can be done to resolve the problems at hand. Obviously, answers to the counselor's questions will vary widely from person to person. No two individuals can possibly display the same collection of problems and life experiences, so no two people can possibly have identical treatment needs. The generalized, lock-step treatment programs frequently offered to substance-abusing clients need to be replaced by approaches that focus on individuals' needs and that recognize the degree to which substance abuse is multivariate in nature.

A BIOPSYCHOSOCIAL APPROACH
TO SUBSTANCE ABUSE

A biopsychosocial approach recognizes the complexity of the issue of substance abuse. Each client who develops a problem related to drug or alcohol use does so because of a combination of biological, social, and psychological factors. There is strong evidence that genetic factors may increase an individual's degree of susceptibility to problems with alcohol (Elliott, 2001) and weaker evidence that there is a genetic role in the abuse of other drugs (Committee on Opportunities in Drug Abuse Research, 1996). Evidence also indicates that substance-use behaviors are affected by cultural, environmental, interpersonal, and intrapersonal factors. Consider, for example, the fact that a young person's risk for using or abusing drugs is affected not only by individual factors but also by peer, family, school, community, societal, and cultural domains (Brounstein, Zweig, & Gardner, 1998; Lane et al., 2001). The same variation exists with regard to adult substance use, abuse, and dependence. Clearly, a substance-abuse problem exhibited by any one individual is affected by the interaction among biological, social, and psychological risk factors.

If the etiology of substance-abuse problems is complex and highly individualized, treatment approaches must take this into account. Lewis, Dana, and Blevins (2002) present the following general guidelines for an individualized counseling process:

1. Use a respectful and positive approach with all clients.
2. View substance-abuse problems on a continuum from nonproblematic to problematic use rather than as an either/or situation.
3. Provide treatment that is individualized, both in goals and in methods.
4. Provide multidimensional treatment that focuses on the social and environmental aspects of long-term recovery.
5. Remain open to new methods and goals as up-to-date research findings become available.
6. Use a multicultural perspective to meet the needs of diverse client populations.

The health counseling model suggests that health and illness should be considered along a continuum between optimal health and serious illness. In a similar fashion, substance-abuse problems should also be considered in terms of a continuum rather than in terms of a dichotomous classification. An attempt to make an either/or diagnosis of alcoholism or addiction risks oversimplification and makes appropriate treatment planning difficult.

> Use of a dichotomous diagnosis, whether of alcoholism or drug addiction, actually interferes with treatment planning by masking individual differences. The simplistic approach to assessment also lessens the potential effectiveness of treatment by discouraging early intervention in cases of problematic drinking or drug use. . . . If we wait until people are ready to accept a diagnosis of "alcoholism" or "addiction," we may be missing an opportunity to help them when they are best able to benefit from counseling. (Lewis, Dana, & Blevins, 2002, p. 7)

Unfortunately, many treatment providers still use a dichotomous classification that disguises individual differences and encourages the belief that one course of treatment could be appropriate for the large number of people who share the same diagnosis. This disease-focused approach assumes a commonality that may not in fact exist and that makes early intervention at the level of risk reduction difficult to accomplish.

Traditional treatments were designed for people who were clustered toward the extreme end of the continuum: those with obvious drug or alcohol dependence. With few alternatives available, people with minor or moderate problems have often been left unserved. In contrast, viewing substance-abuse problems along a continuum makes it possible to respond to a specific client's needs at the time of initial contact rather than wait until problems have become sufficiently severe to warrant heroic interventions. Thus, a college student who has been disciplined for marijuana use in the dormitory may need help with decision making or other life skills. An individual who has lost his or her driver's license because of driving under the influence of alcohol may need to learn impulse control, planning processes, or methods for determining one's blood-alcohol level. A person who has used alcohol or other drugs to cope with anxiety may need assistance in developing healthier relaxation techniques. People should be able to receive counseling without having to accept diagnostic labels that might be inappropriate.

Substance abuse is a male-dominated disorder with upwards of 70 to 80 percent of people abusing drugs being male (Kandall, 1998). The skew in distribution has been reflected in limited research on treatment for and outcomes with women (Moras, 1998). In particular, alcohol abuse tends to be more problematic for men than women; in the United States, alcohol use and dependence are 5 times more prevalent in men than in women (American Psychiatric Association, 2000). Men are 3 times more likely than women to die from alcohol-related ailments (Doyle, 1996), and 39 percent of men experience some kind of psychological dependency on alcohol during their lifetime (Lemle & Mishkind, 1989). It appears that heavy alcohol consumption serves as a manifestation of masculine toughness and as a coping strategy that does not violate traditional masculine norms (Copenhaver & Eisler, 1996).

Additionally, patterns of drug use vary between women and men. Women more often use drugs at home or alone and cite emotional or life-event reasons for beginning substance abuse (e.g., depression, feeling unsociable, worry over health, family pressure); however, men are more likely to cite no specific reason for substance-abuse initiation (Griffin et al., 1989). Women in treatment for substance abuse have been reported to have more severe problems at assessment (Lundy et al., 1995) and fewer positive treatment outcomes than men (Arfken, Klein, di Menza, & Schuster, 2001). Treatment setting, however, may influence the treatment retention rate. Wickizer and colleagues (1994) report that men and women are equally likely to complete treatment in outpatient programs, but women were less likely than men to complete treatment in intensive outpatient programs. Research indicates that Whites generally use alcohol and most drugs at higher rates than other cultural groups, whereas studies on adolescents and youth have found that Whites and Native Americans have the highest rates of lifetime and annual prevalence and the highest rates of heavy use of alcohol.

When counselors base their work on the recognition that clients are complex human beings affected by a variety of factors, they are more likely to develop multidimensional treatments tailored to their clients' individual needs. Although the goals of substance-abuse counseling, by definition, should always include the reduction or elimination of drug or alcohol use, the treatment plan also needs to address other areas of life functioning. Depending on the issues that affect an individual client, the general life areas that should be addressed include the following (Lewis, in press):

- Attaining positive and stable family relationships
- Setting and meeting career goals
- Improving social skills
- Improving life-management skills
- Enhancing physical health and fitness
- Adapting more effectively to work or school
- Developing social-support systems
- Increasing involvement in recreation and other social pursuits
- Dealing with mental health concerns such as depression or anxiety

The specific goals of counseling, as well as the methods to use, depend on the client's own strengths, problem areas, and values.

It is becoming increasingly accepted that treatment must be respectful and empowering to the individual (Center for Substance Abuse Treatment, 2000). One way to demonstrate this approach is to include the client actively in his or her treatment planning. This collaborative effort helps to individualize the process and, at the same time, enhances the individual's sense of self-efficacy. Miller and Rollnick (2002) suggest that the traditional confrontation methods used to force problem drinkers to own the label of "alcoholic" and to accept externally imposed treatment may engender a feeling of helplessness that can become self-fulfilling prophecies. In contrast, treating clients as people who are capable of making responsible and independent decisions about their own drinking improves their self-esteem and self-efficacy and makes positive, self-directed change more likely. Once clients have begun the process of behavior change, their self-efficacy is enhanced as they learn to recognize situations that pose risks for problem drinking and as they acquire skills that they can use to cope with these situations. Self-efficacy is improved further and behavior change is maintained as clients achieve success in coping with difficult situations.

Such opportunities for successful coping are obviously more likely to be available for clients who are being seen on an outpatient basis than for clients who are hospitalized. At the same time, outpatient treatment allows clients to maintain social ties and helps them avoid the sense of powerlessness and dependence that often come with hospitalization. Of course, clients with serious medical problems or highly unstable living conditions may need a period of time under the close supervision that a hospital or residential facility can offer. For many clients, however, less disruptive options would be far more appropriate.

The intensity of treatment required by any one client can be determined only through careful assessment. Fortunately, however, many of the treatment methods with the best research support behind them lend themselves well to short-term, outpatient counseling. Among the most promising methods for positive alcohol-related outcomes are social skills training, behavioral self-control training, brief motivational counseling, behavioral marital therapy, the community reinforcement approach, and stress-management training (Holder et al., 1991). Some of the promising methods for drug-abuse treatment, as identified by the National Institute on Drug Abuse (1999), also lend themselves well to outpatient treatment. These methods include cognitive-behavioral relapse-prevention therapy, motivation enhancement therapy, behavioral therapy, multisystemic therapy, the community reinforcement approach, and voucher systems. These treatments should not become the new "standard program" but should, instead, be seen as alternatives among which counselors and clients can choose. This process helps to make substance-abuse treatment responsive to individual differences and to all types of diversity.

Effective treatment can be possible only when counselors and researchers show sensitivity to the individual, social, and cultural differences among substance-abusing clients. Defining assessment as "an ongoing process through which the counselor collaborates with the client and others to gather and interpret information necessary for planning treatment and evaluating client progress," the Addiction Technology Transfer Centers National Curriculum Committee (1999, p. 35) suggests that counselors should be able to "select and use a comprehensive assessment process that is sensitive to age, gender, racial and ethnic cultural issues, and disabilities that includes, but is not limited to:

- History of alcohol and other drug use
- Physical health, mental health, and addiction treatment history
- Family issues
- Work history and career issues
- History of criminality
- Psychological, emotional, and worldview concerns
- Current status of physical health, mental health, and substance use
- Spirituality
- Education and basic life skills
- Socioeconomic characteristics, lifestyle, and current legal status
- Use of community resources

ASSESSMENT

Individualized treatment planning requires that the counselor develop an understanding of his or her client that goes beyond the narrow limits of information about substance-use behavior. A broad-ranging initial interview can address issues concerning the client's history of drug and alcohol use while eliciting data concerning more general life functioning. This general assessment can lay the groundwork for the treatment planning process and help in decision making as instruments for more specific information are selected.

Drug and Alcohol Assessment Instruments

Before developing a treatment plan, the counselor needs to add to the initial interview by assessing the nature and seriousness of the alcohol or drug problem in more depth. A number of easily administered instruments that focus directly on substance-abuse problems are available for use by counselors, including the Comprehensive Drinker Profile and the Addiction Severity Index.

Comprehensive Drinker Profile.   The Comprehensive Drinker Profile (CDP) is one of the most well-researched instruments currently available. The CDP uses a structured interview format that covers a wide range of issues. An unusual aspect of this instrument is that the counselor who uses it as directed can obtain an exceptionally accurate picture of the amount and pattern of the client's alcohol use. The counselor can also learn a great deal about alcohol-related factors such as range of drinking situations, beverage preferences, reasons for drinking, effects of drinking, and perception of alcohol problems. The instrument also yields several quantitative scores, including a score for physiological dependence on alcohol and a score for general alcohol problems. Detailed information about the instrument, including a manual, can be found at the Center for Alcoholism, Substance Abuse, and Addictions Web site: http://casaa.unm.edu.

Addiction Severity Index.   The Addiction Severity Index (ASI) is also based on a structured interview and is used very widely to assess the treatment needs of people dealing with substance-abuse issues. Unlike the Comprehensive Drinker Profile, which focuses primarily on alcohol, the ASI is useful across all types of drugs. The problems that can be assessed through this instrument are organized into seven categories: (1) medical status, (2) employment status, (3) alcohol use, (4) drug use, (5) legal status, (6) family/social relationships, and (7) psychological status. The interview is structured so that each section covers a separate category, except alcohol and drug use are addressed together. For each issue, a clear distinction is made between problems experienced recently and problems experienced at some time in the person's life.

In each category, clients have an opportunity to express the degree to which they see the issue as problematic—not at all, slightly, moderately, considerably, or extremely—for them. Interviewers take these responses into account when they make their own appraisals in each category. For each section of the instrument, the interviewer devises a severity rating that can guide treatment planning. The severity ratings, which are influenced both by the interviewer's assessments and by the client's ratings, are measured on a 9-point scale, from 0 (no treatment necessary for this issue) to 9 (treatment needed to intervene in a life-threatening situation). The ideal outcome with use of this process is the development of a treatment plan that immediately addresses the most severe issues while placing a lower priority on less pressing concerns. A wealth of information regarding the Addiction Severity Index, including the instrument itself, a manual, and a short guide, can be found at the Treatment Research Institute Web site: http://www.tresearch.org.

The Comprehensive Drinker Profile and the Addiction Severity Index are both comprehensive instruments to be administered in the context of the counseling interview. Counselors often make use of very brief, self-administered instruments as well. These instruments can provide an initial indication concerning the degree to which substance abuse might be a problem for an individual. As needed, the counselor can do a follow-up assessment. Among the brief instruments currently available are the following:

- The Michigan Alcoholism Screening Test (MAST) has 24 yes-or-no items that address alcohol use behaviors. People who score more than 20 points (from a possible 53) are identified as exhibiting "severe alcoholism." See the Web site of the National Institute on Alcohol Abuse and Alcoholism for a review and contact information related to this instrument: http://www.niaaa.nih.gov/publications/mast-text.htm.
- The Alcohol Use Disorders Identification Test (AUDIT) is a brief instrument that has only 10 items and is used in medical settings. People who score 8 or above out of a possible 10 points are considered to have alcohol problems that should be addressed. For a review and contact information related to this instrument, see the National Institute on Alcohol Abuse and Alcoholism Web site at: http://www.niaaa.nih.gov/publications/mast-text.htm.
- The Alcohol Use Inventory (AUI) instrument is more extensive than the AUDIT but is also self-administered. Scales are derived for the quantity and frequency of alcohol use, the client's perception of the benefits and negative consequences of drinking, and the client's awareness of the degree to which an alcohol problem exists. This instrument is available from Pearson Assessments at: http://assessments.ncspearson.com/assessments/tests/aui.htm.
- The Drug Abuse Screening Test (DAST), similar to the MAST, has 20 yes-or-no items; the items are not weighted, so 20 is the highest score. This instrument can be seen in its entirety on the Schick Shadel Hospital Web site at: http://www.schick-shadel.com/drug-test.html.

- The Substance Abuse Problem Checklist (Carroll, 1984) instrument lists more than 300 problems in 8 categories: motivation for treatment; health, personality, social relationship, and job-related problems; misuse of leisure time; religious or spiritual problems; and legal problems. This too can be self-administered.

DSM-IV-TR

The *Diagnostic and Statistical Manual of Mental Disorders (DSM-IV-TR)* published by the American Psychiatric Association (2000) provides a significant addition to the assessment process through its diagnostic guidelines for substance-use disorders. The *DSM-IV-TR* is especially helpful because of the distinction it makes between substance use and substance abuse or dependence. Psychoactive substance use is considered a disorder only (1) when the individual demonstrates an inability to control his or her use despite cognitive, behavioral, or physiological symptoms; and (2) when the symptoms have persisted for at least one month or have occurred repeatedly over a longer period of time.

A client is diagnosed as being *dependent* on the substance only if at least three of the following seven symptoms are present (American Psychiatric Association, 2000, p. 197):

1. Substance often taken in large amounts or over a longer period of time than the person intended.
2. Persistent desire or one or more unsuccessful efforts to cut down or control substance use.
3. A great deal of time spent in activities necessary to get the substance (e.g., theft), taking the substance (e.g., chain smoking), or recovering from its effects.
4. Important social, occupational, or recreational activities given up or reduced because of substance use.
5. Continued substance use despite knowledge of having a persistent or recurrent social, psychological, or physical problem that is caused or exacerbated by the use of the substance.
6. Marked tolerance . . . or markedly diminished effect with continued use of the same amount. . . .
7. Characteristic withdrawal symptoms and substance is often taken to relieve or avoid withdrawal symptoms.

If a person does exhibit three or more of the preceding symptoms, he or she receives the substance dependence diagnosis. Even then, however, differences in the severity of the problem should be taken into account. According to the *DSM-IV-TR,* the following severity distinctions can be made (American Psychiatric Association, 2000, pp. 196–197):

- *Mild*—Few, if any, symptoms in excess of those required to make the diagnosis, and the symptoms result in no more than mild impairment in occupational functioning or in usual social activities or relationships with others.
- *Moderate*—Symptoms or functional impairment between "mild" and "severe."
- *Severe*—Many symptoms in excess of those required to make the diagnosis, and the symptoms markedly interfere with occupational functioning or with usual social activities or relationships with others.

- *Early full remission*—For at least 1 month but less than 12 months, no diagnostic criteria have been met.
- *Early partial remission*—For at least 1 month but less than 12 months, some, but not all, diagnostic criteria have been met.
- *Sustained full remission*—No diagnostic criteria met for a year or more.
- *Sustained partial remission*—Full criteria for dependence not met for 1-plus years, but one or more criteria are met.
- *On agonist therapy*—Using a prescribed medication, like Antabuse, to avoid substance use.
- *In a controlled environment*—For instance, a jail or hospital.

The diagnostic category of *substance abuse disorder* is used for a person whose patterns of use are maladaptive but whose use has never met the criteria for substance dependence.

The *DSM-IV-TR* provides diagnostic criteria without necessarily attaching them to a specific instrument. If the assessment process has been carefully implemented, however, the applicability of the criteria to the specific client will be apparent. A combination of interviewing, history-taking, and administration of assessment instruments should provide both a reasonably accurate picture of the degree to which substance use has interfered with the client's life and an overview of the life problems that should be addressed.

Instruments to Assess Cognitive-Behavioral Factors

Once the client has made the decision to take action toward behavioral change, he or she needs to identify the situations and cognitions that affect drug or alcohol use. Toward this end, counselors can use any or all of three very practical assessment instruments— Inventory of Drinking Situations, Situational Confidence Questionnaire, and Cognitive Appraisal Questionnaire.

Inventory of Drinking Situations (IDS).   The IDS is used to identify situations that the individual client associates with heavy drinking. Drinking situations are divided into 8 categories—5 associated with personal states and 3 associated with other people. The 5 types of situations categorized as relating to personal states involve negative emotional states, negative physical states, positive emotional states, testing of personal control, and urges and temptations. The situations associated with other people involve interpersonal conflict, social pressure to drink, and pleasant times with others. The inventory provides a profile that shows the individual client's high- and low-risk situations. The profile then forms the basis for the client's efforts to understand the antecedents of his or her drinking and to develop mechanisms for behavior change. He or she is encouraged to begin by handling easy tasks and to progress gradually to the more difficult situations. A review and contact information regarding this instrument can be found on the National Institute on Alcohol Abuse and Alcoholism Web site at: http://www.niaaa.nih.gov/publications/ids.htm.

Situational Confidence Questionnaire (SCQ).   This instrument is based on self-efficacy theory. Clients are asked to react to drinking situations (the same situations addressed in the Inventory of Drinking Situations). They are asked to imagine themselves in each situation and to indicate their degree of confidence in their ability to handle it without drinking. This instrument, like the IDS, helps in the design of a hierarchy of drinking situations, and clients are encouraged to work gradually toward involvement in situations about which they feel the least confident. For information about this instrument, see the National Institute on Alcohol Abuse and Alcoholism Web site at: http://www.niaaa.nih.gov/publications/scq.htm.

Cognitive Appraisal Questionnaire (CAQ).   The questionnaire helps clients identify cognitive factors that might interfere with their self-efficacy. Based on a structured interview, the CAQ explores what cognitions are working to influence the individual's appraisal of his or her success. Treatment can then be adjusted so that self-efficacy is enhanced. Helen Annis, who developed this questionnaire, as well as the IDS and the SCQ, places great emphasis on the factor of self-efficacy. According to Annis (1986), "unless a client's experience in drinking situations can be arranged so as to foster gains in self-efficacy, it is unlikely that the changes brought about in drinking behavior during treatment will be maintained after discharge" (pp. 417–418).

TREATMENT STRATEGIES

Because self-efficacy is an important component of long-term recovery, treatment strategies for substance abuse should include interventions that enhance the client's self-management abilities and encourage the perception that change is possible. Behavioral self-control training and skill development programs, along with efforts to help social systems become more reinforcing, are among the promising approaches that tend to lead in this direction.

When developing tailored treatment plans, health counselors need to be constantly aware of cultural issues and concerns that may arise both for the client and for the counselor. Counselors must be careful to not be caught in stereotypes, both positive and negative, which exist around substance use. For example, all Native Americans are not noble warriors, nor are they all "drunken Indians" (Thurman et al., 2000). Because of the diversity between and among ethnic populations, it is necessary to develop an understanding of the target group that comprises the general service delivery area. In addition, counselors need to assess how one's contextual identity (e.g., race, ethnicity, gender, sexual orientation) influences one's substance usage.

The etiology of drug and substance abuse varies greatly across individuals, therefore treatment strategies need to be tailored to address the unique risk factors specific to each client. This uniqueness needs to be considered across large groups, such as minorities, that vary in history, acculturation, experiences, socioeconomic status, values, beliefs, and characteristics. At the same time, however, the treatment needs of each individual must be assessed and taken into consideration. There are client-centered approaches to increase cultural responsiveness that a counselor working with substance abuse can adopt (see Finn, 1994, for a more detailed description). For example, a counselor may choose to accommodate the family values of a client who seeks the opinions of certain family members when he or she makes an important decision. In addition, counselors can look to match client characteristics (e.g., eye contact, speech patterns, confrontational style) to ensure that comfort is met in the treatment setting. Above all, however, interventions should accommodate the cultural variables that clients find salient to their identities. To meet this goal, counselors may need to abandon familiar treatment modes based in a counselor's worldview and adopt other ways of interacting and intervening that are congruent with a client's worldview and treatment expectation.

Behavioral Self-Control Training

Behavioral self-control training is an educational intervention designed to teach clients how to initiate and maintain changes in their own behavior. Clients learn to analyze their drinking or drug-use behavior, to monitor their consumption, and to use self-reinforcement and stimulus-control methods to bring use down to desired levels. The training, which can be provided in either individual or group settings, helps clients work toward their self-selected goals.

This behavior change technique can be used by clients who are working toward either an abstinence or a moderation outcome. One of the most important factors affecting success is the appropriateness of the goal for the individual client. Among clients whose drug of choice is alcohol, controlled drinking may be a good option for some. The client for whom a moderation outcome is most realistic is one who is young and healthy, who has not shown symptoms of physical addiction to alcohol, whose problem is of short duration, who has not yet developed a large number of life problems associated with alcohol, and who objects to abstinence. In contrast, people whose problems are chronic and severe, or who have health problems that are exacerbated by drinking, tend to be poor candidates for controlled drinking. The key to setting appropriate goals involves the recognition of what constitutes non-problematic use for a particular client.

Clients who are attempting to make changes in their substance-use behavior need to monitor their use and to identify the most problematic situations for them. Instruments, such as the Inventory of Drinking Situations, can help in this process, but high-risk situations can also be recognized through clients' day-to-day monitoring of their experiences and recollections of past challenges. When clients are asked to specify incidents of problematic drinking or drug use, whether in the past or in their current lives, they can begin to recognize the cues that tend to trigger problems for them. Situations can vary widely from client to client and may be associated with positive or negative affect, with positive or negative social situations, or with specific times or places.

Once clients have identified the situations that pose risks for them, they need to learn coping strategies. At the most basic level, clients can learn how to anticipate and plan for challenging situations. Clients can choose to avoid certain situations until they have successfully met less difficult challenges, thus, working their way up a hierarchy of situations from those perceived as only moderately difficult to those seen as more formidable. Clients can anticipate situations that are likely to occur in the following week—a party, a wedding, an invitation to drink with colleagues after work on Friday—and plan strategies that may involve either avoidance or active coping.

The active coping strategies that can be used by clients vary according to the individual. Cognitive coping methods involve self-statements that clients can use to remind themselves of their commitment or to reappraise the situation. Behavioral methods can include alternative behaviors or the application of coping skills such as assertion or relaxation. An important component of behavioral self-control training is helping clients increase the repertoire of coping skills available to them, using methods such as instruction, modeling, behavioral rehearsal, and homework assignments. Counselors also need to recognize that clients differ widely in terms of coping styles. Each client's coping skills and deficits should be carefully assessed, with attention being paid to his or her recollection of which strategies have worked most effectively in the past.

Clients' new coping behaviors can be enhanced through self-reinforcement strategies. Clients can control these contingencies both by trying to eliminate environmental cues (e.g., avoiding parties where drugs are likely to be in use) and by arranging their own rewards for positive performance (e.g., purchasing new clothes with the money saved by not buying drugs or alcohol). Positive reinforcement for successful performance should be part of all clients' self-management strategy.

In addition to helping clients cope with high-risk situations, behavioral self-control training should also include attention to the kinds of behaviors directly associated with non-problematic use. If the drug being used is alcohol, clients can learn how to limit their consumption by mixing and diluting their drinks, learning to sip slowly, spacing drinks either by keeping track of the time between them or by alternating with nonalcoholic beverages, consuming food along with alcoholic beverages, and making purposeful attempts to engage in alternative activities. Use of such moderation strategies, which are based on information about nonproblematic, social use of alcohol, are obviously less applicable to other drugs; however, all of the other aspects of behavioral self-control training—functional analyses of substance-use behavior, identification of high-risk situations, and development and reinforcement of appropriate coping behaviors—clearly apply to the whole gamut of substance-abuse problems. For detailed information on behavioral approaches for treating substance abuse, including behavioral self-control training, see the Web site of Reid Hester and his colleagues at: www.behaviortherapy.com.

Skill Development Programs

Self-management and long-term recovery can also be enhanced through training in a number of intrapersonal and social skills. The focus of such skill training depends, of course, on the individual client's needs.

Some clients can benefit by attention to stress management, especially training in relaxation methods. Many substance-abusing clients have learned to use drugs as their only response to stress or anxiety. Their years of drug or alcohol use have masked anxiety, making it unlikely that they have learned to deal effectively with physiological responses to stress. Their efforts to maintain behavior changes are likely to be jeopardized if they become overwhelmed by stressful situations or internal states of anxiety. Relaxation training can be helpful, as long as it is joined by efforts to help clients deal directly with stressful life situations. Clients can gain control over their physical tension through mechanisms such as progressive muscle relaxation, biofeedback, or meditation. If relaxation methods are in clients' skill repertoires, anxiety is less likely to precipitate impulsive drug or alcohol use.

Many clients also need social-skills training, especially in the area of assertiveness. One frequent concomitant of drug or alcohol problems is social pressure to use. Although they may be highly motivated to remain abstinent, clients frequently find themselves engaging in unwanted behaviors because of deficits in assertion. Nonassertive clients also may have general feelings of self-pity, despair, and low self-esteem—all strongly associated with substance abuse. If clients have problems in any of these areas, they can learn to make assertive statements that protect their own decision-making rights and self-esteem. Short-term assertiveness training based on coaching, modeling, behavior rehearsal, and feedback can have an impact on the client's recovery that very much outweighs its costs.

Another skill that has special relevance for substance-abusing clients is problem solving. Clients frequently report a history of having avoided problems by escaping into intoxication. Thus, they should learn the kind of general problem-solving skills needed to function effectively. Training in this area can also help clients solve problems associated more directly with drug or alcohol use. For example, clients may need to learn how to avoid getting into situations that involve drinking and driving or how to plan ahead for dealing with the absence of nonalcoholic drinks at a party. Clients can work on problem-solving strategies in either individual or group counseling settings, developing and judging alternative solutions to a broad range of real and hypothetical problem situations.

Enhancing the Responsiveness of Social Systems

The individual client's recovery depends not just on his or her internal changes but also on the degree to which new behaviors are reinforced in the environment. It is difficult for a person who has used alcohol or other drugs extensively to gain social support for his or her attempts at abstinence. Many drug abusers have become increasingly isolated from mainstream society over their years of drug use, and clients' only associates may be other users. Their best hope for recovery may lie in an attempt to restructure the social systems that affect them.

Community Reinforcement Program.   The Community Reinforcement Program (Meyers & Smith, 1995) prepares clients to face the posttreatment realities of the community environment. This program includes the following components:

- Job counseling
- Couples counseling
- Resocialization and recreation
- Problem-prevention rehearsal
- Early warning system, including a daily "happiness scale"
- Supportive group sessions
- "Buddy" procedures that involve recovering peer advisers
- Written contracts focused on counselor and client responsibilities

One of the things that makes the Community Reinforcement Program effective has always been its emphasis on the individual's reentry into the community. Clients are prepared to cope with the demands of the environment; at the same time, the program tries to make the community itself more reinforcing to clients' recovery through family counseling, group situations, social and recreational activities, and the buddy procedure.

This reinforcement approach was originally designed for inpatient male alcoholics in a state hospital, but such efforts may be even more effective for clients whose health allows them to be treated on an outpatient basis from the beginning. It is unreasonable to expect that clients can be so changed as a result of treatment that they will be able to withstand whatever social pressures are imposed on them. The social systems that affect clients the most must be changed if recovery is to be permanent. Of all of these social systems, the family is probably the most important.

Family Counseling.   If one family member has a substance-abuse-related problem, the entire family is affected to the degree that the problem may become the system's primary organizing factor. In many cases, the family's interactions are built around the substance use, so predictable patterns develop. The drinking or drug-use behavior of one member and the responses of others can allow the family to maintain an unhealthy equilibrium and to avoid change. Because family members play their part in this ongoing pattern of behavior, the substance abuse may not only be allowed to continue but actually may be encouraged.

If family members choose to remove themselves from the established pattern of interaction—if they fail to play their customary roles—the system can be transformed. Individual recovery in fact may depend to a large part on whether such a transformation takes place. Family-counseling interventions should aim toward the long-range goal of systemic change; however, such changes need to take place slowly, through a step-by-step process. The following are the three general stages of change, according to Lewis, Dana, and Blevins (2002):

- *Stage 1*—Interrupting ongoing patterns
- *Stage 2*—Facing the reality of change
- *Stage 3*—Deepening and maintaining change

In the first stage of counseling a substance-abuse-affected family, the counselor's focus should be placed on helping its members interrupt the patterns that have helped maintain the problem. In some cases, change may involve confronting the substance-abusing client and pressing him or her into treatment. If this option is unworkable in a particular situation, family members can interrupt ongoing patterns by disengaging, by withdrawing from the performance of roles that have enabled the substance abuser to avoid negative consequences, and by taking better care of themselves. The purpose of this strategy is not to stop the individual's drinking or drug use but to help the family move away from focusing solely on alcohol or drug abuse, thus achieving an improved level of health.

When an alcohol- or drug-abuser does achieve abstinence, the family is frequently thrown into crisis. Facing the reality of change (Stage 2) involves developing new transactional patterns that are more adaptive to a new reality. It also means recognizing the limitations of change. Family members may be disappointed when they realize that not all of their problems magically disappear with the onset of abstinence. They may be fearful concerning the possibility of relapse or angry about years of abuse-related issues. Expectations may conflict if the former substance abuser expects to regain the power and trust that had been relinquished in the past and if other family members are unable to make sudden changes in their roles and responsibilities. Bepko and Krestan (1985) suggest that the most appropriate goals to help families weather this crisis include keeping the system calm, helping individual family members focus on their own issues, anticipating extreme reactions, addressing concerns about relapse, and teaching new skills that can be used to cope with stress. At this point, structural changes need to be limited to minor adaptations for the purpose of ensuring adequate parenting.

Once these basic steps have been taken and individual members feel that their needs are being addressed, the family as a whole can learn to reframe issues in systems terms. At Stage 3, the counselor can help the family develop deep structural changes that can make the system as a whole more functional for each of its members. The family unit—not just the identified substance-abusing client—is seen as the appropriate target of intervention.

Moore (1992) supports the use of family counseling for substance abuse with African American clients. She noted that one cause for resistance during treatment may be familial. In the families' attempt to protect members from treatment programs under the jurisdiction of Whites, Black parents sometimes participate in the maintenance of the problem. Family counseling is also consistent with the Native American community in that many people are associated with active tribal systems. The use of the extended family in the counseling process can be paramount to treatment success (Choney, Berryhill-Paapke, & Robbins, 1995). For some Asian groups, however, family counseling may not be the best therapeutic strategy due to the cultural norm of not discussing shameful personal experiences in front of strangers, especially if the situation would cast family members in an unfavorable light (Sue & Sue, 2002).

Participation in Self-Help Organizations. "In self-help organizations, people with common bonds can connect with and mutually support one another, request or offer active assistance, and deal with common problems in an understanding but realistic group setting" (Lewis et al., 2003, p. 220). For people with substance-abuse problems, participation in such groups offers a dual reward: (1) the chance to enter a helpful, supportive social system and (2) the chance to help others. If people can enter such equal partnerships, they have the advantage of being useful and valuable to others. This sense of accomplishment can enhance self-efficacy in a way that playing the role of patient or client cannot.

For many years, the fellowship of Alcoholics Anonymous (AA) has provided the kind of social support that enhances the recovery process. More recently, the basic AA model has been adapted to the needs of people who are dealing with related issues. Organizations such as Al-Anon, Alateen, and Families Anonymous give the family members of alcoholics or addicts a chance to help themselves and one another. Narcotics Anonymous, Cocaine Anonymous, and numerous other groups help people maintain abstinence from mood-altering substances. Although the self-help phenomenon should not be considered a form of "treatment," these groups can play a vital role in supporting individuals' long-term recovery.

RELAPSE PREVENTION

Because relapse rates for substance-abusing clients have always been high (Miller et al., 1998), substance-abuse treatment providers have begun to integrate relapse-prevention training into the treatment process for each client as quickly as possible. As clients begin, early in treatment, to identify high-risk situations and to develop methods for coping with them, they are in effect initiating their relapse-prevention efforts.

The Transtheoretical Stages of Change Model provides a good context for examining relapse (Prochaska, Norcross, & DiClemente, 1994). According to this model, people tend to go through stages as they change problematic behaviors. The stages of change include the following:

- *Precontemplation*—People do not intend to change their behaviors in the foreseeable future.
- *Contemplation*—People are aware of the problem and are considering working on it but have not yet made a commitment for action.
- *Preparation*—People plan to take some action within the next month.
- *Action*—People demonstrate their commitment by undertaking changes in the problematic behavior.
- *Maintenance*—People try to consolidate their gains and prevent a return to the problematic behavior.

What is usually called "relapse prevention" is in fact the work of the maintenance stage. For detailed information about this model, as well as instruments being developed for assessing clients' progression through the stages, see the official Web site of the University of Rhode Island center, where Prochaska and his colleagues developed the model, at: http://www. uri.edu/research/cprc/transtheoretical.htm.

The work of Marlatt and Gordon (1985) has been the source of cognitive-behavioral relapse-prevention strategies over the last two decades. Their model is, in effect, a strategy of preparedness based on the notion that clients can develop effective coping responses and plan in advance for their implementation. Each time clients are successful in coping with a high-risk situation, their self-efficacy is enhanced and the likelihood that positive behaviors will be maintained is increased.

Relapse-prevention efforts also address the question of how clients can deal with the times when their coping efforts do not succeed. It is possible for a minor slip to evolve into a full-scale relapse if clients believe that they have failed in their efforts or believe that they have lost control. Clients who believe that abstinence must be total and absolute may experience the abstinence-violation effect following initial use of the substance. The slip is interpreted as a loss of control, and their interpretation may become a self-fulfilling prophecy. The relapse-prevention model encourages clients to think differently about the process, "to realize that lapses are not irreversible, but that instead they can be the occasion for growth, understanding, and learning—a prolapse rather than a relapse" (Curry & Marlatt, 1987, p. 133). Even at this point, preparedness is the key, with each client being armed with concrete plans for coping with substance use.

Case Example

Mary Smith presented herself as a self-referral to a mental health center counselor specializing in substance-abuse issues. In her mid-thirties, married, childless, and employed in a high-powered corporate job, Mary was uncertain whether she had a problem at all. Her husband had been complaining about her drinking, but she felt that this was simply his way of blaming everything that went wrong on this one issue. The incident that made her decide to

seek an assessment involved a friend, Jane, who refused to ride with her to a company pic-
nic because of her fear that Mary would drink too much. Mary drove on her own and was
stopped by a police officer on the way home. She was not charged with driving under the
influence, but the incident frightened her.

Mary agreed to participate in an assessment process and was given the Comprehensive Drinker Profile. The results showed that, in an average week, she consumed between
50 and 60 drinks, well over the norm. The fact that she seldom felt intoxicated indicated a
high tolerance level. The CDP also showed that Mary scored in the significant-problem
range on the measure of general alcohol problems. On the measure of physical dependence
on alcohol, she showed definite and significant symptoms of dependence. Mary believed
that her father, who died young, might have been an alcoholic.

Mary was surprised at the level of her problem, as indicated by the counselor's interpretation of the assessment results. She decided to attempt to make some changes in her
drinking behavior. Because she showed some signs of physical addiction to alcohol and
because of the possibility that alcoholism might be present in her family, the counselor
encouraged her to consider a goal of abstinence, at least for a few months. It was agreed
that, after this period of time, she could reconsider her goal and decide whether to maintain
abstinence or attempt moderate drinking.

Behavioral self-control training was used to help Mary make immediate changes in
her drinking behavior. Among the situations that she found difficult were work-related
drinking occasions and evenings when she arrived home exhausted from a stressful work-
day. She was especially concerned about the work situation, stating that there was very real
pressure to drink with customers and that, as a woman, it was hard enough for her to be
accepted without also going against the social norm. At the same time, she knew that too
much drinking could jeopardize her career. Her workplace was, in a sense, giving her mixed
messages.

Mary worked with the counselor to make some lifestyle changes that were very helpful to her. In job-related drinking situations, she decided to substitute soft drinks for alcohol, and she practiced ways to assert herself so that alternative beverages could be
substituted without calling undue attention to herself. Her friend and colleague, Jane, provided support for Mary's efforts. Mary and Jane decided to join a health club and got into
the habit of working out several evenings a week after work. This practice helped Mary
arrive home refreshed rather than exhausted. Mary's husband agreed to participate in marriage counseling sessions, which helped him become more supportive of her abstinence
efforts.

Mary used several methods to cope with cravings for alcohol. She wrote down her
reasons for making the commitment to address her drinking problems and carried the card
with her as a reminder in difficult situations. She had several sessions of relaxation training
that, in combination with her exercise regiment, helped her cope more effectively with
work-related stressors. She set up a reinforcement schedule, rewarding herself with a small
luxury item after each week of abstinence.

Mary was strongly encouraged to make her own decisions concerning the goals and
methods of the counseling process. It is likely that, if she had been confronted actively and
pushed to admit to an "alcoholic" label, she might have denied the problem, citing her
effectiveness in her work situation and her general good health. The counseling process

helped Mary gain a better balance in her life between work and pleasure, independence and social connectedness. These changes supported her successful efforts at changing her drinking behavior.

■ ■ ■ ■ ■

PREVENTIVE MEASURES

Substance-abuse prevention involves an effort to help people avoid health-jeopardizing behaviors such as overuse of alcohol or other drugs. The only way behavior changes can occur, however, is when individual knowledge and skill are combined with an environment that supports healthful behaviors. Programs aimed toward prevention must be comprehensive efforts that include skill development, self-efficacy enhancement, and social change, along with the provision of information.

The Office of National Drug Control Policy (2003), in reviewing prevention strategies, emphasizes the fact that services should focus both on reducing risk factors and on building protective factors. Strategies that meet these criteria can be directed at any segment of the population. Among the specific strategies recommended are the following:

- *Alternatives*—Provide constructive and healthy activities to meet needs that might otherwise be addressed by use of alcohol and other drugs (e.g., drug-free dances, youth–adult leadership groups, community drop-in centers, and community service activities).
- *Community-based process*—Enhance the ability of the community to prevent substance abuse through activities such as community and volunteer training, systematic planning, multiagency coordination, funding social programs, and community team building.
- *Early intervention*—At the early stages, intervene in problematic drug use through education, intervention, and referral.
- *Education*—Build life and social skills through interventions such as parenting and family management classes, peer leader/helper programs, education programs for youth groups, and groups for children of substance abusers.
- *Environmental activities*—Change community standards, codes, and attitudes regarding drug use (e.g., promoting review of school drug policies, maximizing local enforcement procedures regarding the availability of drugs, modifying advertising practices, and implementing pricing strategies).
- *Information*—Provide knowledge about the nature and extent of drug abuse and the effects of this problem on individuals, families, and communities. Services might include information resource centers and directories, media campaigns, brochures, public service announcements, and health fairs.
- *Problem identification and referral*—Identify problems early through mechanisms such as employee assistance programs, student assistance programs, and programs for people involved in driving under the influence of alcohol or drugs.

If everyone thinks of substance-abuse problems on a continuum, there is no possibility of a clear dichotomy between the methods that can be used for prevention and the techniques that can be used for treatment. Whether the program being implemented is a primary prevention effort in a school or a treatment program for severely addicted individuals, interventions need to teach self-management skills, enhance self-efficacy, and build strong social-support networks.

CONCLUDING NOTE

A biopsychosocial approach to substance abuse is built on the recognition that each client who develops a problem with alcohol or another drug does so because of a complex and highly individualized combination of factors. Substance-abuse counselors can adapt their practices to this conceptualization by using at least the following six general guidelines: (1) use a respectful, positive approach with all clients; (2) view substance-abuse problems on a continuum rather than as an either/or situation; (3) provide treatment that is individualized, both in goals and in methods; (4) provide multidimensional treatment that focuses on the social and environmental aspects of long-term recovery; (5) remain open to new methods and goals as research findings become available; and (6) use a multicultural perspective to meet the needs of diverse client populations.

Such individualized treatment depends on careful assessment linked to comprehensive treatment plans. Treatment strategies should be based on the kinds of interventions that are the most likely to enhance clients' self-management skills and self-efficacy. Interventions should include behavioral self-control training and skill development programs. Strategies should also help make social systems more conducive to clients' recovery. Examples of efforts to enhance the responsiveness of social systems include community reinforcement programs, family counseling, and referrals to self-help organizations.

RESOURCES

Treatment Methods

- Reid Hester and his colleagues' Web site provides information on
  –behavioral approaches for treating substance abuse, including motivational interventions and behavioral self-control training—www.behaviortherapy.com
  –the Drinker's Checkup—http://www.drinkerscheckup.com/index.htm
- For information on motivational interviewing, see http://www.motivationalinterview.org

- Specific approaches to treatment for cocaine addiction can be found in online manuals—http://www.drugabuse.gov/TXManuals
- Empirically-supported treatments for drug addiction are reviewed in *Principles of drug addiction treatment: A research-based guide* on the NIDA Web site—http://www.drugabuse.gov/PODAT/PODATIndex.html

Governmental Organizations

- Substance Abuse and Mental Health Services Administration (SAMHSA)—http://www.samhsa.gov/

- National Institute on Alcohol Abuse and Alcoholism—http://www.niaaa.nih.gov

- National Institute on Drug Abuse—http:// www.nida.nih.gov
- National Clearinghouse for Alcohol Information—http://www.niaaa.nih.gov/other/NCADI-text.htm

- National Office of Drug Policy—http://www. whitehousedrugpolicy.gov/prevent/strategies. html

Self-Help Organizations

- Alcoholics Anonymous—www.alcoholics-anonymous.org
- Narcotics Anonymous—www.na.org

- Smart Recovery—www.smartrecovery.org
- Women for Sobriety—www.womenforsobriety. org/body.html

REFERENCES

Addiction Technology Transfer Centers National Curriculum Committee. (1999). *Addiction counseling competencies: The knowledge, skills, and attitudes of professional practice.* Rockville, MD: U.S. Department of Health and Human Services.

American Psychiatric Association (2000). *Diagnostic and statistical manual of mental disorders* (4th ed.). Washington, DC: Author.

Annis, H. M. (1986). A relapse prevention model for treatment of alcoholics. In W. R. Miller & N. Heather (Eds.), *Treating addictive behaviors: Processes of change* (pp. 407–434). New York: Plenum.

Arfken, C. L., Klein, C., di Menza, S., & Schuster, C. R. (2001). Gender differences in problem severity at assessment and treatment retention. *Journal of Substance Abuse Treatment, 20,* 53–57.

Bepko, C., & Krestan, J. A. (1985). *The responsibility trap: A blueprint for treating the alcoholic family.* New York: Free Press.

Brounstein, P. J., Zweig, J. M., & Gardner, S. E. (1998). *Science-based practices in substance abuse prevention: A guide.* Rockville, MD: Center for Substance Abuse Prevention.

Carroll, J. F. X. (1984). Substance Abuse Problem Checklist: A new clinical aid for drug and/or alcohol treatment dependency. *Journal of Substance Abuse Treatment, 1,* 31–36.

Center for Substance Abuse Treatment. (2000). *Changing the conversation: Improving substance abuse treatment—The national treatment plan initiative, Vol. I.* Rockville, MD: U.S. Department of Health and Human Services.

Choney, S. K., Berryhill-Paapke, E., & Robbins, R. R. (1995). The acculturation of American Indians: Developing frameworks for research and practice. In J. G. Ponterotto, J. M. Casas, L. M. Suzuki, &

C. M. Alexander (Eds.), *Handbook of multicultural counseling* (pp. 73–92). Thousand Oaks, CA: Sage.

Committee on Opportunities in Drug Abuse Research, Division of Neuroscience and Behavioral Health, Institute of Medicine. (1996). *Fetal alcohol syndrome: Diagnosis, epidemiology, prevention, and treatment.* Washington, DC: National Academy Press.

Copenhaver, M. M., & Eisler, R. M. (1996). Masculine gender role stress: A perspective on men's health. In P. M. Kato & T. Mann (Eds.), *Handbook of diversity issues in health psychology* (pp. 219–236). New York: Plenum.

Curry, S. G., & Marlatt, G. A. (1987). Building self-confidence, self-efficacy and self-control. In W. M. Cox (Ed.). *Treatment and prevention of alcohol problems: A resource manual* (pp. 117–136). New York: Academic.

Doyle, J. A. (1996). *The male experience* (3rd ed.). Madison, WI: Brown & Benchmark.

Elliott, V. S. (2001). Addictive cocktail: Alcoholism and genetics. Amednews.com (the newspaper for America's physicians. http://www.ama-assn.org/sci-pubs/amnews/pick_01/hlsa0205.htm.

Finn, P. (1994). Addressing the needs of cultural minorities in drug treatment. *Journal of Substance Abuse Treatment, 11,* 425–437.

Griffin, M. L., Weiss, R. D., Mirin, S. M., & Lange, U. (1989). A comparison of male and female cocaine abusers. *Archives of General Psychiatry, 46,* 122–126.

Holder, H., Longabough, R., Miller, W. R., & Rubonis, A. V. (1991). The cost-effectiveness of treatment for alcoholism: A first approximation. *Journal of Studies on Alcohol, 52,* 517–540.

Kandall, S. R. (1998). Women and addiction in the United States, 1920 to the present. In C. L. Worthington & A. B. Roman (Eds.), *Drug addiction research and the health of women* (pp. 53–80). Rockville, MD: National Institute on Drug Abuse.

Lane, J., Gerstein, D., Huang, L., & Wright, D. (2001). *Risk and protective factors for adolescent drug use.* Rockville, MD: SAMHSA/DHHS.

Lemle, E., & Mishkind, M. E. (1989). Alcohol and masculinity. *Journal of Substance Abuse Treatment, 6,* 213–222.

Lewis, J. A. (in press). Assessment, diagnosis, and treatment planning. In R. H. Coombs (Eds.). *Addiction counseling review.* Boston: Lahaska Press/Lawrence Earlbaum.

Lewis, J. A., Dana, R. Q., & Blevins, G. A. (2002). *Substance abuse counseling.* Pacific Grove, CA: Brooks/Cole.

Lewis, J. A., Lewis, M. D., Daniels, J., & D'Andrea, M. (2003). *Community counseling: Empowerment strategies for a diverse society.* Pacific Grove, CA: Brooks/Cole.

Lundy, A., Gottheil, E., Serota, R. D., Weinstein, S. P., & Sterling, R. C. (1995). Gender differences and similarities in African-American crack cocaine abusers. *Journal of Nervous and Mental Disease, 183,* 260–266.

Marlatt, G. A., & Gordon, J. R. (1985). *Relapse prevention: Maintenance strategies in the treatment of addictive behaviors.* New York: Guilford.

Meyers, R. J., & Smith, J. E. (1995). *Clinical guide to alcohol treatment: The community reinforcement approach.* New York: Guilford.

Miller, W. R., Andrews, N. R., Wilbourne, P., & Bennett, M. E. (1998). A wealth of alternatives: Effective treatments for alcohol problems. In W. Miller & N. Heather (Eds.), *Treating addictive behaviors* (2nd ed.; pp. 203–216). New York: Plenum Press.

Miller, W. R., & Rollnick, S. (Eds.) (2002). *Motivational interviewing: Preparing people to change addictive behavior* (2nd ed.). New York: Guilford.

Moore, S. E. (1992). Cultural sensitivity treatment and research issues with Black adolescent drug users. *Child and Adolescent Social Work Journal, 9,* 249–260.

Moras, K. (1998). Behavioral therapies for female drug users: An efficacy-focused review. In C. L. Worthington & A. B. Roman (Eds.), *Drug addiction research and the health of women* (pp. 197–222). Rockville, MD: National Institute on Drug Abuse.

National Institute on Drug Abuse. (1999). *Principles of drug treatment: A research based guide.* Bethesda, MD: National Institutes of Health.

Office of National Drug Control Policy (2003). Prevention strategies. Retrieved April 2003, from http://www.whitehousedrugpolicy.gov/prevent/strategies.html.

Prochaska, J. O., Norcross, J. C., & DiClemente, C. C. (1994). *Changing for good: A revolutionary six-stage program for overcoming bad habits and moving your life positively forward.* New York: Avon Books.

Sue, D. W, & Sue, D. (2002). *Counseling the culturally different* (4th ed.) New York: Wiley.

Thurman, P. J., Plested, B., Edwards, R. W., Chen, J., & Swain, R. (2000). Intervention and treatment with ethnic minority substance abusers. In J. F. Aponte & J. Wohl (Eds.), *Psychological intervention and cultural diversity* (pp. 214–233). Boston: Allyn & Bacon.

Wickizer, T., Maynard, C., Atherly, A., Fredrick, M., Koepsell, T., Krupski, A., & Stark, K. (1994). Completion rates of clients discharged from drug and alcohol treatment programs in Washington State. *American Journal of Public Health, 84,* 215–221.

CHAPTER SEVEN

EXERCISE

The labor of the human body is rapidly being engineered out of working life.
—John F. Kennedy

The nature of human activity has radically changed since the Industrial Revolution. Most people do not have to chop wood, plow fields, or carry water; instead they are required to sit at a desk or in a vehicle for long hours or to stand on the assembly line or behind a store counter. With few exceptions, life today calls on us to physically move very little. Cars, buses, planes, trains, and computers seem to do all the work.

Despite a marked growth of interest in physical fitness and exercise in the United States over the past 25 years, the contemporary lifestyle of most people is still sedentary. Low levels of physical activity continue to be a major public health concern for almost all population groups of developed counties (Dubbert, 2002). Recent data consistently estimate that only about one third of the population exercises regularly, and most of these people do not exercise in such a way as to achieve maximum benefits. Even though physical fitness has become a significant public health intervention area as well as an economic industry (e.g., fitness apparel, exercise videos, health clubs, magazines and books, etc.), the number of active exercisers represents a minority of the population.

The cardiovascular system, muscles, ligaments, tendons, and bones are meant to be used. Throughout most of human history, people weren't really aware of that fact, but they used their bodies anyway. Today, regular participation in physical activity is frequently cited by the general public as an important habit in maintaining good health, but relatively few people do it. Interestingly enough, success seems to be measured by lack of physical exertion. Pushing paper affords a person more status than hammering a nail into a board. Machines are designed with an eye toward lessening or altogether alleviating manual effort. As more and more goods and services are readily available without the need for physical activity, people experience a loss in the capacity to physically perform. A clear case of the proverbial axiom "use it or lose it" seems to be occurring. Unfortunately, it appears that more people are losing the capacity to use their bodies to the fullest potential.

Science and the general public seem to accept the notion that physically active people of all ages generally tend to be healthier than their sedentary counterparts. The health benefits attributed to regular physical activity are diverse and include the enhancement of both physical, psychological, and social functions. Research during the 1990s on the association of physical activity and health outcomes underscored the health risks faced by a society that has been successful in engineering the necessity for physical activity out of most people's daily lives.

The 1996 U.S. Surgeon General's *Report on Physical Activity and Health* (USDHHS, 1996) included an extensive review of the effects of physical activity and exercise on health. This review noted that taking into account all different causes of death, moderate to high physical fitness was associated with lower mortality than was low fitness. Higher levels of activity and fitness have a protective effect on older as well as younger populations; and in longitudinal studies, people who became more fit over time reduced their risks in comparison with those who remained at low levels of fitness. This review also noted the positive influence of an increase in physical activity on the primary or secondary prevention of specific diseases such as cardiovascular disease, coronary heart disease, non-insulin-dependent diabetes, and different forms of cancer.

The health benefits of physical activity and exercise have also been linked to less perceived stress (Stetson et al., 1997), lower anxiety, depression (Salmon, 2000), and improvements in cognitive functioning (Emery et al., 1998; Kramer et al., 1999). On the other hand, a growing amount of research has established physical inactivity as an important risk factor for a range of diseases and deleterious physical conditions, such as coronary heart disease, stroke, some forms of cancer, non-insulin-dependent diabetes mellitus, osteoporosis, obesity, as well as a range of negative psychological outcomes (Bouchard, Shepard, & Stephens, 1994).

Although the health benefits of engaging in physical activity and exercise have been well established, 75 percent of U.S. adults are inactive or insufficiently active (CDC, 2001). Analyses of adults' physical activity survey data have provided a detailed picture of who is active at different intensities and in different settings. The proportion of the population over the age of 18 who reported engaging in light-to-moderate physical activity at least 5 days per week has remained at about 25 percent since 1990, and the prevalence of those reporting insufficient activity was about 45 percent (CDC, 2001). Fewer still, only 16 percent to 17 percent, reported engaging in vigorous physical activity. About 25 percent of all adults reported *no* leisure-time physical activity.

The documentation of the mental and physical benefits of a regular program of exercise shows the difficulties in establishing and maintaining such programs (Dubbert, 2002). To receive the benefits, exercise must be done properly and on a regular basis. Yet, according to Dishman (1988), of those individuals who initiate an exercise program, approximately 50 percent drop out within 3 to 6 months. Further, half of those enrolled in some of the best equipped and staffed programs drop out within the first few months, and the majority of participants cease to exercise within 1 to 2 years. The picture is probably much worse for those who undertake fitness programs on their own.

Significant differences by ethnic and age groups and between men and women (Bolen et al., 2000; National Center for Health Statistics, 1999) may provide clues to variables that control level of participation. Most studies confirm that there are substantial age and gender variations in participation in exercise. During adolescence, there is a steady decline in physical activity. Surveys in North America estimated that while 70 percent of 12-year-olds participate in physical activity, this declines to 42 percent of men and 30 percent of women by age 21 (NIH Consensus Development Panel, 1996). People 50 years of age and older are the most sedentary population group, and by age 75, one in three men and one in two women engage in no regular physical activity (USDHHS, 2000).

The relationship between cultural factors (e.g., race, ethnicity, gender, social class, education level, and age) and participation in exercise is multifaceted with few clear patterns. It has been observed for many years that leisure-time physical activity is most prevalent among younger, male, better educated, White adults with higher incomes (USDHHS, 1996). In general, Whites exercise more than people of other racial groups, although this phenomenon may have more to do with socioeconomic status than ethnicity (Fitzgerald et al., 1994). Several studies found that African American women are less active than White women (Folsom et al., 1991). The Behavioral Risk Factor Surveillance System (CDC, 1993) found that ethnic minorities in general were less involved in physical activities. Among women, a sedentary lifestyle was reported by 68 percent of African Americans compared to 56 percent of non-Hispanic Whites. A similar pattern was noticed for men. In addition, there is reported higher prevalence of physical inactivity among rural Americans than those living in urban settings (CDC, 1998).

Participation in exercise has been linked to socioeconomic and educational background. The proportion of adults reporting a sedentary lifestyle in the U.S. National Health Interview Survey (National Center for Health Statistics, 1994) was 32 percent among lower income people compared to 24 percent in the general population, yet these numbers may be misleading. Airhehenbuwa, Kumanyika, Agurs, and Lowe (1995) interviewed African Americans of limited economic means whose work included physical labor. The participants equated their vocation with physical activity and felt that exercise was a physical stressor. Interestingly, participants felt they had little leisure time and considered rest, as a means of compensating for their physical labor, more worthwhile than exercise. Many studies on exercise behavior ignore occupational behavior as exercise activity, yet a 1990 survey (CDC, 2000) showed that approximately half of the adults with no leisure time reported at least 1 hour per day of hard physical work. Occupational activity was greater for minorities and for those with less than a high school education and decreased with age. Thus future research needs to put more attention on the measurement of occupational physical activity as exercise as opposed to definitions that equate exercise with a leisure-time activity.

Sex differences in exercise can be viewed as a function of the social construction of gender rather than due to sex differences per se (Hays, 1999). Traditionally, the physical meaning of gender has been strikingly different. Masculinity has been associated with energy, strength, and physical labor, whereas femininity has been associated with serenity, limitation, and passivity (Gilbert & Scher, 1999). For men, body-image issues tend to focus on strength whereas for women body concerns relate to appearance and weight. While boys consider excess fat as being related to muscle mass, girls often view it as being fat. In the realm of weight loss, when men want to lose weight they typically begin to exercise whereas women often start to diet (Hays, 1999). Girls and women, compared to boys and men, tend to be more sedentary; less involved in physical activities; and less engaged in organized, competitive sports (Duda, 1991, as cited in Hays, 1999). One of the predictors of lack of exercise initiation is being a woman (Dishman, 1994). Hays (1999) identified the essential paradox for women and exercise: Exercise is extremely valuable for women while underappreciated by the same group.

At this point it should be clear that most members of the population do not engage in physical activity and exercise even though participation could dramatically influence everyone's health status and quality of life. The role of exercise in health promotion and disease prevention has become very important. Counselors are beginning to be asked to develop and conduct programs that emphasize the behavioral and motivational aspects of initiating and maintaining a physically active and healthful lifestyle. Although there is a great deal of knowledge about why one should exercise regularly, little information is available about how best to start and continue such a program.

THE GOALS AND BENEFITS OF EXERCISE

There are many possible goals for exercise. In health-related settings, however, research (e.g., Dubbert, 2002) supports the following objectives:

1. Cardiovascular research/improvement
2. Caloric expenditure/weight management
3. Cardiovascular risk-factor modification
4. Cardiac rehabilitation
5. Adjunctive treatment for blood pressure and diabetes control
6. Reduction of anxiety, depression, and other mental health concerns
7. Rehabilitation of specific joint and muscle functions that have become limited by disease or injury

Various forms of exercise affect the body differently. For example, walking and swimming improve cardiovascular fitness, endurance, and muscle strength. Weight lifting, however, primarily improves muscle strength. Therefore, programs must be tailored to each client's needs. For further discussion of the physiology of exercise, interested readers are referred to texts such as Cerney, Burton, and Armstrong (2001); McArdle, Katch, and Katch (2001); and/or Housh, Housh, and Devries (2002). Physicians, exercise physiologists, or physical therapists develop most exercise programs. Recently, however, health counselors are being consulted to ensure that the program is properly tailored to each individual in order to create optimal adherence to the prescribed program.

THE BODY'S RESPONSE TO EXERCISE

Before examining how health counselors can tailor exercise interventions, a brief explanation of the body's response to exercise may be helpful. When an individual engages in an exercise such as walking, running, cycling, or swimming, the contraction of skeletal muscles that produce movement requires an immediate increase in energy. To supply the energy, the muscle cells begin to increase their rate of metabolism through the use of available metabolic substrates, which include muscle glycogen and fat, blood glucose, and free fatty acids that are transported to the blood from fat stores to the working muscles. To maintain this increase in metabolic activity, oxygen also has to be provided to the working muscles or fatigue will develop rapidly. This increase in metabolic rate by the muscles, the need to transport substrates and oxygen to the muscle tissue, and the need to rapidly remove the metabolic waste products all produce a variety of adaptive responses by the body.

To meet these demands, the central nervous system also changes. There is a reduction in the parasympathetic tone and a rapid rise in the sympathetic nervous system drive. These two component systems act in opposition to each other in order to keep balance. The magnitude of these responses is directly proportional to the intensity of the exercise. To facilitate the delivery of extra oxygen and remove carbon dioxide, the rate and depth of breathing increases. When a person feels short of breath during exercise, this has nothing to do with lung function; rather, it is the result of the inability of the heart and the blood vessels to transport sufficient oxygen to the working muscles. During vigorous exercise, metabolic demands rise rapidly, and the blood flow to the working muscles must rise to meet these demands; this produces an increase in cardiac performance. Blood pressure rises during exercise; the result is a greater driving pressure, which increases blood flow. Heart rate reflects (more or less) the amount of effort being expended during the exercise. The body's responses to low-resistance, dynamic exercise—running, swimming, cycling—are usually considered to place a high load on the heart and vascular system. More static or heavy resistance exercise, such as weight lifting, creates a pressure load that exerts a relatively small increase in cardiac output but a large rise in blood pressure (Housh et al., 2002). This type of exercise will increase the strength of the muscle being contracted but has very few, if any, health-related benefits. Thus, it is usually not included in health-oriented exercise programs.

EXERCISE AND MENTAL HEALTH

Common sense dictates that improved mental health is a natural outcome of exercise (Glenister, 1996), and research has attempted to identify potential psychological benefits that may be related to regular exercise. It has been claimed that mental health in both clinical and nonclinical populations is positively affected by regular vigorous physical activity (Dubbert, 2002). Specifically, exercise appears to be useful for the management of anxiety, depression, anger, tension, reaction to stress, self-efficacy, and self-esteem (Dubbert, 2002; Hansen, Stevens, & Coast, 2001; Tkachuk & Martin, 1999). Research studies on anxiety tend to support the hypothesis that *state anxiety* (anxiety related to specific life events) is more responsive to exercise than *trait anxiety* (persistent anxiety that appears to be related to one's personality). Exercise programs of moderate intensity, frequency, and duration appear to be far more effective in reducing anxiety and tension than does a single episode of exercise (Salmon, 2000). Other researchers (Blumenthal et al., 1999) provide evidence of the effectiveness of exercise in reducing mild-to-moderate depression. Physical activity and exercise appear to alleviate some of the symptoms of depression, particularly for people whose level of depression is higher than normal before the start of the exercise program.

Research also suggests that physical exercise may be a beneficial adjunct for alcoholism and substance-abuse programs; improve self-image, social skills, and cognitive functioning; and reduce the symptoms of anxiety and stress. (For a complete review of the use of exercise therapy for psychological disorders, see Tkachuk and Martin, 1999.) In nonclinical populations, weekly exercise seems to consistently contribute to reinstating positive moods (Steinberg et al., 1998).

In addition, the important preventive role of exercise in making people less suscepti-ble to factors that might produce mental illness seems apparent. Sime (1996) notes that avid exercisers frequently report an improved quality of life; an increased sense of accomplish-ment, worth, and well-being; and feelings of relaxation, euphoria, and elation during and after exercising.

Although there is little doubt that exercise improves mental health, the exact mecha-nisms by which psychological improvements are accomplished are unclear. Some suggest that moderate exercise activates the neurotransmitters enkephalin and beta-endorphins that contribute to feelings of euphoria, better self-esteem, and higher tolerance for pain (Housh, Housh, & Devries, 2002). Moving away from biochemical explanations, many researchers believe that psychosocial aspects of activity, such as increased social contact, perceived mastery, or distraction from daily stressors, can contribute to the beneficial effects. Estivill (1995) hypothesizes that exercisers may achieve temporary relief from daily stress and that any sense of depression is replaced by a pleasant and calm state of awareness similar to that found with spiritual practices. In addition, aerobic exercisers may get a boost of virtuous-ness akin to the work ethic demanded by traditional religion. Courneya (1995) suggests that the positive effect associated with exercise is related to the cohesiveness of the group in which one participates. Of course, another explanation is that exercise acts like a placebo in enhancing the perceived improvements of one's well-being. What is clear from these hypotheses is that the relationship between exercise and mental health is complex with mul-tiple pathways; however, the bottom line is that exercise helps people feel better.

THE EFFECT OF EXERCISE ON THE AGING PROCESS

The human body is designed for the enjoyment of physical activity. If it is not used, the indi-vidual is denied enjoyment and can expect that the body will degenerate more quickly. The signs of physical degeneration are what is usually called *aging*. The effects of aging include slumped shoulders, sagging skin, loss of vitality, stiff joints, weakness, fatigue, and decreased libido. Of course, such changes are inevitable, but exercise seems to serve to mit-igate the effects of the aging process. A major determinant of the rapidity of aging is the individual and the way one takes care of oneself.

An important consideration about exercise is the effect that it has on the circulatory system as well as on the aging process. The maintenance of optimal health requires that tis-sues both receive fresh nutrients and excrete waste sufficiently. When an individual remains sedentary, the circulatory system maintains a level of efficiency that will sustain the current level of activity (inactivity) but nothing extra. The end result is that when an extra burst of energy is needed, it just isn't there—no reserves of energy exist because there isn't a higher degree of circulatory efficiency.

ASSESSMENT

Before beginning any exercise program, proper assessment is necessary to determine cur-rent levels of fitness and to establish appropriate training goals. The following section will outline some different assessment techniques.

Although research and experience indicate that exercise programs are not very dangerous, it still is recommended that medical clearance be obtained before beginning any exercise program. This is for the safety and protection of the client, as well as the counselor.

Exercise Program Screening

Once an exercise program has been prescribed for an individual, it is necessary to consider safety precautions related to the client's capacities and limitations. For example, someone with high blood pressure should not be involved in strenuous weight-lifting activity because it increases blood pressure. Counselors who supervise exercise programs need to be aware of methods to determine high-risk candidates who need medical screening and assessment so that they can decide which clients would not be good candidates for unsupervised exercise programs. Thus, to prevent potential ethical and legal conflicts, counselors who have not received the necessary training in exercise physiology may want to set up interdisciplinary liaisons with physicians and exercise physiologists.

The following statements, which require the client to answer yes or no, have been taken from a variety of sources and can be used as a brief screening tool to highlight areas of risk that may require consultation or further assessment by a medical professional. Counselors at least need to ask these questions before clients go through exercise assessment, prescription, or establishment of a program.

—————————   You are over 35 years old and physically inactive.

—————————   You have been told that you have heart trouble, heart disease, a heart murmur, or that you have had a heart attack.

—————————   You frequently have pains or pressure in the left or midchest area or in the neck.

—————————   You often feel faint or have spells of severe dizziness.

—————————   You experience extreme breathlessness after mild exertion.

—————————   Your doctor says your blood pressure is too high and is not under control, or you do not know whether your blood pressure is normal.

—————————   You have bone or joint problems such as arthritis.

—————————   Your family has a history of early heart attacks or strokes.

—————————   You have another medical condition, such as diabetes or asthma, that may need special attention in an exercise program.

—————————   You are significantly overweight.

—————————   You have an old, serious injury (knee, back) that might warrant special precautions, a special exercise evaluation or prescription, or be worsened by a strenuous exercise program.

If a "yes" answer is given for any of the questions, a physician's opinion and often a medical evaluation are warranted. It is the physician who must decide whether a complete physical and/or "stress" test is warranted. Physician consultation is strongly recommended before any strenuous exercise or fitness testing or whenever there is any doubt about the appropriateness of a particular client beginning an exercise program.

In addition to the medical doctor, exercise physiologists specialize in screening and assessing individuals at various risk levels. Exercise physiologists are often an important resource for the health counselor for information or consultation. More and more exercise physiologists are interested in using counselors to help them construct effective exercise motivation packages that make use of modern behavioral technology to increase exercise adherence and compliance.

Assessing Exercise Needs

Assessment is a complicated process that includes an evaluation of the individual's current state of physical health and a projection of future potential, as well as an appraisal of which interventions would be the most beneficial. It is also necessary to assess the level of cooperation that can be expected from the client. Accurate assessment can lead to more effective tailoring of a client's exercise program.

It is important to note that physical activity and exercise are conducted within a cultural context that promotes different ideals. Participation in exercise and sports is primarily promoted in North American society where the muscular physique has emerged as the ideal body form (Marks, Murray, Evans, & Willig, 2000). The ability to attain the physical ideal is often promised to those who go to fitness gyms; however, this may be limited by financial resources and enough leisure time to exercise. An understanding of the variations in the extent of participation in exercise requires not only attention to the various physical and psychological processes, but also a keen awareness of the sociocultural context—either promotes or discourages physical activity—that has meaning for each client. Therefore, when conducting an assessment, be sure to account for cultural variations in the way exercise is perceived and defined, and the role it plays in clients' lives.

Measuring an individual's habitual exercise pattern is difficult. It is very difficult, if not impossible, to obtain a "gold standard" measurement because it is tough to ascertain the truth about a person's exercise habits. Using paper-and-pencil instruments or other self-report devices to estimate exercise is also problematic. As was indicated in the previous section, it is essential to assess the client's current state of physical fitness *before* an exercise program can be employed. Without an adequate assessment of his or her current physical condition, counselors runs the risk of actually creating more problems for the client. It is germane to note at this point that the most effective counselors work in tandem with a physician or a physician's assistant. The components that the physician most often assesses are cardiovascular fitness, muscular fitness, and flexibility, which are briefly explained next.

Cardiovascular Fitness.   When cells in the human body combine oxygen with nutrients, they produce energy. The body can store some nutrients, but it must replenish others with each new breath inhaled. An efficient cardiovascular system supplies each cell with an optimal amount of oxygen and removes the maximum amount of waste possible each time the lungs are used. Exercise that develops an efficient cardiovascular respiratory system is known as *aerobic*. This type of exercise is an excellent source of stimulation for the lungs and the heart. Not surprisingly, many physicians suggest an aerobic activity for patients who have recently suffered from heart attacks or who currently have high blood pressure. Clinical studies have shown that aerobic exercise, such as running, walking, cycling, or swimming, helps the entire cardiovascular system work more efficiently. This in turn builds up heart muscles, and changes in the heart's rate can be measured when the heart is at rest. Those who engage in regular aerobic activity, for example, can expect to have a lowered resting heart rate. In assessing cardiovascular fitness, the physician must get an accurate reading of the patient's heart rate and blood pressure, and a stress electrocardiogram to determine the current condition of the heart (Cerney et al., 2001).

Muscular Fitness.   *Muscular fitness* refers to the strength, endurance, and power of the muscle, and physicians often test this area as well. Muscle *strength* refers to the amount of force that the muscle produces when it contracts. Development of strength is directly related to the number of trials that the muscle endures against resistance; that is, people become stronger as they keep lifting heavier and heavier objects. Another component of muscular fitness is endurance, which refers to the ability of the muscle to work overtime. Specifically, *endurance* is the ability to repeat an activity or to continue one for a long span of time. Muscular endurance is something that increases with concentrated use of the muscles (McArdle et al., 2001). *Power* is the speed at which the muscle can contract and apply a measure of strength. Different exercises provide very different benefits for muscular development. If an individual is involved in only one sport or one activity, he or she is likely to gain benefits from it but not develop the overall fitness that may be needed to ensure the maintenance of good health.

Flexibility.   The assessment of *flexibility* is concerned with the range of movement of a joint. Inactivity reduces the flexibility of a joint. Many people make the mistake of assuming that older people have lost some mobility of their joints as part of the aging process whereas, in reality, their loss has more to do with their level of activity than with the aging process. Lack of flexibility is usually preceded by a decline in physical activity. It is well documented that less active people have a more limited range of motion than do those who exercise regularly (Cerney et al., 2001). Even regular use of the muscles, if restricted to one pattern because of limited activity or a sedentary lifestyle, often results in a restricted range of movement.

Readiness to Change

Counselors are ultimately change agents who work with clients at points when something needs to be different. Even though they may indicate a willingness to exercise or the desire to exercise, not all clients enter into a counseling relationship ready to actually change behavior. Therefore, to ensure that counselors adequately create exercise interventions that match clients' readiness to change, the assessment process should include an analysis regarding their commitment to exercise behavior change. Helpful for understanding readiness to change is the transtheoretical model of behavior change, which depicts behavior change as a process that involves progression through a series of five stages (see Prochaska, Norcross, & DiClemente, 1994, for a summary of this theory). The stages include precontemplation (no intent and no exercise), contemplation (considering exercise but no intent), preparation (intent to exercise and occasional exercise), action (implementing regular exercise), and maintenance (avoidance of relapse by exercising months or more). The transtheoretical model contains three basic assumptions about change: (1) it involves more than an all-or-nothing or on–off action, (2) at any time people are in one or another stage of change, and (3) specific interventions are more or less relevant at different stages.

The transtheoretical model has been applied to as many as 12 health behaviors, including exercise activity (Marcus & Simkin, 1993; Rosen, 2000). Perception of benefits of and barriers to behavior change has been shown to vary systematically across the stages of change. For example, for most of the 12 behaviors investigated by Prochaska and colleagues (1994), precontemplators reported more barriers to behavior change than benefits, whereas individuals in the action stage reported more benefits than barriers. The key for health counselors in using this model is to assess how ready a client is to begin exercise and thus tailor the exercise prescription to match his or her readiness. For example, a client at the precontemplation level would need psychoeducation and cognitive strategies to recognize that exercise is a useful activity whereas a client at the maintenance stage would need much more tailoring in the area of relapse prevention as opposed to basic exercise information.

Other Assessment Concerns

In addition to determining one's fitness level and exercise capacity, a thorough initial assessment with regular follow-up sessions can document changes in health status for clients who do not feel that they are changing. Clients often report no change in weight but their physical measurements indicate that they have lost inches and that clothes no longer fit the same way. Additionally, clients may notice a decrease in resting and exercise heart rates. Failure to show change after a reasonable time can cue the counselor to explore the following possibilities:

1. The client is not adhering well enough to the exercise prescription (exercise mode or type, frequency, intensity, and duration) to produce the desired change.
2. The exercise prescription itself is faulty or inadequate.
3. The measures are not sensitive enough to the changes and perhaps need to be altered, replaced, or supplemented by others.

It is important to mention again that performing an exercise fitness test is a complicated task, and health counselors who have no medical or exercise physiology training should *never* attempt exercise testing on clients without direct supervision by medical or exercise physiology specialists. Interested readers are encouraged to consult the publications of the American College of Sports Medicine (ACSM) on exercise testing and prescriptions (ACSM, 1998a; 1998b). Numerous special training courses on exercise testing, prescription, and program implementation are provided around the country by the ACSM. Contact information is available in the Resources section at in the end of this chapter.

Attitudes and Beliefs about Exercise

King, Rejeski, and Buchner (1998) suggest that believing in the value of physical activity, perceiving fewer barriers, and having higher self-efficacy for physical activity participation are important psychosocial determinants (consistent predictors) of activity in adults of all ages. Thus, those who believe in the value of exercise for *their* specific benefit have a greater likelihood of incorporating and maintaining exercise as part of their daily routine. One might expect that the dissemination of knowledge testifying to all the positive effects of exercise would be effective in increasing the number of frequent exercisers, yet education has not been demonstrated to be enough to get people exercising (Dishman & Buckworth, 1996). Although researchers are quick to note that education is not a salient factor in individuals' motivation to engage in exercise, education is an element in clients' choice to participate in an exercise program. In particular, it is important for people to have the most current details about exercise in order to create or to modify their beliefs based on accurate information.

Few people would disagree that Americans are underexercised. Often, excuses and faulty beliefs for neglecting exercise are at the root, including the following:

- "It's no fun."
- "It's for kids."
- "I'm too busy."
- "I'm too tired."
- "I'm too fat."
- "I look awful in running shorts."
- "I can't afford it."
- "I don't have anybody to play with."
- "I tried it once and it didn't work."
- "I don't know how."
- "I'm afraid."

Further, the high prevalence of inactivity may be related, in part, to the perception that a high frequency of vigorous exercise is required to achieve significant health benefits (Pate et al., 1995; Sallis & Owen, 1999). Whereas it is true that activities of higher intensity may produce greater health benefits than low-intensity activities, sedentary individuals are less likely to adhere to a prescription for high-intensity activities. Instead, greater increases in physical activity are found for those who participate in low-intensity rather than moderate- or high-intensity activities (Dishman & Buckworth, 1996; 1997). The bottom line is that any exercise is good exercise when starting out; intensity can then be increased when exercise has become a regular habit.

What this means is that many people have the wrong information or high expectations for exercise that often leads to the creation of beliefs or excuses that serve as barriers to exercise. It is important to remember that health beliefs about exercise are part of the individual's value system at the personal, interpersonal, and cultural levels. This system often serves as a substantial factor in creating positive exercise attitudes. In the same way that they create cognitive schemas about other health behaviors (e.g., beliefs about nutrition, effective health habits), most people have complex belief systems about exercise and their relationship to physical activity. These cognitive schemas are the result of early childhood experiences, family values and beliefs about exercise, and other formative events that create filters through which exercise in the current context can be understood. Beliefs are especially important at the contemplation stage when people are working through initial involvement in an exercise program, yet often are not an effective indicator in identifying those who will adhere to a prescribed exercise regimen (Carter, Lee, & Greenockle, 1987).

INTERVENTIONS

Although the evidence supports the many benefits of exercise, the bottom-line effectiveness of any exercise program depends on ensuring sufficient adherence to the regimen to produce the desired health benefits (Sallis & Owen, 1998). General counseling, training principles, and developing a prescription and goals and objectives are all part of the intervention process.

Counseling

As previously discussed, research strongly suggests that the majority of people who begin a systematic exercise program, either on their own or in a structured program, will stop before any lasting benefits occur. This is probably the result of inappropriate, inadequate, or inefficient counseling, both in the very important habit-acquisition stage and during the maintenance stage, or during transition from a formal program to a self-managed program. It is likely that poor attention to the learning environment, personality characteristics, and behavioral techniques are responsible for these statistics. It is difficult to accurately determine exactly what factors are related to regular exercise participation. Sallis and Owen (1998) outline nearly 40 variables, which were identified from reviewing almost 300 exercise adherence studies, that can possibly influence participation in physical activity by adults.

With multiple variables contributing to exercise participation, experience shows that one of the best tools to help clients begin and then maintain exercise programs is the use of counseling to support their efforts. Sime (1996) provides the following guidelines that can help counselors develop and implement effective exercise programs:

1. Explore the client's exercise history to determine current exercise habits as well as past enjoyable activities that may contribute to exercise adherence.
2. When possible, participate in early training sessions to serve as a model and guide for the activity and appropriate client behavior.
3. Educate the client about the possible physical, psychological, and social benefits of exercise as a way to enhance commitment.
4. Consider options to make exercise more functional and a part of the client's daily activity routine (e.g., commute to work by walking, running, or bicycling; include household chores in the exercise prescription; or create activities that can be completed over a lunch period).
5. Take advantage of a client's environmental surroundings (e.g., trails, parks, lakes, community swimming pools, home or worksite exercise equipment) in tailoring exercise activities.
6. Provide the client a wide range of exercise alternatives.
7. Prescribe the type, duration, frequency, and intensity of exercise in terms of the client's current level of conditioning.

8. Attempt to facilitate exercise within a positive social milieu.
9. Assist the client with development of behavioral self-control (e.g., behavioral contracting, stimulus control, positive reinforcement) and cognitive strategies to improve program adherence.
10. Prepare the client for relapse and recidivism using relapse-prevention strategies.

Most of the strategies listed here are addressed in the remainder of this chapter. Remember, creating effective exercise programs is a long-term process with multiple positive outcomes besides exercise adherence; Martin and Dubbert (1987) note:

> Exercise programmers often view adherence to the program as the natural outcome of initial health education and the motivation provided by improved performance and fitness. In our opinion, more often the opposite is true: fitness improvement and health education are the inevitable by-products of exercise programs that ensure long-term adherence. Reinforcement can come from being with others, from easy invigorating activity, or from praise by family and program members. (p. 368)

General Principles of Training

According to Prentice, Arnheim, and Hall (2002), three important principles—overload, progression, and specificity—provide guidance for the design of exercise programs. For an adaptive response to occur, a system must be subjected to a load significantly greater than the load to which it is accustomed. This is the essence of the *overload* principle. At the initial stages of an exercise program, when a client is "deconditioned" from sedentary living, very little exercise is enough to create an overload. As the client's fitness level improves, greater amounts of work are necessary to create an overload and to produce change. Thus, training must gradually increase in duration and intensity to maintain overload.

The principle of *progression* states that an exercise program should be applied in a gradual, progressive manner in accordance with the client's level of fitness. This principle directly relates to overload. At the beginning of an exercise program, the rate of progression should be relatively slow. The program should last for several weeks, especially for an individual who has been sedentary for a long period of time, because any change produces muscle soreness and injury to muscles that are unaccustomed to the stress and strain of vigorous exercise. To keep the client's attitude positive and his or her enthusiasm high, effective counselors work hard to minimize discomfort and soreness at the early stages of a training program. This is often a difficult challenge, because this is an age of "drive-thru" living in which everything has to be done right away. It is important for the counselor to stop an individual from doing too much too soon which can lead to physical pain, discomfort, and thus loss of interest.

The third principle, *specificity,* is based on the fact that the body adapts to an overload stimulus in a manner that is specific to the type of training (aerobic or anaerobic) as well as to the muscles involved in the training. There is little transfer of training effects, either from one type of training to another or from one muscle group to another. It appears that different types of exercise place different demands on the mechanisms for energy production. It is perhaps with this thought in mind that many exercise trainers are urging cross-training to develop whole-body fitness.

Developing the Exercise Prescription

In developing an exercise prescription, the counselor needs to tailor the program to each client to maintain his or her adherence to the program. The major components of an exercise prescription include the type or mode of exercise, its frequency, its intensity, and its duration. Whereas suggested standards exist in terms of components, counselors' tailoring of an exercise program will be as varied as each individual because interventions should meet a client's specific needs and differences. Current recommendations for physical activity and health follow, then there is a further break down of each facet to facilitate a greater understanding of tailoring.

Exercise and physical fitness recommendations have been developed over time and adjusted to meet current information about exercise. In 1978, the American College of Sports Medicine published guidelines on the frequency (3–5 days per week), intensity (60–90 percent of maximum heart rate reserve), duration (15–90 min per session), and type (rhythmic use of large muscle groups in activities such as running or swimming) of exercise needed for cardiorespiratory fitness and optimal body composition (ACSM, 1978). These guidelines became the widely recognized standard for both exercise and good health; they were updated in 1990, with the ACSM adding the area of resistance training and recognizing that moderate exercise may reduce the risk of chronic disease even though it may not improve cardiovascular fitness (ACSM, 1990).

In 1995, the American College of Sports Medicine and the Centers for Disease Control and Prevention (CDC) published new recommendations for physical activity and health (Pate et al., 1995) designed to help Americans find a way to make healthy physical activity part of their lifestyles. Guidelines were revised as a result of research suggesting that an accumulation of short (8–10 min) active periods over the course of a day could approximate the benefits from a sustained period of activity (Pate et al., 1995). This scientific evidence, coupled with the desire to provide recommendations that could realistically be reached by the general public, resulted in the recommendation that U.S. adults should accumulate 30 minutes of moderate-intensity physical activity on either most days of the week (USDHHS, 1996) or on a minimum of 3 days per week (Fletcher et al., 1996). Examples of moderate-intensity activity include walking briskly (3–4 mph; 4.8–6.4 kpm), general calisthenics, painting and home repair work, lawnmowing with a power mower, washing windows, and other heavy cleaning in the home (Pate et al., 1995). The first Surgeon General's *Report on Physical Activity and Health* (USDHHS, 1996) added that moderate-level activity has significant health benefits but that vigorous activity should only be encouraged for those who are able and willing to increase the intensity of their effort.

The following sections further examine ideas around the mode, frequency, duration, and intensity components of exercise programs.

Mode of Exercise.   It is important to choose exercises that will be appropriate and also appeal to the individual. The process of tailoring the mode of exercise to an individual significantly contributes to program effectiveness. Research indicates that clients who believe that exercise programs have been specifically designed for them often continue with the prescription longer than those not given that same impression (Thompson & Wankel, 1980). To determine the appropriate mode of exercise, counselors need to assess a client's previous exercise history, home and work schedules, home and work environments (e.g., access to walking paths and trails, places to bicycle, availability of swimming pools, availability and access to fitness centers and gymnasiums), and individual goals and preferences as part of the assessment process. Tailoring exercise to the client's personal goals, history, and lifestyle is extremely important.

For an activity to be considered satisfactory aerobically, several criteria must be met. The exercise must involve moderate-to-vigorous activity of large muscle groups, be rhythmic in nature, and be performed aerobically. The activities that best meet these criteria are aerobic dancing, bicycling, cross-country skiing, racquet sports, rope skipping, swimming, walking, jogging, and running. Among adults, walking is often the preferred mode of physical activity, and most prefer to walk on their own rather than in a supervised group (King et al., 2000). Many other activities could be used to complement these activities, but most are probably not vigorous enough to produce an adequate aerobic benefit, including backpacking, golfing, hiking, downhill skiing, and skin diving.

In some cases, the exercise mode is not a matter of choice. Clearly, some exercises have superior efficiency, and some might be the only feasible alternative. For example, for those in the Midwest, winter weather restricts many clients to inside exercise, and often the only feasible alternative is stationary biking or walking on a treadmill. However, when the seasons change, clients should be encouraged to move outdoors to walk or ride bicycles. When not able to tailor the mode of exercise to the individual client, work with him or her to reframe the available exercise options in order to see the potential positive features.

Frequency of Exercise.   As noted before, researchers consistently report that the ideal frequency of aerobic exercise for improving cardiovascular fitness is 3 times per week. This allows the client time to complete the exercise and gives the body a reasonable period of time to recover and rejuvenate. Less frequent exercise produces minimal gains in fitness, endurance, and other health benefits. A bigger problem, however, is that a lower frequency program prevents the establishment of exercise as a habit. It is important for the counselor to help the client develop an exercise pattern that will be continued and adhered to for years so that he or she is working on lifestyle change. Unless a person is in competitive sports training, exercising 3 to 4 times per week seems optimal. When one exercises more than 4 times per week, the likelihood of injury, fatigue, and nonadherence increases.

Most researchers believe that exercising briskly every other day and resting on alternate days is the preferred schedule. This system is relatively easy to keep track of and easy to manage. There are exceptions to this suggestion. Some clients find it helpful to exercise on a daily basis, perhaps just after awakening, whereas others enjoy working out on weekdays and resting on weekends. The important point is to understand each individual's lifestyle and to develop a schedule of no less than 3 times per week. If an individual chooses to exercise on a daily basis, it may be important to suggest a lower intensity workout. Counselors should carefully monitor those clients who engage in extreme physical activity to ensure that they are not becoming exercise-dependant (Hausenblas & Downs, 2002).

Another consideration in exercise frequency is the availability of programs. Large metropolitan areas may have around-the-clock fitness clubs, whereas in smaller urban and rural areas, programs may be limited. When tailoring an exercise program, counselors need to choose one that is realistic for an individual's schedule in order to create programs that are attainable within his or her time frame.

Intensity of Exercise.   It is important to note that many of the changes in exercise recommendations specifically relate to the question of exercise intensity. Clearly, a dose–response relationship exists between physical activities and health outcomes, meaning that greater health benefits result from engaging in physical activity that is more vigorous or of longer duration (USDHHS, 1996; Fletcher et al., 1996). However, in more current guidelines and recommendations the accrual of beneficial health outcomes associated with higher levels of physical activity was given less emphasis because of the hope that a prescription for moderate activity, as opposed to intense, would result in greater exercise adoption and maintenance, thereby ultimately producing greater improvements in the health of the population. These recommendations are supported by research indicating that there are greater increases in physical activity for low-intensity than for moderate- or high-intensity activities (Dishman & Buckworth, 1996). In addition, there is often greater adherence to exercise programs when the exercise prescriptions are for moderate versus higher levels of intensity and frequency (Perri et al., 2002). Thus, although activities of higher intensity may produce greater health benefits than low-intensity activities, sedentary individuals are less likely to adhere to a prescription for high-intensity activities.

There are many suggestions for assessing the proper level of intensity for an exercise program. A general rule is for one to exercise at a level that is around 70 percent higher than the client's resting heart rate. Exercising at this target heart rate will produce an aerobic, or cardiovascular, benefit. Researchers believe that lower intensities produce significantly fewer benefits but that exercising too intensely can be counterproductive; that is, the benefits are not any greater, and the increased intensity greatly increases the risk of injuries, which can lead to poor treatment adherence. A simple rule to follow with clients is: if they find it difficult to talk while exercising, then it is likely that they are working out at too high a level of intensity.

To determine and monitor heart rate, follow these suggestions. Obtain a maximum heart rate by having a physician administer a stress electrocardiogram. For those clients for whom this would be too costly or not warranted, use a simple general calculation: take the number 220 and subtract the client's age from it. The number obtained is termed the *maximum heart rate.* To determine the *target heart rate,* subtract the individual's resting rate from the maximum rate; calculate 70 percent of that difference and add it back to the resting heart rate. The result represents the target heart rate. For example, the maximum heart rate of a 50-year-old woman with a heart rate of 80 beats per minute is 170 (220 – 50 = 170). Her target heart rate is 143 (170 – 80 = 90; 70% of 90 = 63; 63 + 80 = 143).

Urge individuals to operate within 65 to 75 percent of their maximum heart rate. Clients need to stop periodically and take their heart rate for 10 seconds, then multiply by 6 to determine the current rate per minute. This should be done throughout an exercise program until they are comfortable just "feeling" what their proper exercise intensity level is. Individuals who have a difficult time taking their own heart rate can use any of the low-cost monitors available commercially, plus many exercise machines now have heart rate monitors embedded.

Counselors can usually observe that the intensity level is too great by checking to see whether the client's face is bright red or whether there is profuse sweating or heavy breathing. If so, the exercise is probably being done too intensely. Recommend that clients begin to keep an exercise log of their activities—recording data such as duration, distance, subjective perception of the exercise (how did it feel?), mode, and intensity. This data can then be used to monitor progress over time and to make adjustments in intensity. It is also important to caution all clients to be sure to drink plenty of fluids before, during, and after exercise to avoid dehydration. This is especially important during the summer months or in hot climates.

Duration of Exercise.   The duration of exercise is closely related to mode, frequency, and intensity. The general rule is that exercise needs to be done for about 30 or more minutes; however, it may be necessary to gradually move up to that level. Clients should begin at durations that are comfortable and match their current level of fitness. An early goal of any exercise program should be to gradually increase duration to reach the 30-minute standard.

The duration of exercise will relate directly to how much time individuals have available. Many people in today's high-efficiency, fast society want to get the most out of an exercise program in the least amount of time. On the basis of experience, although 15 to 20 minutes is the minimum recommended exercise duration, it is more likely that a duration of 30 to 45 minutes will produce the necessary aerobic effect. Also, whereas some individuals may want to rush and complete exercise as if it was a daily task, counselors should encourage clients to set aside and protect exercise time in order to enjoy the process of exercising while allowing it to be a break from daily demands.

In summary, selecting the proper mode, frequency, intensity, and duration can help health counseling professionals tailor the exercise prescription and increase treatment adherence. Once an appropriate format for an exercise program has been chosen, the counselor needs to encourage the client to think in a fashion that views exercise as an important part of daily living in order to facilitate a true lifestyle shift.

Developing Goals and Objectives

The importance of goal setting in exercise performance cannot be stressed enough. Common goals and objectives are to improve flexibility, muscular strength and endurance, cardiovascular endurance, and body composition and weight. However, some clients may start an exercise program with the intent of improving stress management, increasing social contacts, improving self-esteem, and so on. It is important to clearly identify the client's goals and, as noted earlier, to tailor the exercise prescription. Thus, the goal-setting process involves setting the specific goal, such as increasing endurance by being able to run 5 miles, and then identifying the behavior—running daily—to use to achieve the goal. The more flexible, individually tailored, and achievable the goals are, the better the ensuing adherence. Goals should be measurable so that progress can be monitored.

It is important to educate clients about reasonable goals and reasonable timetables for achieving results. Most clients expect immediate changes and benefits and are often quickly discouraged when they do not reach lofty goals. Therefore, when helping a client establish overall exercise goals, it is necessary to help him or her set subgoals along a continuum (e.g., running 2 miles after 2 weeks, 3 miles after 6 weeks, 4 miles after 12 weeks) and to establish how the mental aspects of setting, achieving, or failing to achieve the goals might affect being able to stick with the program.

By talking about potential pitfalls, clients can begin to troubleshoot and create exercise interventions that will work for them. Often individuals who create exercise goals on their own continue patterns of failure—setting unobtainable and unrealistic goals—that have plagued their entire exercise history. It is important therefore for counselors to help clients formulate short-term and long-term goals to break old, ineffective patterns of behavior and thinking about exercise. Experience shows that the more flexible the goals are, in terms of both specific sessions and hopes for performance across time, the more effective clients are in minimizing the occurrence of failures. For example, it is best to urge clients to state long-term goals such as "I want to be able to run the Chicago Marathon in eight months" or "I want to be able to run three miles to my brother's house without stopping within six weeks." For short-term goals, however, ideas like these are best: "In two months I want to be able to run five miles four days a week" or "In three weeks I want to be able to run one mile without stopping." In addition, counselors should encourage clients to concentrate more on adherence and regularity than on performance, because performance generally will be the by-product of adherence. Thus, recommend that clients initially set goals that focus on exercising 3 to 4 days each week rather than setting specific time, distance, or intensity goals.

COGNITIVE STRATEGIES DURING EXERCISE

One of the most effective ways to begin to exercise is by using the cognitive strategy of dissociation, or *distraction,* which is the purposeful distancing of attentional focus from potentially displeasing sensory stimuli (e.g., exercise-induced discomfort) (Masters & Ogles, 1998). During the initial stages of exercise, the feedback that the body provides is often negative, and individuals who pay attention to these signals may quickly stop a program that appears so discouraging. Through the use of distracting cognitive strategies, such negative feedback can be minimized. Distraction should help clients feel reduced perceived exertion and more positive affect and enjoyment from the exercise. Whereas elite athletes often do the opposite—use association, the increase of focus on bodily sensations—to improve performance (Scott et al., 1999), nonelite exercisers usually gravitate toward the use of distraction. This suggests that typical exercisers often prefer to distance themselves from pain and discomfort, thus clients distract their thoughts during exercise and focus on more enjoyable ideas.

Research by Martin and his colleagues (1984) found that individuals who were taught to dissociate their thoughts from the actual exercise or the bodily sensations connected with the exertion had significantly better class attendance, exercise adherence, and long-term maintenance of their regimen than did those who were taught to associate thinking about the exercise and how it felt and act as their own coach. Whereas some have questioned (Kimiecik, 1999) whether distraction is an effective long-term strategy for building adherence to exercise, others (e.g., Masters and Ogles, 1998, contains an extensive review) suggest that distancing minimizes feelings of discomfort during exercise and that over time this allows exercise to tap into the self-reinforcing properties of exercising and identifying as an exerciser. Thus, distraction can be viewed as a cognitive technique for building adherence to exercise, enjoyment while exercising, increasing exercise duration, and even maximizing physical output (Annesi, 2001).

Some of the distraction methods include positive self-talk, exercising with others and talking, reading or watching TV while doing stationary exercise, participating in an exercise class, exercising in a pleasant setting, and/or using music or visual distraction (e.g., virtual-reality machines). Music can be a means of keeping the focus off internal sensations, as well as enhancing enjoyment of exercise (Wankel, 1993). Music can be particularly important for new exercisers during the initial months of attempting to adapt to the demands of a regular exercise program (Boutcher, 1993). Virtual-reality machines have been shown to lead to higher physical exertion and greater adherence to exercise programs when compared to no distraction method (Annesi & Mazas, 1997; Porcari, Zedaker, & Maldari, 1998). Further, Annesi (2001) found that the combination of both music and TV was most effective in curbing the exercise dropout rate and increasing physical output when compared to no distraction technique or the use of just music or TV. It is important to mention that distraction activities, such as those listed here, would *not* be appropriate for clients with serious physical problems who have been taught to be, or need to be trained to become, very sensitive to their body signals.

PSYCHOEDUCATIONAL STRATEGIES

Theoretical ideas from social learning theory and behaviorism can be highly effective when applied to exercise. Enduring patterns are sustained because they are cued and reinforced as aspects of the environment. This basic paradigm of antecedent behavior–consequence is a fundamental psychological principle. The basic strategy necessary in modifying behavior is to make changes in the environment that will both support the desired behaviors and weaken the competing—unwanted—behaviors. The process involved in identifying cues that will enhance the desired outcome while subsequently noting the cues that result in competing or less desirable behaviors is a complex task. In the lives of sedentary individuals, few effective cues for promoting exercise exist, as compared to the numerous cues for the competing behaviors. There are plenty of cues in the environment to remain on the couch and to not get up and start jogging or going to the gym. Therefore, the counselor's job is to help the client build on and increase the effective cues. The more often a behavior occurs in a particular stimulus situation, the more powerful a cue the stimulus situation becomes. The counselor can help the client recognize the very process of conditioning that is occurring on a daily basis. Once he or she is cognizant of this, the client can be more open to the psychoeducational process of exercise.

The initial step in the psychoeducational process is to have clients spend a discrete period of time engaged in self-monitoring. To do this, clients should log their exercise behavior over a set period of time. After they have had sufficient time to observe and record their exercise behaviors, the antecedent variables, and any cueing that they may have been aware of, clients can work with the counselor to arrange an environment that is conducive to promoting exercise while eliminating cues to remain sedentary (Dishman, 1988). As with any self-monitoring activity, the performance of the desired behavior, almost predictably, increases when attention is paid to it.

When beginning a structured exercise program, the time, place, and people involved in the program will come to represent the cues for those who want to adhere to the program.

Yet, structured exercise programs have a built-in, unfortunate drawback; that is, once the structured program ends, so do the cues it provides. Thus, clients and counselors have to work to build and create cues in the environment that will continue to serve as a reinforcement when the structured program ends. One way to address this problem is to provide a variety of cues within the environment that remind clients to exercise. These can include magazines and posters about the exercise activity, setting out exercise clothes the night before, or even having a friend or spouse call as a reminder. The counselor should attempt to generalize the stimulus control of exercise to other settings before the program concludes. To expect people to continue to exercise following the sudden withdrawal of their cues is naïve, so advance planning is necessary.

Another important factor to attend to is the decreasing of cues for competing behaviors. The counselor can promote this process by helping the client identify concretely the specific time and location that he or she will be relatively isolated from competing cues and able to engage in exercise. Picking a consistent time and location can help one build the exercise program into a schedule and allow the client to actively protect the time from competing cues. There are different ideas with regard to the best time for exercise based on circadian rhythms and body temperature, yet for those who are trying to build exercise patterns and are less concerned about ideal performance, the best time is a consistent set time. Another idea is to have the client set up an elaborate set of environmental cues to decrease competing cues (e.g., equipping one's office with exercise photos and carrying a gym bag complete with exercise clothes for any occasion). By doing this, the client creates an environment that actively promotes exercise and eliminates possible excuses.

In general, punishment without simultaneous reward for the desired behavior is ineffective in eliminating a high frequency of undesired behavior. Therefore, the elimination of the natural discomforts that accompany increased physical activity is essential. Intervention at the level of the behavior itself, in the form of an individualized exercise prescription and an educative process, may help lessen the natural discomforts associated with increased physical activity. Cognitive restructuring that eliminates negative self-talk ("I hate running," "I'm so tired," or "Why does this have to hurt so much?") and then teaches some much needed skills in temporary dissociation appear to be the most effective interventions (Dishman, 1988).

Reinforcement and encouragement are another important aspect of the psychoeducational process. Again, it is important to encourage clients not to rely on the counselor as the primary agent of change. For example, clients are often encouraged to sign written contracts that serve as reinforcement for exercise adherence. A commonly overlooked disadvantage of written contracts is that clients become dependent on external forms of reinforcement; when they are without an external reinforcement agent, clients will almost certainly relapse. A further complication of the contract system is that clients may come to view the counselor as responsible for their success and may find themselves unable to gain a sense of self-efficacy that will allow them to succeed independently. One way to address this is to help clients begin to identify internal rewards and look for encouragement resources in their own home and work environments. This can be done by exercising with another person, thus one reward becomes social contact and one reforcement is not wanting to cancel a social obligation.

Preventive and therapeutic exercise programs are increasingly found in the community at large—in the school, at the worksite, and in some health-care settings. Few exercise programs are available in medical settings, such as hospitals or outpatient clinics, yet some studies show at health-care settings are an effective place to deliver exercise-related information (Dubbert, 2002). Often, however, physicians prescribe exercise programs for few of the patients they see, and a number of studies suggest that part of the reason is that physicians do not believe that they can alter the behaviors of their patients. Interestingly, patients want their physicians to be concerned about their health habits, and it seems quite likely that the influence that physicians have on their patients' behavior is substantially greater than physicians themselves believe.

Most people who are trying to locate physical activity programs for maximum benefit conclude that the single most important setting for such programs is the school. Well-run physical education programs for school-age children can set the stage for a lifetime of interest and involvement in exercise. Yet, in spite of the fact that most states require the teaching of physical education at some point in the school curriculum, participation in physical education classes continues to decline. In a 1997 survey, 64 percent of adolescents reported 20 minutes of vigorous activity at least 3 times a week (USDHHS, 2000). Other studies have shown as few as 10 percent of youth engaging in physical activity for at least 10 minutes at a time (Armstrong & Van Mechelen, 1998).

The newest setting for the development of physical activity programs is the workplace. Since approximately 70 percent of the adult population is employed and workplace physical activity programs have been shown to provide health and economic benefits to employees and both economic and noneconomic benefits to employers, it is likely that worksite wellness programs are here to stay (Taylor, 1999). Some large companies have exercise gymnasiums and structured exercise programs as part of a larger package of workplace wellness interventions. Other companies make private arrangements with fitness gyms in the community to provide memberships and monthly dues at a reduced rate.

A successful exercise intervention that has been adopted by many worksites is the 10,000 steps to health program. To achieve good health, this program suggests striving to take 10,000 steps a day (the equivalent of walking roughly 5 miles). Two recent *Journal of the American Medical Association* studies have confirmed that this lifestyle approach can be as effective as a traditional exercise program. Many doctors and researchers have found that wearing a pedometer is a great way to track daily activity in order to count how many steps are taken each day (Zipes, 2002).

Other community resources are YMCA and YWCA facilities. Both organizations have been involved with the development and implementation of exercise programs across the United States for years and provide a great variety of exercise-related facilities, classes, and instruction. For contact information, see the Resources section at the end of this chapter.

Case Example

Bill is a 31-year-old married White male who sought out counseling for depression. The precipitating event was a physical exam in which his physician felt that Bill was at considerable risk for cardiovascular problems. Bill, apparently, was confronted with his mortality for the first time in his life. Bill reported that he was a good high school athlete and that he had participated in three different sports events. He attended a state college and earned a business degree. Since graduating from high school, he has participated in physical activities only on an irregular basis. He has been relatively successful in business and was receiving a routine executive fitness exam when he learned of his high risk for cardiovascular problems.

In addition to describing his high-stress job and lack of exercise, Bill reported tension in his marriage of 7 years and stress because of his three preschool-age children. Although Bill did say that he loved his wife, he also indicated that he didn't like her all the time. There is a history of cardiovascular problems in Bill's family of origin; his father suffered a near-fatal heart attack at age 52 and had died of cardiovascular complications at age 56.

The biopsychosocial treatment formulation addressed the many problem areas that Bill faced. The counselor believed that Bill, as had his father, had taken his physical health for granted and had focused heavily on being a good provider. Although his health habits were not necessarily bad, they were not very good either, and it was likely that he did have some inherited cardiovascular weakness. It was also likely that, given the high stress caused by Bill's current living situation—three young children, a high-pressure job, and some marital conflict—he might be reluctant or incapable of taking on any new challenges such as an exercise program.

With this information in mind, the counselor began to talk with Bill about the kind of exercise program that he could realistically become involved in. Bill indicated that two of his close friends had been skipping business lunches and going to the local YMCA, riding the stationary bicycles and using the rowing machines. He thought that this was something that he too would be able to do on roughly four out of every five working days. He indicated that he was not too interested in either rowing or biking but did feel that the Y was convenient and that having his close friends along would make the whole experience more enjoyable. The counselor suggested that Bill talk specifically with the director of the Y and ask him or her to contact his physician regarding setting up a specific exercise program. Bill and his counselor eventually decided that he would begin slowly, riding the bike for 7 minutes and do some walking, and then gradually build up his workout to be in the 35- to 40-minute range at the end of 4 months.

The counselor helped Bill figure out what might be a good reward if he was successful in his exercise program. Bill indicated that he was planning to go to the Caribbean on business and that he was thinking of taking his wife along. He thought that just feeling good while outdoors and being comfortable in summer clothes might be worthwhile. Bill agreed to meet with the counselor on a weekly basis to deal with other presenting issues; 5 minutes of each session would be devoted to reporting on and continuing to tailor the exercise prescription. The ongoing contact would also help eliminate and fend off problems of relapse.

■ ■ ■ ■ ■

ADHERENCE TO EXERCISE PROGRAMS

Regardless of the setting in which physical activity and exercise programs take place, researchers consistently express a major concern with the low rate of adherence to such programs (Dubbert, 2002). Whereas some people are able to immediately find the correct exercises and have no trouble with adherence, many others have problems starting and sticking to exercise programs. Studies show that 40 to 65 percent of people who start a new program will drop out within 3 to 6 months (Annesi, 1998) and that the mean exercise dropout rate has remained stable at 50 percent over the past 25 years (Dishman & Buckworth, 1997). These numbers are consistent across age and gender and between structured and nonstructured exercise programs (Dishman & Buckworth, 1997). Clearly, health counselors must pay specific attention to creating programs that address exercise adherence. The factors that contribute to both exercise participation and adherence are complex and multifactoral; three sets of factors have been studied in terms of their roles in predicting adherence: personal factors, social/environmental factors, and characteristics of the exercise program itself. The next sections explore these areas, followed by a discussion of some adherence-promoting structures.

Personal Factors

Unfortunately, the most obvious personal factor—attitude toward exercise—appears to be unrelated to whether a person adheres to an exercise program; that is, most people who lead sedentary lives have extremely favorable attitudes toward exercise. Of the personal factors, perhaps the most accurate predictor of nonadherence is low motivation. A second personal factor is the extent to which the person is achieving his or her exercise objectives. Low motivation and the failure to appear to be making progress toward one's goals may be a near-fatal combination. In the client's behavioral domain, predictors of dropping out of exercise programs include smoking, having inactive leisure-time pursuits, and exhibiting Type A behavior. Being overweight is a biological factor associated with a high dropout rate. Combining the measures of body weight, motivation, and smoking behavior results in 80 percent accuracy in predicting who will adhere to an exercise program and who will drop out (Dishman & Buckworth, 1997). For exercisers of all ages, influences contributing to exercise continuance include believing in the value of physical activity, perceiving fewer barriers to completing exercise, and having higher self-efficacy for exercise participation (King et al., 1998). These are all areas that health counselors can specifically target with clients.

Social/Environmental Factors

Whether perceived or actual, environmental factors are among the significant barriers to exercise adherence. Environmental factors include issues of access to an exercise setting or equipment due to expense or physical location (Dishman, 1994), or the basic logistical dilemma of how to fit exercise into one's busy daily schedule. The major social/environmental factors that appear to predict adherence to an exercise program include support by family members, geographic stability, absence of family problems, and whether exercise is done in a group setting as opposed to exercising alone.

Characteristics of a Program

With regard to the characteristics of the exercise program, adherence is highest when the program is conveniently located and when the program is moderate in intensity. Pollack (1988) notes that moderate exercise prescriptions are associated with greater adherence because less injury occurs when compared to high-intensity prescriptions. Dishman and Buckworth (1997) add that injury occurrence may have a strong influence on maintenance of exercise activity. A more obvious, but often overlooked, characteristic of programs has to do with how fun and enjoyable they are for participants. Enjoyment is a central variable that affects adherence (Wankel, 1993). To address fun and enjoyment, many structured exercise classes located at private gyms look to adopt new formats (e.g., kickboxing aerobics, bootcamp/ station training) to keep participants interested and the activity new and enjoyable.

Adherence-Promoting Program Structure

Martin and Dubbert (1987) explain that, if clients are to establish the exercise habit effectively, their specific concerns about the program and the facility need to be addressed; several considerations and recommendations follow:

1. The overall convenience of the program facility and regimen
2. The use of a group exercise format
3. The supervision of participants by counselors
4. An emphasis on shaping individual responsibility for the exercise program
5. The liberal use of behavioral technologies to prompt and reinforce the exercise habit
6. The utilization of early generalization training
7. The use of continued contact and testing for those who have graduated from the program

Even in the best prescribed programs, it is important that individual clients be prepared to take responsibility for self-motivated home- or work-based exercise programs. As part of this preparation, clients need to be "inoculated" against relapses or slips. Counselors' concern should be not whether clients will slip; a period of time in which they will stop exercising is to be expected. More concern needs to be placed on what clients can do when this occurs and the ways to curb the degree of backsliding. One of the best methods of relapse prevention is relapse prediction (Hays, 1999). Experience shows that it is often helpful to rehearse with clients, *before* the termination of counseling, how relapses will be dealt with when they happen. Strategies and ideas about relapse prevention follow.

Many breaks in the exercise routine are due to injury or sickness, much of which is in turn the result of exercising too intensely (Dishman & Buckworth, 1997). Therefore, a number of relapses might be prevented through more careful shaping and monitoring of the exercise program design. The remainder of the slips or relapses are generally related to (1) work and home changes (e.g., a job transfer, marital conflicts) or (2) motivational problems and loss of interest in the exercise. If slips or relapses do occur Martin and Dubbert (1987) note that it may be helpful to use the following strategies.

1. Participants should admit and take responsibility for the exercise slip, which includes letting go of guilt, blame, and so on. They are to be encouraged to call a friend and talk about the slip in objective (not self-loathing) terms: "It happened"; "it was no one's fault, now what do I do about it?"
2. Participants should plan to exercise the following day or as soon as possible. This includes planning when, where, what, for how long, and with whom. Encourage clients to write these plans down and/or share them with another.

3. Participants could arrange to exercise with someone else. Exercising with someone who is at an equal fitness level or who will agree to exercise at the same intensity enhances reinforcement and distraction. The first day after the slip, the individual should not attempt the highest level of intensity, frequency, or duration of exercise previously achieved, especially after an extended layoff. This would be courting trouble, burnout, and injury. The first several weeks of exercising should be easy and enjoyable to solidly reshape the exercise habit.

4. Participants should prepare completely for exercise on the planned return day, both cognitively and physically. They should get a good night's rest, eat well, go over each step of the return event mentally, lay out proper clothing, clear away competing events, show up early, warm up properly, and give it their best.

5. Participants should be reinforced for showing up. No matter how little or how much they accomplish during the early return-to-exercise sessions, clients should praise themselves and encourage others to praise them for their positive steps. Participants could plan some reinforcing event following each session (e.g., going to the movies or to a favorite healthy dinner spot or taking a nice, hot bath).

Relapse prevention is not something that rests exclusively within clients but is more about a cooperative effort in which both clients and counselors work to overcome potential troubles. Counselors should address relapse head-on by stating: "Most people stop and resume exercising many times before they are able to develop an effective exercise habit and pattern. What situations might get you off track? How long would it last? What has gotten you off track before? What has been helpful in getting you started again?" (Hays, 1999). These types of questions can not only normalize the relapse process but also create adaptive responses that clients can use when they experience periods of relapse. In addition, by addressing relapse, clients begin to focus on their own motivational forces that can contribute to exercising.

One frequent oversight in the process of relapse prevention is the failure to identify conditions that militate against adherence to treatment (Dishman & Buckworth, 1997). Fatigue, sore muscles, and time spent away from the favorite TV shows can be powerful aversive factors in treatment adherence. Without proper identification of these factors, no interventions or "inoculation" measures can be instituted. Questions (e.g., "What will you miss by exercising?" or "What will be the worst part about starting to exercise?") should help pinpoint troublesome areas. Counselors can also ask clients to role-play how they can stand up to aversive factors. Clients may want to make people close to them aware of the aversive factors in an attempt to remove them from their immediate environment and to get support in addressing some of them.

Little research exists to provide specific information on the best adherence program. Several characteristics of successful exercise programs have already been mentioned. Additional characteristics that receive considerable attention in the literature are locus of control, perceived self-efficacy, and the exercise setting.

Locus of Control.   Studies note that individuals who are best able to internalize their own reinforcements, or are able to better motivate themselves, experience a higher internal locus of control than those who are primarily other-oriented in their reinforcement process

(Dishman & Buckworth, 1997). Not surprisingly, Carter, Lee, and Greenockle (1987) found that the expected adherence of clients who are engaged in the exercise program is consistent with their understanding of how able they are to control the outcome of their efforts. Subjects in the study who saw themselves as able to change, particularly with regard to exercise-related behaviors, had the highest actual performance rate.

Perceived Self-Efficacy.   Perceived self-efficacy is the internalization of the concept that one can succeed at a given task with a given set of circumstances. Research supports self-efficacy as an essential component in the process of treatment adherence and relapse prevention (Dishman & Buckworth, 1997). The self-evaluative process is a part of the client's set of expectations for treatment, and it is an area that deserves considerable explanation at the beginning of treatment. Although a client may have a firm sense of his or her ability to be efficacious in an exercise program, this does not mean that the counselor and the client cannot make the appropriate interventions that would affect the continuation of this motivation positively early in the program. One suggestion is that clients learn some cognitive-restructuring techniques to address self-defeating or negative beliefs, which tend to erode self-efficacy. Attempts at altering the client's self-perception should be made with his or her knowledge and, perhaps more important, cooperation. In addition, guided imagery is an excellent way to intervene on a cognitive level. The counselor can also carefully arrange exercise assignments that are easily attainable, thereby enhancing the client's sense of self-efficacy.

Exercise Setting.   Writers and researchers have identified the exercise setting as one of the more problematic areas in relapse prevention and exercise adherence. It should be noted, however, that while it certainly is an important component, it is not the only one that affects adherence. A crucial component to tailoring exercise programs is paying close attention to varying the setting in which the exercise is performed in order to alleviate boredom. If enjoyment and fun is one of the most important factors in terms of adherence, then whenever possible the exercise setting should be fun. Ardell (1986) suggests that counselors use a variety of exercises and be careful not to rely on just one or two modalities of exercise.

An immediate intervention to address boredom is cross-training, which involves using several exercise modalities as part of an exercise program (e.g., bike one day, run another, swim on a third day, and so on). Encourage people to exercise in interesting locations (e.g., on bike paths, alongside a lake or ocean, in parks) as opposed to remaining indoors; also, periodically change the route to create new visual stimuli. Of course, when selecting the setting, be sure that it is readily accessible and an almost obvious choice for clients. Counselors must be very sensitive to individual needs and develop an exercise location that is convenient; a program based solely on one's physical ailments and exercise needs has a high probability of failure.

CONCLUDING NOTE

The Surgeon General's *Report on Physical Activity and Health* (USDHHS, 1996) provided ample justification for the continued emphasis on physical activity objectives that are in

Healthy People 2010 (USDHHS, 2000). For 2010, physical activity is once again the first health indicator listed. Specific objectives call for increasing the proportion of adolescents who engage in vigorous physical activity and for increasing the proportion of adults who engage in regular, preferably daily, moderate physical activity. Whereas these objectives make clear sense in light of the physical, health, social, and psychological benefits associated with exercise, it is unlikely that the general public will immediately reverse the current sedentary behavior that plagues the U.S. population. Questions remain as to how these objectives can be reached.

Health counseling professionals can play an important role in helping people develop the necessary behavioral and motivational aspects to initiate and maintain an exercise program. By tailoring exercise prescriptions with regard to mode, frequency, intensity, and duration, counselors can increase the likelihood of habit formation. When they apply the tools of the profession (i.e., behavior and cognitive interventions, appropriate goal setting, effective intervention tailoring, attention to relapse prevention, etc.) to the area of exercise, clients can be empowered and effectively prepared to meet their exercise goals and adherence.

RESOURCES

Web Sites

- American College of Sports Medicine, P.O. Box 1440, Indianapolis, IN 46206, (317) 637-9200—www.acsm.org.
- American Psychological Association, Division 47: Exercise and Sport Psychology—www.psyc.unt.edu/apadiv47
- Exercise Guidelines for Physical Fitness—www.mckinley.uiuc.edu/health-info/fitness/exercise/exercise.html
- Exercise Information for Women—www.womensexercisenetwork.com

- Information about children and exercise—http://kidshealth.org/index.html
- YMCA of the U.S.A., Program Resources, 6400 Shafer Court, Rosemount, IL 60018—www.ymca.net.
- YWCA of the U.S.A. 1015 18th Street, NW, Suite 1100 Washington, DC 20036, (800) YWCA US1—www.ywca.org.

REFERENCES

Airhehenbuwa, C. O., Kumanyika, S., Agurs, T. D., & Lowe, A. (1995). Perceptions and beliefs about exercise, rest, and health among African-Americans. *American Journal of Health Promotion, 9,* 426–429.

American College of Sports Medicine (ACSM). (1978). The recommended quantity and quality of exercise for developing and maintaining fitness in healthy adults. *Medicine and Science in Sports and Exercise, 10,* vii–x.

American College of Sports Medicine. (1990). The recommended quantity and quality of exercise for developing and maintaining cardiorespiratory and muscular fitness in healthy adults. *Medicine and Science in Sports and Exercise, 22,* 265–274.

American College of Sports Medicine. (1998a). ACSM on exercise and physical activity for older adults. *Medicine and Science in Sports and Exercise, 30,* 975–991

American College of Sports Medicine. (1998b). The recommended quantity and quality of exercise for developing and maintaining cardiorespiratory and muscular fitness in healthy adults. *Medicine and Science in Sports and Exercise, 30,* 992–1008.

Annesi, J. J. (1998). Effects of computer feedback on adherence to exercise. *Perceptual and Motor Skills, 87,* 723–730.

Annesi, J. J. (2001). Effects of music, television, and a combination entertainment system on distraction, exercise adherence, and physical output in adults. *Canadian Journal of Behavioural Science, 33,* 193–202.

Annesi, J. J. & Mazas, J. (1997). Effects of virtual reality-enhanced exercise equipment on adherence and exercise-induced feeling states. *Perceptual and Motor Skills, 85,* 835–844.

Ardell, D. B. (1986). *High level wellness.* Berkeley: Ten Speed Press.

Armstrong, N., & Van Mechelen, W. (1998). Are young people fit and active? In S. Biddle, J. F. Sallis, & N. A. Cavill (Eds.), *Young and active? Young people and health enhancing physical activity: Evidence and implications* (pp. 69–97). London: Health Education Authority.

Blumenthal, J. A., Babyak, M. A., Moore, K. A., Craighead, W. E., Herman, S., & Khatri, P. (1999). Effects of exercise training on older patients with major depression. *Archives of Internal Medicine, 159,* 2349–2356.

Bolen, J. C., Rhodes, L., Powell-Grner, E. E., Bland, S. D., & Holtzman, D. (2000, March 24). State-specific prevalence of selected health behaviors, by race and ethnicity—Behavioral risk factor surveillance system, 1997. *Morbidity and Mortality Weekly Reports, 49*(SS02), 1–60.

Boutcher, S. (1993). Emotion and aerobic exercise. In R. N. Singer, M. Murphey, & L. K. Tennant (Eds.), *Handbook of research on sport psychology* (pp. 799–814). New York: Macmillan.

Bouchard, C., Shephard, R. J., & Stephens, T. (Eds.). (1994). *Physical activity, fitness, and health: International proceedings and consensus statement.* Champaign, IL: Human Kinetics.

Carter, J., Lee, A., & Greenockle, K. (1987). Locus of control, fitness values, success expectations, and performance in fitness class. *Perceptual and Motor Skills, 65,* 777–778.

Centers for Disease Control and Prevention (CDC). (1993). Prevalence of sedentary lifestyle—Behavioral risk-factor surveillance system: United States, 1991. *Morbidity and Mortality Weekly Report, 42,* 576–579.

Centers for Disease Control and Prevention. (1998, December 25). Self-reported physical inactivity by degree of urbanization—United States, 1996. *Morbidity and Mortality Weekly Report, 47*(50), 1097–1100.

Centers for Disease Control and Prevention. (2000, May 19). Prevalence of leisure-time and occupational physical activity among employed adults—United States, 1990. *Morbidity and Mortality Weekly Reports, 49*(19), 420–424.

Centers for Disease Control and Prevention. (2001, March 9). Physical activity trends—United States, 1990–1998. *Morbidity and Mortality Weekly Reports, 50*(9), 166–169.

Cerney, F. J., Burton, H. W., & Armstrong, L. E. (2001). *Exercise physiology for health care professionals.* Champaign, IL: Human Kinetics.

Courneya, K. S. (1995). Cohesion correlates with affect in structured exercise classes. *Perceptual and Motor Skills, 81,* 1021–1022.

Dishman, R. (1988). *Exercise adherence: Its impact on public health.* Champaign, IL: Human Kinetics.

Dishman, R. K. (1994). Introduction: Consensus, problems, and prospects. In R. K. Dishman (Ed.), *Advances in exercise adherence* (pp. 1–27). Champaign, IL: Human Kinetics.

Dishman, R. K., & Buckworth, J. (1996). Increasing physical activity: A quantitative synthesis. *Medicine and Science in Sport and Exercise, 28,* 706–719.

Dishman, R. K., & Buckworth, J. (1997). Adherence to physical activity. In W. P. Morgan (Ed.), *Physical activity and mental health* (pp. 63–80). Philadelphia: Taylor & Francis.

Dubbert, P. M. (2002). Physical activity and exercise: Recent advances and current challenges. *Journal of Consulting and Clinical Psychology, 70,* 526–536.

Duda, J. (1991). Editorial comment. *Journal of Sport Psychology, 3,* 1–6.

Emery, C. F., Schein, R. L., Hauck, E. R., & MacIntyre, N. R. (1998). Psychological and cognitive outcomes of a randomized trial of exercise among patients with chronic obstructive pulmonary disease. *Health Psychology, 17,* 232–240.

Estivill, M. (1995). Therapeutic aspects of aerobic dance participation. *Health Care for Women International, 16,* 341–350.

Fitzgerald, J., Singleton, S., Neale, A., & Prasad, A. (1994). Activity levels, fitness status, exercise knowledge, and exercise beliefs among healthy, older African-American and white women. *Journal of Aging and Health, 6,* 296–313.

Fletcher, G. F., Balady, G., Blair, S. N., Blumenthal, J., Caspersen, C., & Chaitman, B. (1996). Statement on exercise: Benefits and recommendations for physical activity programs for all Americans. A statement for health professionals by the Committee on Exercise and Cardiac Rehabilitation of the Council on Clinical Cardiology, American Heart Association. *Circulation, 94,* 857–862.

Folsom, A. R., Cook, T. C., Sprafka, J. M., Burke, G. L., Norsted, S. W., & Jacobs, D. R. (1991). Differences in leisure-time physical activity levels between blacks and whites in population-based sample: The Minnesota Heart Survey. *Journal of Behavioral Medicine, 14,* 1–9.

Gilbert, L. A., & Scher, M. (1999). *Gender and sex in counseling and psychotherapy.* Boston: Allyn & Bacon.

Glenister, D. (1996). Exercise and mental health: A review. *Journal of the Royal Society of Health, 116,* 7–13.

Hansen, C. J., Stevens, L. C., & Coast, J. R. (2001). Exercise duration and mood state: How much is enough to feel better? *Health Psychology, 20,* 267–275

Hausenblas, H. A., & Downs, D. S. (2002). Relationships among sex, imagery, and exercise dependence symptoms. *Psychology of Addictive Behaviors, 16,* 169–172.

Hays, K. F. (1999). *Working it out: Using exercise in psychotherapy.* Washington, DC: American Psychological Association.

Housh, T. J., Housh, D. J., & Devries, H. A. (2002). *Applied exercise and sport.* Scottsdale, AZ: Holcomb Hathaway.

Kimiecik, J. C. (1999, April). Associative and dissociate behavior modification strategies to promote regular exercise. *IDEA Health and Fitness Source,* 37–43.

King, A. C., Castro, C., Wilcox, S., Eyler, A. A., Sallis, J. F., & Bronson, R. C. (2000). Personal and environmental factors associated with physical inactivity among different racial–ethnic groups of middle-aged and older-aged women. *Health Psychology, 19,* 354–364.

King, A. C., Rejeski, W. J., & Buchner, D. M. (1998). Physical activity interventions targeting older adults: A critical review and recommendations. *American Journal of Preventive Medicine, 15,* 316–333.

Kramer, A. F., Hahn, S., Cohen, N. J., Banich, M. T., McAuley, E., & Harrison, C. R. (1999). Ageing, fitness, and neurocognitive function. *Nature, 400,* 418–419.

Marcus, B. H., & Simkin, L. R. (1993). The stages of exercise behavior. *Journal of Sports Medicine and Physical Fitness, 33,* 83–88

Marks, D. F., Murray, M., Evans, B., & Willig, C. (2000). *Health psychology: Theory, research, and practice.* London: Sage.

Martin, J. E., & Dubbert, P. M. (1987). Exercise promotion. In J. A. Blumenthal & D. C. McKee (Eds.), *Applications in behavioral medicine and health psychology: A clinician's source book*

(pp. 361–398). Sarasota: Professional Resource Exchange.

Martin, J. E., Dubbert, P. M., Catell, A. O., Thompson, J. K., Raczynski, J. R., Lake, M., et al. (1984). Behavioral control of exercise in sedentary adults. Studies 1–6. *Journal of Consulting and Clinical Psychology, 52,* 795–811.

Masters, K. S., & Ogles, B. M. (1998). Associative and dissociate cognitive strategies in exercise and running: 20 years later, what do we know? *The Sport Psychologist, 12,* 253–270

McArdle, W. D., Katch, F. I., & Katch, V. (2001). *Exercise physiology: Energy, nutrition, and human performance* (5th ed). Philadelphia: Lippincott/Williams & Wilkins.

National Center for Health Statistics. (1994). *Healthy people 2000 review, 1993.* Hyattsville, MD: Public Health Service.

National Center for Health Statistics. (1999). *Healthy people 2000 review, 1998–99.* Hyattsville, MD: Public Health Service.

NIH Consensus Development Panel on Physical Activity and Cardiovascular Health. (1996). Physical activity and cardiovascular health. *Journal of the American Medical Association, 276,* 241–246.

Pate, R. R., Pratt, M., Blair, S. N., Haskell, W. L., Macera, C. A., & Bouchard, C. (1995). Physical activity and public health: A recommendation from the Centers for Disease Control and Prevention and the American College of Sports Medicine. *Journal of the American Medical Association, 273,* 402–407.

Perri, M. G., Anton, S. D., Durning, P. E., Ketterson, T. U., Sydeman, S. J., Berlant, N. E., et al. (2002). Adherence to exercise prescriptions: Effects of prescribing moderate versus higher levels of intensity and frequency. *Health Psychology, 21,* 452–458.

Pollack, M. L. (1988). Prescribing exercise for fitness and adherence. In R. K. Dishman (Ed.), *Exercise adherence: Its impact on public health* (pp. 259–277). Champaign, IL: Human Kinetics.

Porcari, J. P., Zedaker, J. M., & Maldari, M. M. (1998). Virtual motivation. *Fitness Management, 14,* 50–51; also http://www.fitnessworld.com/library/virtual1298.html.

Prentice, W. E., Arnheim, D. D., & Hall, S. (2002). *Arnheim's principles of athletic training* (11th ed.). New York: McGraw-Hill.

Prochaska, J. O. (1994). Strong and weak principles for progressing from precontemplation to action on the basis of twelve problem behaviors. *Health Psychology, 13,* 47–51.

Prochaska, J. O., Norcross, J. C., & DiClemente, C. C. (1994). *Changing for good.* New York: William Morrow.

Rosen, C. S. (2000). Integrating stage and continuum models to explain processing of exercise messages and exercise initiation among sedentary college students. *Health Psychology, 19,* 172–180.

Sallis, J. F., & Owen, N. (1998). *Physical activity and behavioral medicine.* Thousand Oaks, CA: Sage.

Salmon, P. (2000). Effects of physical exercise on anxiety, depression, and sensitivity to stress: A unifying theory. *Clinical Exercise Review, 21,* 33–61.

Scott, L. M., Scott, D., Bedic, S. P., & Dowd, J. (1999). The effects of associative and dissociative strategies on rowing ergometer performance. *The Sport Psychologist, 13,* 57–68.

Sime, W. E. (1996). Guidelines for clinical applications of exercise therapy for mental health. In J. L. Van Raalte & B. W. Brewer (Eds.), *Exploring sport and exercise psychology* (pp. 159–187). Washington, DC: American Psychological Association.

Steinberg, H., Nicholls, B. R., Sykes, E. A., LeBoutillier, N., Ramlakhan, N., Moss, T. P., & Dewey, A. (1998). Weekly exercise consistently reinstates positive mood. *European Psychologist, 3,* 271–280.

Stetson, B. A., Rahn, J. M., Dubbert, P. M., Wilner, B. I., & Mercury, M. G. (1997). Prospective evaluation of the effects of stress on exercise adherence in community-residing women. *Health Psychology, 16,* 515–520

Taylor, S. (1999). *Health psychology* (4th ed.). New York: McGraw-Hill.

Thompson, C. E., & Wankel, L. M. (1980). The effects of perceived activity choice upon frequency of exercise behavior. *Journal of Applied Social Psychology, 10,* 436–443.

Tkachuk, G. A., & Martin, G. L. (1999). Exercise therapy for patients with psychiatric disorders: Research and clinical implications. *Professional Psychology: Research and Practice, 30,* 275–282.

U.S. Department of Health and Human Services (USDHHS). (1996). *Physical activity and health: A report of the Surgeon General.* Atlanta, GA: Author.

U.S. Department of Health and Human Services. (2000). *Healthy people 2010* (Conference ed.). Washington, DC: U.S. Government Printing Office.

Wankel, L. M. (1993). The importance of enjoyment to adherence and psychological benefits from physical activity. *International Journal of Sport Psychology, 24,* 151–169.

Zipes, D. (2002). 10,000 steps to health. *Medical Update, 28,* 4.

CHAPTER EIGHT

SLEEP

'Tis sleep that knits up the ravell'd sleave of care . . . balm of hurt minds, great nature's second course, chief nourisher in life's feast.
—Shakespeare

For many, good health has become a preoccupation and, even an obsession for some. Today, people count calories, jog, eat healthy food, work out with weights, practice yoga, and take their own pulse and blood pressure readings. Yet, the quest for fitness by day can be undermined by poor or lack of sleep at night. Sleep loss can shatter an individual's timing, resilience, zest for life, and sense of well-being. Good sleep appears to be a basic requirement for feeling aware, energized, and healthy. Disturbed sleep, however, is one of the most common health complaints noted in surveys of the general population. In the United States, about 80 million people experience a variety of sleep problems. Some have problems going to or staying asleep (insomnia), others stop breathing in their sleep (sleep apnea), some go from being awake to very deep sleep quickly without any warning (narcolepsy), and about 25 percent of children have sleep disturbances (Carskadon & Taylor, 1997). Whereas short-term or transient insomnia is virtually a universal human experience, chronic and severe insomnia affect 15 to 30 percent of U.S. adults (Maxmen & Ward, 1995). In fact, one poll found that 58 percent of adults report some type of insomnia (Hellmich, 2000).

When compared with the prevalence of major psychiatric disorders—depression, anxiety, schizophrenia, and alcohol and substance dependence—the prevalence of chronic insomnia and other sleep disorders is greater. Not surprisingly, research indicates that sleep disorders are relatively common among individuals who manifest psychiatric disorders (Pallesen et al., 2001). Further, insomnia is one of several criteria for different anxiety and affective disorders (American Psychiatric Association, 2000) and constitutes a symptom in several other organic difficulties (e.g., allergies, chronic pain, cerebrovascular diseases)—see Wooten (1994).

Although individuals with sleep disorders typically seek treatment from physicians, health counselors and mental health clinicians can play an important role in treatment for these problems. It is unlikely, however, that many mental health counselors will work in sleep clinics or specialize in the treatment of sleep disorders. But it is quite likely that counselors will encounter disordered sleep, particularly insomnia, among the concerns of clients who seek counseling for other reasons. Thus, this chapter focuses on background information and treatment strategies for sleep (especially insomnia) that are applicable, in both individual and group settings, to clients who present with various health and/or mental health concerns.

CHARACTERISTICS OF SLEEP

Despite the importance of sleep in our lives, researchers have not been able to answer the basic question: Why do we sleep? The function of sleep has been the basis for much speculation and investigation. There currently are two popular theories—adaptive and repair—as to why people spend about a third of each day sleeping (Plotnik, 2002). The *adaptive theory* suggests that sleep has evolved because it prevents humans and animals from wasting energy and exposing themselves to the dangers of nocturnal predators. Support for this theory is found in observations that large predatory animals often sleep wherever they wish, whereas smaller prey sleep far less and in protected areas. In addition, Hirshkowitz, Moore, and Minhoto (1997) note that animals (including humans) who rely primarily on visual cues and have little night vision have also evolved a circadian clock for sleep at night to avoid becoming prey. The *repair theory* suggests that activities during the day deplete key factors in one's body and brain and that sleep serves a replenishing or reparative function.

Support for the repair hypothesis comes from multiple findings. It appears that the brain and body need sleep to grow, repair the immune system, and maintain an optimal mood. During sleep there is an increase in the secretion of growth hormone, which controls aspects of metabolism, physical growth, and brain development. In addition, during sleep there is an increase in the production of immune cells to fight off infections (Born et al., 1997). Finally, it has been observed that moderate changes in sleep cycles resulted in reports of decreased happiness and cheerfulness (Boivin et al., 1997). Other theories include the *ethologic theory,* which holds that sleep is a controlled system that enhances survival; and the *instinctive theory,* which postulates that sleep is an instinct such as migration, courtship dances, or imprinting.

All of these theories are compatible, and it seems likely that sleep serves multiple functions. It may well be that a certain minimal amount of sleep is required to restore some bodily processes and that additional sleep may vary according to ethological requirements or specific needs to conserve energy. The following three sections discuss the stages of sleep, individuals' sleep needs, and the circadian rhythm.

Stages of Sleep

When you go to sleep each night, it may feel like your sleep is unbroken for 8 hours and then you wake up. Sleep is not one unbroken state but a series of recurring stages and types that are traditionally measured and defined by an electroencephalogram (EEG). The EEG measures the changes in brain waves that occur during sleep, thus your brain never really sleeps but instead goes through different stages. The two basic types of sleep are rapid eye movement (REM) and non-rapid eye movement (NREM), as well as a transition phase between sleep and wakefulness. NREM sleep is where people spend most of their time and it begins when a person falls asleep—becomes disengaged or decreasingly conscious of the outside world. This moment of disengagement is sudden, precise, and signals the onset of sleep. Following the onset of sleep, the NREM stage involves a descent into periods of decreasing brain activity that are categorized into four stages (Hirshkowitz, Moore, & Minhoto, 1997).

Stage one sleep is the transition from wakefulness to sleep, which often lasts 1 to 7 minutes. EEG activity slows from alpha waves, which are the dominant resting–waking pattern, to theta (3–7 cycles per second). Activity slows further with the onset of stage two sleep, which occurs within several minutes after falling asleep. A person awakened from stage one sleep usually reports a feeling of having been awake all along.

Stage two sleep is the longest of the sleep stages and occupies 50 to 70 percent of adults' sleep. EEG activity at this stage consists largely of beta waves and two electrical phenomena called spindles and K-complexes, which are thought to be a response to both external and internal stimuli. As people pass through stage two sleep, muscle tension, heart rate, respiration, and body temperature general decrease, and it is harder to be awakened (Plotnik, 2002). People awakened from this stage usually report having had short, fragmented, and mundane thoughts, but they report having been asleep.

Stage three sleep is characterized by the presence of slow, high-amplitude delta waves (1 to 4 cycles per second). Delta sleep is the deepest type of sleep and is commonly believed to be the most restorative. It occurs primarily in the early part of the night and occupies 20 to 50 percent of adults' sleep.

Stage four sleep is considered to have the lowest level of physiological, neurological, and psychological activity. The threshold for arousal by external stimuli is higher at stage four than at any other time, and sleep-deprivation studies suggest that this stage may be the most necessary element of sleep. After several nights of total sleep deprivation, the length of stage four sleep increases dramatically on the first recovery night. So, a person permitted only 4 or 5 hours of sleep over several nights will soon exhibit a "rebound" effect, meaning that when allowed to sleep undisturbed, he or she will compensate by having about 60 percent more REM sleep than the person normally would.

REM sleep is characterized by rapid eye movement (eyes move rapidly back and forth behind closed lids), which usually occurs in short bursts. REM sleep makes up about 20 percent of sleep time (Plotnik, 2002). Although muscle tone is lowest during REM sleep, small twitches may be noted in many muscle groups. Heart rate and blood pressure may be twice as high during REM sleep (Dement, 1999). The stage is associated with dreaming, and 80 percent of those awakened from REM sleep report having had vivid dreams. The strange combination of being asleep yet remaining physiologically aroused during REM sleep is often called paradoxical sleep.

Now that you understand the types and stages of sleep, it is important to understand a typical sleep cycle. A single night of sleep consists of 4 to 6 cycles of NREM/REM sleep. The first sleep cycle is as follows: stage one, stage two, stage three, stage four, stage three, stage two, and REM. On going to bed, the normal sleeper enters stage one and then passes into stage two; after 10 to 30 minutes in stage two, the sleeper gradually enters delta sleep in stages three and four. Within 90 minutes, the sleeper cycles to stage two and then enters a REM period that lasts only a few moments. This first REM period is the least intense REM stage in terms of both physiological manifestations and dream intensity. The remaining sleep

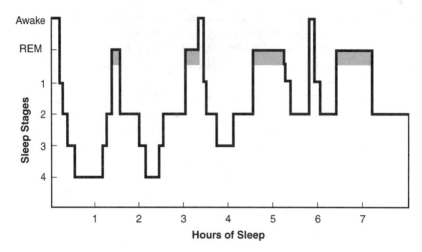

FIGURE 8.1 **Sleep Cycles in a Normal Adult**

cycles are the same, but they follow a slightly different course: REM, stage one, stage two, stage three, stage four, stage three, and stage two. Each sleep cycle lasts approximately 90 minutes and, as the night progresses, stages three and four decrease, but each REM episode lasts longer. REM sleep becomes more intense both physiologically and psychologically toward morning; whereas delta sleep is rarely seen during the latter sleep cycles (Dement, 1999). Five or more spontaneous awakenings are spread throughout these sleep cycles. For good sleepers, awakenings typically last for a few seconds to a few minutes each. Although the sleeper is responsive to environmental stimuli during these periods of arousal—for instance, removing a blanket if it is too warm in the room—the brief awakenings are seldom recalled in the morning. Figure 8.1 visually depicts the sleep cycles of a normal adult.

Sleep Needs across the Lifespan

Sleep is not a constant phenomenon but changes noticeably across the developmental lifespan. With the changes in sleep across the lifespan come different percentages of time spent sleeping, time in REM sleep, and the types of sleep problems. Total sleep time increases as the individual matures and then gradually decreases. From infancy to adolescence, the amount of time spent sleeping and the amount of REM sleep gradually decreases. A child sleeps about 18 hours a day when newborn (about 50% of that time in REM sleep), 10 to 12 hours a day by age 4 (25–30% of that time in REM sleep), 9 to 10 hours at age 10, and about 7½ to 8 hours by adolescence. By the age of 20, adolescents have adopted the sleep pattern of adults, which is about 7 to 8 hours of sleep (20% or less being REM sleep). By the age of 60, total sleep need has dropped to about 6 hours with the amount of REM sleep remaining constant (Plotnik, 2002). Although time spent asleep decreases over the adult years, time spent in bed increases after about age 40, so adults spend more time in bed but get less sleep. The configuration of sleep for the older adult is unlike that of the adolescent or young adult. Typically, older people experience decreases in periods of deep, or delta stage, sleep and experience increases in light, or stage one and two, sleep. At age 70, the delta stage makes up less than 10 percent of sleep, as compared with 15 to 25 percent during adolescence and young adulthood. As a result of this increased percentage of light sleep, older adults find themselves awakening more often during the night (Dement, 1999).

One of the enduring questions about sleep is: Exactly how much sleep does the average individual need to be alert and energetic throughout the day? The consensus in Western culture is that 8 hours is the optimum amount of sleep. However, evidence shows that the answer to the question is that individuals require smaller or larger amounts of sleep depending on age. Many people needlessly worry because their sleep pattern does not match the norm of 8 hours. Normal sleep across individuals ranges from 3 to 10 hours per night. Each individual, whether child or adult, has a personal ideal for the amount of sleep needed. The best measure of sufficient sleep is adequate daytime functioning; that is, an individual who remains alert and energetic during wakefulness is probably getting sufficient sleep (Coren, 1996). Recent research, however, notes that when compared to adults, adolescents need more sleep (almost 10 hours) and that their circadian clocks favor going to bed later and getting up later (Carskadon, 2000). Thus, adolescents who must get up early for school are often sleep-deprived.

As the type and amount of sleep changes with age, the incidence of sleep dysfunction increases. Typical sleep dysfunction in young children includes nightmares, enuresis (bedwetting), and bedtime fears. Because adolescents often underestimate their sleep needs and become sleep deprived, they may have difficulty getting up in the morning. For young and middle-age adults, transient and chronic insomnia are common. Among older adults, there is a sharp increase in the incidence of sleep apnea (cessation of breathing), nocturnal myoclonus (muscle spasms), and chronic insomnia. With reference to insomnia, older people suffer more from frequent and longer mid-cycle awakenings or early morning awakenings, whereas insomnia in younger adults is characterized by initial insomnia (i.e., difficulty failing asleep). In people over 60, about 30 percent report trouble getting to sleep, and 65 percent report difficulties staying asleep, which is often due to daytime napping (Bliwise, 1997). All of these changes seem to occur at an earlier age in females than in males (Dement, 1999).

Circadian Rhythms

There are many biological "clocks" in the brain that must be regularly synchronized for one to remain in a state of good health. *Biological clocks* can be understood as internal timing devices that are genetically set to regulate various physiological responses for different periods of time (e.g., the secretion of urine is an hourly biological clock, the rise and fall of body temperature is a single-day clock, and the menstrual cycle is a monthly clock; see Plotnik, 2002). *Circadian rhythms* are biological cycles that require about 24 hours to complete, and of the body's various circadian rhythms, the sleep–wake cycle is one of the most important. When normal individuals live with no time cues, they usually show a sleep–wake rhythm that lasts around 24 hours and 18 minutes (Czeisler et al., 1999). Most individuals who work in the daytime have a circadian system with a diurnal orientation—they sleep at night and are awake during the day. Individuals who work at night must acclimate to a nocturnal orientation, which often results in being awake at night and asleep during the day. Over time, this circadian system can accommodate a change from a diurnal to a nocturnal orientation. But the inborn clock that controls the circadian system does not reset itself immediately after abrupt changes in the sleep–wake cycle. Until it does, the individual may experience sleep deprivation, mood changes, difficulty with concentration, and poor work performance. In short, the circadian system has a profound influence on sleep–wake cycles.

Entrainment is the mechanism that keeps the circadian system on a 24-hour diurnal orientation. Entrainment relies on *zeitgebers*—a German word for time giver—to allow the circadian system to become oriented accurately. Zeitgebers can be physical phenomena, such as the alternation of daylight and darkness, or social practices involving cultural patterns and knowledge of clock time. Zeitgebers must be experienced by the individual for entrainment to follow. Entrainment is particularly important because a day is agreed to be exactly 24 hours long, but the genetically set sleep–wake circadian clock, as noted before, is set for an average of 24 hours and 18 minutes. Thus, the sleep–wake cycle needs to be reset about 18 minutes each day. For most people, this reset occurs automatically, yet for individuals who are socially isolated, have an irregular routine, or have little exposure to daylight, they could not be entrained to a 24-hour cycle. When entrainment does not occur, people often experience decreased cognitive performance, work-related and traffic accidents, jet lag, and various sleep disorders (Young, 2000).

SLEEP DISORDERS AND IRREGULAR SCHEDULES

The endogenous, self-sustaining nature of the circadian system and the need for an entrainment mechanism to keep it cycling on time suggest how sleep disorders can arise from irregular schedules. When major changes in the sleep–wake cycle occur, significant changes in the circadian system can be expected. Accordingly, the individual's biological clock will no longer be running "on time," so sleep, daytime alertness, and well-being become impaired; often, that impairment is chronic. Lifestyle changes, jet lag, shift work, and depression are all associated with circadian dysfunction.

Changes in Lifestyle

If an individual's lifestyle is such that the normal and necessary physical and social zeitgebers are disregarded and replaced with a cavalier attitude toward the timing of sleep, insomnia is likely to occur. On the other hand, a regimen of both indoor and outdoor activity that allows an adequate exposure to the necessary zeitgebers and ensures a regular daily pattern of sleep is often all that is necessary to realign the circadian system.

Jet Lag

Because of the increase in air travel across many time zones in one day, jet lag is becoming a major source of circadian deregulation. *Jet lag* refers to a state experienced by travelers in which their circadian clock is out of sync with the external clock at their destination (Plotnik, 2002). Jet lag often results in fatigue, disorientation, lack of concentration, reduced cognitive skills, irritability, and slowed physical reactions. Further complicating matters, sleeping is often difficult, fragmented, and not very restful. The severity of these problems generally depends on the number of time zones crossed (Coren, 1996). A distinction must be made between the effects that result from the particular environmental conditions of air travel and the effects that result from the need to realign the circadian system, because it is the latter that has the most direct and longer term impact on the individual's sleep. Jet lag is not limited to sleep deprivation; it is also a problem of daytime functioning, which is affected by two other processes.

The first process concerns inappropriate phasing and the physiological and psychological functions associated with alertness, well-being, and performance efficiency exhibiting endogenous, self-sustaining circadian rhythms. These rhythms are timed in such a way that the down phase of the sleep–wake cycle normally coincides with the timing of sleep. But, after a flight to a new time zone, the down phase may coincide with a time that is normally meant for daytime activities. Therefore, performance and mood can be impaired by the individual's shift into the down phase of the cycle. The second process that affects daytime functioning is called *dissociation*—there is rhythmic disharmony in the circadian rhythms. A good analogy is that of a symphony orchestra that is not playing in concert. Circadian dissociation is characterized by feelings of tiredness and malaise, gastrointestinal dysfunction, and irritability.

For most travelers, jet lag is an acute problem that lasts only a few days. The sleep pattern can be improved by speeding up the process of circadian realignment and it generally takes about one day to reset the circadian clock for each hour of time zone change (Plotnik, 2002). Regardless of the time zone, travelers have the advantage of physical and social zeitgebers working on their behalf. Thus, by rigidly avoiding daytime napping and maximizing exposure to physical and social zeitgebers, travelers can greatly reduce the duration of circadian misalignment and its adverse effects. But resolving the sleep problem eliminates only one of the three components of jet lag. Inappropriate phasing and circadian dissociation can be improved only by speeding up the process of circadian realignment or, in the case of inappropriate phasing, by careful scheduling of activities.

Shift Work

When compared to jet lag, the sleep problems of workers on rotating or night shifts are far more complex. For people engaged in shift work, sleep deprivation is chronic, and physical and social zeitgebers are impervious to nocturnal circadian realignment. At this point, it is not clear whether a perfect realignment can ever be accomplished. The primary impact of the circadian system on sleep results from the system's inability to adjust instantly to the change from a diurnal to a nocturnal routine. However, circadian factors are not the only determinants of the shift-worker's sleep problems. The worker's ability to cope with the rotating or permanent night-shift schedule is influenced by three interrelated factors: circadian realignment, sleep hygiene (the behaviors and rituals involved in falling and staying asleep), and domestic and social factors.

As with jet lag, during the adjustment period, there are three mechanisms by which mood, well-being, and performance efficiency can be greatly affected. First, sleep becomes disrupted, which results in a stage of partial sleep deprivation. Second, nighttime wakefulness overlaps with the down phases of various psychological functions normally associated with sleep in the day-oriented individual. Third, the various components of the circadian system become disordered so that the normal harmony of appropriate phase relationships is significantly changed.

If the shift worker resides in a well-adjusted household, sleep is likely to be interrupted by the demands of childcare, shopping, and household management. Unfortunately, domestic disharmony is frequently blamed on the shift-worker's need for sleep at a time when households are usually rather noisy. The worker is also socially isolated from day-working friends, which compounds shift-work intolerance. On the other hand, in "company towns" where working different shifts is the rule rather than the exception and social and community events are scheduled accordingly, shift work seems to be better tolerated.

Staying awake when one's sleep clock calls for sleep results in decreased performance and impaired cognitive and motor skills. Employees who work the graveyard shift tend to experience a high number of accidents. The worst time tends to be 5 A.M., when it is difficult to stay awake (Luna, French, & Mitcha, 1997). One reason shift workers have so many accidents is that the sleep–wake clock has prepared the body for sleep (i.e., feeling sleepy, less attentive and alert, etc.) at the very moment when the workers are required to be the most awake (Boivin et al., 1997).

If only shift workers and their families felt the effects of shift work and circadian disregulation, the general public might be disinterested. But the fact of the matter is that shift work and circadian disregulation have profound implications for the environment and the world's population. It may be a coincidence, but some of the most renowned disasters or near disasters at nuclear power plants, such as Chernobyl, Three Mile Island, Davis-Besse (Ohio), and Rancho-Seco (California), occurred during the early morning hours and involved human error. In addition, reports about tragedies (e.g., Bhopal, the *Valdez*–Alaskan oil spill, and even the decision to launch the 1986 *Challenger* Space Shuttle) cite the contribution of human error and poor judgment related to sleep loss and shift work (Coren, 1996; Harrison & Horne, 2000). All of these disasters occurred around 4 A.M. (or involved crucial decisions around that time) and have been attributed to errors in judgment by shift workers.

Treatment for shift-workers' sleep deprivation is not only complex but also difficult, because of chronic sleep loss and the inability of natural daytime zeitgebers to realign the circadian system to a nocturnal orientation. Other factors, such as daytime, domestic, and social functions, can encroach on shift-workers' sleep time and further compound the problem. In addition, shift workers find it difficult to remain on a night-shift schedule on their days off. Research shows that most revert to a day-oriented routine and fail to maintain their nocturnal circadian orientation. Shift workers must be encouraged to adhere to a regular sleep schedule and to receive sufficient support and cooperation—honor the sleep schedule—from those with whom they live. Further, supervisors and those involved with scheduling workers' shifts should become more knowledgeable about the effects of shift work on circadian rhythms. Those who work in law enforcement and in the nursing and medical fields are prime candidates for chronic sleep disturbances since they are often asked to work on rapidly rotating shifts.

Depression

In addition to irregular lifestyles, jet lag, and shift work, certain illnesses are greatly influenced by the circadian system. In particular, depression is strongly linked to circadian system dysfunction (Empson, 2002). Although there is not a one-to-one correspondence between circadian disregulation and depression, it is clear that inappropriate circadian functioning is a primary symptom of depression and may also be a contributing factor. Circadian-related symptoms of depression include early morning awakening (leading to fatigue and lethargy), diurnal mood swings, and insomnia or hypersomnia. Clearly, the sleep patterns of depressed clients are significantly changed. For many, *sleep latency*—the amount of time required to move from wakefulness to the onset of REM sleep—is reduced. Those experiencing depression must be educated in the importance of sleep hygiene to help reduce depressive symptoms. The use of tricyclic antidepressant medication over time has been shown to be useful in regulating circadian rhythms and sleep patterns (Wilson et al., 1995).

In short, sleep deprivation involves a major disruption in the sleep–wake cycle and is a common problem for travelers and shift workers. In some cases, it is a symptom of an underlying illness—depression. The difficulties in adjusting to an altered sleep–wake schedule are closely related to an endogenous circadian system that can be very resistive to change. Proper exposure to physical and social zeitgebers encourages circadian realignment to normalcy.

BIOPSYCHOSOCIAL FACTORS IN SLEEP

Numerous factors have been found to relate to sleep difficulties. By taking a biopsychosocial perspective, it is possible to consider these factors in an orderly and comprehensive fashion. The discussion here begins with biological factors, followed by sections about psychological and social factors.

Biological Factors

Medical conditions that cause pain, breathing difficulties, and/or other discomfort can disrupt sleep; such conditions include asthma, ulcers, arthritis, angina, migraines, and cluster headaches. Some medications used to treat these problems can also adversely affect sleep. For instance, prescription medication for the treatment of asthma often contains adrenaline, which causes arousal and interferes with sleep. Other medications that interfere with sleep include the thyroid medications Synthroid and Cytomel, cancer chemotherapy agents, oral contraceptives; anticonvulsant agents, such as Dilantin, and Inderal—a beta-blocker commonly used for hypertension and other cardiovascular conditions. These medications interfere with sleep onset and often cause frequent sleep interruptions. In addition, sleep problems can develop from withdrawal of some medications such as Valium, Librium, Tranxene, and other minor tranquilizers; sedating tricyclic antidepressants such as Elavil and Sineqaun; and street drugs such as marijuana, cocaine, and heroin (Empson, 2002). Some of these medications also suppress REM sleep, which leads to intense and vivid dreaming during withdrawal from them. Further, some drugs used to treat insomnia can actually worsen other medical disorders. Finally, some sleeping medications suppress the brain's respiratory centers, compounding the breathing difficulties of asthmatics.

Another cause of sleeping difficulty is the regular use of central nervous system stimulants. The most common of these is caffeine, whether in the form of coffee, tea, soft drinks, and even chocolate. The effects of caffeine tend to peak within 30 minutes to 1 hour, yet it can take up to 8 hours for the drug to leave the body (Coren, 1996). Caffeine does not just keep people awake, it reduces the amount of deep slow-wave sleep; increases the amount of arousals; and, in amounts equivalent to three cups of coffee, caffeine increases awakenings from sleep (Empson, 2002). Understanding the influence of coffee on sleep is particularly relevant with the understanding worldwide that outside of water, coffee is the most consumed beverage, and that the United States has the highest per capita consumption rate (Coren, 1996).

Cigarette smoking has also been associated with sleep difficulties. For instance, when smokers and nonsmokers with sleep problems were matched in terms of personality pattern and drug consumption and compared, the smokers spent an average of 15 minutes longer falling asleep and nearly 20 minutes longer being awake during the night than did nonsmokers. Presumably, these differences were caused by the stimulative effects of nicotine (Soldatos et al., 1980). Smokers who consume about one pack per day typically have difficulties falling asleep and do not sleep as deeply (Coren, 1996). It has also been noted that smoking cessation leads to improved sleep patterns

The most commonly self-prescribed drug to induce sleep is alcohol. Although the occasional use of alcohol can help some individuals get to sleep, excessive alcohol intake has been shown to severely interfere with normal sleep patterns. Those who regularly use alcohol complain that, although they may fall asleep quickly, they experience frequent episodes of awakening during the night and have difficulty falling back to sleep, often sleeping no more than 2 to 4 hours a night. EEG sleep recordings of these individuals show fragmented REM sleep and reduced total REM. In addition, deep NREM sleep has been shown to be diminished during withdrawal from alcohol (Coren, 1996; Empson, 2002).

One of the recent surprises in sleep research has been the discovery of a use for melatonin. Melatonin is hormone secreted by the pineal gland and it is sensitive to light fluctuations. Melatonin secretion increases with darkness and decreases with light. Arendt, Middleton, Stone, and Skene (1999) note that the primary function of melatonin is to convey information about the length of daylight, so it helps people achieve entrainment to the solar day. Melatonin has been used to control the effects of jet lag and to help reset the sleep–awake cycle (Empson, 2002).

Medications aimed at relieving insomnia have also been shown to disrupt sleep. This rebound phenomenon is called *drug dependency insomnia*. Typically, sleep medications are effective for the first few nights but become less effective after about 14 days of continuous use. In fact, larger and larger doses of medication are required to achieve sleep, which means that drug tolerance has developed. When the medication is abruptly withdrawn, the result is *rebound insomnia*—the reappearance of disturbed sleep but now with frightening nightmares. These disturbing experiences reinforce the individual's sense of need for the medication. Not surprisingly, the individual continues to take the medication (often in larger doses) despite obtaining only light, disturbed sleep (Coren, 1996).

Finally, external factors can affect biological and physical processes and subsequently alter the quality of sleep. Bedroom ventilation, humidity, temperature, and similar conditions and irritating noises can all alter the quality of sleep. The comfort of one's bed, especially the softness or hardness of pillows and mattress, can affect sleep. For some sleep problems, a simple environmental modification of one or more factors may be sufficient to reestablish a restful pattern of sleep.

Psychological Factors

Most sleep problems involve an interaction between physiological and psychological factors. When an individual undergoes serious and prolonged stress, such as with the loss of a job or the ending of a relationship, the brain's arousal system responds with increased activity, which results in changes in one's sleep pattern. If the stress continues for several weeks, other factors usually interfere to cause temporary insomnia. Frequently, a dysfunctional habit of "trying too hard to fall asleep" develops. The more individuals are sleep-deprived, the harder they try to sleep, which further increases arousal and results in less sleep. Such individuals usually fall asleep easily when not trying to sleep, but become alert whenever they make a conscious decision to fall asleep.

Maladaptive conditioning often results when an individual lies in bed unable to sleep. When this occurs, the bedroom environment becomes associated with frustration and arousal rather than with relaxation and sleep. Similarly, the individual's usual bedtime rituals, such as brushing teeth and setting the alarm clock, become stimuli that anticipate frustration and tension rather than relaxation. Often, a person who suffers from such conditioned insomnia sleeps better away from the usual sleep environment, such as in the living room or in a hotel. In addition, when one sleeps poorly because of stress, he or she often falls asleep in the early morning hours and then oversleeps or needs daytime naps to "catch up." Not surprisingly, these behaviors lead to circadian disregulation.

As long as sleep is basically adequate, an occasional poor night's sleep is usually tolerated. However, for individuals who believe that they suffer from insomnia, a poor night's sleep only serves to reconfirm this belief, and the fear of insomnia becomes a self-fulfilling prophecy (Empson, 2002).

Such behavioral factors contribute to almost all chronic insomnia. Whether insomnia results from psychological upheaval, environmental stress, a medical condition, or medication, behavioral factors reinforce the pattern of insomnia. Therefore, behavioral factors need to be considered and treated even if the original cause of the insomnia was not behavioral in nature. It should not be surprising, then, that the treatment of chronic insomnia requires behavioral interventions in addition to treatment of the primary cause of the insomnia.

Social Factors

There has been relatively little written about the social factors involved in sleep disorders, with the exception of some research that reported on marital functioning and the effects of shift work on marital and family life.

Marital problems have been shown to be commonly associated with insomnia, and various explanations for this association have been given. One explanation is that poor sleepers are frequently unable to express their feelings and consequently have unsatisfactory interpersonal relationships (Kales, Soldatos, & Kales, 1981). Another explanation is that the partner who anticipates problems with sexual performance may consciously or unconsciously delay going to bed to avoid sexual intimacy, which then leads to a sleep disorder. Furthermore, couples with poor sexual relations tend to suffer from continuous deprivation of affection and closeness, which leads to tension and feelings of being neglected that in turn result in insomnia (Kales & Kales, 1984). A third explanation involves social support factors. Berkowitz and Perkins (1985) found that interpersonal role conflicts, lack of support from their husbands, and decreased marital satisfaction were associated with increased reports of insomnia and other psychosomatic symptoms in wives.

Another explanation for marital disharmony involves the degree to which spouses or partners are out-of-phase with each other's circadian rhythms. There is extensive research comparing "larks," morning individuals, with "owls," late-night individuals (Monk & Folkard, 1983). Larks tend to live by the maxim "early to bed and early to rise," whereas owls tend to retire late and arise late. Needless to say, out-of-phase couples tend to have fewer serious conversations; fewer shared activities, including time together in bed; more marital conflicts; and less frequent sex (Larson, Crane, & Smith, 1991). Not surprisingly, shift workers are often owls. They tend to sleep less than 7 hours and have more health complaints. Monk and Folkard (1983) have shown that shift work not only exacerbates existing health and relational problems but also creates new problems and sets the stage for conflicts not likely to be faced by couples who are in-phase. One of the most common problems is that the shift-worker's need for peace and quiet conflicts with the spouse's and family's normal morning activities, which are usually noisy and chaotic. In addition, the female shift worker is often expected to attend to housekeeping responsibilities in addition to her job, which adds to her sleep debt.

Sleep apnea is a more serious disorder characterized by breathing cessation that occurs more than 5 times per hour during sleep and can last for more than 10 seconds (Plotnik, 2002). People with sleep apnea tend to snore loudly, which disturbs the sleep of their bed partners. Although marriage generally buffers the impact of external stressors for spouses, this is seldom the case for individuals with sleep apnea. People with sleep disorders, such as sleep apnea, often experience significant marital dissatisfaction. Spouses with sleep apnea are generally significantly more depressed, exhausted, and socially isolated than are their divorced counterparts. Also, both partners show poor adjustment in their marital, social, and leisure activities, and the sleep apneic spouse also shows poor adjustment in parental growth (Cartwright & Knight, 1987).

The way that couples sleep together may change dramatically over time, and sleep positions that couples choose at the start of the night may reflect their relationship during the day. According to Dunkell (1978), new couples sleep nestled together, with one spouse tucked into the contours of the other spouse's body. This coziness provides each spouse with reassurance by offering maximum physical intimacy. After 5 years or so, spouses begin to drift apart, and there is a widening gulf between their bodies when they sleep. This physical retreat does not necessarily represent an emotional separation, but it may indicate a mutual security that the couple has achieved. Finally, many believe that sex is an effective sleep inducer; however, research suggests that having sex makes no difference in either aiding or interfering with sleep in men or women (Coren, 1996).

Little has been written on the influence of cultural variables on sleep disorders. Still, as with all health concerns, cultural factors may have a considerable effect on the maintenance of symptoms and the alleviation of distress. It is important to note that sleep complaints may be viewed as less stigmatizing in some cultures than other mental disorders (Paniagua, 2001). For this reason, individuals from some cultures (e.g., Southeast Asia) may be more likely to show complaints of insomnia or hypersomnia than complaints involving symptoms of mental disorders such as depression and anxiety (APA, 2000).

Some sleep problems, such as nightmares, may vary depending on cultural background. In some cultures, nightmares are strongly associated with spiritual or supernatural phenomena; in other cultures, nightmares may be viewed as an indicator of other mental disturbances. One cultural factor that can influence sleep or sleep patterns is the role of *acculturative stress*—the difficulties encountered in the process of adapting and acculturating to a new cultural surrounding (Smart & Smart, 1995). This process can lead to increased stress and tension, which can influence sleep patterns.

ASSESSMENT

Before proceeding, it is important to define and classify insomnia. *Insomnia* refers to difficulties of either going to sleep or remaining asleep throughout the night (Plotnik, 2002). Usually, sleep experts acknowledge three categories: transient insomnia, short-term insomnia, and chronic insomnia. *Transient insomnia* is sleep loss that lasts 1 to 3 days and is triggered by excitement, nervousness, or travel. Christmas Eve, jet lag, the night before a key meeting, or the prospect of having surgery can trigger transient insomnia. By definition, transient insomnia is insomnia that clears spontaneously. *Short-term insomnia,* on the other hand, disturbs sleep for up to 3 weeks and is common during times of personal stress or serious medical illness. It is often resolved when the stress is alleviated or the illness is treated. *Chronic insomnia,* however, may persist for years. In the face of chronic stressors, some individuals develop insomnia, whereas others develop anxiety or tension headaches (Hauri, 1989).

On the other hand, many insomniacs are not overly stressed but develop sleep problems as a result of "learned" or *conditioned insomnia*. Further, insomnia is typically described in relation to when and how it disrupts the process of sleeping. The usual division is: sleep onset insomnia (difficulty falling asleep), sleep maintenance insomnia (difficulty getting back to sleep), terminal insomnia (inability to return to sleep, even for a short while, after waking up), and nonrestorative sleep (waking up in the morning feeling unrefreshed after sleeping) (Pallesen et al., 2001).

An Assessment Strategy

As noted earlier, individuals with sleep problems usually present themselves to physicians for assessment and treatment. Over the past 10 years, sleep disorders clinics staffed primarily by physicians have helped thousands of individuals with serious and relatively rare sleep conditions return to a more normal pattern of life. There are times when referral to a sleep disorders clinic is essential, particularly when excessive daytime sleepiness is reported or when there are indications of sleep apnea. Generally speaking, health counselors and therapists should be able to recognize and treat most cases of insomnia.

Speilman (1986) describes a conceptual strategy for the assessment of insomnia and suggests that case material be categorized into a scheme of predisposing conditions, precipitating circumstances, and perpetuating factors. The following paragraphs briefly review this assessment scheme.

Predisposing conditions are those that precede the onset of the sleep disturbance and set the stage for recurrence by lowering the thresholds for triggering insomnia. Although the intensity of a predisposing condition is not sufficient to produce insomnia, it establishes vulnerability or serves as a contributing factor in its development. *Precipitating circumstances* are the triggering events of the symptoms of insomnia. They are traditionally at the center of the assessment process because triggering factors often provide the best clue as to pathophysiology and subsequent treatment. In chronic insomnia, however, the current sleep problem may function autonomously from its origins. *Perpetuating factors* are those features that sustain or support insomnia.

Thus, assessment should focus on determining the influences that maintain insomnia and treatment should focus on the reduction of these influences. For example, insomnia triggered by the anticipation and worry involved in buying a new house may persist for a number of months after the excitement and turmoil have subsided. If the precipitating influences are no longer present and an irregular sleep–wake schedule can be assessed as the factor responsible for the persistence of the insomnia, effective treatment for the current problem can disregard the initial reason for the development of the sleep problem. By the same token, if the house purchase has turned out to be a disaster and the ruminative worrying continues, then features of the precipitating condition have become perpetuating factors, and treatment needs to focus on these problems. Factors that may perpetuate insomnia include excessive time in bed, irregular timing of retiring and arising, unpredictability of sleep, worry over daytime deficits, maladaptive conditioning, increased caffeine consumption, sedative hypnotics, and alcohol ingestion, and multiple episodes of sleep (e.g., naps or fragmented sleep).

Biological Assessment

The biological assessment of insomnia should include a health history, drug history, family history, and possibly a referral for a medical evaluation. The assessment of insomnia should begin with a review of clients' health history. It is common practice for medical and health practitioners and clinics to have clients complete a standardized health history form. This form can be a useful screening device for the health counselor to use to collect additional information from clients.

The pain and discomfort associated with a number of medical conditions, such as arthritis, asthma, angina, cancer, and various types of headaches, often contribute to insomnia. Pain experienced during the day may intensify at bedtime because environmental stimuli are diminished and the client's attention becomes more internally focused. An individual with cancer, in addition to being in pain, is often overwhelmed with fear and anxiety about the ultimate consequences of the illness. Similarly, someone with angina or cardiac arrhythmia often fears going to sleep, afraid of a possible attack during the night, which makes her or him feel even more vulnerable and helpless.

As described earlier, sleep can be disturbed by a number of medications, including sleep medications that are misused. An evaluation of insomnia should therefore include a thorough drug history. Stimulant drugs, steroids, antidepressants like Prozac, and beta-blockers like Inderal are likely to cause sleep problems when they are taken close to bedtime, even if taken in therapeutic doses. Caffeine-containing substances ingested close to bedtime can also cause difficulty falling asleep (though caffeine as a whole influences sleep), whereas drinking alcohol can result in an inability to stay asleep. Rebound insomnia may follow the withdrawal of even a sedative hypnotic (such as Valium or Halcion) for more than a few nights. The abrupt withdrawal of high doses of other sleeping medications may cause both insomnia and nightmares. Finally, improper doses or scheduling of certain sleep medications or sedating antidepressants can cause excessive daytime sleepiness. Since this can be mistaken for the excessive sleep of hypersomnia or narcolepsy, the health counselor needs to inquire not only about the type of drug but also about dosage and scheduling of the drug. It is here that the *Physicians' Desk Reference* or a call to a pharmacist or physician may be useful and necessary.

A history of family sleep disorders should be obtained from anyone in whom insomnia is suspected, since it can aid in the diagnosis of the client's problem and could uncover treatable sleep problems in other family members. Families of both narcoleptic and hypersomatic clients have been found to have a higher incidence of sleep disorders as compared to the general population. Similarly, individuals who experience sleep apnea, nightmares, and somnambulism (sleepwalking) often have positive family histories (Empson, 2002).

To help individuals assess their sleep patterns, health counselors should obtain a 24-hour sleep–wake history, not just learn about one's 8-hour sleep period. For instance, older clients often complain of severe listlessness at night, but they take several naps during the day. Insomniacs frequently have a history of irregular habits, including erratic bedtime schedules; they also report low or inconsistent levels of physical activity during the day. In addition, the 24-hour sleep–wake history may reveal that excessive physical exercise or stimulating mental activity close to bedtime is causing initial insomnia (difficulty falling asleep).

Sleep Disorders Clinics.   As previously noted, excessive daytime sleepiness; excessive snoring, which may indicate sleep apnea; myoclonus; and narcolepsy are common indicators for referral to a sleep clinic. To this, it would be good to add impotence, which can have either psychological or physiological origins. Occasionally, clients with psychological impotence can be convinced of the nonorganic nature of their disorder only when confronted with laboratory evidence of nighttime erections, which rules out the possibility of an organic cause for impotence.

The mainstay of sleep centers is polysomnogram (PSG) equipment. PSGs monitor brain waves, heart rhythm, respiration, temperature, and body movement throughout the night. Typically, a client reports to the sleep clinic late in the evening, changes into bedclothes, and has several electrodes applied to the face and body. The electrodes are arranged in pairs and are placed on the chin to record muscle tone, on the corners of the eyes to measure eye movement, on the top of the scalp to detect brain waves, and on the upper-right and lower-left areas of the chest to measure heartbeats. Temperature-sensitive devices are taped under the nostrils and mouth to record the rate and volume of inhaled air, and electrodes on each leg record leg movement before and after sleep. Finally, a beltlike gadget placed around the lower chest monitors the movement of the diaphragm. If sleep apnea is suspected, a small microphone is placed underneath the nose to record breathing.

The PSG records continuously throughout the night, and electrical impulses appear as wavy lines on a continuous sheet of paper fed into the machine. The data is processed by computer, which calculates sleep latency, time in each sleep stage, number of awakenings, number of breathing stoppages, changes in heart rate, and final awakening. It is an expensive method to use to assess insomnia. Because insomnia is such a common disorder, PSG evaluations are rather impractical (Reite et al., 1995). Although routine use to assess insomnia is not recommended, a PSG evaluation is of vital importance in other cases of sleep disorders such as sleep apnea (Pallesen et al., 2001).

Pallesen and associates (2001) note that another objective measure of sleep is a wrist actigraph that measures a person's movements during the night. On the basis of data taken from these movements, a variety of sleep parameters can be conducted. The wrist actigraph is less expensive than the PSG and is noninvasive and easy to use.

Psychological Assessment

Psychological assessment of insomnia usually includes information gathered from sleep diaries, rating scales, behavioral observations, psychological inventories, and interview data (Pallesen et al., 2001), which are described next.

Sleep Diaries.   Having clients keep a sleep diary for a 1- or 2-week period can help the counselor assess clients' 24-hour sleep–wake patterns. The sleep diaries or logs are filled out each morning. Lichstein and Riedel (1994) suggest that clients self-monitor behavior such as the time they entered and left bed, the time they fell asleep, the number and duration of times they awakened during the night, time of final awakening, subjective sleep ratings, daytime sleepiness, napping, and medication and alcohol usage. The health counselor may also want clients to monitor their physical activity throughout the day and record any nightmares that occurred.

For cases of insomnia, the client's sleep diary may be particularly useful in detecting sleep difficulties related to disordered schedules and routines. When excessive sleep is the problem, the diary documents not only the symptomology of the condition but also the number of naps taken and the client's general activity pattern. The health counselor will have to determine whether a client with an obsessive–compulsive disorder or hyperchondriacal traits should be asked to keep a sleep diary, as it could reinforce the tendency to focus and ruminate on sleep difficulties. A spouse or roommate may be asked to verify the accuracy of the client's sleep diary. The counselor can provide them with a separate diary on which to record sleep data.

Rating Scales.   A variety of rating scales have been developed to measure various sleep difficulties. These scales are primarily useful in evaluating the subjective feelings of clients when more objective measures are not possible. Scales typically measure the degree of "restedness" in the morning, general satisfaction with the night's sleep, difficulty in getting to sleep, and pleasantness of dreams. Four- to 9-point scales generally are used. Two such rating scales are highlighted here.

The Sleep Impairment Index (Morin, 1993) is a broad measure that is helpful with older adults. Another broad and general sleep rating scale is the Pittsburgh Sleep Quality Index (Buysse, Reynolds, Monk, Berman, & Kupfer, 1989). The major drawback of sleep rating scales is their retrospective approach to assessing sleep and their susceptibility to the bias of the client (Pallesen et al., 2001).

Behavioral Observations.   Aside from having irregular and inconsistent bedtimes, the insomniac may engage in daytime napping, which further disturbs circadian rhythms. Other poor sleep habits may include using the bed for purposes other than sleep such as reading, watching television, eating, conversing, or worrying about the next day's events. As a result, the bed becomes a cue for a variety of activities other than sleep. Although it is useful to elicit information of this nature from the client, it is also helpful to have corroborating data from another party (e.g., a spouse, significant other, family member, or roommate). Health counselors should suggest that this individual, typically a spouse, be interviewed independent of the client for purposes of collecting corroborating information. Again, the most objective behavioral observation occurs in sleep clinics, where a continuous videotape recording is made of the individual concurrent with PSG monitoring.

Psychological Inventories.   The experience of disrupted sleep is often associated with anxiety, mood changes, ruminations, and psychopathology—particularly depression. To aid in the assessment of insomnia, the health counselor may consider the use of psychological inventories to better understand some clues to causes as well as implications related to a client's sleep problems. The most frequently used inventory for the description of personality and the diagnosis of psychopathology is the Minnesota Multiphasic Personality Inventory (MMPI). If depression is suspected, the Beck Depression Inventory (Beck, 1967) can be useful. Remember, insomnia may develop either independently or as a result of depression. Thus, it is important to determine whether the course of the sleep problem parallels the course of the mood disturbance, or whether the sleep problem predated the depression. Subsequently, health counselors should be aware that many depression inventories include sleep disturbance items that may artificially increase the depression scores of individuals who suffer from insomnia. Another inventory, such as the Symptom Check List 90-Revised (Dergoatis, 1992), can also be used to assess general symptomology.

Interview Data.   The sleep interview plays a significant role in the assessment of sleep disorders, particularly of insomnia. In addition to collating and clarifying data from health history forms, sleep diaries, rating scales, and personality inventories, interviews can supply other important information. The sleep interview may cover an examination of a client's view of etiology of current sleep difficulties and treatment options. Since insomnia is common in many psychiatric conditions, including anxiety and depressive disorders, mania, acute schizophrenia, and organic brain syndrome, determining whether a sleep difficulty is associated with psychological problems is critical. The interview, much like a clinical interview, should review historical and current factors, focusing on general health, prior sleep history, circumstances that instigated the sleep disturbance, psychiatric issues, and prior treatment attempts (Pallesen et al., 2001).

Since a variety of cognitive factors are implicated in sleep disorders, health counselors need to be aware of maladaptive cognitions. Many chronic insomniacs typically blame their insomnia on cognitive arousal rather than on somatic factors. The following are some of the insomnia-producing dysfunctional beliefs or misconceptions:

- "Everyone needs eight hours of sleep."
- "We have to think, worry, analyze, and plan while lying in bed."
- "We can't function well after a poor night's sleep."
- "We should keep the same sleep schedule as others in our family."

- "All sleep difficulties are stress-related."
- "Occasional insomnia indicates chronic insomnia."

Assessment of specific cognitive factors related to sleep difficulties suggests that cognitively oriented interventions, such as cognitive restructuring, paradoxical intention, and thought stopping, can be particularly useful for insomnia clients.

Assessment of Social Factors

As mentioned in the Behavioral Observations section, other important information that the client might not be able to provide can sometimes be obtained from a corroborator—a significant other, spouse, or roommate. For example, when a client complains of sleeping too much during the day, the corroborator can be questioned about the possibility of sleep apnea. If the corroborator indicates that the client snores heavily and that periodic snorting sounds occur in intervals of more than 10 seconds, sleep apnea can be suspected. Similarly, regarding complaints of insomnia, the corroborator could provide useful information about the quantity and quality of the client's sleep.

An earlier discussion about the impact of marital functioning on sleep indicated that it is essential that the insomniac's spouse be interviewed. It is best for him or her to be interviewed separately regarding the marital relationship, family stresses, work demands and stresses, the regularity or irregularity of daily schedules, the use of prescription medications and other substances that could interfere with sleep, as well as sleep and sexual activity styles and patterns. In a conjoint interview, a counselor should be able to ascertain the degree to which the couple's energy levels are in-phase or out-of-phase and the extent to which each is a lark or an owl.

Finally, an assessment of social factors should include a review of relevant cultural factors that can influence sleeping concerns. Whereas this assessment can be brief, health counselors should look to ascertain the role of multicultural variables in the maintenance and resolution of sleep concerns.

TREATMENT STRATEGIES

There are a range of strategies and interventions for the treatment of sleep disorders. In the next section the chapter will review a variety of biological, psychological, and social interventions.

Biological Interventions

Three types of medication are generally used to induce sleep. Nonprescription or over-the-counter sleep aids can cause drowsiness but do not directly induce sleep. Such medications sometimes allow the individual who tries too hard to fall asleep to actually relax and then fall asleep. Prescription medications, often referred to as hypnotics or benzodiazepines, are a second type of sleep medication. Valium, Dalmane, Halcion, Xanax, and others, which were originally marketed as medications to relax muscles and relieve anxiety, have replaced barbiturates as the most frequently prescribed hypnotics. Barbiturates are the third type of sleep medication; however, because of their high potential for abuse and overdose, they are seldom prescribed today.

Hypnotics, which reduce anxiety, worry, and stress, are commonly prescribed for and effective in the short-term (3–4 weeks) treatment of insomnia (Plotnik, 2002). Whereas the occasional use of hypnotics is considered quite acceptable, the chronic use of these drugs to treat insomnia should be avoided due to side effects. As already noted, the efficacy of hypnotics decreases over time, most hypnotics distort natural sleep, and hypnotics often result in rebound insomnia when medication is withdrawn or wears off. In addition, it should be noted that hypnotics can impair wake time performance of activities such as driving and mental concentration. In fact, there are a number of reported cases of transient amnesia associated with the use of medications (e.g., Halcion and Valium). There is also concern that hypnotics mask the insomniac's medical, behavioral, and psychological problems, thus delaying appropriate treatment. Finally, sleep medications carry the risk of medical complications, including overdose, adverse interactions with other medications, and withdrawal symptoms (Pallesen et al., 2001).

It is currently considered acceptable medical practice to prescribe hypnotics to help clients get through an acute crisis as long as they are also followed and supported through the withdrawal period. A nightly prescription of hypnotics over months or years is rarely indicated, although a few clients seem to benefit from long-term low doses of a hypnotic. On the other hand, occasional use of hypnotics, such as once or twice a week, sometimes helps to reduce insomniacs' fear that they may never sleep again and allows them to get some much needed rest. Benzodiazepine medications, such as Halcion and Dalmane, are now generally preferred over other types because of their relative safety and lack of interaction with other drugs. However, benzodiazepines should not be taken with alcohol, which could result in a lethal overdose. More recently, several nonbenzodiazepines have been introduced (e.g., Ambien, Sonata) and have proved effective in treating insomnia with fewer side effects (Roan, 1999). As previously mentioned, another natural drug that has been used is melatonin.

Psychological Interventions

The use of medications remains a widely used treatment for sleep disturbances despite the fact that long-term efficacy has not been established (Currie, Wilson, Pontefract, & deLaplante, 2000). At the same time, there is growing evidence supporting the efficacy of nonpharmacological treatments (Morin et al., 1998). The psychological approaches and interventions that have been useful in the treatment of insomnia include relaxation training, cognitive-behavioral strategies, stimulus control, sleep restriction, homework, and psychotherapy. Each of these is briefly described in the following sections.

Relaxation Training.   Teaching clients to relax is probably the most common behavioral treatment for insomnia. The rationale for relaxation training is based on the theory that all insomniacs are muscularly tense or physiologically aroused at the time of desired sleep onset. Accordingly, relaxation training focuses on decreasing anxiety and reducing cognitive and physiological arousal and tension. The type of relaxation training to choose is relatively unimportant. Progressive muscular relaxation, controlled breathing, hypnosis, and EMG (electromyography) biofeedback have all proved effective (e.g., Lichstein & Johnson, 1993). It seems that these relaxation techniques are effective mainly because they focus the insomniac's attention away from tension-inducing thoughts and onto a repetitive, nonthreatening stimulus.

The health counselor is cautioned that relaxation training is considerably more of a challenge for the insomniac than for other anxious clients. Simply giving someone a relaxation tape or conducting a single practice session is rarely sufficient; Hauri (1989) notes two reasons for this difficulty. First, insomniacs seem to be much slower to learn relaxation techniques than are clients with other physiological disorders, and they need to apply these skills around desired sleep onset, at a time when voluntary control is waning.

Cognitive-Behavioral Strategies. For many insomniacs, anxious concerns and ruminative thoughts are the most distressing signals that sleep will not come easily. Their worry may reflect realistic reactions to external events such as real or imagined interpersonal, financial, or health problems. Not surprisingly, some insomniacs report that their worries focus primarily on whether they will be able to fall asleep. Whatever the source of anxiety, a vicious cycle occurs; concern over not sleeping leads to a disruptive night of sleep, which in turn reinforces the conviction that insomnia persists.

Cognitive-behavioral strategies can be helpful in allaying these concerns and ensuring the onset of sleep (Currie et al., 2000; Morin et al., 1998). For instance, if the insomniac is overwhelmed with tension-inducing thoughts, a distraction procedure might be used. Clients might be advised to read or watch TV in bed until sleep overcomes them. Similarly, the insomniac typically looks at the clock every 5 to 10 minutes and then becomes upset about the fact that sleep is not forthcoming; simply removing the clock may be more important than extensive training and relaxation.

On the other hand, if specific anxious thoughts keep the insomniac awake, these thoughts need to be dealt with individually. For example, one might prescribe a 20-minute, presleep worry time, during which the client sits—undistracted—and writes down all random thoughts, and then deals with or thinks about each troubling thought. In contrast to good sleepers who think nonthreatening thoughts when they awake in the middle of the night, poor sleepers immediately become angry and upset that they are awake. Such arousing thoughts then turn a 5-second period of arousal into a 2-hour catastrophe. In this situation, cognitive reframing techniques are quite effective. However, other cognitive methods, such as thought-stopping, may be contraindicated when the client is at the threshold of sleep.

Stimulus Control. In those clients for whom the maladaptive, conditioned association between bedroom stimuli and arousal is the major problem, stimulus control may be effective. This association is typically diagnosed in clients who sleep well away from their own bedrooms but poorly in their usual environment. When this is the case, the counselor educates clients about the mechanisms that keep them awake. Stimulus control increases the association between being in bed and being asleep, and it strengthens the consistency of the sleep–wake cycle. Based on operant behavioral techniques, it involves instructing clients to greatly limit their activities in the bed and bedroom. Stimulus-control instructions have been developed to ensure that bedtime becomes associated with rapid sleep onset; the following are some instructions to help insomniacs:

1. Go to bed only when sleepy.
2. Use the bed for no other purpose than sex and sleep. Do not read, eat, watch TV, knit, or talk with your bed partner.
3. If you are not asleep within 10 minutes of getting into bed, get up and leave the bedroom. Stay in another room until you feel sleepy; engage in a nonstimulating activity until you become sleepy, then go back to bed.
4. Set the alarm and get up at the same time every morning.
5. Do not nap during the day.
6. Fill out a sleep log each morning.

Sleep Restriction.   It is common for insomniacs to believe that extending time in bed will help compensate for long sleep latencies or disrupted sleep—that this will mean they have an opportunity to "catch up" on lost sleep. Although extra time spent in bed may yield more sleep, it adds potentially deleterious effects. An assumption of sleep-restriction therapy is that extra bed time often leads to increased wakefulness and results in fragmented sleep and variability in the timing of sleep and wakefulness. The aim is to consolidate sleep and constrain its occurrence to a specific period by restricting time spent in bed. Sleep restriction is especially appropriate for clients with insomnia who nap frequently during the day or who spend an excessive amount of time in bed at night (Stepanski et al., 2003).

Clients are first asked to fill out a 1- or 2-week sleep log describing each night. A strict schedule of bedtimes and arising times is prescribed to try and consolidate sleep and decrease time spent awake at night. Clients are instructed to stay in bed only for as long as they are actually sleeping. For instance, suppose an insomniac reports that he sleeps only 2½ hours per night and gets up around 6:30 A.M. During the first week of treatment, this client would be asked to remain out of bed and awake until 4:00 A.M. He would then still have to rise at 6:30 A.M. and would not be allowed to take any naps. Each morning clients on a sleep-restriction regimen report their sleep to their counselor (or to the counselor's answering machine). When they report at least 90 percent sleep efficiency (i.e., when they spend at least 90 percent of their restricted time in bed actually sleeping), their bed time is lengthened in 15-minute intervals until they can sleep normal amounts again (Hauri & Linde, 2000).

Homework.   Monitoring and charting sleep-related behaviors is necessary not only to develop a sense of self-control but also to develop new and better sleep habits. As in other lifestyle-change and health-promotion programs, homework tasks are a cornerstone for the treatment of insomnia and other sleep disorders. Clients must learn that they may need to spend up to an hour a day monitoring and practicing behaviors if they are to be successful in overcoming their insomnia. Similarly, the health counselor needs to establish and to reinforce the expectation that homework and other between-session tasks are vital to the change process.

Psychotherapy.   Because psychopathology reflects unresolved emotional conflict that can underlie chronic insomnia, psychotherapy can play an important role in its treatment.

The general goals of psychotherapy for insomniacs include the clients': (1) improvement in the ability to express emotions appropriately, (2) development of insight regarding personal vulnerability, (3) improvement in the quality of interpersonal relationships, and (4) restructuring of the lifestyle so that it no longer revolves around the symptom of insomnia. A number of common psychotherapeutic issues are involved in the treatment of insomnia: (1) denial of problem areas other than insomnia; (2) strong resistance to the exploration of other problem areas; (3) a need for control, which is often expressed in demands for sleeping medications, failure to stay on medication withdrawal regimens, or lack of compliance with homework assignments; (4) excessive dependence on the counselor and/or reluctance to become an active participant in the therapy process; and (5) withholding of direct expression of negative feelings. As such, psychotherapy can be an effective treatment strategy to help clients understand their sleeping difficulties while invention can tailor cognitive and behavioral techniques to each client.

Social Interventions

Earlier sections noted the impact that the marital/partner relationship can have on the disorders of sleep, such as insomnia, and suggested that insomnia and other sleep disorders can influence relationships. Therefore, it is essential that the spouse or significant other be involved in the treatment process. The health counselor should first interview the spouse individually and then conjointly with the client about the nature of the insomnia and its impact on the relationship. In some cases, it may be necessary to address relationship issues with the couple. At other times, a referral for therapy can be made when discord is an important factor in the insomnia.

Traditionally, treatment for insomnia has taken place within an individual format. Lacks (1987) argues that the group format is superior to individualized insomnia treatment. She compared insomniacs treated with the same therapy protocol in individual formats and in group formats and concluded that, on measured treatment outcomes, individually treated clients fared the same as clients who were treated in groups. She believes, however, that the group participants appeared to profit more from treatment than those in an individual format because of group cohesion and mutual problem solving and support.

Lacks (1987) outlined a four-session treatment protocol involving five to seven clients in which a single therapist facilitates the group and noted that the more homogeneous the group, with respect to background and type of sleep problem, the better the result. The program combines psychoeducation, self-monitoring, stimulus control, and cognitive methods. Clients are expected to have been weaned off of any sleeping medications and to be drug-free before beginning the program.

The first session should last approximately 90 minutes and subsequent sessions require about 60 minutes. The first session is the most important because the behavioral treatment of insomnia is explained and the concept of stimulus control is highlighted. Group members are instructed in the rules of sleep hygiene and the expectation that they will monitor their sleep patterns by means of a sleep diary and complete other homework assignments during the course of the group. The next three sessions should focus on collaborative troubleshooting of problems that group members have encountered in adhering to the treatment during the previous week. Although new material is introduced into each of the three sessions, problem solving and troubleshooting are their mainstay.

Typically, the second session is the most difficult. Many clients feel frustrated and discouraged, particularly if their symptoms and distress have worsened during the previous week. Issues of treatment adherence or noncompliance, especially with self-monitoring, need to be addressed. An important part of the second session is to help group members establish a set of prebedtime routines. It is during this session that the stimulus-control theory of insomnia becomes personalized in the "sleep life" of each group member. As in the other sessions, the expected minimum homework involves a daily sleep diary, which logs the number of hours of sleep and the number of times that the client is out of bed each night, as well as responses to the following items:

- How sleepy were you when you first went to bed last night (on a 1- to 5-scale from "not too sleepy" to "very sleepy")?
- What time did you get up this morning?
- Briefly list your activities while getting ready for bed.
- Briefly list your activities from dinner to bedtime.
- List any activities you carried out in bed yesterday.
- What were you thinking about in bed last night?

Session three begins with the review of the sleep diaries and the troubleshooting of any problems clients encountered. The new material for the session involves discriminating behaviors associated with good and poor sleep. Clients discuss ways to make behaviors associated with good sleep a part of their daily routines.

The problem-solving/troubleshooting format that Lacks (1987) described continues in session four. In addition, clients should be prepared for the maintenance and follow-up phase of treatment. Clients continue to fill out sleep diaries during this last week and then begin to phase them out as new routines become automatic parts of their behavior. The group counselor then approaches the subject of relapse. Clients are told that, from time to time, everyone has a night or a brief period of sleep difficulty, especially during periods of increased stress. It is good to tell clients that, if they use the techniques they have learned during the sessions and can avoid the tendency to develop performance anxiety, they are very likely to avert any more serious or persistent sleep disturbances. Finally, clients are expected to participate in a 6-week follow-up to give the counselor feedback about their continued progress.

Lacks notes that 4 weeks is the average length of time for improvements in sleep to become apparent, even though some individuals take less and some take more. In short, this treatment protocol combines stimulus-control techniques with cognitive methods and psychoeducation.

RELAPSE PREVENTION

Relapse does not appear to be as problematic in the treatment of insomnia as it does in exercise programs, weight control, smoking cessation, and/or pain control. Thus, relatively little written has been in the treatment manuals on this subject. Lacks (1987) indicates that the group process has a distinct impact on treatment adherence. When seen individually, clients who are noncompliant in self-monitoring or in following treatment instructions are accountable only to a counselor. However, in the group format, the same nonadhering clients meet with a more forceful reaction from other group members who seem to be less willing to tolerate nonadherence from each other.

CASE EXAMPLES

Case 1

Ms. Y is a 36-year-old attorney who sought counseling to understand "why I'm so driven" and to get relief from her insomnia. She reports having had difficulty falling asleep most nights since she was a law student. She indicates that she is "mentally hyperactive" at bedtime and is unable to stop thinking about the day's significant events, particularly those involving her courtroom performance. When she feels she has not been very effective in court, she believes she does not deserve to fall asleep. Any evening excitement, such as a movie or a lively conversation, leaves her unable to unwind for several hours. Occasionally, in the middle of the night, she awakens and begins ruminating about the day's events. On the nights when she sleeps poorly, she feels high-strung and tense the following day.

Because many of her clients are corporate executives, she has a number of dinner engagements each week. She notices that, on the days when she has had wine or a mixed drink with dinner, she invariably awakens in the middle of the night aroused and slightly sweaty. Business travel also seems to worsen her sleep pattern. Ms. Y is unmarried and has a wide circle of friends and enjoys socializing with them. However, relaxing alone has always been anxiety-producing for her; so, if she finds herself at home alone, she immerses herself in her work. Over the years, she has tried a variety of prescription and over-the-counter sleeping medications, which had left her feeling "hungover" the next day.

Ms. Y's excessive devotion to work and productivity to the exclusion of leisure activities is suggestive of an obsessive–compulsive personality style. In addition, her long-standing problems with falling asleep and frequent midcycle awakenings with ruminations are characteristic of insomnia. In this regard, Ms. Y presents with the most prevalent personality style among chronic insomniacs. Subsequently, the counselor negotiated a combined treatment of both compulsive and insomnia features with Ms. Y. The counselor emphasized a "here-and-now" rather than an in-depth therapeutic approach, which could further reinforce her obsessive thinking. The counselor also interpreted Ms. Y's excessive feelings of insecurity, which reinforced her need for guarantees before taking any action, and encouraged her to verbalize and work through her aggressive ambivalence and other feelings.

In the course of treatment, Ms. Y learned to self-monitor her sleep pattern and to use relaxation techniques to reduce her anxiety and center herself. She was advised to avoid stimulating evening activities, discontinue the use of alcohol, and reduce her intake of caffeine. She easily learned stimulus-control techniques and, with some difficulty, was able to apply thought-stopping to the ruminations she experienced when she awakened in the middle of the night. Finally, she was able to decrease her night-work obligations and replace them with more pleasurable leisure activities. Within 6 weeks, her insomnia had greatly improved and within 6 months of weekly sessions, she was able to terminate treatment and feel much less "driven."

■ ■ ■ ■ ■

Case 2

Mr. Q is a 32-year-old computer programmer who presented to an outpatient psychiatry clinic at a local hospital with complaints of difficulty falling asleep and staying asleep, combined with dependence on sleeping medication. The problem began approximately 18 months earlier; at that time Mr. Q received a job promotion to supervisor. A brief 3-week period of emotional turmoil ensued, with anxiety symptoms accompanying the difficulty initiating and maintaining sleep. His family physician prescribed 10 mg of Valium a day with a dose of .25 mg of Halcion at bedtime. Initially, he reported symptomatic improvement and, as the job stress subsided, he was able to discontinue the Valium. His attempts to stop the nightly Halcion, however, resulted in severe sleeplessness, nightmares, and daytime agitation. Mr. Q resumed the bedtime Halcion and, 2 months later, had to double the dose because the insomnia worsened.

Before the onset of the sleeping problem, Mr. Q had always preferred to stay up late to do his programming, sleeping from 3:00 A.M. to 10:00 A.M. He reported logging 6½ hours of sleep followed by a sleep latency of 15 to 30 minutes. Bouts of initial insomnia had occurred intermittently since his early teen years.

It appears that Mr. Q's delayed phase sleep pattern—3:00 to 10:00 A.M.—was a predisposing condition as well as a major component in the circumstances that initiated the insomnia. The job promotion was the precipitant, or the trigger, of the insomnia. Dependence on Halcion appeared to have perpetuated and as well as exacerbated his sleep problem.

After an extensive physical and psychiatric evaluation, Mr. Q was put on a weaning schedule of the Halcion. The counselor assigned to work with Mr. Q described the expected withdrawal reactions and, along with the attending psychiatrist, closely monitored the gradual withdrawal of the medication over the course of 2 weeks. The counselor also explained how Mr. Q's delayed sleep pattern had led to the recurrence of insomnia and discussed the value of keeping regular sleep–wake patterns in light of Mr. Q's tendency to stay up late at night. In 2 weeks, the Halcion was successfully discontinued. For the next 2 weeks, Mr. Q was asked to monitor his sleep in a sleep diary and he then began a course of group treatment for insomnia based on the treatment protocol developed by Lacks (1987). By the third week of the program, Mr. Q reported the return of normal sleep with no episodes of insomnia.

■ ■ ■ ■ ■

PREVENTION STRATEGIES

Although most of the scientific knowledge about good sleep is common sense, it is surprising how often individuals who suffer from serious insomnia do not follow the rules for good sleep hygiene. Pallesen and associates (2001) suggest briefly reviewing the following sleep hygiene recommendations.

Sleep Hygiene Principles

1. Curtail the time physically spent in bed because excessive time can lead to sleeplessness, many awakenings, and a more shallow sleep.
2. Never make an effort to sleep because the more a person tries to sleep, the more aroused one becomes. If you are awake and cannot sleep, reading or watching TV often have a paradoxical effect and initiate sleep.
3. Put the bedroom clock out of sight because time pressure is not conducive to sleep.
4. General exercise is recommended but not within 4 hours of bedtime. Exercise can help one relax and tends to deepen sleep.
5. Avoid coffee, soda containing caffeine (or any beverage or food containing caffeine), alcohol, and nicotine. Avoid any stimulants and although alcohol in limited amounts can promote sleep, it often fragments sleep.
6. Eat a light low-calorie bedtime snack because hunger can disrupt sleep.
7. Explore napping; for most people, afternoon naps disrupt nighttime sleep, but for others, an afternoon nap results in relaxation, which can facilitate sleep in the evening.
8. Consider the use of hypnotics on a limited basis.
9. Sleep only as long you need to feel refreshed the next day.
10. Maintain a regular wake-up time because this helps you synchronize circadian rhythms.
11. Try to establish a simple routine about going to bed.
12. Create a conducive environment for sleep—fresh air and little noise are very helpful.
13. Interrupt ruminative worry about personal or business problems by cognitive refocusing or thought-stopping. For those who worry excessively during the night, prescribe a set "worry time" early in the evening and work toward solutions before getting in bed.

Lacks and Rotert (1986) studied the knowledge and practice of sleep hygiene of poor sleepers compared with good sleepers. They found that poor sleepers have more knowledge about sleep hygiene than good sleepers but practice it less often. Poor sleepers have more awareness of the effects of caffeine and other stimulants on sleep disruption but continue to use stimulating substances one or two nights a week.

Because shift work and jet lag represent two very common phenomena among clients who work with counselors on a variety of health concerns, the following primary insomnia-prevention suggestions should be useful.

Preventing Shift-Workers' Insomnia

The following preventive measures are suggested for individuals who work nights or on rotating shifts:

1. Eat meals at the same time each day to make as little change in the circadian rhythms as possible.
2. Sleep at least 4 hours during the same time each day.
3. When sleeping during the day, darken the room with heavy drapes or shades.

4. Experiment with ways to block out daytime noise (e.g., with earplugs, white-noise machines, an air conditioner, or a fan).
5. Restrict the use of stimulants—don't drink coffee, tea, or cola drinks or smoke heavily in the hours just before going to bed.
6. Try not to shift gears by changing wake–sleep schedules on weekends or brief holidays.
7. Try to reduce family stress related to shift work. Discuss the resentment your spouse and children feel about your absence at night, and enlist the family's help in finding ways to spend some time together each day.

These measures focus primarily on the individual; the following are some suggestions for preventive measures at a systemic level.

Some guidelines for scheduling shift rotations have been suggested. For routine jobs, daily shifts may be better than weekly ones. Workers should report for the day shift on Mondays, switch to evenings on Tuesdays, work nights on Wednesdays, take Thursdays off, then work again during the day on Fridays. Popular in Europe, this schedule allows employees to stay "tuned" to a standard time frame and to eat at least one meal a day with their families. For jobs that require more concentration or decision-making abilities, much longer shifts—of months rather than days or weeks—may be better because they allow the body clock to catch up with the time clock (Harrison & Horne, 2000; Hauri & Linde, 2000; Monk, 1986).

Preventing Jet Lag

Jet lag can hardly be avoided; however, some of its effects can be minimized. To address jet lag, Hauri and Linde (2000) suggest the following:

1. Begin the time shift before leaving home. The week before the trip, gradually begin going to bed and getting up earlier if traveling east or staying up later if traveling west.
2. Leave home rested; avoid last-minute hassles.
3. Dress comfortably, stretch occasionally, and alternately tense and relax muscle groups while in flight.
4. Eat lightly during the flight and for a few days afterward. Don't drink alcohol or caffeinated beverages—substitute with water, soft drinks, or fruit juices.
5. Do not smoke or smoke infrequently.
6. Schedule arrival for late in the day, close to normal bedtime at home. Spend the first day after arrival in a quiet and relaxed manner.
7. On short trips, stay on "home time"; on longer trips, start living by the new time frame immediately; and if traveling halfway around the world, stop at some point for one or two days of rest.
8. Rely on sleep rituals and relaxation exercises to ease into sleep; avoid sleeping medications because they only mask rather than treat jet lag.
9. Try using melatonin.

CONCLUDING NOTE

This chapter reviewed biopsychosocial aspects of sleep and sleep disorders, particularly the circadian disregulation noted in chronic insomnia. Some of the theories of sleep and the methods for the assessment of and intervention in chronic insomnia were also discussed. Because primary care physicians and sleep disorders clinics are the usual places of referral for sleep problems, health counselors ordinarily will not be consulted by clients who complain primarily of insomnia. More likely, clients will present with another health problem or a psychological issue, and only during the course of the assessment will the counselor find out that an "undercurrent" sleep problem, such as chronic insomnia, is present. For this reason, the treatment protocol and suggestions here for assessing and intervening in chronic insomnia were geared to this treatment setting. Relapse is considerably less of a problem for sleep disorders than it is in most of the other health counseling areas. A number of specific suggestions presented for the primary prevention of insomnia involve common principles of sleep hygiene, individual and systemic guidelines for reducing the incidence of insomnia among shift workers, and specific recommendations about preventing or reducing the impact of jet lag.

RESOURCES

Web Sites

- American Academy of Sleep Medicine, One Westbrook Corporate Center, Suite 920, Westchester, IL 60154; (708) 492-0930—www.aasmnet.org.
- American Insomnia Association, One Westbrook Corporate Center, Suite 920, Westchester, IL 60154—www.americaninsomniaassociation.org.
- American Sleep Apnea Association, 1424 K Street NW, Suite 302, Washington, DC 20005; (202) 293–3650—www.sleepapnea.org.
- National Sleep Foundation, 1522 K Street, NW, Suite 500, Washington, DC 2005; (202) 347-3471—www.sleepfoundation.org.
- Sleepnet.com™ has everything you wanted to know about sleep, including disorders, research, sleep labs, support groups, and professionals—www.sleepnet.com.

Organizations

There seem to be 12-step groups and national organizations for every imaginable health concern except insomnia. Your local sleep clinic might be able to refer you to a local group. On the other hand, there are narcolepsy support groups as well as A.W.A.K.E Network groups (www.sleepapnea.org/awake.html) for sleep apnea clients in most cities. They can be found by consulting the local phone directory.

Client Education Publications

- Ferber, J. (2004). *Solving your child's sleep problems* (Rev. ed.). New York: Fireside—

This is one of the few books that focus on sleep disturbances among children from infants to adolescents, with specific suggestions for parents who need to deal with these problems.

■ Hauri, P., and Linde, S. (2000). *No more sleepless nights workbook.* New York: Wiley—Dr. Hauri, a well-regarded sleep researcher and head of the Mayo Clinic's insomnia program, has written a very readable account of treatment for insomnia. A unique feature of this self-help book is the emphasis on preventing

and reducing the effects on sleep of jet lag and shift work.

■ Jacobs, G. (1999). *Say goodnight to insomnia.* New York: Owl Books—Helpful self-help book with basics about sleep disorders and other information. Jacobs is a sleep researcher and writes from a knowledgeable position. There are plenty of exercises and experience summaries to help people address sleep concerns.

REFERENCES

American Psychiatric Association (APA). (2000). *Diagnostic and statistical manual of mental disorders* (4th ed., *DSM-IV-TR*). Washington, DC: Author.

Arendt, J., Middleton, B., Stone, B., & Skene, D. (1999). Complex effects of melatonin: Evidence for photoperiodic responses in humans. *Sleep, 22,* 625–635.

Beck, A. (1967). *Depression: Clinical, experimental and theoretical aspects.* New York: Harper & Row.

Berkowitz, A., & Perkins, W. (1985). Correlates of psychosomatic stress symptoms among farm women. *Journal of Human Stress, 17,* 76–81.

Bliwise, D. L. (1997). Sleep and aging. In M. R. Pressman & W. C. Orr (Eds.), *Understanding sleep: The evaluation and treatment of sleep disorders.* Washington, DC: American Psychological Association.

Boivin, D. B., Czeisler, C. A., Kijk, D. J., Duffy, J. E., Folkard, S., Minors, D. S., Totterdell, P., & Waterhouse, J. M. (1997). Complex interaction of sleep-wake cycle and circadian phase modulates mood in healthy subjects. *Archives of General Psychiatry, 54,* 145–152.

Born, J., Lange, T., Hansen, K., Molle, M., & Fehm, H. L. (1997). Effects of sleep and circadian rhythm on human circulating immune cells. *Journal of Immunology, 158,* 4454–4464.

Buysse, D. J., Reynolds III, C. F., Monk, T. H., Berman, S. R., & Kupfer, D. J. (1989). The Pittsburgh Sleep Quality Index: A new instrument for psychiatric practice and research. *Psychiatric Research, 28,* 193–213.

Carskadon, M. A. (2002). Adolescent sleep patterns: Biological, social, and psychological influences. *Adolescence, 37,* 855–856.

Carskadon, M. A., & Taylor, J. F. (1997). Public policy and sleep disorders. In M. R. Pressman & W. C. Orr (Eds.), *Understanding sleep: The evaluation and treatment of sleep disorders.* Washington, DC: American Psychological Association.

Cartwright, R., & Knight, S. (1987). Silent partners: The views of sleep apneic patients. *Sleep, 10,* 244–248.

Coren, S. (1996). *Sleep thieves.* New York: Free Press.

Currie, S. R., Wilson, K., Pontefract, A. J., & deLaplante, L. (2000). Cognitive-behavioral treatment of insomnia secondary to chronic pain. *Journal of Consulting and Clinical Psychology, 68,* 407–416.

Czeisler, C. A., Duffy, J. F., Shanahan, T. L., Brown, E. N., Mitchell, J. F., Rimmer, D. W., et al. (1999). Stability, precision, and near-24 hour period of the human circadian pacemaker. *Science, 284,* 2177–2181.

Dement, W. C. (1999). *The promise of sleep.* New York: Random House.

Derogatis, L. R. (1992). *SCL-90-R: Administration, scoring, and procedures: Manual-II.* Towson, MD: Clinical Psychometric Research.

Dunkell, S. (1978). *Sleep positions: The night language of the body.* New York: North American Library.

Empson, J. (2002). *Sleep and dreaming* (3rd ed.). New York: Palgrave.

Harrison, Y., & Horne, J. A. (2000). The impact of sleep deprivation on decision making: A review. *Journal of Experimental Psychology: Applied, 6,* 236–249.

Hauri, P. (1989). Primary insomnia. In T. Karasu (Ed.), *Treatment of psychiatric disorders,* Vol 3. Washington, DC: American Psychiatric Association.

Hauri, P., & Linde, S. (2000). *No more sleepless nights workbook.* New York: Wiley.

Hellmich, N. (2000, March 29). One way to get to sleep: Get up. *USA Today,* 1A.

Hirshkowitz, M., Moore, C. A., & Minhoto, G. (1997). The basics of sleep. In M. R. Pressman & W. C. Orr (Eds.), *Understanding sleep: The evaluation and treatment of sleep disorders.* Washington, DC: American Psychological Association.

Kales, A., & Kales, J. (1984). *Evaluation and treatment of insomnia.* New York: Oxford University Press.

Kales, A., Soldatos, C., & Kales, J. D. (1981). Sleep disorders: Office evaluation and management. In S. Arieti & H. Brodie (Eds.), *American handbook of psychiatry,* Vol. 7 (2nd ed.). New York: Basic Books.

Lacks, P. (1987). *Behavioral treatment of persistent insomnia.* New York: Pergamon.

Lacks, P., & Rotert, M. (1986). Knowledge and practice of sleep hygiene techniques in insomniacs and good sleepers. *Behavioral Research and Therapy, 24,* 365–368.

Larson, J., Crane, D., & Smith, C. (1991). Morning and night couples. *Journal of Marital and Family Therapy, 17,* 53–65.

Lichstein, K. L., & Johnson, R. S. (1993). Relaxation for insomnia and hypnotic medication use in older women. *Psychology and Aging, 8,* 103–111.

Lichstein, K. L., & Riedel, B. W. (1994). Behavioral assessment and treatment of insomnia: A review with an emphasis on clinical application. *Behavior Therapy, 25,* 659–688.

Luna, T. D., French, J., & Mitcha, J. I. (1997). A study of USAF air traffic controller shiftwork: Sleep, fatigue, activity, and mood analyses. *Aviation, Space, and Environmental Medicine, 68,* 18–23.

Maxmen, J. S., & Ward, N. G. (1995). Essential psychopathology and its treatment (2nd ed.). New York: Norton.

Monk, T., & Folkard, S. (1983). Circadian rhythms and shift work. In R. Hockey (Ed.), *Stress and fatigue in human performance.* New York: Wiley.

Monk, T. H. (1986). Advantages and disadvantages of rapidly rotating shift schedules—A circadian viewpoint. *Human Factors, 28,* 553–557.

Morin, C. M. (1993). Insomnia: Psychological and physiological differences between good and poor sleepers. *Journal of Abnormal Psychology, 72,* 255–264.

Morin, C. M., Colecchi, C., Stone, J., Sood, R., & Brink, D. (1998). Behavioral and pharmacological therapies for late-life insomnia: A randomized controlled trial. *Journal of the American Medical Association, 281,* 991–999.

Paniagua, F. A. (2001). Culture-bound syndromes. In I. Cuellar & F. A. Paniagua (Eds.), *Handbook of multicultural mental health* (pp. 142–170). San Diego: Academic.

Pallesen, S., Nordhus, I. H., Havik, O. E., & Nielsen, G. H. (2001). Clinical assessment and treatment of insomnia. *Professional Psychology: Research and Practice, 32,* 115–124.

Plotnik, R. (2002). *Introduction to psychology* (6th ed). Belmont, CA: Wadsworth.

Reite, M., Buysse, D., Reynolds, C., & Mendelsen, W. (1995). An American Sleep Disorders Association review: The use of polysomnography in the evaluation of insomnia, *Sleep, 18,* 58–70.

Roan, S. (1999, October 25). Elusive sleep, elusive cure. *Los Angeles Times,* S1.

Smart, F. J., & Smart, D. W. (1995). Acculturative stress of Hispanics: Loss and challenge. *Journal of Counseling and Development, 73,* 390–396.

Soldatos, C., Kales, J., Scharf, M., et al. (1980). Cigarette smoking associated with sleep difficulty. *Science, 207,* 551–552.

Speilman, A. (1986). Assessment of insomnia. *Clinical Psychology Review, 6,* 11–25.

Stepanski, E., Rybarczyk, B., Lopez, M., & Stevens, S. (2001). Assessment and treatment of sleep disorders in older adults: A review for rehabilitation psychologists. *Rehabilitation Psychology, 48,* 23–36.

Wilson, S. J., Bell, C., Coupland, N.J., & Nutt, D. J. (1995). Sleep in depressed outpatients during treatment with fluvoxamine—A home based study. *European Neurospsychopharmacology, 5,* 303–307.

Wooten, V. (1994). Medical causes of insomnia. In M. E. Kryger, T. Roth, & W. C. Dement (Eds.), *Principles and practice of sleep medicine* (2nd ed., pp. 509–522). London: Saunders.

Young, M. W. (2000, March). The tick-tock of the biological clock. *Scientific American,* 64–71.

CHAPTER NINE

SEXUAL HEALTH

What we're born with, what we experience all through infancy and
childhood is a sexuality that isn't concentrated on the genitals: It's
a sexuality diffused through the whole organism. That's the paradise
we inherit. But the paradise gets lost as the child grows up.

—Aldous Huxley

The so-called sexual revolution has certainly had many positive effects on the social climate. It has paved the way for more frank and open discussions about sex and sexual problems; has made it easier to get needed information on sexual matters; and has fostered a more tolerant attitude toward behaviors that in previous times would have been condemned as unhealthy, deviant, or criminal. Unfortunately, this new openness has not solved everyone's problems; in fact, the sexual revolution has created a few new ones. A quick glance at the newspaper; an overheard conversation; discussions with friends; and/or perhaps, an examination of your own thoughts will reveal that problems, misconceptions, and fears about sex and sexuality still abound (Travis & Ryan, 1988).

Research and popular books both focus on human sexuality as an experience commonly beset by one problem after another. These problems are presented in stereotypical fashion: women are lacking in physical arousal, unable to reach orgasm, or just plain uninterested in sex; men are required to endure infrequent sex, impotence, and problematic premature ejaculation.

All people in our society have been or will be involved in sexual behavior. The professional literature and public media conclusively document the confusion and distress couples feel regarding their ability to fully utilize and express their sexual potential. The extent of these widespread problems would seem to mandate that counselors develop diagnostic and therapeutic skills to meet clients' needs. Unfortunately, too few counselors have the skills to feel comfortable working in the area of sexual counseling.

Although interventions to deal with problems of sexual functioning date back to earliest recorded history, sex therapy as an independent discipline was not introduced until the early 1970s. From the beginning of this century until the latter part of the 1960s, any treatment of sexual dysfunction was approached primarily from a psychoanalytic viewpoint.

Dysfunctions were viewed as the result of deep-seated personality conflicts—specifically, as a failure to resolve the Oedipal complex. This therapeutic orientation viewed unconscious conflicts as the underlying cause of sexual problems and the resolution of these conflicts as the cure. However, empirical outcome studies of analytical psychotherapy applied to sexual problems failed to demonstrate that psychotherapy was an effective intervention (Cooper, 1971; Reynolds, 1977). In the late 1950s, learning theory and behavioral therapy were introduced and Masters and Johnson's *Human Sexual Inadequacy* was published in 1970. With the publication of this book, sex and sexuality counseling and therapy became established as a distinct therapeutic discipline.

It is undeniably important for counselors to be aware of the assessment issues and intervention strategies that are required in the treatment of sexual dysfunction. Yet, although it is important to remain mindful of what might go wrong, it is equally important to be aware of ways in which counselors can help clients enjoy and enhance their sexual health.

Sexuality is a basic part of our humanness. Through sexuality, people can experience a greater repertoire of communication than is otherwise available. Desire to be interconnected, unfulfilled longing, and pure ecstasy are but a few of the emotions experienced—all often difficult to put into words. Sex as a vehicle of expression is said to be the barometer of a marital relationship. When issues of sexual health are explored, good sex is seen as not just an expression but also as an amalgam of beliefs, attitudes, physiology, and communication. When sexuality is viewed as a communication process, the quality of the relationship can be assessed by examining satisfaction with the sexual experience.

THE COMPONENTS OF SEXUALITY

Because sexuality is a complex blend of beliefs and attitudes, physiology, and communication, this chapter begins by exploring each of these components.

Beliefs and Attitudes

An undeniable force in an individual's sexuality is the ideas espoused, either directly or indirectly, by the family. These attitudes influence the "when" and "how" of sexual behaviors as well as what is acceptable and unacceptable for expression. It has often been said that when a couple gets into bed, there are actually six people present: the man, the woman, and both sets of parents.

The earliest attitudes about sexual behavior are rooted in body image (Fisher, 1989). Individuals' body images often contain gross distortions because of the discomfort that many parents experience when discussing the body. Further distortions can also occur depending on the degree of parental acceptance of early (but phase-appropriate) masturbation. Although infants may revel in the discovery of their genitalia, parents usually do not. Mothers and fathers may be equally uncomfortable with acknowledging the mere existence of genitals, not to mention discussing their relative functions (Johnson, 1999).

Early experiences of disappointment in the acceptance of the genitalia lead to a sense of discomfort and possibly even a sense of alienation from one's own body (Johnson, 1999). How this influences a person's self-concept as a sexual being is readily apparent. One way that a healthy self-image is expressed in sexuality is in the ability to give and receive plea-sure. If the self-concept of the individual is plagued by sexual embarrassment, then sexual expression is hindered. Early memories of severe disapproval or punishment for masturba-tion can also impede the healthy sexual feelings that develop during adolescence. How can one enjoy something that is wrong and still see himself or herself as good? The idea that sex is sinful or bad can translate into later problems with the individual's own capability for sexual expression.

When considering personal beliefs, counselors must also look at cultural differences. The sexual relationships, customs, and attitudes of a particular society are an integral, func-tional element in that culture. Therefore, what might be seen as sexually permissive or repressive in one culture may appear natural and normal in others (Caplan, 1987). Cultural variations can affect sexual desire, expectations, and attitudes about sexual performance. When considering sexual health behavior and beliefs, the ethnic and religious backgrounds of clients must be considered. It is also important to explore how gender expectations may contribute to clients' sexual beliefs and attitudes.

In particular, counselors need to determine whether a client's cultural background emphasizes male dominance and control of female sexuality versus those cultures that reward the opposite view (Paniagua, 2001). In some cultures where procreation and fertility is a primary concern, female sexual desire is not considered very important (Castillo, 1997). In Latina cultures, women are often referenced in terms of *marianismo,* which espouses that women are morally superior and semi-divine compared with men. Connected with Catholi-cism, this view suggests that women are expected to remain virgins until they marry. Unmar-ried women who lose their virginity are labeled as promiscuous (Arrendondo, 1996).

Thompson and Pleck (1995) note that traditional Western masculine ideology promotes the idea of nonrelational, objectifying attitudes toward sexuality, including the fear and hatred of homosexual attitudes and beliefs. These gender norms for men often teach them to equate sexual behavior with intimacy and can create rigid sexual expectations, which are often related to men's sexual performance. When men experience concerns about their sexual behavior, they may fear seeking help or speaking about their concerns for fear of not meeting male gender-role expectations. In Latino cultures, gender identity in men can strongly be associated with *machismo,* which places an emphasis on arrogance and sexual aggression in male–female relationships, sexual attraction, and physical strength (Arrendondo, 1996).

Physiological and Biological Factors

The exploration of the physiological component of sexual health requires a thorough health screening. The screening should encompass as many variables as possible, including the client's past illnesses, current subjective state of health, body deformities, and current med-ications. It is also appropriate for the counselor to note whether any early illnesses resulted in developmental or physical limitations. Any kind of disability can have a significant impact on all of the developmental processes of an individual. Someone who has a disabil-ity is often regarded as asexual, and this cultural attitude, as well as people's behavior toward such people, have been known to seriously interfere with the social and sexual development of people who are ill or have disabilities. Whether the limitation should be of prime consideration with regard to sexual functioning needs to be seen as the subjective opinion of the client. If he or she does not view the particular problem as challenging, then it is unlikely to impinge of the client's sexual identity or functioning (Maier, 1984).

Current complaints of ill health should be carefully investigated as either the cause of or a contributing factor to sexual dysfunction. For example, certain illnesses create respiratory problems that can impede the flow of oxygen throughout the body, creating temporary erectile dysfunctions. Although the incident is still disconcerting, the client's fears are greatly alleviated once the temporary nature of the condition is understood.

Certain drugs induce biochemical changes in the body that result in diverse complaints such as decreased sexual drive, erectile dysfunction, premature ejaculation, and painful coitus (dyspareunia). Alcohol and various legal and illegal drugs also can create sexual problems. Many research studies have been successful in identifying the medications that cause sexual dysfunction (Ferguson, 2001; Masand & Gupta, 2002; Mullen et al., 2001; Pesce, Seidman, & Roose, 2002; Targum, 2000; Wirshing et al., 2002). Counselors need to be aware of both the possible side effects of medications and the possible alternative procedures that will not affect clients' sexual functioning.

Another assessment issue is the growing incidence of infertility. *Infertility* is defined as the inability to conceive within a 1-year period of time. The prevalence of infertility has risen dramatically in the past several decades, with estimates of infertility ranging from 15 to 20 percent for couples in their childbearing years. Numerous factors have been cited as causally related, including increased incidents of sexually transmitted diseases (STDs), increased medication or drug usage, and increased popularity of having children later in life. Clearly, infertility will continue to be a treatment issue for counselors (Sadler & Syrop, 1987).

A process of evaluation for infertility includes a health history (e.g., contraceptive usage, prior exposure to STDs), a detailed list of coital frequency (and how it corresponds to the ovulatory cycle), and a complete physical examination of both partners. This may include a postcoital examination as well as a semen analysis. The actual treatment of infertility has some significant psychological implications (Turkington & Alper, 2001). When couples decide to undergo infertility treatment, their lives are often taken over by the mechanization of a treatment team. Their privacy ceases to be of concern to the physicians who care for them. Focus on the genitals ceases to be sexual and is transformed into a purely mechanical reproductive one—sexuality is out and babymaking is in. Having sex ceases to be an enjoyable and spontaneous event as every sex act becomes the ultimate test of fertility. Sexuality is no longer a dimension of a relationship but has been reduced to its elemental form—reproduction. The strain that this poses on the relationship is often enormous.

Communication

Couples who are in the process of changing their sexual behavior must also change their relationship. At the heart of any relationship is the ability to communicate. Couples need to evaluate their relationship on many levels, and communication is at the core of this process. Assessment of this issue is complex.

Couples who request help for sexual problems often have difficulty communicating, but they may not realize it because the patterns are an established part of their overall interaction. To work on sexual issues, couples must first address the underlying purpose served by their communication process. The process of discovery could easily double the length of time that they will need to engage in counseling. Most likely, couples will not want to waste time on this issue and will request more direct treatment of the sexual problem. The counselor therefore may need to use sexual exercises designed to enhance couples' communication.

It is important to stress again that sexuality is much more than a mechanical interaction of bodies. It is actually a complex interaction of beliefs, attitudes, and communication, as well as physiology. Without assessing the influence of the salient cultural variables (e.g., gender role beliefs, sexual orientation, ethnicity, etc.) of each couple, health counselors may miss crucial information that guides, dictates, and mediates sexual behaviors and attitudes.

There is a very interesting system that assesses sexual behavior by focusing on the purposiveness of the actions, as opposed to their causes (Shulman, 1967). This strategy looks at sex from the point of view of the goal of sexual behavior and assesses the social purpose, or effect, of the sexual behavior. Social purposes are not difficult to judge—behavior is either socially useful or socially useless. Destructive sexual behavior would always seem to be useless, and so, one would think, is unethical sexual behavior. Furthermore, the existence of sexual drives is taken for granted, as is the idea that sexual behavior is under the individual's control. Sex is therefore something a person does, not just something that happens to her or him. Why a person uses sex in one way rather than another is related to her or his personal opinion of sex and of life. For example, if a client sees life as a competitive striving to get, to have, and to achieve, then his or her sexual behavior will reflect these attitudes; an individual may have trained herself over the years to use sex for personal triumph in a competitive manner.

Sex is useful when it promotes what people ordinarily consider good: social harmony, pleasure, love, and so forth. Sex is useless when it is destructive, socially isolating, produces suffering, and so on. There are at least six useful ways to use sex: (1) for reproduction, (2) for pleasure, (3) to create a feeling of belonging, (4) as a cooperative endeavor to create a feeling of sharing, (5) for the purpose of consolation, and (6) for self-affirmation. In addition, sex can be abused by using it for the following purposes: (1) to make mischief, (2) to create distance, (3) to dominate, (4) to serve, (5) to demonstrate success or failure, (6) to express vanity, (7) to get revenge, and (8) to prove abnormality (Shulman, 1967).

ASSESSMENT

The three major methods of assessing sexual dysfunction are the interview, psychometric testing, and medical evaluation; the next sections describe each of these.

Interview

The initial interview is used to help determine the nature of the dysfunction and whether sex therapy would be an appropriate intervention. Areas for the counselor to consider in making this determination include the following:

1. A description of the sexual difficulty or difficulties
2. What attempts have been made to resolve difficulties

3. A description of the current sexual activity of the couple, including coital and non-coital activities
4. An assessment of the overall quality of the relationship
5. The presence or absence of an individual psychopathology
6. A medical history and physical status
7. The individual and joint motivation for treatment
8. A detailed assessment of functioning during each phase of the sexual-response cycle—desire, arousal, and orgasm

A counselor can also gain information from the manner in which the responses are conveyed by observing the couple's interaction and other nonverbal communication.

If sex therapy is deemed appropriate, the next step is for the counselor to obtain a detailed history of each individual. The purpose of such an interview is to help the counselor obtain information about factors, which may contribute to the maintenance of the dysfunction, that can help in creating an intervention strategy. As any skilled counselor knows, additional information is gathered throughout the therapeutic process, as each individual's personality and the couple's interactive dynamics become more and more observable.

Information required for an adequate evaluation includes a general individual history, a sexual history, a relationship history, and an assessment of current status. The general history should provide the counselor with the following:

1. Information on the family structure and background over the past two generations
2. An assessment of current psychopathology
3. Individual interactive styles—how communicative and how assertive the person is, how he or she goes about getting needs met
4. Identification of the values, morals, and religious beliefs that guide each individual
5. Identification of individual life goals
6. A determination of each one's the level of anxiety, both in general and in response to sexual and other life events
7. Answers to questions about extramarital relationships and love for the partner
8. An assessment of each individual's view of the world and whether there is a positive or negative focus

The individual's sexual history could also include assessment of early sexual learning, early sexual experiences, frequency of and desire for sexual activities, masturbation history and current behavior, sexual attitudes and fantasies, and gender preference.

The relationship history should include assessment of the couple's skills in conflict resolution, communication, decision making, and responsibility sharing, as well as assessment of affection; sexual satisfaction; relationships with children and parents; ability to express anger, love, and attraction to the partner; the power structure in the relationship; and future relationship goals (Friedman & Czekala, 1985). Throughout the assessment phase, continue to address salient cultural variables that may comprise a client or couple's belief system about sexual behavior, beliefs, and attitudes. Continue to be attentive to cultural variations while being open to suggest that culturally influenced beliefs can both be limiting and enhancing in designing interventions.

Psychometric Testing

A number of paper-and-pencil tests have been developed to aid in the assessment of sexual dysfunction, including ones to identify arousal deficits as well as to isolate problem behaviors. Attitudinal tests and other instruments intended to measure sexual capability, sexual experience, pleasure, fear, anxiety, and guilt are also available. An excellent review of these instruments can be found in a 1979 special issue of *The Journal of Sex and Marital Therapy* (vol. 5, no. 3).

Medical Evaluation

Accepted clinical opinion states that almost all sexual dysfunctions are psychogenic. Recent evidence, however, suggests that the arousal and orgasm responses are vulnerable to impairment of three functions: hormonal (Munarriz et al., 2002), vascular (Graziottin, 1998), and neurological (Kalayjian & Morrell, 2000). All clients should be asked about their medical history and current health. A thorough evaluation by a gynecologist; urologist; or, preferably, a specialist in sexual medicine should be performed in cases of erectile dysfunction, painful coitus, subjective loss of genital sensation, reduction in intensity of orgasm, or for anyone who has a history of diabetes, alcoholism, spinal cord trauma, or takes medications that might affect sexual functioning (Schover, 1982).

For further information on the advancement in knowledge, and for techniques regarding the physical contributions to sexual dysfunction, see Charlton and Yalom (1997); Leiblum and Rosen (2000); Love (2001); Kolodny, Masters, and Johnson (1979); Krone, Siroky, and Goldstein (1983); Renshaw (1996); Schnarch (1998); and/or Yaffe and Fenwick (1988).

INTERVENTIONS

Before discussing specific intervention strategies, this section reviews the major concepts of modern sex therapy. Although the concepts have been chosen and developed primarily to help people who experience sexual dysfunctions, they will be of interest and value to health counselors because of their proven relevance in treating many types of relationship conflicts. The following list—developed by Humphrey (1983)—identifies the major concepts of sex therapy.

1. Sex is a natural function. In healthy partners, male and female sexual-response cycles occur as a result of normal erotic stimulation just as naturally as heavy breathing follows vigorous exercise.
2. Every human being has his or her own unique SVS—sexual value system. If a person does not act in accordance with his or her SVS, conflict, guilt, and other such negative consequences will occur.
3. Sexual intercourse involves a mutual activity between two persons—hence, there is no such thing as an "uninvolved" sexual partner who can blame the other for all the couple's sexual troubles.

4. First events carry special meanings for each person, so things such as first orgasms, first acts of intercourse, and so on are especially significant events in the lives of individuals and couples.

5. Sex is a medium of exchange between persons. Partners must *give* pleasures in order to *get* pleasures themselves.

6. Authoritative "command" concepts (musts, shoulds, oughts) have no place in sexual activity. For instance, an attitude of "I must have an orgasm or I'll be unhappy" places excessive pressure on sexual performance. Sexual functioning cannot be forced or ordered. An attitude of openness, neutrality, and vulnerability is necessary for one to completely "surrender" oneself sexually to one's partner.

7. Feelings are facts. For example, a man may be very upset because his wife feels that his sexual language is crude, but her feeling is a fact. He must therefore talk "appropriately" if he is going to be able to communicate sexually with her on a positive basis.

8. Intercourse does not occur in a psychosocial vacuum. What goes on outside the bedroom has a direct bearing on what goes on sexually within the bedroom.

9. Each sexual partner needs to speak for himself or herself, not for the partner. People should learn to use "I" statements to achieve this and to avoid "mind reading," second-guessing, or blaming their partners. Instead of saying "you weren't turning me on," people can be taught to reframe the message by saying "I wasn't feeling turned on by you . . ."—thus acknowledging their feeling but not blaming the partner.

10. Good communications are of vital importance to the maintenance of any relationship. They are especially critical in communicating attitudes, feelings, and wishes about sexuality.

11. Good marital sexual intercourse is most likely to occur if it is engaged in regularly over the years. The adage of "use it or lose it," referring to a person's ability to respond sexually, holds true.

Most therapists use a multifaceted package of interventions that range from a psychodynamic exploration of the individual through relationship restructuring to a prescription of direct changes in sexual behavior. The following principles currently underlie most sex therapy interventions:

1. Mutual responsibility
2. Elimination of performance anxiety
3. Education
4. Attitude change
5. Improved communication
6. Enhanced relationships
7. Physical and medical evaluations
8. Behavior change

Sexual problems can be divided into two categories: primary and secondary. Primary sexual problems arise from sex-related stimuli and occur only in sexual situations. Secondary sexual problems are only one manifestation of a larger personal relationship problem. Classifying cases as primary or secondary helps the counselor determine the appropriate counseling strategy. Primary problems usually respond well to brief counseling. Secondary problems usually require intensive counseling or therapy. The major focus of health counselors, therefore, is on brief therapy. The next section describes a process that should be sufficient to alleviate many of the sexual problems that counselors encounter. It is based on psychological learning theory and can be used compatibly with all major intervention systems. Learning is emphasized as the means of changing both overt and covert sexual behavior. One to five visits of 30- to 60-minute duration are involved. An extended version of this material is available in Pion, Annon, and Carlson (1982).

The Four-Levels-of-Intervention Model

This treatment model was developed to aid counselors in helping clients with sexual problems (Annon, 1974; Pion & Annon, 1975). The model, referred to as P-LI-SS-IT, provides for four levels of intervention, with each letter or pair of letters designating a suggested method for handling particular sexual concerns. The four levels are: (1) *P*ermission, (2) *Li*mited *I*nformation, (3) *S*pecific *S*uggestions, and (4) *I*ntensive *T*herapy.

To attempt to assess and treat each sexual concern in exactly the same way would be inappropriate. The model, both flexible and comprehensive, provides a framework for distinguishing problems that are amenable to brief therapy from others that require intensive therapy. The first three levels can be viewed as brief therapy, as contrasted with the intensive therapy of the fourth level.

This model has a number of distinct advantages. It may be applied in a variety of settings and adapted to whatever client time is available. Theoretically, each ascending level of approach requires increasing amounts of knowledge, training, and skill on the part of the counselor. Because each level requires increased experience, the model allows professionals to gear their approach to their own particular level of competence. This also means that counselors now have something to help them determine when referral elsewhere is appropriate. Most important, the model provides a framework for discriminating between and among problems. How many levels counselors will feel competent to use directly depends on the amount of interest and time they are willing to devote to expanding their knowledge, training, and skill.

The First Level of Treatment: Permission Giving.   Sometimes all that people want to know is whether they are normal or "okay," not perverted, deviant, or abnormal. They would like to find this out from someone with a professional background or from someone who is in a position of authority. Many times clients are not bothered by their specific behavior but, rather, by the thought that something may, be "wrong" or "bad" about what they are doing or not doing. Frequently, clients just want an interested professional as a sounding board for expressing their concerns. In these cases, the counselor will probably be able to tell them that they are not alone or unusual in their concerns and that many people share them. Reassurance of normality and permission to continue doing exactly what clients have been doing are often sufficient to resolve what might eventually become a major problem.

Permission giving will certainly not solve all sexual problems, but it will resolve some. It has the advantages that it can be used in almost any setting at any time (given some measure of privacy) and that the counselor needs only minimal preparation. Finally, it may be used to cover a number of areas of concern, such as thoughts, fantasies, dreams, and feelings (covert behaviors), as well as overt behaviors.

Concerns about sexual thoughts and fantasies are common. For example, both men and women periodically have sexual thoughts and fantasies about people other than their partners; about people of the same sex; or even about their own parents, brothers or sisters, sons or daughters, or friends. Letting clients know that this is not unusual may relieve some of the anxiety or guilt about being abnormal. Only when such thoughts or fantasies become persistent or begin to interfere directly in some way with other areas of functioning do they create a problem.

Permission giving may also be appropriate for handling dream concerns. Individuals may have occasional dreams involving sexual activity with a wide variety of people other than their partners. At times, the dreams may also involve sexual activity with partners of the same sex, even though the dreamer may never have had such actual experiences. Reassurance that such dreams are perfectly normal and not unusual or indicative of abnormality is usually sufficient to relieve the anxiety or guilt associated with them. Often, permission giving is sufficient to stop the recurring dream that initially caused the anxiety.

Another common concern is clients' anxiety over experiencing sexual arousal to what they consider to be inappropriate stimulation. Many of these concerns arise from the failure to discriminate between arousal that results from sexual thoughts and fantasies and arousal that results from direct tactile stimulation. For example, a mother who is breast-feeding her baby might experience some degree of sexual arousal because of the direct tactile stimulation to her breasts. A father may experience an erection when playing with a young child on his lap. Reassurance that these are normal, involuntary responses to tactile stimulation may reduce clients' unnecessary anxiety and prevent a minor happening from developing into a major concern. Similar permission giving for such feelings can apply to horseback and motorcycle riding; tree and rope climbing; the use of tampons, douches, and enemas; or any other circumstance that involves tactile stimulation of the breasts, genitals, or anal area.

Permission giving can be applied to a wide range of sexual behaviors that the counselor recognizes as common and normal but that the client does not. Take, for example, the case of the couple who read in their favorite magazine that the average frequency of sexual intercourse for people of their age and education is 2½ times a week. Their own frequency may be 8 times a week or 8 times a year, but now they begin to worry whether they are normal, oversexed, or undersexed. A counselor's response that, in essence, gives them permission to continue with their own preferred frequency may be all that is necessary to relieve anxiety.

Many sexual concerns can be handled by giving the client permission to not engage in certain sexual behaviors unless he or she chooses to. An example might be the young woman who is receiving pressure from her partner to experience multiple orgasms or who has read or heard that every woman has the right to expect and demand them. However, she is satisfied with the one orgasm that she experiences with her partner and does not really care whether she is multiorgasmic or not. Giving this woman permission to not experience multiple orgasms may be helpful to her. Conversely, in the case of the woman who would really like to experience multiple orgasms but is fearful or hesitant that she might then become a "nymphomaniac," giving permission to be multiorgasmic, if she chooses to, might be a helpful approach.

Permission giving is most appropriate and helpful when used in direct relation to the client's goals. By keeping this in mind, the counselor will be able to decide what form of permission giving will be the most beneficial for a particular client.

On the surface, the basic assumption underlying the permission-giving approach may appear to be that the counselor should sanction whatever sexual thought, fantasy, or behavior a consenting adult wishes to engage in. In a general sense, this may be correct, but such an assumption has some definite limitations. Although an individual client ultimately has to decide on his or her own behavior, a counselor's blanket permission may not be appropriate if the person is not making an informed choice. The counselor is responsible for informing the client of the possible adverse consequences of engaging in certain thoughts, fantasies, or behaviors.

A number of books have "given permission" for the indiscriminate use of any fantasy a person may desire while engaging in masturbation or sexual behavior with a partner. Learning theory suggests, and clinical evidence substantiates, that systematically associating thoughts and fantasies with sexual activity is a powerful means of conditioning sexual arousal to almost any stimulus (Annon, 1973). This fact has been used to therapeutic advantage. In certain circumstances, however, if someone who is uninformed engages in such activity there may be undesired results. Informing clients of the possible consequences of their behavior and leaving the ultimate choice to them seems more appropriate than blanket permission giving.

Limitations.   The extent to which counselors feel comfortable with and are willing to use the permission-giving approach depends in general on their breadth of sexual knowledge, orientation, and value system. The more knowledge that counselors have of sexual behavior in their own and other cultures, the more comfortable they feel in applying this level of treatment. Counselors' theoretical or professional orientation can also place limits on how appropriate permission giving may be for a particular thought, fantasy, dream, feeling, or behavior. Counselors with a psychoanalytic background may wish to withhold permission giving for recurrent sexual dreams, preferring to work through such material in therapy with clients. Obviously, that is the individual counselor's choice.

There is no intent to suggest here that counselors change their viewpoint to that of a learning-oriented approach. Counselors should use only those suggestions that they think are appropriate to their frame of reference. At the same time, however, counselors should be willing to experiment a little.

Ideally, the counselor will not try to impose a personal value system on the client intentionally. In practice, however, this is sometimes difficult to achieve. Of course, the counselor should not give up his or her own value system. At times, the client's stated goals may come into direct conflict with the counselor's value system. When this happens, the counselor's responsibility is to clearly inform the client of this and refer him or her elsewhere.

A final important point is that of self-permission. Counselors should be able to give permission to themselves to not be experts. They must not be afraid to say they do not know the answer when they do not. No one person is an expert in this field. Theory, research, and practice in the sexual area are so far-ranging that no individual or group of individuals can be expected to know or keep abreast of even a sizable fraction of the information in this area. Counselors do what they can for their clients on the basis of their own knowledge and experience. In some cases, the most important thing a counselor has to offer is himself or herself—someone who will listen; who can communicate interest, understanding, and respect; and who will not label or judge the client.

If permission giving is not sufficient to resolve the client's concern, and if the counselor is not in an appropriate setting or does not have sufficient time or relevant knowledge and skills, the client should be referred elsewhere. Otherwise, the counselor can combine permission giving with the next level of treatment—limited information.

The Second Level of Treatment: Limited Information.   In contrast to permission giving, which basically is telling clients that it is all right to continue doing what they have been doing, limited information means giving them specific factual information directly relevant to sexual concerns. This may result in clients continuing to do what they have been doing, or it may result in something different. Limited information is usually given in conjunction with permission giving. Each can be used as a separate treatment level, but considerable overlap exists between the two.

Common Areas of Sexual Concern.   Providing limited information is an excellent method for dispelling sexual myths, whether they are specific ones (e.g., those that pertain to genital size) or more general ones (e.g., men and women differ markedly in their capacity to want and enjoy sexual relations and to respond to sexual stimulation). Other common sexual concerns are about breast and genital shape and size, masturbation, intercourse during menstruation, oral genital activities, sexual frequency, and sexual performance.

A great deal of evidence indicates that men and women are far more similar than dissimilar in their capacity for and experience of sexual desire, arousal, and orgasm. Numerous cross-cultural studies from various fields, such as anthropology and sociology consistently reveal that cultures that encourage women to be free in sexual expression produce sexually responsive women who are as uninhibited and responsive as males. Cultures that encourage and expect women to experience orgasm yield women who do experience orgasm.

Limitations.   The extent to which counselors are willing to use limited information in handling sexual concerns depends on their breadth of knowledge about the area. How they offer information to clients depends on the individual style with which counselors feel most comfortable and the manner of presentation that they feel will be most helpful to their clients. With a conservative-appearing, middle-aged couple who hesitantly ask if anal contact is normal, the counselor might reply, "Such activity is not considered unusual or abnormal. In fact, a recent national survey of married persons under 35 indicated that half of them experienced manual anal foreplay." With a young couple who casually asks if germs can be transferred through oral genital contact, the counselor may respond, "Yes, it is possible. The mouth has a very high bacteria count."

Whatever their style, counselors now have two strategies for approaching sexual concerns. As with permission giving, the degree to which counselors feel comfortable with and are willing to use the second treatment level also depends on their theoretical orientation and value system. The limitations imposed by the factors discussed in the first level of treatment apply here as well.

The addition of this treatment level may resolve some concerns that could not be handled by application of the first level of treatment alone. If giving limited information is not sufficient to resolve the client's sexual concern, the counselor has two additional options. He or she can refer the client for treatment elsewhere or, with the appropriate setting, knowledge, skills, and experience, the counselor can proceed to the third level of treatment—specific suggestions.

The Third Level of Treatment: Specific Suggestions.   Before they can give specific suggestions to clients, counselors must first have detailed information. The assumption here is that offering specific suggestions would not be therapeutically appropriate or helpful to the client without having first obtained information about the client and his or her unique set of circumstances. If the counselor were to immediately launch into a number of suggestions after hearing the initial description of the problem (not the "label" for the problem), the counselor may not only waste the client's time (e.g., offering suggestions he or she has already tried) but may also further compound the problem. By suggesting inappropriate and possibly useless treatment procedures based on insufficient data, the counselor may overlook other more necessary and/or appropriate treatment.

The Sexual-Problem History.   At this stage, the counselor should elicit a sexual-problem history. This is not to be confused with a comprehensive learning-about-sex history. The model proposed here assumes that a comprehensive learning history may not be relevant or necessary for instituting effective brief therapy. Application of the specific suggestions approach may resolve a number of problems that filtered through the first two levels of treatment but, needless to say, it is not expected to successfully dispense with all such problems. If this third level of treatment is not helpful to the client, a complete sexual history may be a necessary first step toward intensive therapy.

Guidelines for obtaining a sexual-problem history, which is a necessary part of the brief therapy approach to treatment, are outlined here.

1. Description of current problem
2. Onset and course of problem
   a. Onset—gradual or sudden, precipitating events, consequences
   b. Course—changes over time: increase, decrease, or fluctuation in severity; frequency; intensity; functional relationships with other variables
3. Client's concept of cause and continuation of the problem
4. Past treatment and outcome
   a. Medical evaluation—specialty, date, form of treatment, results, current medication for any reason
   b. Other professional help—specialty, date, form of treatment, results
   c. Self-treatment—type and results
5. Current expectations and goals of treatment—concrete versus general

How such a history is taken has to be adapted to the counselor's setting and the amount of time available. The problem history is easily adapted to sessions of 5 minutes or of several hours. Making up a form with these sexual-problem history guidelines may be helpful because the counselor can use it as a general guide while interviewing and/or write the client's responses directly on it for future reference. Either way, using a form should help the counselor become comfortable and experienced with the preceding guidelines until they are memorized.

Self-Recorded Problem History. Over the years, considerable research has been done on the use of self-recorded (audiocassette) problem histories. In this method, the couple is requested, at the time of the first interview, to prepare a tape before the next visit. The purpose of doing so is explained to the client as follows:

- To describe the problem(s) for which the person(s) is seeking help.
- To describe the possible influences that relate to or have preceded the onset of the problem.

The counselor provides an introductory letter and a guideline that outlines a satisfactory method of tape preparation, and the client is asked to read them in the office. In the letter, the client is told: (1) that the tape is a means of describing the problem and its history, (2) that listening to the tape again after the therapy is over may help give the person a measure of self-growth and understanding, and (3) that preparation of the tape at home can save treatment hours and thus lessen expense. (The client is also assured that the counselor will maintain the material's confidentiality and will adhere to professional standards.) Experience has shown that permitting the client a greater amount of responsibility for history-taking can actually facilitate the therapeutic process.

Providing Treatment. Once the counselor feels comfortable in obtaining the problem history from clients in whatever fashion, he or she is ready, to offer specific suggestions. In contrast to the permission giving and limited information treatments, which generally do not require that clients take any active steps to change their behaviors unless they choose to, specific suggestions are direct attempts to help clients alter their behaviors to reach their stated goals.

Most of the suggestions that may be given can be used by a counselor who has only 10 to 30 minutes for a client interview. Furthermore, they can be used even when the counselor is able to see the client on only one or a few occasions at the most. Obviously, these are minimum time limits that can be expanded and adapted to the time available, but the specific suggestions level is intended for use within the brief therapy framework proposed. If the suggestions are not perceived as potentially helpful within a relatively brief time period, intensive therapy is probably more appropriate.

As with the methods in the previous levels of treatment, specific suggestions may be seen as a preventive measure as well as a treatment technique. For example, suggesting specific ways to avoid pain associated with genital intercourse may prevent a woman from experiencing vaginismus—painful vaginal spasms. Or a direct treatment approach to ejaculation problems may prevent an eventual occurrence of a man's erection difficulties. This level of treatment can be combined easily and advantageously with the previous two levels.

Two common sayings are helpful when applying the specific suggestions approach. One, which is particularly beneficial for clients with concerns about a particular feature of their body, is: "What you do with what you have, rather than what you have, is what counts!" The second has even broader applications. Many clients who have sexual concerns tend to see each forthcoming sexual event with their partners as the "final test." If the man once again ejaculates too soon or does not obtain an erection, he often feels as though he has lost his last chance. Similar concerns are reported by women in search of orgasms. "Will it happen this time?" or "It's got to happen this time or I'll just die!" thoughts are not conducive to success in attaining desired goals. Helping clients learn to say and believe that "There is always another day (another time, another occasion)" can do a great deal to modify some of the self-defeating attitudes of many individuals.

This level of treatment is particularly effective for dealing with heterosexual problems involving arousal, erection, ejaculation, orgasm, or painful intercourse. The specific suggestions to offer (e.g., redirection of attention, sensate focus techniques, interruption of stimulation, squeeze technique, vaginal muscle training) will depend on the information obtained in the sexual-problem history. In general, they fall into three categories: (1) suggestions to the male, (2) suggestions to the female, and (3) suggestions to the couple.

Often, the counselor sees a client who has no immediate partner available. In such cases, a number of suggestions can be made for self-stimulation procedures. The counselor may encounter other situations in which a client is involved in a relationship with a person who has a problem but who is not able or willing to come in for a consultation. Assuming that the second person is open to suggestions, the client can pass along whatever information he or she feels might be appropriate under the circumstances.

The most helpful suggestions are usually those that can be made when both partners are present. Clients should be encouraged to have their partners come in with them. When couples come in together and are willing to cooperate with treatment suggestions, the probability that mutual goals will be realized is much greater. Working with one person on a problem that involves two is always more difficult.

Limitations.   Efficient use of the specific suggestions treatment level depends largely on the counselor's breadth of knowledge, skill and experience, and awareness of relevant therapeutic suggestions. The limitations discussed under the other treatment levels apply here as well. For interested readers, Annon (1974) provides a detailed description of the application of suggestions to the more prevalent heterosexual problems encountered by males and females.

Readings.   Counselors can suggest that clients read material related to their concerns. Using reading materials is another means of providing permission or limited information about a certain sexual area or client concern, and they can be used to supplement specific suggestions or promote new client-initiated procedures. Because of time limitations on either the counselor's or the client's part, the counselor may need to suggest readings in lieu of other specific suggestions. The counselor, of course, should not suggest any readings to clients unless he or she is well acquainted with their content and feels comfortable recommending them. The following are helpful materials for both clients and counselors: *The Last Sex Manual* (Pion & Hopkins, 1978), *For Each Other* (Barbach, 1982), *Falling in Love Again* (Barbach, 1990), *Taking Time for Love* (Dinkmeyer & Carlson, 1989), *Super Marital Sex* (Pearsall, 1987), and *Sexual Happiness* (Yaffe & Fenwick, 1988).

The third level of treatment—specific suggestions—concludes the presentation of the brief therapy approach of the P-LI-SS-IT model. A number of sexual concerns may be treated successfully through such an approach. Those that cannot be resolved will filter through, at which point the counselor can refer the client for appropriate treatment elsewhere. If the counselor has the requisite time, knowledge, experience, and skills, he or she can proceed to the fourth level of treatment for clients—intensive therapy.

The Fourth Level of Treatment: Intensive Therapy.   This section does not describe or attempt to outline the specifies of the intensive therapy approach to the treatment of persisting sexual problems. However, for the counselor who has already received training for intensive therapy, this is the appropriate time to initiate such treatment.

Counselors need to realize that involving a client in an expensive, long-term treatment program without first trying to resolve the problem using a brief therapy approach may be unethical. A number of sexual concerns can be treated successfully using the brief approach if counselors are willing to apply it. Specific suggestions that work for one client may not always be effective for another. Sometimes, interpersonal conflicts prevent the suggestions from being carried through. When this happens, and when counselors believe they have done as much as they can from within the brief therapy approach, the time has come for intensive therapy.

In the model proposed here, intensive therapy does not mean an extended standardized program of treatment. By their nature, standardized programs are not of help to some people, and they may not be necessary. Be aware that many of the essential elements of some of the current standardized programs can be successfully used within a brief therapy approach.

In the P-LI-SS-IT model, intensive therapy is seen as highly individualized treatment that is necessary because standardized treatment was not successful in helping the client reach his or her goals. Within the present framework, intensive therapy means undertaking a careful initial assessment of the client's unique situation to devise a therapeutic program that is unique to the individual involved.

COMMON SEXUAL DISSATISFACTIONS AND TREATMENT STRATEGIES

There are a number of complaints about sexuality that counselors hear over and over again. These include inability to communicate about sexual likes and dislikes, lack of skill in initiating sexual activity, disagreements about the extent of foreplay or nonsexual expression of physical affection, discrepancies in the partners' desires to experiment with new sexual activities, boredom with the sexual relationship, disagreements about frequency of sexual activity, inability to find time for sex, or differing preferences for the location or times of day for sexual activity (Schover, 1982). Each of these dissatisfactions is discussed and treatment techniques are suggested in the following suggestions.

Difficulty with Sexual Communication

The following is a common story, even today, when sexual freedom and performance are constantly touted.

My partner and I just don't talk about sex. In our entire marriage, we've seldom said anything about it. I think I know what she likes, because after fifteen years with someone, you really get to know them; but I'm not always sure if she's turned on, and I don't know if she has orgasms. She says she does. If I want something to happen during sex, I usually just wait and see if she does it. I wouldn't know how to ask for it, as we would both be embarrassed.

The first thing to do is to make sure that both partners wish to change their sexual communication. To focus on what each could gain, counselors will find it helpful to ask partners to write down the three things they would most like to change about their own sexual behavior and the three things they would most like to change in their partner's behavior. Many clients will just write down "nothing." In that case, the counselor may need to explain that the goals should be small and specific. Examples can be given—"say something romantic to me during intercourse," "spend more time touching my penis," or "be able to ask him to bring me to orgasm after intercourse." The goals can be shared with the partner later as part of the communication training exercise.

If the clients have difficulty with using sexual terms, a desensitization exercise may be useful. In one session, each partner is asked to provide as many synonyms as possible for the words *penis, vagina, clitoris,* and *intercourse.* The counselor keeps a written list for each word provided and may model relaxed use of sexual terms by adding some slang words. Further discussion can focus on the humorous aspects of sex, any feelings of shame about the genitals, or the words that feel most comfortable to each partner and in different situations (e.g., in discussing sex with the counselor, in talking to each other at home).

Another in-session technique is couple communication training (Jacobson & Margolin, 1979; Stuart, 1980; Dinkmeyer & Carlson, 1989). Partners are taught to present their points of view in the form of an "I" message such as, "When you do X, I feel Y." The other partner accurately reflects the message given and then has the opportunity to respond in the same mode. The couple is taught to ask for things that are specific ("I would like you to stroke my back gently," as opposed to "Why don't you touch me?"), positive ("I like it better when you use a harder grip on my penis," instead of "Stop touching me so lightly. It tickles!"), and focused in the present ("I would like to take more time in foreplay tonight," rather than "You never give me a chance to get turned on! I don't think we've spent more than two minutes in foreplay during the last five years"). The couple can begin by using these techniques to discuss a sexual topic that is not a point of conflict. The partners can then proceed to communicate about their goals for sexual behavior change. After they have had successful communications within a session, the couple can be assigned to have a discussion at home, which they can audiotape for the counselor.

Other homework assignments include using sensate focus exercises and gradually building in immediate feedback. Complete instructions for sensate focus can be found in Kaplan (1975) or Dinkmeyer and Carlson (1989). In the most basic version, the couple is requested to take turns being the giver and receiver of nongenital body caresses. The task of the giver is to focus on his or her own sensations as the partner's body is touched for a set period of time. The receiver also focuses on his or her own body rather than worrying about the giver's feelings.

At this stage, there is no verbal or nonverbal feedback during the touching, unless the stimulation is painful. After being the receiver, each client should tell the partner the best three touches and the one kind of caress they liked the least. Feedback should specify the part of the body and the type of touch. The next task is for the receiver to give immediate positive feedback. Again, comments should be specific. If one partner does not enjoy a caress as the receiver, the partner should ask for something that he or she liked better rather than just requesting that the giver stop the stimulation.

The caressing steps are then repeated with the breasts and genitals. The couple is cautioned not to focus exclusively on the genitals, now that they are allowed to touch them. Some nonverbal communication techniques can also be demonstrated, such as guiding the giver's hand.

Lack of Skill in Initiating Sexual Activity

Many clients have difficulty initiating sex or doing so in a way that evokes a positive response in their partners. Often, the place to begin treatment is with a discussion of how clients express their wishes for sex and how they know when their mates are likely to be responsive.

> My wife never initiates sex. It's always my job. I get tired of always being the aggressive one. It makes me wonder whether she really likes sex, even though she seems to enjoy it. It would turn me on if she let me know she was in the mood once in a while.

> He just doesn't know how to get me ready for sex. He always seems to wait until I'm busy with something else, and then he just comes up behind me and grabs me. Then he's hurt if I don't respond right away. Or else he just turns around and says, "Let's go to bed."

Many clients have never identified their own sexual signals. One spouse may also have no idea how to tell whether his or her partner is feeling sexually receptive. If a wife often goes up to bed with the expectation that her husband will follow her upstairs to make love but he watches TV until midnight, it is not surprising that her frustration and anger build up. The first step is for the couple to recognize each other's signals. The next step is to build some pleasurable strategies for sexual initiation into the couple's interaction.

Each partner should offer some suggestions during the counseling session on ways that the other can initiate sex. The counselor can also offer strategies that have been successfully used by other couples (e.g., giving a kiss and a whisper in the ear, having dinner by candlelight, or wearing sexy apparel). Schover (1982) suggests giving the following assignment:

> This week I would like each of you to practice initiating sex at least three times. That doesn't mean I want you to have sex six times. I just want you to think of some different ways to ask your partner for sexual activity, and to carry them out. Probably this will not lead up to having sex on most of the occasions. I want you to try something different each time you initiate, including some things that usually might make you feel silly, or embarrassed. The partner's task is to write down afterwards how you felt when your mate initiated. Say a little about the things you did and did not like about the approach (p. 61).

This assignment often brings out conflict about being assertive, both in asking for what the partner would like and in refusing the mate's requests. An assignment that Zilbergeld (1978) calls "yes's and no's" can help the couple explore these issues further. Each partner is asked to make three requests during the week for something he or she would like but usually would not demand. In addition, each is asked to say "no" 3 times to something he or she does not want to do but would usually agree to do. If the couple's difficulty in assertion is mainly in the sexual area, the yes's and no's can be restricted to sexual situations. The important task for the counselor when discussing the results of these assignments is to reinforce new positive behaviors and to help clients become aware of self-statements and feelings that prevent them from being assertive.

Disagreements about Foreplay and Nonsexual Physical Affection

Unlike difficulties with communication or initiation, which are seen equally often in men and women, disagreements about the length of foreplay and the amount of nonsexual touching and cuddling in a relationship are often (but not always) gender-specific. The following is a typical pattern:

> **She:** "He never really gives me time to warm up for intercourse. All he wants to do is kiss me once or twice, and maybe feel my breasts, and then he's ready. It's frustrating, because I want more touching, and more tenderness. He never even likes to sit with his arm around me in the evening. He only touches me when he wants sex."

> **He:** "She just wants to hang on me all the time. I'm tired when I get home from work and I don't feel like hugging and kissing. I just want to read the paper after dinner. And I suppose I should spend more time on foreplay, but I get impatient for the real thing. Anyway, I'm afraid I would just come too fast if we spent more time touching first."

Munjack and Oziel (1980) provide a practical outline for counseling clients on increasing foreplay. They suggest educating the couple in the woman's slower time to arousal and in her need for more genital stimulation while limiting genital stimulation during foreplay for the man. The man can also be taught simple methods of delaying ejaculation (Zilbergeld, 1978).

In addition, some exploration of each partner's subjective experience during nonsexual and sexual touching should be undertaken. What is perceived as relaxed tenderness to one person may seem overwhelming and intrusive to the other. The counselor may find it helpful to assign 15 minutes of kissing and cuddling, with each partner being asked to examine what personal thoughts occur during the experience. As a result, new self-talk may replace the less-productive messages. For example, a husband who finds himself thinking, "Ugh, I feel smothered. I wish I could go watch the football game," might be asked to focus on his wife's soft skin or to ask her to rub his back instead of kissing him passionately. Or he may be asked to say to himself, "I can stop this stimulation any time I wish, so I might as well try it a little longer and see if there is any part of it that I enjoy."

Again, sensate focus exercises can be a useful way for the couple to try new kinds of nongenital stimulation. The structure provided by the counselor can short-circuit arguments about how much touching is enough. The counselor might also assign kissing, hugging, and genital and nongenital touching, for a maximum of 15 minutes, outside the bedroom with some clothes on and with the stipulation that the activity will not lead to intercourse. This may help the couple rediscover some of the excitement felt while dating. This exercise also combats the stereotype that all sexual activity must be an elaborate routine of foreplay that ends in intercourse and orgasm for both partners.

Another useful technique is to assign a "quickie"—a sexual session in which only a minimal amount of preparation and foreplay is included. The couple's task is to see how quickly each can get in the mood for intercourse. The ultimate goal is flexibility in choosing to have a romantic atmosphere or take all evening for sex sometimes and to enjoy each other in an uncomplicated way at other times.

In this same vein, the partner who is pushing for more physical affection and/or foreplay can be asked whether there are nonsexual activities that would serve as a substitute for these ways of demonstrating caring. Sometimes, either setting aside 15 to 30 minutes in an evening just to talk or going out on a "date" together may fulfill cravings for attention and contact that were perceived as sexual frustration.

Disagreements about the Variety of Sexual Activities

A wish for more sexual variety can arise from a number of issues. One partner may be somewhat depressed or feel unstimulated in the nonsexual areas of life and seek diversion in the bedroom. There may be unrealistic expectations for sexual pleasure, fed by media myths. Other clients may have cherished certain sexual fantasies for many years and finally have gotten up the nerve to ask their spouses to try them out. Often, however, the sexual routine has really become rigid and boring, so the sense of playfulness and exploration has disappeared.

> We just do the same thing each time we have sex. We kiss for a few minutes, touch each other in the usual places, and then go on and start intercourse, either with him on top or with me on top. I tried to get him to read some books about sex or go to an X-rated movie, but he says he's satisfied with things the way they are. Sex is OK, but I want it to be more like what I read about.

When one partner wishes to try a particular sexual activity that the other finds distasteful, the counselor has a dilemma. As Munjack and Oziel (1980) point out, no one should be forced (or even coaxed) into an activity that is personally unpleasant or painful. Often the reluctance to be involved is for other relationship reasons, and the counselor can help the couple discover what the real issue is. When the desired behavior is something that one partner is ambivalent about trying, however, that partner should first identify what he or she finds negative about it.

Emotional Issues about the Sexual Relationship

Another area for therapeutic exploration is the couple's subjective emotional experience during sexual activity. If one or both partners are feeling bored or constrained, building in some playfulness may provide relief. The partners could be assigned to do some physical activity of their choice that would put them in a playful mood before having sex (e.g., taking a shower together, wrestling, tickling, or having a pillow fight) or to play at taking certain roles during sex (e.g., being very shy and innocent or very seductive).

Sometimes, verbally sharing a sexual fantasy with a partner may increase arousal and can substitute for activities that could have a negative impact on a relationship (e.g., joining a mate-swapping club or trying something that one partner finds frightening). Clients who have difficulty fantasizing can be encouraged to read anthologies of fantasies, such as *In the Garden of Desire* (Maltz & Boss, 1997), or columns in magazines such as *Penthouse.* The counselor may ask each person to write his or her own sexual fantasy and then allow the partner to read it. If both partners feel comfortable with these activities, they may try telling fantasies to one another before or during sexual activity.

Disagreements about the Frequency of Sexual Activity

Sometimes, neither partner in a couple has a real lack of sexual desire, but both disagree about the frequency for sexual activity; for example:

> "We don't get enough sex. Our lives are so busy with work and the kids. I also think my partner is happy with sex once a week or once every two weeks, but I'd like it more often."

Zilbergeld and Ellison (1980) provide a cogent discussion of the causes of this situation and some good treatment suggestions. They point out that sex counselors have been biased in trying to increase the desire of the partner who wants sex less often rather than suggesting that the more "lusty" client examine the reasons for wanting sex so frequently. As mentioned before, sometimes sexual desire may mask a longing for more affection or time shared with the partner. One assignment that may help increase nonsexual expression of affection is "Encouraging Days" (Dinkmeyer & Carlson, 1989); that is, both partners identify small ways that their mates can express caring, and then they are asked to increase their rates of the desired behaviors.

When it does seem important to increase a couple's frequency of sexual activity, there are exercises to aid clients in discovering what brings on a sexual mood. One exercise is having clients keep a daily "desire diary" to record all sexual feelings and thoughts, where they occurred, who was present, and what the other person's reaction was. Another exercise is to have clients list as many things as they can that make them feel more sexual, including physical activities, such as playing sports and dancing; dressing certain ways; looking at erotic materials; and so on. Clients are then assigned to try several of these activities during the week. Once they realize which situations elicit a sexual mood, they can use that knowledge to create arousal when their partners are available.

Inability to Find Time and Agree
on Location for Sexual Activity

Many couples complain that they cannot find the time for sex. Sometimes, this complaint generalizes into a situation in which the only time spent together is taken up with household tasks or childcare. When asked to set aside an evening to go out on a "date," such a couple may insist that it is impossible to take the time off from errands or to afford a babysitter. Sometimes the counseling needs to focus on a reassessment of priorities, including how the clients' current emotional distance affects the future of their relationship. Realistically, some couples may have to choose between having the added income from extra jobs and having enough time to be alone with each other. Couples with children may need to consider getting some childcare or letting the children know that the parents need private time.

Other couples complain that they cannot agree on a time of day for sex. One is a "night person" and the other is a "morning person." Often, sexual moods correspond to their periods of high energy. Some discussion and eventual compromise is needed.

Some couples disagree about the location for sex. One person feels most comfortable in bed, whereas the other enjoys having sexual encounters on the living room rug, in the bathtub, and/or in the backyard. The couple may need to deal realistically with one partner's concern about being "caught in the act" by children or neighbors. The couple also may need to make the environment comfortable for both partners, perhaps by putting big cushions in front of the fireplace or by having curtains around the porch; more ideas can be found in *Hot Monogomy* (Love, 1999).

SEXUAL DESIRE AND HEALTH

Although sexual desire may have nothing at all to do with the state of one's health, there are some cases in which health does affect sexual desire. This is particularly so if a client's level of desire has dropped off after a period of higher desire and the drop cannot be attributed to any significant changes in his or her life; the counselor should recommend a full check-up to determine whether the change in desire is due to physical factors. Some health conditions and some medications have a detrimental effect on sexual desire. Depression can also cause a drop in desire, as can extreme fatigue or tension. Endocrinological problems, such as changes in the flow of particular hormones, can also affect sexual desire. It is important to inform a medical doctor about a change in desire so that the possibility of medical causes can be examined. The rest of this section discusses different levels of desire and offers suggestions for communication and compromise.

Differences in Sexual Desire

A common complaint in relationships is that one partner wants sex more often than the other does. Many people are able to reach some kind of compromise and make a satisfactory adjustment. For others, however, the differences in desire continue to be a troublesome aspect of their relationship that can often lead to other distresses. It is practically impossible to state what "normal" desire is. Each person has a different "appetite" for sex, just as for food. Individuals have different needs for intimacy and for romance as well as for sexual contact. Differences in sexual desire may be so serious that anger and resentments carry over into other areas of a couple's life (Friedman, 1984; Love, 1999).

For many, the early stage of a relationship contains sexual novelty and discovery. Once the "honeymoon" period comes to an end, couples are forced to confront each other on a wide variety of issues. When the novelty of the relationship wears off, people may discover each other's imperfections and annoying habits and attitudes. The media—particularly television and men's and women's magazines—tend to present relationships in an extremely unrealistic manner. Conflict is rarely seen in any form that is comparable to people's personal experiences, and it is easy to become disappointed and unhappy when problems occur for which there may be no immediate and/or effective resolution. It is not surprising that disappointment, disillusionment, and unhappiness often translate into a lack of desire for sex with one's partner. Imbalance of power in a relationship can also have a negative influence on sexual functioning. If one partner has all the power or makes all the decisions, the other partner may feel that the only power he or she has is to not want sex. One of the biggest stumbling blocks to a close sexual relationship is a lack of trust. People have to be willing to become vulnerable with one another to enjoy sex together.

For other individuals, low desire has nothing to do with the partner in particular but is just a general state. Perhaps the individual has had some negative experiences or has been brought up to believe that sex or pleasure in general is wrong. Others who just have a lower appetite for sex are perfectly happy when they do have sex, they just do not want it very often. Although this is not a problem for them, it may become a problem for their partners.

Suggestions for Clients with a Higher Level of Desire.   The suggestions and questions presented in this section are not meant to imply that one partner is at fault for his or her partner's more infrequent desire for sex. It is important for both partners to cooperate in finding ways to make the overall and sexual relationship more comfortable and enjoyable. Some people are able to leave their individual and relationship problems outside the bedroom door, whereas others find it difficult or impossible to want and enjoy sex if things are not going well in other aspects of their lives. Some people can use sex to make up after a fight; others can only enjoy sex if they are feeling good about themselves and about their partners.

Counselors often find it is helpful to encourage the couple to carefully choose the times to initiate sex. If either partner is excessively tired or rushed, it is difficult for sex to be a relaxed and enjoyable experience. It is important to make time to be together for other activities, as well as for sex, and for the sexual time to be relaxed, warm, romantic, and intimate. Couples might consider preparing for sex by putting on some soft music, lighting candles, or making some other romantic gesture that will indicate that they are thinking about and planning time together.

Communication during sex—what each likes and what feels good—is also extremely important. When it is placed within the context of a romantic setting, is leisurely, and some imagination and variety is associated with it, sexual activity often becomes more enjoyable for both partners.

If one partner has a lot of worries and stresses in other areas of life, he or she often finds it difficult to take time to relax and enjoy sex. The other partner can help by providing an environment that is calm and relaxing and letting him or her know that time together can be a haven from the stresses of everyday life. Finally, if the relationship is generally poor, if the two cannot communicate, and if they frequently argue and disagree about important issues, it may be necessary to alleviate some of the problems before the partners can become confident and relaxed enough to be sexual.

Suggestions for Clients with a Lower Level of Desire.   Again, the suggestions here do not imply that there is anything wrong with an individual because he or she has less desire for sex than his or her partner. However, if the partners would like to resolve their different needs, have sex more frequently, or increase their desire, the following suggestions may be helpful. An important first step is to spend some time thinking about how they really feel about sex in general and about sex with their partner in particular. Is sex a neutral experience that they can take or leave, or is it something that they find aversive?

If most of one's difficulties are partner-specific, then the focus needs to be on making sex better and more enjoyable with that partner. Communication is the key to any good relationship in general and to good sex in particular. Partners should be able to tell each other what they want, what they would like, and what would make sex more relaxing and more enjoyable. Sex is a lot more than intercourse and orgasm, and if partners can communicate and share other sexual activities and other ways of being intimate, they may find that desire increases. If both partners would like to be better lovers, they must give each other feedback on what feels good and what is most arousing.

Couples should be assertive but not use sex as a way of expressing anger. People need to learn to express feelings directly to partners. If they have difficulty trusting and being intimate with one another, clients need to develop ways of increasing trust and intimacy.

It is important to focus on the positive rather than on the negative when engaging in sexual activity. Although focusing on the unattractive aspects of one's partner may be easy, this focus can be redirected; for example, rather than focusing on the "roll of fat around the waist," focus on the "beautiful blue eyes." The choice of focus helps to determine each partner's sexual desire.

Some people find that their desire is low in general but that it is not directly related to sex with their partners. The following are several questions that can be used to help explore the role of sex in clients' lives:

- Are you under a good deal of stress?
- Are you willing and able to take time for yourself and to look toward your own needs and pleasures?
- Are there things in your life that are making you feel depressed?
- When you do engage in sexual activity, do you enjoy it and wonder why you do not pursue it more often, but then find yourself reluctant to initiate or accept your partner's initiation?

Life stress and depression are frequently incompatible with sexual desire and often explain why one partner's desire is lower than the other's.

Taking time for oneself and for one's own pleasure is an important component in the enjoyment of sexual activity. Sometimes, "old messages" intrude and keep people from enjoying their own sexuality; for example, if one partner learned that sex was wrong, dirty, or immoral when he or she was young. It may be difficult for that individual to give up the feelings associated with those messages, even though those beliefs are no longer held. Reminding oneself that old messages need not currently influence one's life can often have a healthy impact on changing sexual desire. Sex should be fun, not a chore. Counselors should "give" couples permission to have fun and to play so that they can start treating sex as a more pleasurable activity. This focus on play often makes a significant difference when treating clients with low desire.

Suggestions for Both Partners

It is unfair to assume that the partner with a lower desire has to make all the changes in the relationship. Compromise—both partners making changes—is necessary to make any sexual desire change work. Frequently, it seems that the partner with a higher desire wants sex all the time. However, in many cases, if sex occurred more frequently, the partner with more desire would decrease the number of requests. The actual frequency of sex will determine who has to make the most changes. Clearly, if one partner wants sex once a week and the other wants it every day, it should be possible to compromise on 2 or 3 times per week. However, if one partner wants sex once a week and the other partner wants it once a year, compromise will be more difficult.

Working together, both partners can increase their communication and try to resolve other issues in their relationship so that sexual activity is not used to act out power struggles, control conflicts, and/or deal with anger. Sometimes sexual desire disappears because of other concerns. For example, if there is conflict over having or not having children or over who is responsible for contraception, sexual desire may decrease. Again, if issues can be discussed openly and a compromise reached, sexual desire is likely to return.

Frequently, who initiates sex and how sex is initiated and refused are issues for couples. If one partner tends to turn down sex because of the way it is initiated, it is important for that partner to say so. However, when refusing an invitation for sex, the individual needs to let the partner know that it is not a rejection of him or her but simply a statement about how the partner is feeling at the moment. By making another "date" for sexual activity or by making a point to initiate sex at some later time, the refusing partner can help prevent the other's feelings of anger and frustration. Communication and compromise can go a long way toward improving a couple's sexual relationship. It is important that both partners learn to focus on what each of them can do to make things better rather than on what their partner should do.

PSYCHOSEXUAL DISORDERS AND TREATMENT STRATEGIES

This section reviews the major categories of psychosexual disorders and reviews treatment strategies.

Male Sexual Dysfunction

There are three main types of male sexual dysfunction: erectile dysfunction, premature ejaculation, and retarded ejaculation.

Erectile Dysfunction. This term refers to the ongoing inability of a male to have or maintain an erection throughout intercourse. The dysfunction may be primary or secondary. In primary dysfunction, the man has never been able to sustain an erection long enough to complete intercourse. Secondary erectile dysfunction, also known as impotence, applies to the man who enjoyed the ability to gain and sustain an erection for intercourse before but is currently experiencing difficulties.

McCarthy and Perkins (1988) suggest an eclectic therapeutic approach to secondary erectile dysfunction. Techniques such as stop/slash intromission and sensate focus have been successfully employed (Brown & Field, 1988). Counseling can help the individual overcome the underlying dynamics of secondary sexual dysfunction.

Premature Ejaculation.   Another common male sexual dysfunction is premature ejaculation. Two variations of this dysfunction have been observed. If the man reaches an orgasm and loses his erection before inserting his penis into the vagina, this is known as "too early orgasm." If the man can achieve vaginal penetration but experiences orgasm very quickly or significantly earlier than his partner climaxes, this is known as "too quick orgasm."

It is important to note that there is a subcategory called situational premature ejaculation, which is temporary and can occur for a variety of reasons. For example, if a man is enjoying a sexual experience after a long period of abstinence, he may ejaculate too quickly. These types of situations are to be placed in a separate category from the individual who has continuous problems with premature ejaculations. Although disquieting, these experiences are normal and occur with relative frequency for all males.

Retarded Ejaculation.   The third type of male sexual dysfunction is retarded ejaculation, and it is relatively uncommon. Although the male is able to reach orgasm through masturbation, he is unable to climax through any form of vaginal stimulation. Some researchers (e.g., Kaplan, 1979, and Newcomb & Bentler, 1988) take issue with the whole concept of retarded ejaculation. They argue that if a man is able to achieve orgasm through a form of stimulation other than vaginal, then the only dysfunction that exists is psychodynamic.

Much has been written about the remediation of male sexual dysfunction by Masters and Johnson (1970). Their literature on the effectiveness of the "squeeze technique" has been widely written about. Other methods for treating male sexual dysfunction have made a concerted effort to include the partner in the treatment plan; the most popular current form is the stop/slash technique. When the man is about to reach orgasm, his partner stops stimulation. As soon as the urge to ejaculate subsides, the man and his partner resume stimulation. This technique has gained wide approval from counselors because it focuses on the couple instead of treating the man as an instrument to be acted upon. McCarthy and Perkins (1988) also suggest that couples are more receptive to this intervention than to others because of the role of the woman as an active agent of change. This heightens the sense of unity within the couple and prevents the focus from being placed on the male as the identified "patient."

Another common and effective behavioral technique is to prohibit intercourse and substitute touching exercises. This technique allows the partners to learn to listen to their bodies and to get in touch with what feels pleasurable to each other (Dinkmeyer & Carlson, 1989). Since many men are apt to move toward intercourse shortly after gaining an erection, a series of nondemand exercises allows the man to experience a wider range of sensation and arousal patterns. Sensate focus also enjoys a high degree of use as a relaxation technique.

Female Sexual Dysfunction

Women experience three main sexual dysfunctions: painful intercourse (dyspareunia), orgasmic dysfunction, and vaginal spasms.

Dyspareunia.   Painful intercourse occurs during the arousal phase. The lack of vaginal lubrication or the presence of a vaginal infection are the predisposing factors of dyspareunia. Although painful intercourse can be experienced by men, it is much more common for women. The general antecedent for women is insufficient vaginal lubrication. Many times this dysfunction is further complicated by the inability of the woman to articulate specifically what she wants sexually. Such a communication problem can be explored through counseling. Psychoeducation, along with assertiveness training, can also be valuable for helping the woman learn to express her needs.

Orgasmic Dysfunction.   The term primary orgasmic dysfunction applies when a woman has never experienced orgasm, as opposed to secondary anorgasmia in which the woman previously was orgasmic but currently is experiencing difficulties. Women who masturbate to orgasm but are unable to achieve orgasm through a partner's stimulation fall into the second category. Another category of female orgasmic dysfunction is classified as random, which describes women who experience orgasm but only on an occasional basis.

For the purpose of remediation, anorgasmia and dyspareunia share some common elements. Practical suggestions are that the couple practice touching exercises and abstain from intercourse for a predetermined amount of time. This in and of itself may allow the woman to relax and lubricate sufficiently. Other techniques include additional stimulation of the genital area, and oral stimulation paired with manual stimulation can be an effective arousal technique (Kaplan, 1979). The point of this intervention is that the partners are to experiment and discover what works for them.

It is essential that counselors be aware of sexual stereotypes. The importance of the female orgasm is often considered unnecessary to female fulfillment (Masters & Johnson, 1970). The Masters and Johnson (1970) data indicate that what women really wanted from sex was closeness and love. What counselors see is that women want those things plus an orgasm (McCarthy & Perkins, 1988).

Vaginal Spasms.   Clinically known as vaginismus, vaginal spasms are the spastic contractions that prevent the insertion of the penis into the vagina. This dysfunction is quite rare, occurring in approximately ¼ of 1 percent of the population. But another associated problem, functional vaginismus, occurs with greater frequency. The difference is that "true" vaginismus actually prevents the intromission of the penis, whereas lesser versions of vaginismus create extreme discomfort but do allow penetration to occur.

Treatment for vaginismus is similar to the desensitization process used in phobias (Masters & Johnson, 1970). The woman is first led through guided imagery activities, whereby she learns to relax when envisioning intercourse. Then the counselor suggests a series of exercises to implement at home, either alone or with a spouse. The woman or her partner insert first one finger and then two fingers into her vagina, gradually increasing the dilation of the vaginal muscles. This exercise then proceeds to the insertion of a vibrator until the vaginal muscles are sufficiently relaxed to accommodate the man's penis.

An important consideration in the female sexual disfunction treatment process is the possible interplay of emotional factors. Earlier traumatic experiences, such as rape or incest, may have led to the symptom cluster known as vaginismus. Sprei and Courtois (1988) indicate that in the case of early trauma, intense counseling is indicated to dissipate the factors that precipitated the vaginismus. Behavioral interventions only alleviate the symptoms. Another possible contributory feature is the individual's faulty sexual beliefs and attitudes. The best course for remediation of misconceptions is psychoeducation, through which the counselor is able to help the client both identify and explore faulty beliefs.

TREATMENT ADHERENCE AND RELAPSE PREVENTION

Treatment adherence can be increased when counselors use brief therapy that employs the use of contracts. Masters and Johnson (1970) utilize a brief, intensive therapeutic model that includes a contract stipulating that the couple will be seen every day for 2 weeks, at which point the treatment ends. The contract enforces the notion that the couple and not the counselor is responsible for each other's continuing growth toward sexual health. Self-responsibility is an important and often underutilized component of therapy; it has been emphasized throughout this book and is at the heart of effective sexual therapy.

The essential components of relapse prevention and treatment adherence are part of the therapeutic process. Effective psychoeducation may be one of the best strategies to prevent relapse. Research often considers the most effective forms of psychoeducation that can be utilized (McCarthy & Perkins, 1988). Experience shows that it is helpful to use sexual intimacy activities, such as the following from the book *Taking Time for Love* (Dinkmeyer & Carlson, 1989):

Activity #1:	Be informed—In this exercise, couples read books and watch films together.
Activity #2:	Touch—Couples are taught how to use intimate focus, a technique very similar to sensate focus.
Activity #3:	Learn to pay attention to your sex life.
Activity #4:	Make time for sex.
Activity #5:	Continue to court each other.
Activity #6:	Fantasize.
Activity #7:	Learn how to say yes or no to sexual activity.
Activity #8:	Avoid falling into rigid or boring routines.
Activity #9:	Learn to give positive feedback.
Activity #10:	Feel fit and sexy.
Activity #11:	Take responsibility for your own sexual pleasure.

CONCLUDING NOTE

This chapter described brief strategies that apply a biopsychosocial understanding to the creation and maintenance of sexual health. The extent of clients' sexual problems is widespread and, unfortunately, counselors are often unprepared for (or uncomfortable) working in this area. Through the use of the P-LI-SS-IT model, with psychoeducational supplements, many concerns about sex and sexuality can be alleviated.

RESOURCES
Treatment Professionals

It is often difficult to locate a counselor, and/or it may seem to be an overwhelming task. In most states, anyone can hang out a shingle that says "therapist" and can advertise and begin counseling. It is important to be sure to contact a professional who has training in sexual counseling. It might be helpful to get in touch with the appropriate certifying organization for each of the various professions.

- Marriage and family therapists are clinically certified by the American Association of Marriage and Family Therapy (AAMFT—www.aamft.org), 112 South Alfred St., Alexandria, VA 22314; (703) 838–9808.
- Social workers are certified by the National Association of Social Workers (NASW—www.naswdc.org), 750 First St., NE, Suite 700, Washington, DC 20002.
- Psychologists are members of the American Psychological Association (APA), 750 First St., NE, Washington, DC 20002.
- Sex therapists are certified by the American Association of Sex Educators, Counselors, and Therapists (AASECT—www.aasect.org), P.O. Box 5488, Richmond, VA 23220-0488 as well as by the American Board of Sexology (ABS—www.sexologist.org), 2431 Aloma Ave., Suite 277, Winter Park, FL 32792.
- Psychiatrists are certified by the American Psychiatric Association, 1000 Wilson Blvd., Suite 1825, Arlington, VA 22209 (www.psych.org).
- Professional counselors are certified by the American Counseling Association (ACA—www.counseling.org), 5999 Stevenson Ave., Alexandria, VA 22304.

These organizations are good sources for referrals to counselors in your area. If you cannot locate a local chapter, write to the national headquarters and ask for the name of a qualified person.

One thing to consider when referring the client to a treatment facility is its location. Although Masters and Johnson are well regarded, they are not easily accessible to everyone. The easiest and most reliable way to refer a client is to consult the major medical center in your area. The chances are excellent that if they do not have a sexual treatment program, they will know how to link you up with one. The following is a partial list of the facilities that offer treatment within the continental United States.

- Johns Hopkins University, Sexual Disorders Clinic, Meyer Building, Room 101, 600 North Wolfe Street, Baltimore, MD 21205 (Fred S. Berlin, M.D., Director)—This clinic offers treatment for sexual dysfunctions as well as a comprehensive program for sex offenders. Johns Hopkins also participates in ongoing research on the effects of medications on sexual behavior.
- The Kinsey Institute for Research in Sex, Gender, and Reproduction, 313 Morrison Hall, Bloomington, IN 47405 (June Reinisch, M.D., Director)—The Kinsey Institute always has ongoing research about gender-based differences in attitudes to sexuality as well as beliefs and attitudes. Although the clinic currently does not offer direct treatment as one of its services, the Kinsey Institute is an excellent referral service for those based in the heartland of the United States.

- Masters and Johnson Institute, 24 South Kings Highway, St. Louis, MO 63108 (Virginia Johnson Masters, Director)—The clinic offers both direct service, which it is well noted for, and an excellent research facility. The direct-service component is an intensive 2-week program that employs behavioral techniques aimed at remediation of the dysfunction within the brief time-limited program.
- Sexual Dysfunction Program (www.lumc.edu/programs), Loyola University Health System, 2160 S. First Avenue, Maywood, IL 60153; (708)216–3752 (Domeena Renshaw, M.D., Director)—Married couples with sexual problems are provided 7 weeks of counseling by a multidisciplinary team of health-care professionals. Single clients are also counseled individually or in a 6-week, all-female or all-male small-group counseling setting. Loyola also provides training for counseling professionals.

Publications

- Barbach, L. (1990). *Falling in love again.* Los Angeles: Venus Group.—This is a multimedia program that helps couples who have sexual problems. The kit consists of a 1½-hour videotape, a pair of identical manuals—one for each partner—and two audiocassettes. The program is designed for couples who are having common problems.
- Barbach, L. (2000). *For yourself: The fulfillment of female sexuality.* New York: Anchor Press/Doubleday.—This book made a significant contribution by giving women permission to enjoy their sexuality. It remains an important contribution to women's understanding of their own sexuality.
- Comfort, A. (2003). *The joy of sex: Fully revised and completely updated for the twenty-first century.* New York: Pocket Books.—This book is designed to help couples alleviate the boredom in their sexual experiences. Replete with a smorgasbord of new positions for intercourse, it is much more than a "how-to" book—it celebrates the overall experience of our sexuality.
- Dinkmeyer, D., and Carlson, J. (1989). *Taking time for love: How to stay happily married.* Englewood Cliffs, NJ: Prentice-Hall.—This book is a solid resource guide for partners who wish to enrich their marriage. Written by two psychologists, it will show you how to enrich your relationship in just a few short minutes a day.
- Pearsall, P. (1989). *Super marital sex.* New York: Doubleday.—This book is also about much more than sex; it is a guide for the couple to attain satisfaction in the overall relationship.
- Ortiz, E. T. (1989). *Your complete guide to sexual health.* Englewood Cliffs, NJ: Prentice-Hall.—This book was designed for Planned Parenthood of San Diego and Riverside Counties and provides a complete guide to reproductive health. High school and college students will find it useful because the book provides practical information on sex and birth control.
- Yaffe, M., and Fenwick, E. (1988). *Sexual happiness: A practical approach.* New York: Henry Holt.—A thorough guidebook on how to achieve and maintain sexual happiness.

REFERENCES

Annon, J. S. (1973). The therapeutic use of masturbation in the treatment of sexual disorders. *Advances in Behavior Therapy* (Vol. 4, pp. 199–215). New York: Academic.

Annon, J. S. (1974). *The behavioral treatment of sexual problems, Vol. 1: Brief therapy.* Honolulu: Enabling Systems, Inc.

Arrendondo, P. (1996). MCT theory and latina(o)-American populations. In D. W. Sue, A. E. Ivey, & P. B. Pedersen (Eds.), *A theory of multicultural counseling and therapy* (pp. 217–235). Pacific Grove, CA: Brooks-Cole.

Barbach, L. (2000). *For yourself: The fulfillment of female sexuality.* New York: Anchor/Doubleday.

Barbach, L. (1982). *For each other: Sexual intimacy.* New York: Doubleday.

Barbach, L. (1990). *Falling in love again.* Los Angeles: Venus Group.

Brown, R. A., & Field, J. R. (Eds.). (1988). *Treatment of sexual problems in individual and couples therapy.* Baltimore: PMA Press.

Caplan, P. (1987). *The cultural construction of sexuality.* London: University of London.

Castillo, R. J. (1997). *Culture and mental illness.* Pacific Grove, CA: Brooks-Cole.

Charlton, R. S., & Yalom, I. D. (1997). *Treating sexual disorders.* San Francisco: Jossey-Bass.

Cooper, A. J. (1971). Treatments of male potency disorders: The present status. *Psychosomatics, 12,* 335–344.

Dinkmeyer, D., & Carlson, J. (1989). *Taking time for love: How to stay happily married.* Englewood Cliffs, NJ: Prentice-Hall.

Ferguson, J. M. (2001). The effects of antidepressants on sexual functioning in depressed patients: A review. *Journal of Clinical Psychiatry, 62*(3), 22–34.

Fisher, S. (1989). *Sexual images of the self: The psychology of erotic sensations and illusions.* Hillsdale, NJ: Erlbaum.

Friedman, J. M. (1984). Differences in sexual desire. In *Innovations in clinical practice: A sourcebook* (Vol. 3, pp. 464–467). Sarasota: Professional Resource Exchange.

Friedman, J. M., & Czekala, J. (1985). Advances in sex therapy techniques. In *Innovations in clinical practice: A sourcebook* (Vol. 4, pp. 187–200). Sarasota: Professional Resource Exchange.

Graziottin, A. (1998). The biological basis of female sexuality. *International Clinical Pharmacology, 13*(6), 515–522.

Humphrey, F. G. (1983). *Marital therapy.* Englewood Cliffs, NJ: Prentice-Hall.

Jacobson, N. S., & Margolin, G. (1979). *Marital therapy: Strategies based on social learning and behavior exchange principles.* New York: Brunner/Mazel.

Johnson, T. C. (1999). *Understanding your child's sexual behavior: What's natural and healthy.* Oakland, CA: New Harbinger.

Kalayjian, L., & Morrell, M. (2000). Female sexuality and neurological disease. *Journal of Sex Education and Therapy, 25*(1), 89–95.

Kaplan, H. S. (1975). *The illustrated manual of sex therapy* (2nd ed.). New York: Brunner/Mazel.

Kaplan, H. S. (1979). *Disorders of sexual desire and other new concepts and techniques in sex therapy.* New York: Simon & Schuster.

Kolodny, R. C., Masters, W. H., & Johnson, V. E. (1979). *Textbook of sexual medicine.* Boston: Little, Brown.

Krone, R. J., Siroky, M. B., & Goldstein, I. (Eds.). (1983). *Male sexual dysfunction.* Boston: Little, Brown.

Leiblum, S. R., & Rosen, R. C. (2000). *Principles and practices of sex therapy* (3rd ed.). New York: Guilford.

Love, P. (1999). *Hot monogamy: Essential steps to more passionate, intimate lovemaking.* New York: Plume.

Love, P. (2001). *The truth about love.* New York: Simon & Schuster.

Mair, R. (1984). *Human Sexuality in Perspective,* Chicago: Nelson Hall.

Maltz, W., & Boss, S. (1997). *In the garden of desire: The intimate world of women's sexual fantasies.* New York: Broadway Books.

Masand, P., & Gupta, S. (2002). Long-term side effects of newer-generation antidepressants: SSRIs, venlafaxine, nefazodone, bupropion, and mirtazapine. *Annals of Clinical Psychiatry, 14*(3), 175–182.

Masters, W. H., & Johnson, V. E. (1970). *Human sexual inadequacy.* Boston: Little, Brown.

McCarthy, B. W., & Perkins, S. (1988). Behavioral strategies and techniques in sex therapy. In R. Brown & J. Field (Eds.), *Treatment of sexual problems in individual and couples therapy.* Baltimore: PMA Press.

Mullen, B., Brar, J. S., Vagnucci, A. H., & Ganguli, R. (2001). Frequency of sexual dysfunction in patients with schizophrenia on haloperidal, clozapine, or risperidone. *Schizophenia Research, 48*(1), 155–156.

Munjack, D. J., & Oziel, L. J. (1980). *Sexual medicine and counseling in office practice: A complete treatment guide.* Boston: Little, Brown.

Munarriz, R., Talakoub, L., Flaherty, E., Gioia, M., Hoag, L., Noel, K., et al. (2002). Androgen replacement therapy with dehydroepiandrosterone for androgen insufficiency and female sexual dysfunction: Androgen and questionnaire results. *Journal of Sex and Marital Therapy, 28*(1), 165–173.

Newcomb, M., & Bender, P. (1988). Behavioral and psychological assessment of sexual dysfunction: An overview. In R. Brown & J. Field (Eds.), *Treatment of sexual problems in individual and couples therapy.* Baltimore: PMA Press.

Paniagua, F. A. (2001). Culture-bound syndromes. In I. Cuellar & F. A. Paniagua (Eds.), *Handbook of multicultural mental health* (pp. 142–170). San Diego: Academic.

Pearsall, P. (1987). *Super marital sex.* New York: Doubleday.

Pesce, V., Seidman, S. N. & Roose, S. P. (2002). Depression, antidepressants and sexual functioning in men. *Sexual and Relationship Therapy, 17*(3), 281–287.

Pion, R. J. (1975). Diagnosis and treatment of inadequate sexual response. In J. Sciarra (Ed.), *Gynecology and obstetrics,* Vol. 2. New York: Harper & Row.

Pion, R. J., & Annon, J. S. (1975). The office management of sexual problems: Brief therapy approaches. *Journal of Reproductive Medicine, 15*(4), 127–144.

Pion, R. J., Annon, J. S., & Carlson, J. (1982). Brief sexual counseling. *Counseling and Human Development, 14*(8), 1–8.

Pion, R. J., & Hopkins, J. (1978). *The last sex manual.* New York: Wyden Press.

Renshaw, D. (1996). *Seven weeks to better sex.* New York: Dell.

Reynolds, B. S. (1977). Psychological treatment models and outcome results for erectile dysfunction: A critical review. *Psychological Bulletin, 84,* 1218–1238.

Sadler, A. G., & Syrop, G. H. (1987). The stress of infertility: Recommendations for assessment and intervention. *Family Stress Journal, 1*(1), 1–17.

Schnarch, D. (1998) *Passionate marriage: Love, sex and intimacy in emotionally committed relationships.* New York: Henry Holt.

Schover, L. R. (1982). Enhancing sexual intimacy. In *Innovations in clinical practice: A sourcebook* (Vol. 1, pp. 53–66). Sarasota: Professional Resource Exchange.

Shulman, B. H. (1967). The uses and abuses of sex. *Journal of Religious Health, 6,* 317–325.

Sprei, J., & Courtois, C. (1988). The treatment of women's sexual dysfunction arising from sexual assault. In R. Brown & J. Field (Eds.), *Treatment of sexual problems in individual and couples therapy.* Baltimore: PMA Press.

Stuart, R. B. (1980). *Helping couples change: A social learning approach to marital therapy.* New York: Guilford.

Targum, S. D. (2000). SSRIs and sexual dysfunction. *Drug Benefit Trends, 12*(9), 3–12.

Thompson, E. H., & Pleck, J. H. (1995). Masculine ideology: A review of research instrumentation on men and masculinities. In R. F. Levant & W. S. Pollack (Eds.), *A new psychology of men* (pp. 129–163). New York: Basic Books.

Travis, J. W., & Ryan, R. S. (1988). *Wellness workbook* (2nd ed.). Berkeley, CA: Ten Speed Press.

Turkington, C., & Alper, M. M. (2001). *The encyclopedia of fertility and infertility.* New York: Facts on File.

Wirshing, D., Pierre, J. M., Marder, S. M., Saunders, C. S., & Wirshing, W. C. (2002) Sexual side effects of novel antipsychotic medications. *Schizophrenia Research, 56*(1–2), 25–30.

Yaffe, M., & Fenwick, E. (1988). *Sexual happiness: A practical approach.* New York: Henry Holt.

Zilbergeld, B. (1978). *Male sexuality.* Boston: Little, Brown.

Zilbergeld, B., & Ellison, C. R. (1980). Desire discrepancies and arousal problems in sex therapy. In S. R. Leiblum & L. A. Pervin (Eds.), *Principles and practice of sex therapy.* New York: Guilford.

CHAPTER TEN

CHRONIC PAIN

*Pain is perfect misery, the worst of evils,
and excessive, overturns all patience.*

—Milton

Pain is the sensory and emotional experience of discomfort associated with actual or threatened tissue damage or irritation (Sanders, 1985). Nearly everyone reports the experience of pain sometime during the course of life. Pain is the most pervasive symptom in medical practice, the most frequently stated "cause" of disability, and the single most compelling force underlying a person's decision to seek medical care. Since the first edition of this book, there have been significant scientific breakthroughs in understanding the neural pathways involved in the complex experience of pain and the contributions of psychosocial factors to the pain experience. Not surprisingly, such findings have led to further advances in the development of pharmacological, surgical, and psychological treatment modalities. In recognition and support of the clinical and research breakthroughs, the U.S. Congress has designated the first decade of the twenty-first century as "The Decade of Pain Control and Research."

The purpose of this chapter is to survey the various factors and methods for assessing and treating clients with chronic pain. As with other health counseling issues, the approach here emphasizes a biopsychosocial perspective. There are reviews of the various theories of pain; the individual and group intervention strategies for managing pain; and the issues of relapse, adherence, and prevention. Since the two most common chronic pain syndromes are headaches and back pain, the discussion concentrates on these two complaints.

Before proceeding further, an important distinction must be made—pain is usually characterized as either acute or chronic. Whether it is mild or severe, and whether the cause is known or unknown, the duration of acute pain usually is only a few days. Sufferers expect relief through some kind of medical intervention, and the health-care provider expects pain to decrease as the affected area heals. Whether it is sunburn, toothache, or postsurgical pain, acute pain can be either recurrent or progressive. With intermittent pain, such as in arthritis, there are pain-free intervals. With progressive acute pain, such as in cancer, the pain is ongoing and increases in intensity.

Pain is a complex perceptual experience influenced by a wide range of psychosocial factors—including emotions; social and environmental context; sociocultural background; the meaning of pain to the person; and one's beliefs, attitudes, and expectations—as well as biological factors. When it is present, chronic pain influences all aspects of an individual's functioning: emotional, interpersonal, physical, and occupational. Thus, successfully treating chronic pain requires attention not only to the organic basis of the symptoms but also to the range of factors that modulate pain transmission and moderate the pain experience and related disability (Turk, & Feldman, 2000).

Chronic pain and the chronic pain syndrome are characterized by disability and suffering of more than 6 months in duration that are disproportionate to detectable, undetectable, or remedial disease. Chronic pain syndrome is benign but correctable, and so it excludes the pain of cancer. It can be initiated by acute trauma or disease, such as back injury or heart attack, or it can develop in association with an intermittent disease such as angina or rheumatoid arthritis (Sternbach, 1968). The most common forms of chronic pain syndrome are low back pain and headache (Gatchel & Turk, 1999).

Chronic back pain originates with injury to soft tissue or to bony structures, and the frequency of occurrence of back pain is high. Svensson and Anderson (1982) estimate that 50 to 80 percent of the population will have back complaints at some time. Most problems that lead to back pain resolve themselves within a matter of days or a few weeks: however, many do not. Hullard (1954) found that approximately 20 percent of the population is incapacitated because of back pain for periods ranging from 3 weeks to 6 months, and 4 percent is incapacitated for more than 6 months. Johnson (1978) reports similar findings from a worker's compensation sample, suggesting that chronic back pain affects about 4 percent of the working population.

Headache is even more common than back pain. It has been estimated that as many as 80 million Americans—one third of the population—experience headaches. Americans lose in excess of 700 million workdays a year at a cost of $65 billion for health care. In addition, Americans spend more than $2 billion a year on over-the-counter headache remedies. For many, headaches are minor occurrences that can be relieved with aspirin, acetaminophen, or ibuprofen. However, not all headaches are alike, and some may be so frequent and severe that the sufferer is unable to function in daily activities. Approximately 20 percent of Americans experience severe headaches and approximately 10 percent of visits to family physicians are precipitated by headache complaints (Diamond et al., 1999).

BIOPSYCHOSOCIAL ASPECTS OF PAIN

Unlike the biomedical perspective, which focuses on pathophysiological explanations for chronic pain, or the psychogenic perspective, which assumes that pain is a physical manifestation of psychological difficulties, the biopsychosocial perspective provides an integrative model; it incorporates physiological processes, as well as psychological and social-contextual variables, that may cause and perpetuate chronic pain. Whereas the biomedical model emphasizes disease processes, the biopsychosocial model views illness as a dynamic and reciprocal interaction between biological, psychological, and sociocultural variables that shape the person's response to pain (Turk & Flor, 1999). Thus, the biological substrate of a disease affects psychological factors such as mood, and the social context within which the individual functions, particularly in interpersonal relationships.

The biopsychosocial perspective is essential to understanding the relationship among the physiological, psychological, and social factors. A number of researchers have described models that attempt to integrate physiological, psychophysiological, psycholosocial, and behavioral variables to explain symptoms, perception of pain, disability, and response to treatment (Price, 1999; Turk & Flor, 1999). Technological advances in the recent decades in medicine, such as functional magnetic resonance imaging (MRI) and positron emission tomography (PET), permit researchers to examine brain activity noninvasively (Rainville, Duncan, Price, Carrier, & Bushnell, 1997). Research utilizing such technology is necessary to increase knowledge of the effects of psychological factors on brain structures. Greater understanding of the reciprocal interactions among neurological, hormonal, endocrine, and psychosocial factors hopefully will increase health-care professionals' capacity to treat pain more effectively.

What is the biopsychosocial view of the experience of pain? Briefly, this model assumes some form of physical changes—or even pathology—in the muscles, joints, or nerves that travel to the brain. Pain perception involves the interpretation of the painful stimuli, while appraisal involves the meaning attributed to the pain. These appraisals are influenced by one's beliefs and schemas. On the basis of beliefs and the appraisal process, the individual can choose to ignore the pain and continue previous activity or can choose to stop or diminish the activity and assume the "sick" role. Subsequently, the interpersonal role is shaped by how significant others respond (Turk & Okifuji, 2002).

Biological Factors

Various primary anatomical and biochemical processes as well as a number of secondary factors can contribute to the experience of pain (Wall & Melzack, 1999). High fatigue and subsequent low stamina enhance sensitivity to or decrease tolerance of pain, which in turn initiate a vicious cycle of decreased activity and increased perception of pain. Similarly, the physiological effects of alcohol or other substances can further complicate the experience of pain and can seriously hamper rehabilitative efforts. Finally, there is considerable variability among individuals in the threshold of pain, which cannot be accounted for entirely by social and psychological variables.

Psychological Factors

In addition to biological factors, a number of psychological factors influence the experience of pain. These include self-efficacy, beliefs and attributions about pain, alexithymia, and psychological predictors of long-term disability.

Self-Efficacy.   Self-efficacy has become a central construct of pain management in the past several decades. *Self-efficacy* is defined as a personal conviction and expectation that one can successfully perform certain behaviors in a given situation (Bandura, 1977). Bandura proposed that given sufficient motivation to engage in a behavior, individuals' self-efficacy beliefs determine whether that behavior will be initiated, how much effort will be expended, and how long effort will be sustained. Accordingly, individuals with low or negative self-efficacy expectations will cope less effectively than those with positive efficacy expectations.

Not surprisingly, the role of self-efficacy in the perception of and adjustment to pain and possible subsequent disability is of great interest to both researchers and clinicians. Individuals who believe that they can alleviate suffering will likely mobilize whatever coping skills they have learned and will persevere in their efforts. Those who doubt their controlling efficacy are likely to give up readily in the absence of rapid results. A sense of coping efficacy also reduces distressing anticipations that create aversive physiological arousal and bodily tension, which further exacerbate pain sensation and discomfort. Bandura (1977) suggested further that those techniques that enhance mastery experiences the most will be the most powerful tools for bringing about behavior change.

Numerous studies have confirmed that self-efficacy, coping style, and cognitive distortions affect an individual's reports of pain intensity, activity, and response to treatment (Jensen, Turner, & Romano, 1994). Higher levels of self-efficacy have been linked with greater pain control, more adaptive psychological functioning, improved treatment outcome, and reduced disability (Turk, 1996). Maladaptive cognitive strategies, such as catastrophizing, have been linked with increased pain and generalized distress (Silverman, 2001; Turk & Feldman, 2000). Other studies have noted that the higher rate of affective distress common to chronic pain populations can lead to more negative cognitive appraisals of the impact of pain, and influence one's ability to control pain and response to treatment (Gatchel & Turk, 1999). As a whole, however, depression appears to be highest among chronic pain patients (Banks & Kerns, 1996).

Beliefs and Attributions about Pain.   There is growing evidence about the clinical value of understanding an individual's beliefs regarding chronic pain. Beliefs about the meaning of symptoms, the individual's ability to control pain, the impact of pain on his or her life, and worry about the future have been shown to play a central role in chronic pain. Such beliefs have been found to be associated with psychological functioning, physical functioning, coping efforts, and response to treatment (Turk & Okifuji, 2002).

Research on attribution about pain also has clinical relevance. For example, the belief that activity might aggravate the initial injury often results in fear of engaging in rehabilitative efforts, and leads to preoccupation with bodily symptoms and to physical deconditioning, which in turn can exacerbate pain and maintain disability. Individuals who attribute their symptoms to an injury are more likely to view any physical sensation as harmful which increases anxiety levels. Consequently, these changes can lower pain thresholds and tolerance, which further increase activity avoidance and functional limitations and foster physical deconditioning (Turk & Okifuji, 1996).

Studies of individuals diagnosed with fibromyalgia syndrome have demonstrated that traumatic onset is associated with greater perceived severity of symptoms even when there is no difference in physical pathology between those who attribute symptom onset to a traumatic event and those who perceive their symptoms as having an insidious onset. Moreover, individuals whose painful symptoms follow an accident are more likely to be refractory to treatment than those with nontraumatic onset. It is also noteworthy that people's beliefs about the cause of pain onset can influence clinicians' diagnosis and treatment. For example, individuals who describe their pain as a consequence of trauma are more likely to be prescribed physical and pharmacological treatments for symptomatic relief. Thus, health-care providers treat individuals who report traumatic onset of their symptoms differently, even though signs and symptoms do not necessarily reflect differences in the extent of detectable physical pathology.

Alexithymia.   In addition, chronic pain sufferers have been shown to be predisposed to *alexithymia*—they have relatively restricted emotional vocabularies and a tendency to communicate their distress in somatic terms. For example, alexithymic individuals may say "I've got a terrible headache" instead of more accurately indicating that "I'm really afraid and worried." Such indirect and displaced expressions further exacerbate their experience of pain (Blackwell, 1989).

Predictors of Long-Term Disability.   Certain psychological factors have been reported to be predictive of long-term disability (Johansson & Lindberg, 2000). Such predictors include recovery versus continued disability, maladaptive attitudes and beliefs, lack of social support, heightened emotional reactivity, job dissatisfaction, substance abuse, and compensation status. The prevalence of pain behaviors and psychiatric diagnoses seem to be the best predictors of the transition from acute injury to chronic disability. Interestingly, physical factors, such as severity of injury and physical demands of the job, are less predictive of chronicity and disability (Turk & Okifuji, 2002).

Social Factors

Various social factors influence the experience of pain. These include ethnic differences, gender differences, family relationships, and sick-role and illness behavior.

Ethnic Differences.   Not all social or cultural groups respond to pain in the same manner. How clients perceive pain, both within themselves or in others, and how they communicate their pain to health practitioners is often dependant on cultural factors such as race, ethnicity, age, gender, sexual orientation, disability, and social class (Chaplin, 1997; Turk, 1996; Webb, 1983). For example, Jewish clients may show pain more openly than Asian clients. This may be due to the fact that Asians "in general are taught self-restraint and may be more reluctant to express pain" (Castillo, 1997, p. 196). It is possible to exhibit pain behavior in the absence of a painful stimulus and vice versa; that is, because pain is essentially a personal experience, outsiders depend on verbal and nonverbal cues to determine if another is in pain. Whether pain is revealed depends on cultural conditioning and has to do with issues of pride (De La Cancela, Jenkins, & Chin, 1998).

The communication of pain is often dependant on whether a client is from a culture where restraint, stoicism, and fortitude are valued, hence reserve is exhibited in the face of suffering; whether help-seeking or self-caretaking is valued; whether pain is viewed as normal or abnormal; or whether pain is viewed as a type of divine punishment that must be experienced (Helmen, 1985). For example, traditional Western gender roles for men suggest that men do not ask for help, show tears, and that they endure pain (Brannon, 1976;

O'Neil, 1981; Pleck, 1995). The availability of healers can also determine whether pain behavior will be displayed, as clients may gauge their responses based on the setting and the personnel present (De La Cancela et al., 1998).

Gender Differences. Researchers have investigated sex variations in the prevalence rates of various chronic pain conditions. Women are more likely than men to experience a variety of recurrent pains; many have moderate or severe pains from menstruation, pregnancy and childbirth. In most studies, females report more severe levels of pain, more frequent pain, and pain of longer duration than do males. Women may be at greater risk for a pain-related disability than men but women also more aggressively seek relief from pain through health-related services. Women may be more vulnerable than men to health-care providers' unwarranted psychogenic attributions for pain (Unruh, 1996). Whereas females show a higher prevalence of headaches, it has been suggested that males report more episodic and chronic cluster headaches. Additionally, men are vulnerable to pain associated with their anatomy—for example, testicular pain following infection or trauma (Unruh, 1996).

Along psychosocial dimensions, women with chronic pain report higher levels or affective distress (e.g., depression, generalized anxiety) than men. Similar rates of disability from chronic pain have been found among men and women. Unruh (1996) suggests that men may possess a limited range of skills for coping with chronic pain. These coping skills include direct action, problem-focused coping, talking problems down, denial, positive thinking, and resorting to substance abuse to reduce tension. On the other hand, women tend to possess greater coping flexibility and rely on active cognitive-behavioral coping, emotion-focused coping, relaxation, and social support.

Family Relationships. A large body of research that documents the role of family relationships and chronic pain has accumulated over the past 20 years. Spouses have been shown to serve powerful roles as the primary source of social reinforcement (Kerns & Payne, 1996). Positive attention from a spouse or significant other that is contingent on overt expressions of pain is associated with higher levels of pain intensity and pain behaviors as well as higher levels of disability and negative responses to treatment. Spousal reinforcement of pain behaviors has been linked to increased severity of depressive symptoms and other affective distress (Turk, Kerns, & Rosenberg, 1992).

Sick-Role and Illness Behavior. There are a number of other social factors, including the concept of the "sick-role" and the influences of spouse, family, friends, and culture, that can shape both the experience of chronic pain and its treatment. Shared beliefs and reward systems can play a crucial role in the client's own attributions and behaviors. An overly solicitous spouse/partner can systematically encourage the client to adopt a sick-role, seek further medical treatment, or pursue litigation. In all cases, illness rather than wellness behavior is being reinforced.

Health-care professionals can also contribute to illness behavior by ordering excessive diagnostic evaluations and treatment regimens that reinforce the client's perception that he or she has a serious, undiscovered disease that must be identified and treated. Finally, society reinforces chronic pain behavior through financial compensation for injury or disability. Litigation frequently places the individual in the position of needing to remain in the sick-role in order to qualify for compensation (Blackwell, Galbraith, & Dahl, 1984).

ASSESSMENT

The emphasis of any procedure counselors use will depend on the purpose of the assessment. Broadly speaking, the three main aims in an assessment of chronic pain are: (1) to determine the client's suitability for treatment, (2) to determine the client's strengths and deficits so that the program can be tailored to his or her needs, and (3) to evaluate change over the course of treatment. Unfortunately, very little is known about which clients are likely to respond quickly to specific psychological, biological, or social interventions. Thus, at this stage in the development of health counseling, it is not possible to list a number of guidelines on client suitability. However, this section offers the counselor a number of considerations about the overall client assessment process.

Assessing cultural variations in chronic pain may be difficult and limiting because of the individual differences in the expression of pain across cultures (Paniagua, 2001). Another reason for this limitation is that it is extremely difficult to assess the severity of pain with objectivity (Castillo, 1997), which might prevent counselors from distinguishing pain from culturally related pain symptoms.

A comprehensive, biopsychosocial assessment involves data from four different sources: (1) the health conselor's observation and interview data; (2) the client's self-report on various inventories, grading forms, and questionnaires; (3) the information provided by a spouse or other significant person; and (4) the associated physiological theories. Each of these four sources is elaborated on in the following sections.

Health Counselor's Perspective

The clinician's impression of the client's pain will come primarily from the interview and from direct behavioral observation. Ideally, the clinical interview should involve the client as well as significant others (e.g., spouse, family members, or friends) with whom he or she spends a lot of time. If treatment is to be successful, both counselor and client must arrive at a "meeting of the minds" regarding the meaning or model of pain for the client. The initial interview should therefore involve considerable information-giving and education about pain mechanisms.

Clients with a long history of pain are likely to have been given different and sometimes conflicting explanations of their problem by other health professionals. It is important, then, to discuss these and any worries that they may have about their condition. Clients will also have their own theories about the physical and psychological bases of their pain, which they may never have shared with others for fear of being labeled "crazy." A health counselor's failure to explore these issues at the beginning of the interview may render any detailed inquiries about pain factors or personal history of limited value. Once a shared model of pain has been established, it is much easier to take clients' case history.

To treat chronic pain effectively, a health counselor needs to have a detailed description of the client's pain symptoms and history. (For reference, various kinds of headache pain are described in Table 10.1.) The client is queried about the presentation of pain as well

TABLE 10.1 Common Types of Headaches

TYPE	SYMPTOMS	PRECIPITATING FACTORS
Tension headaches	"Hatband" distribution, associated with tightness of scalp or neck; nonthrobbing pain, dull, frequently bilateral. Degree of severity remains constant.	Hidden depression; emotional stress.
Common migraines	Lightheadedness, blurred vision; ringing in ears; severe, one-sided, throbbing pain, often accompanied by nausea, vomiting, dizziness, tremor, sensitivity to sound and light, cold hands, hot and cold flashes.	Excessive hunger, change in weather or altitude, excessive smoking, use of oral contraceptives, flashing or bright lights, foods containing tyramine or other vasoactive substances.
Classic migraines	Same as common migraine, except for warning symptoms, which may include the smelling of strange odors, visual disturbances, hallucinations, and numbness in arms or legs. Preliminary reaction subsides within half an hour and is followed by severe pain.	Same as for common migraine.
TMJ headaches	TMJ (tempromandibular joint) dysfunction can occasionally produce a muscle contraction type of pain, sometimes accompanied by a "clicking" sound on opening the jaw. Infrequent cause of headache.	Stress, jaw clenching, and malocclusion (poor bite).
Cluster headaches	Tearing of eyes, excruciating pain around or behind one eye, flushing of face, nasal congestion. Attacks occur every day for weeks or months, then disappear for up to a year. Pain frequently develops during sleep and may last for several hours. Ninety percent of cluster victims are male.	Excessive smoking, ingestion of alcoholic beverages.
Caffeine headaches	Actually caffeine withdrawal headaches; throbbing headaches caused by rebound dilation of the blood vessels several hours after consumption of large quantities of caffeine.	Caffeine.
Hypertension headaches	"Hatband" or generalized type pain. Pain is most severe in the morning, then diminishes as the day goes on.	Severe hypertension (more than 200 systolic and 110 diastolic).

as what he or she takes or does to relieve it (Blackwell et al., 1984). It is suggested that the following 10 areas be targeted during the assessment interview.

1. The history of the pain problem, including when it started, how it has progressed, and when help was first sought for it.
2. The client's explanatory model or beliefs about the cause of the pain.
3. The pain syndrome and the pain's impact on the client's current lifestyle, interpersonal relationships, hobbies, and work.
4. The client's previous history, which should include how the client approached and coped with stressors before the onset of the chronic pain. It also needs to include family structure, social supports, recreational and exercise patterns, diet, and vocational patterns.
5. The client's current recreational interests, exercise patterns, diet, family structure, social supports, and vocational activities.
6. The social context of pain episodes—what happens in the family before an attack, and what the response of family members is when pain occurs. It is also important to inquire as to whether the client knows anyone else who has a chronic pain syndrome. Finally, be sure to inquire about the client's early childhood models of illness behavior.
7. The factors that seem to trigger attacks or make them worse.
8. How the client typically tries to cope with the pain, and what he or she fears most about the problem.
9. The use of prescription medications for pain; the use of nonprescription medications (e.g., medications that have been prescribed to a family member or a friend); the use of over-the-counter medications; and the use of alcohol, caffeine, nicotine, and other addicting substances.
10. The client's expectations about treatment—what the client thinks will help the pain, what results the client hopes to receive from treatment, and what expectations the client has of the counselor as the professional and of himself or herself as the client. In other words, what is the client's receptivity and capacity for treatment?

Professionals who work with chronic pain sufferers have found that it is useful to conduct a separate interview with the client's spouse or partner to clarify any issues and to determine how the client's pain affects him or her and how the spouse responds to the sufferer. Then, a joint spouse–client assessment interview needs to be held to observe and assess marital and interpersonal dynamics (Turk, Meichenbaum, & Genest, 1983).

Since individuals tend to exhibit pain behaviors when they are in discomfort, it is possible to assess their pain by observing and assessing their behavior. An individual with intense pain behaves different from someone with moderate pain, just as an individual with headache pain tends to behave different from a person with low back pain. The observant counselor will see the range of the client's affect and behavior, noting the appropriateness of both with regard to the content of the interview. The counselor also should ask the client to walk, pick up an object on the floor, remove his or her shoes while sitting, or perform several exercises such as trunk rotations, toe-touches, and sit-ups. During the exercises, the health counselor needs to rate pain indices such as wincing and grimacing, sighing, or rubbing the painful areas. This behavioral assessment could also be compared with the client's self-ratings of these movements (Karoly & Jensen, 1987).

Client Self-Reports

One of the more obvious ways of measuring people's pain is to ask them to describe their discomfort, either in their own words or by filling out a form, rating scale, or questionnaire. Pain-intensity rating forms are useful for revealing the course of pain over time, the fluctuations in pain intensity, and the times when medications are needed and used. It is common in pain clinics to have all clients complete a pain diary, which is designed to provide information concerning the times, places, and presence of others during pain episodes; and information about thoughts and feelings before, during, and after severe pain episodes. In addition, the pain-allaying techniques—the things clients do to cope with pain—are also noted in the diary.

A number of formal rating scales have been used to assess a client with chronic pain. The Profile of Mood States (POMS) has a range of scales to assess different emotional states—such positive mood states as vigor as well as such negative mood states as depression. The *Beck Depression Inventory* is useful for eliciting some of the cognitive components of depression and pain. The MMPI-2 (the second version of the Minnesota Multiphasic Personality Inventory) is a widely used formal instrument in clinical practice with pain clients. The *Pain Stages of Change Questionnaire* (PSOCQ) can be used to assess readiness for change, particularly regarding willingness to adopt a self-management approach to treatment (Kerns et al., 1997; Jensen et al., 2000). Perhaps the most commonly used self-report device is the *Multidimensional Pain Inventory* (MPI), which classifies pain sufferers into three subgroups. Research on this inventory suggests that it can predict treatment outcomes (Jamison et al., 1994).

Chronic pain clients frequently display a characteristic MMPI-2 profile with elevated scores on scales 1, 2, and 3, which measure hypochondriasis, depression, and hysteria. (This triad is often referred to as the psychosomatic V.) It is important to note that the validity of these three scales is reduced when organic disease is present. Scale 1 suggests a deep-seated conviction that something is wrong in the body, and scale 3 reflects the tendency to somatize. An increased awareness of symptoms may also be related to previous experience of disease or similar symptoms in a relative or a loved one. Pain and depression, as measured by scale 2, frequently coexist, and they appear to amplify each other. Among chronic pain clients, depression may either occur simultaneously with the pain symptoms or follow the onset of pain by several weeks or months. Health counselors have also noted that some chronic pain patients have elevated scores on scales 8 (schizophrenia) or 9 (mania) on the MMPI. This elevation usually suggests that the experience of pain is being influenced by cognitive distortions or defects in information processing rather than indicating true schizophrenia or a bipolar disorder. Elevations on scales 8 and 9 are more likely to occur when the client's symptoms are vague or ambiguous (Blackwell et al., 1984).

One of the most direct and simple ways to assess pain is to have clients rate some of their discomfort on a self-rating scale (Karoly & Jensen, 1987). Two types of self-rating scales to measure pain intensity are commonly used. The visual analog scale is a 10-centimeter line with endpoints of "no pain" and "worst pain ever"; the client marks a point on the line that describes the pain's intensity at a given moment. The category rating scale also uses a line, but it is divided into sections with designations such as "no pain," "mild," "discomforting," "distressing," "horrible," and "excruciating." The client checks the sections that correspond to the pain experience. Because these self-rating scales are relatively quick and easy to use, clients are asked to rate their pain frequently, usually on an hourly basis. Repeated ratings reveal how the pain changes over time and what patterns occur in the timing of severe pain. For example, pain may be more severe in the evening on certain days and not on others, or when certain other people are around.

Unlike the *POMS* or the *Beck Depression Inventory,* which assess general mood states, the *McGill Pain Questionnaire* (MPQ) primarily assesses the affective (emotional) component of the pain experience itself. The MPQ consists of 78 pain adjectives separated into a total of 20 subclasses. The test instructs the individual to select the best word to describe his or her pain from each subclass. Each word in each class has an assigned value based on the degree of pain it reflects. Melzack (1975) developed the instrument based on his belief that pain involves three broad categories: affective (emotional/motivational), sensory, and evaluative. Subsequently, of the 20 subgroups, some describe sensory experiences of pain (e.g., prickling, hot, scalding), others describe its affective qualities (e.g., sickening, fearful, punishing, cruel), and others still describe the evaluative aspects of pain (e.g., annoying, miserable, troublesome). The MPQ yields both a pain-rating index and a present pain-intensity score. The MPQ has a number of strengths and weaknesses as an instrument for assessing chronic pain; it does differentiate among categories of pain, such as headache, arthritis, cancer, and phantom-limb pain. However, the MPQ requires that the client have an extensive English vocabulary. For instance, the questionaire includes words such as "taut" and "lancinating," and it requires the client to make a fine distinction between words such as "throbbing," "beating," and "pounding." Thus, the MPQ may not be particularly useful across all cultural and subcultural groups, and it cannot be used with individuals under the age of 12.

Spouse/Partner Information

Assessment of a client's everyday activities, especially those within the home, can provide significant information to the health counselor. It is useful to know how much time is spent in bed, how often the client complains of discomfort, how much help he or she seeks, and how often the person walks with a limp. Family members or significant people in the client's life may be the best individuals to provide information on everyday pain behaviors.

As in other treatment programs, it is useful for the client's spouse or partner to fill out a diary for a 2-week period. This pain diary is designed to record episodes when another person is aware that the client's pain is very severe. A record should be made of the date and time, as well as where the episode occurred, and also a description of observed behaviors that suggest that the client was in pain. The other person should indicate what he or she thought and felt while observing the client and what response was made to help. Effectiveness of actions is rated on a scale ranging from "did not help at all" to "seemed to stop the pain completely." This diary provides additional data that, when compared to the client's diary, can be of help when dealing with interpersonal issues that can influence the pain experience.

Physiological Measures

A biological approach for assessing pain involves taking measurements of physiological activity. The most common physiological measure for assessing pain is the electromyograph (EMG). The EMG records the electrical activity in muscles, which reflects their tension. Because muscle tension has been associated with various pain states such as headache and low back pain, health counselors assumed that EMG recordings could provide objective evidence for the presence or absence of pain. In fact, headache sufferers do show different EMG patterns when they have headaches than when they do not (Blanchard & Andrasik, 1985). Biofeedback technology is, in large part, based on EMG recordings; unfortunately, more research is needed to verify that such recordings provide a useful measure of pain.

Another physiological measure is the electroencephalograph (EEG). When a client's sensory system detects a stimulus, such as a clicking sound, the signal to the brain produces a change in EEG voltage. Electrical changes produce evoked potentials that show up on the EEG recording as sharp peaks in the graph. Research has demonstrated that pain stimuli produce evoked potentials that vary in size with the intensity of the stimuli, decrease when patients take analgesics, and correlate with the individual's subjective report of pain (Chapman et al., 1985). It should be noted that, even though psychophysiological measures provide objective assessments, these measures may be affected by other factors (e.g., attention, stress, and diet). Accordingly, psychophysiological measures are best used as adjuncts to direct observation, self-report, and other standard assessment approaches.

TREATMENT PLANNING AND
SELECTION AND INTERVENTIONS

While psychological treatments are important in managing chronic pain, not all clients benefit equally. Because individuals with chronic pain syndromes are a very heterogeneous group even though they may have the identical medical diagnosis, it is not uncommon to assume that they should respond similarly to interventions. Although individuals in treatment for chronic pain become active participants in their treatment, such efforts may not necessarily eliminate pain. Pain-management programs foster self-management and self-efficacy with physical approaches such as exercises and pacing, as well as psychological approaches. Even though such programs require clients to make a number of lifestyle changes, these individuals often experience significant relapse following initially successful outcomes. Accordingly, it is useful to identify those prone to treatment rejection, dropout, and relapse, as well as to prepare individuals for treatment and to tailor it so as to promote positive outcomes.

Readiness for Change

Individuals' beliefs and expectations about how their pain should be treated as well as their readiness to accept and adopt a self-efficacy approach to manage their pain can have an important influence on treatment outcome (Kerns et al., 1997). According to the readiness-for-change model, individuals who firmly believe that their pain is "medical" and requires physical treatment are not likely to accept a self-management approach. In contrast, those who acknowledge that medical interventions are limited, tend to be more willing to accept self-management of their treatment. Kerns and colleagues (1997) developed the *Pain Stages of Change Questionnaire* (PSOCQ) to assess individuals' readiness to adopt a self-management approach to chronic pain and have demonstrated that the concept of readiness for treatment can identify individuals at risk of prematurely terminating their treatment (Kerns & Rosenberg, 1999). Their findings suggest that increased commitment to a self-management approach may serve as a predictor of successful treatment.

Tailoring Treatment

One of the most frequently used pain inventories, the *Multidimensional Pain Inventory* (MPI) classifies pain sufferers into three subgroups: (1) "dysfunctional" characterized by severe pain, compromised life activities and enjoyment, reduced sense of control, and high level of emotional distress; (2) "interpersonally distressed" characterized by relatively high degrees of pain and affective distress, and experiences of low levels of perceived support from significant others; and (3) "adaptive copers" characterized by low levels of pain, functional limitations, and emotional distress—they cope relatively well despite their long-standing pain (Jamison et al., 1994). Several studies using the MPI support the need for tailoring treatment to individual characteristics (Turk & Okifuji, 2002).

Indications for Inpatient Treatment.   The question of whether pain sufferers would be better served by a course of inpatient treatment must be considered. Indications for inpatient treatment include serious substance dependency, severe physical disability, multiple somatic complaints that require medical evaluation, and overwhelming environmental influences such as an overly solicitous spouse/partner. By contrast, clients with localized pain, less severe limitations, and cooperative relatives can usually be managed as outpatients (Blackwell, 1989).

Because chronic pain is a multiply determined condition, it is not unreasonable to conclude that a multimodal intervention will be needed for successful treatment. Much of the success reported in the pain-management literature is attributed to the fact that several treatments are used in combination or in sequence. These treatments include a wide range of biological, psychological, and social interventions.

Biological Interventions

Depending on the severity of the chronic pain sufferer's symptoms, biological treatment interventions may be necessary to produce at least partial relief from pain and suffering. Thus, the health counselor will need to work collaboratively with the client's neurologist or primary care physician. Unfortunately, biological interventions may unduly contribute to the client's hope of a magical cure instead of increasing the client's autonomy and commitment to learning to live with and adapt to pain. This section reviews a number of the common biological interventions that can serve as useful adjuncts to psychosocial interventions.

Psychotropic Medications.   The effectiveness of psychotropic medications, particularly antidepressants, has been widely studied (Sindrup & Jensen, 1999; Ansari, 2000). It has been noted that approximately 60 to 80 percent of individuals with chronic pain benefit, to some degree, from treatment with a tricyclic antidepressant, which appear to be more consistently effective than the newer serotonin reuptake inhibitors (Jung, Staiger, & Sullivan, 1997; Ansari, 2000). The only exception seems to be venlafaxine—Effexor (Pernia et al., 2000). At doses of 50 to 75 milligrams per day, the tricyclic antidepressant amitriptyline (e.g., Elavil) appears to be the optimal dose.

Because many chronic pain sufferers display depressive symptoms, it was assumed that antidepressants should be an essential component of treatment for all or most of them. Recent data, however, seem to indicate pain relief is not necessarily dependent on improved mood (Ansari, 2000).

Physical Rehabilitation.   Many inpatient and day-hospital pain programs include a stepwise plan of physical retraining to help reverse the effects of muscular atrophy, fatigue, and lack of stamina that normally discourages activity in patients with chronic pain. Specific goals or quotas are set for clients to reach whatever activity level is required to restore functional independence at home or on the job.

Sensory Stimulation.   Massage, heat, cold, vibration, acupuncture, and various forms of electrical stimulation have a place in the biological treatment of chronic pain. Transcutaneous nerve stimulators (TENS) are lightweight units that stimulate the skin through electrodes and offer effective pain relief when there is skin sensitivity or nerve damage. Acupuncture is now regarded as a form of low-frequency stimulation that produces some relief in about 60 percent of clients, particularly those with musculoskeletal conditions.

Relaxation Training and Biofeedback.   Because muscular contractions, vascular dilatation, is believed to worsen certain forms of pain, biofeedback may be a useful treatment. This is particularly the case with headache sufferers for whom there is EMG evidence of an abnormal level of activity in response to stressful stimuli. Studies indicate that, instead of biofeedback, generalized relaxation training may be a simpler, less expensive, and equally effective form of treatment (Blanchard & Andrasik, 1985). Nevertheless, temperature-regulation, or thermic biofeedback, in which clients learn to increase and decrease body temperature in their fingertips, is the mainstay of treatment for migraine sufferers at many headache clinics.

Drug Detoxification.   Approximately one third of chronic pain clients use no addicting substances, one third are dependent on narcotics alone, and one third are addicted to both narcotics and sedatives. Physiologically dependent chronic pain sufferers need to be weaned from medications by tapered withdrawal over a 10- to 14-day period. When there is also psychological dependence, which is often the case with drugs such as Valium, self-regulated reduction is negotiated with the client, who may be asked to set goals, keep records, and be given positive reinforcement for abstinence.

Nerve Blocks and Neurosurgery.   Nerve blocks are used for both diagnosis and treatment and are specifically indicated for pain that is caused by injury to the sympathetic nervous system. Neurosurgical techniques are usually the treatment of last choice. Some clients with chronic pain have benefited from neurosurgical techniques, but it is unclear whether this can be attributed to the techniques, to relief of severe depression, or to extensive personality change.

Psychological Interventions

Psychological interventions have been found to be quite effective in influencing clients' tolerance of pain as well as their willingness to complete a treatment program. Yet, psychological interventions are often difficult to implement initially because chronic pain clients typically resist psychological concepts. The following sections describe some common psychological interventions.

Behavioral Techniques.   The aim of behavioral techniques is to increase the frequency of wellness behaviors and decrease pain and illness behaviors. The client must come to accept that the aim of treatment is not to remove pain but, rather, to help him or her cope with it and resume normal activities despite it. Reinforcement, shaping, and extinction techniques are used extensively. Generally, the client is given no attention for pain behavior or for requests for pain medication but is provided considerable social reinforcement for wellness behaviors. Physical therapy and exercise quotas are developed to encourage an increase in the client's activity level (Kroenke & Swindle, 2000).

Cognitive Techniques.   Cognitive techniques are various methods by which individuals learn to distract or distance themselves from pain. Imagery and cognitive restructuring are used to reframe the experience of pain or to replace it with more pleasant thoughts or sensations. Cognitive techniques appear to work best for pain of mild to moderate intensities (Holzman, Turk, & Kerns, 1986; Morley, Eccleston, & Williams, 1999).

Cognitive-Behavioral Therapy.   Cognitive-behavioral therapy appears to be moderately effective for chronic pain. Such therapy significantly decreases pain-related distress and disability in the range of 30 to 60 percent (Kroenke & Swindle, 2000). It should be noted that such therapy has less effect on actual pain intensity. Specific cognitive-behavioral techniques that have been found to be useful are relaxation training, activity scheduling, reinforcement for non-pain behavior, behavior activation, and cognitive restructuring (Morley et al., 1999).

Hypnosis.   Hypnosis and posthypnotic suggestion are methods by which some clients can learn to evoke images or metaphors to distract them from, or to reframe, pain sensations. It appears that hypnosis alone is seldom effective; therefore it is used in combination with other psychological interventions.

Individual Counseling.   Clients who experience chronic pain often possess psychological characteristics and defensive styles that limit the usefulness of traditional individual counseling interventions. The presence of alexithymia (i.e., difficulty feeling or expressing emotions), overcritical superego, and defense mechanisms (e.g., denial, rationalization, projection, or suppression) make it difficult to engage these clients in treatment. Therefore, counseling goals and strategies must be tailored to their needs and styles. The major goals of counseling are to increase self-awareness, build ego support, and enhance coping skills.

Self-awareness can be fostered through cognitive-learning and pattern-recognition techniques that, over time, allow the client to become aware of the linkages between feelings, autonomic (involuntary) arousal, and painful sensations. Strategies for strengthening healthy defenses, enhancing coping skills, and supporting the ego in the here and now have been found useful for the chronic pain sufferer. In time, some clients become more verbally skilled and able to internalize the counselor's benign, nonjudgmental qualities and to develop trust. This then makes it possible for the client to discuss deeper-seated conflicts, explore face-saving avenues to escape psychological predicaments, and relinquish the secondary gains of pain (Blackwell, 1989).

Group Therapy.   Group approaches have been particularly effective for chronic pain clients in inpatient, day-hospital, and outpatient settings. The therapeutic factors of cohesiveness, altruism, universality, hope, guidance, and identification are particularly pertinent to pain sufferers. Since loneliness and helplessness are often accompaniments of chronic pain, the group process helps clients feel understood and empowered. In addition to giving support, groups also provide invaluable opportunities for modeling wellness behavior. Once norms that affirm wellness and coping behaviors are established, the group itself becomes a powerful reinforcer of change for pain sufferers (Pearce & Erskine, 1989).

Social Skills Training.   Clients experiencing chronic pain often lack the ability to assert themselves to get their needs met. Instead, they use illness behavior to control or avoid situations and to solicit attention and care from others. Assertiveness training, problem-solving training, and role-playing are methods used to help clients express their needs more directly. Other social skills may be lacking in communication, vocational, or sexual areas that are also amenable to specific social skills training (Turk & Holzman, 1986).

Combining Cognitive-Behavioral Therapy and Medications.   There is some research evidence—randomized-controlled trials—that confirms counselors' clinical experience that the combination of cognitive-behavioral therapy and amitriptyline positively influences treatment efficacy. It appears that the amitriptyline increases the client's activity level and reduces pain intensity while the cognitive-behavioral therapy improves the client's productivity (Pilowsky et al., 1995). In short, strong evidence supports the effectiveness of both cognitive-behavioral therapies and tricyclic antidepressants across a wide range of chronic pain conditions, including headache.

Clinical Outcomes.   Psychological interventions have been used alone as well as an essential modality in the comprehensive, multidisciplinary treatment of chronic pain. A large volume of research exists demonstrating the efficacy of the psychological treatments for low back pain, arthritis, headaches, temporomandibular disorders, and whiplash-associated disorders. In addition, cognitive-behavioral approaches appear to prevent the development of long-term disability due to chronic pain syndrome. Generally speaking, psychological treatments for chronic pain are most effective when incorporated with other treatment components or modalities such as physical therapy and patient education (Turk & Okifuji, 2002).

Social Interventions

Social interventions are useful for reducing the influence of the environmental, communicative, and behavioral aspects of pain. Generally speaking, social interventions require the cooperation and involvement of the family, the community, and/or governmental agencies. Couples and family therapy, peer support groups, social security disability or worker's compensation, and reentry planning are some examples of the points of entry for social interventions (Blackwell, 1989).

Couples and Family Therapy.   Since relatives play a significant role in shaping a client's behavior in response to pain, they may be willing to learn alternate ways of helping the client develop a more healthy adaptation to pain. As treatment progresses, couple or family sessions are scheduled to reward and to encourage healthy new behavior while ignoring the pain behaviors (Pearce & Erskine, 1989).

Peer Support Groups.   As in support groups for overeaters, cancer patients, and the like, groups for chronic pain sufferers can provide an inexpensive and effective method of producing sustained encouragement and support. Owing to their emphasis on mutual problem solving and acceptance of personal responsibility, peer groups have been unusually effective in helping pain sufferers cope with their difficulties and learn or reinforce healthy skills (Pearce & Erskine, 1989).

Compensation and Disability Payments.   Another consideration in treatment planning is the role that financial reward plays in perpetuating pain behaviors. An important step in rehabilitation is the settlement of lawsuits or disability claims. Yet, it is unrealistic to assume that pain behavior will be resolved by financial settlement. Because chronic pain is multiply determined, removing a single source, or reward, is unlikely to produce a dramatic change. As Fordyce (1985) implies, social security disability payments have unintentionally and unfortunately reinforced the sick-role in many chronic pain sufferers.

Reentry Planning.   Because chronic pain clients often display anxiety, a reappearance of somatic symptoms, and complaints at the time of discharge or at the end of outpatient treatment, reentry planning is crucial. When planning for reentry into social and occupational roles, stressors need to be anticipated and clients should be prepared for brief relapses. The counselor also needs to confer with employers and shop stewards if job changes or accommodations are indicated.

Chronic Pain Control in a Group Format

Pearce and Erskine (1989) offer a group approach to chronic pain control based on cognitive, behavioral, psychoeducational, and group techniques. The groups consist of 8 to 10 male and female chronic pain clients. Each group meets once a week for 7 successive weeks. Each session begins with group education and cognitive pain-control training, which lasts for an hour and is followed by a half hour of relaxation and stress management. This is followed by 45 minutes of physical therapy or exercise and a 15-minute coffee break, which provides an opportunity for clients to socialize informally. The last hour focuses on lifestyle restructuring and general goal setting. Each of the four treatment components is now described briefly.

Group Education and Cognitive Pain-Control Training. The group begins with a detailed explanation and rationale for the cognitive-behavioral approach as the basis of the course. This establishes the validity of the various group components and begins to shift clients' focus from passive helplessness toward active responsibility. Presentations are made to outline the gate-control theory and the notion of pain as a multiply determined, multidimensional phenomenon. Clients are asked to make free associations with the word *pain,* and the adjectives are categorized into three sections: physiological, subjective, and behavioral manifestations. In this way, a multidimensional view of pain is reinforced. The rest of the first session and the next two focus on techniques aimed at altering the subjective component of pain. Distraction and reframing are two such techniques. Each technique is illustrated and individualized for each group member who then chooses a technique or techniques to practice daily at the first sign that pain intensity is on the increase. Specific homework assignments are given and checked at subsequent sessions (Pearce & Erskine, 1989).

Relaxation and Stress Control. Progressive relaxation and self-induced relaxation are both taught to and practiced by chronic pain clients. Self-hypnotic relaxation training has been found to be useful, and clients practice at home by listening to a tape recording of a counselor's instructions. The ultimate goal of this training is for clients to learn to achieve deep states of relaxation without cues from either the group counselor or the tape (Turk et al., 1983).

Exercise Therapy. This part of a group session is structured around a core of exercises that involve all the major muscle groups and is designed to promote increased flexibility and stamina. Every client is given a booklet in which he or she can write down individualized, weekly homework goals and record the progress made. Specifically, the group aims to decrease the level of fear surrounding movement and activity and to increase the client's level of physical activity and fitness. In addition, the exercises alert each client to posture problems and the benefits of good posture while reinforcing an improved body image.

Analgesic Reduction and Lifestyle Restructuring. Goal setting is the basic technique utilized for reducing the use of analgesics and eliminating avoidance behavior over a wide range of activities—self-care work, social interaction, and leisure pursuits. A case for discontinuing analgesics is made by emphasizing the potential advantages of alternative methods of pain control. For those clients who are on medications, reassurance is given that a gradual reduction rather than an immediate cutoff is the aim. Long-term goals to change medication intake and lifestyle are then negotiated individually. Once formulated, these goals are specified in clear and specific language.

In the group, each client's goals are shared and written on a large sheet of paper. The chart is referred to in future sessions so that individual progress is constantly monitored. Each week, homework tasks related to the goals are set and then checked the following week. Clients are warned about vicious cycles between avoidance behavior and certain cognitions. Clients often expect pain to increase on exposure to some feared stimuli, or, because of past experiences, believe that they will be incapable of controlling pain. Exposure to the feared stimuli through graded tasks, which progress from less to more fearful, provides an invaluable way of testing and challenging these cognitions and thereby improving self-efficacy. The group itself acts as a powerful reinforcer once norms about task completion are established. Finally, issues of relapse are discussed.

Although there is some evidence (Pearce & Erskine, 1989) that group treatment of chronic pain is effective, more research is needed to establish this conclusion. Pearce and Erskine (1989) offer some indications and contraindications for group treatment. The indicators for group treatment are broad: The client should be an adult with significant chronic disability for which all conventional physical treatments have been tried and have failed. Excluded are individuals who have a history of severe mental illness, a terminal disease, or strong suspicions about the efficacy of psychologically based approaches.

Chronic Pain Control in an Individual Format

Effective individual health counseling for chronic pain clients can be done. Turk and colleagues (1983) and Holzman, Turk, and Kerns (1986) give detailed accounts of individual cognitive-behavioral and psychoeducational treatment of pain sufferers. Usually, 6 to 10 individual weekly sessions are scheduled. Sessions with a clinician can be scheduled back-to-back with sessions with a physical therapist, who focuses on the graded exercise component; or the clinician can incorporate both the cognitive-behavioral and psychoeducational interventions into the exercise training.

Pearce and Erskine (1989) outline a typical program of weekly sessions. In the first session, psychoeducation is used to reframe pain problems, and the client is introduced to long-term goal setting and homework to monitor the intensity of pain and the tension level. The second session is devoted to relaxation training, analysis of homework, and identification of major stressors. Goal setting to increase exercise and physical activity levels is also addressed. In the third session, the client begins to learn stress inoculation, and goals are adjusted for increased exercise and physical activity. In the fourth session, specific cognitive pain-control techniques are taught, practiced, and assigned for homework, and goals are set again to increase physical and social activities. In the fifth session, previously learned cognitive-control techniques are monitored and new ones are taught. Once again, goal setting increases both physical and social activities. In session six, all techniques previously learned are reviewed. A discussion about relapse prevention and the importance of planning follow-up sessions is held. Finally, additional goal setting is established.

TREATMENT NONCOMPLIANCE AND RELAPSE PREVENTION

Achieving optimal treatment outcomes may not occur because of treatment noncompliance—nonadherence—and relapse. This section describes both of these phenomena in pain management, and then discusses relapse prevention.

The risk of relapse among clients with chronic pain is high. While nearly all psycho-logical interventions for persistent pain have been shown to be effective, at least for some clients, the duration of the benefits varies. Just as it is important for health counselor to be able to use strategies for enhancing treatment adherence, it is also essential to focus on enhancing the maintenance of therapeutic gains.

Treatment Noncompliance or Nonadherence

Clients' beliefs about their pain play an important role in their adjustment to chronic pain. Beliefs also influence compliance with or adherence to treatment recommendations, improvement in depressive symptoms, increases in physical functioning, and health-care use (Jensen, Turner, & Romano 1994). There is a tendency for health counselors to be more focused on the details of treatment and less on whether clients adhere to the demands of the treatment. Thus, health counselors make recommendations for significant changes in behaviors and expect that clients will continue to engage in the behaviors prescribed. Despite this expectation, the long-term rate of adherence to treatment by chronic pain clients is reportedly low (Lutz, Silbret, & Olshan, 1983). Moreover, a health counselor may conclude that a particular treatment is ineffective when it may be quite effective, but only for clients who comply with it. Thus, it is incumbent on clinicians to use strategies that enhance treatment adherence.

Relapse Prevention

Marlatt and Gordon (1985) developed a relapse-prevention model to address the problem of long-term maintenance of new health behaviors. It was created to aid clients acquire new coping skills that would reduce the risk of an initial relapse or recurrence and to prevent minor lapses from escalating into total relapse. The major element of the model is that the problem of possible lapses and relapses is neither ignored nor attributed to failures of the treatment program or the client. Such lapses and relapses are viewed as an important part of the learning required for long-term successful behavioral change and thus should be included in treatment programs (Keefe & Van Horn, 1993).

To prevent relapse once treatment has been completed, Marlatt and Gordon (1985) recommend a series of techniques for use with clients, including: (1) identification of indi-vidual high-risk situations, (2) development of coping skills for high-risk situations, (3) practice in coping with potential lapses, (4) development of cognitive coping strategies for use immediately after a lapse, and (5) development of a more balanced lifestyle. Dis-cussion about preventing relapse is a usual part of the last stage of treatment. Because relapse is common for chronic pain clients, the health counselor urges them not to panic or "catastrophize." Instead, they need to be encouraged to use a relapse-prevention strategy and the skills that have been worked on in treatment. This is particularly important to ensure that any setbacks are not viewed as a failure of counseling or of the clients.

Turk and Feldman (2000) believe that any discussion of relapse must be done in a "delicate" fashion. On the one hand, the counselor does not want to convey an expectancy of treatment failure; but, on the other hand, he or she does want to anticipate and include in treatment the client's possible reaction to the likely recurrence of pain. These researchers suggests two techniques. First, the counselor should reanalyze, with the client, reactions that have followed previous relapses. Second, the counselor can suggest the types of thoughts and feelings that imaginary pain clients might have had upon experiencing pain again and what they might have done to cope with it. The counselor can mention that he or she does not know whether the client will have such feelings or thoughts but that it is worthwhile to determine possible reactions to similar situations.

CASE EXAMPLES

Case 1

Ms. C is a 32-year-old married female referred by her neurologist for a combination of muscle contractions and migraine headaches. She reported that her headaches of 15 years' duration had recently worsened. Ms. C added that she was ingesting an alarming amount of narcotic analgesics and was fearful of becoming a drug addict.

She denied any difficulties in her personal life but expressed a great deal of puzzlement about the exacerbation of her pain symptoms over the past several months. She indicated that her physician recently placed her on Elavil, a tricyclic antidepressant, but she did not believe she was depressed, and she thought the medication was another form of analgesic. Upon further inquiry, it was learned that Ms. C had experienced two recent deaths in her extended family—her maternal grandmother and maternal aunt. She admitted that both had been very close to her. Also, she had returned to university studies after several years' absence to finish a degree. Her husband was completing his last year of medical school; they have two children, aged 6 and 4, and Ms. C's return to school had unbalanced the family's homeostasis. She found herself facing a variety of conflicts. In addition to doing her schoolwork, she insisted on maintaining her household responsibilities. Although she found it increasingly difficult to meet all these obligations, she was unable to make any demands on her husband.

A mutual agreement about treatment was reached in which Ms. C's goals were to reduce and eliminate her medication under the guidance of her prescribing neurologist; to reduce her narcotic analgesics under the guidance of her prescribing physician; and to decrease family conflicts and increase her self-efficacy. Within 6 weeks, Ms. C had been weaned completely from her narcotic analgesics. At the same time, she made steady progress in relaxation training and in temperature-regulation biofeedback. Ms. C proved she was adept at learning self-regulatory skills, and she experienced considerable reduction in her headaches.

She also discovered, as a result of keeping her headache diary, that some of her headaches were strongly associated with interactions with her rather dominating husband and with the male instructor in one of her courses. Treatment to explore these problems and their similarities included specific assertiveness training that focused on dealing with her instructor. As this problem improved, Ms. C noted improvement in her relationship with her husband. Next, Ms. C was assisted in analyzing and changing her perfectionistic and unrealistic expectations for herself by cognitive reappraisal and the use of positive, coping self-statements. The counselor also pointed out that all the changes in her family situation and the deaths of her grandmother and aunt had failed to make any impression on her. The counselor helped her to see that her headache pain masked much of the grief and unhappiness in her life. Subsequent sessions focused on other issues, and Ms. C was able to recall that her first migraine headache occurred during adolescence when one of her close friends died in a car accident.

In all, Ms. C met with the counselor for 10 sessions and set up a follow-up appointment for 3 months later. At the last contact, Ms. C described herself as being more in control of her headaches and better able to handle emotional upsets. Her headaches were much less frequent and, when present, were significantly reduced in duration and intensity. Her medication had been completely eliminated and, although she continued in her university courses, her expectations for her household responsibilities became more realistic.

■ ■ ■ ■ ■

Case 2 _____

Mr. F is a 51-year-old construction worker who incurred a work-related injury involving his right hip and lower back for which he was awarded Workers' Compensation. A predictable pattern of seeking medical help, blaming physicians for their inability to cure him, and facing limited prospects of returning to work ensued. Subsequently, he neglected his family responsibilities, lost interest in sex, and began consuming large quantities of tranquilizers and narcotic analgesics to control his pain. He had become irritable and impatient with his wife and children. He denied his problems by attempting to undertake tasks that could not possibly be completed, such as painting his house. His wife assumed the major responsibility for running the affairs of the family, which involved assuming a mediating role between her husband and the two children.

Mr. F began group treatment similar to that described by Pearce and Erskine (1989) and, by the seventh session, had not only learned cognitive skills to sufficiently distract himself from his pain but was also able to be weaned from all his addictive medications. After the group treatment, he followed through with the counselor's referral to the state Division of Vocational Rehabilitation (DVR). Subsequently, he began a job-retraining program, which would conceivably lead to employment in a less physically demanding job.

■ ■ ■ ■ ■

PREVENTION STRATEGIES

There are a number of preventive measures that chronic pain clients or potential clients can use. This section briefly discuss two of them: one for clients with back pain and one for those who suffer from migraine headaches.

Exercise is a major factor in the prevention of back pain. First, it can strengthen abdominal muscles and thus relieve excess demands on the back muscles. Any number of exercises, including graduated sit-ups, have been recommended. Most communities have hospitals or clinics that offer a "back college" for people to learn appropriate exercises, posture, and bending movements tailored to those who suffer back pain. Orthopedic specialists and physical therapists can recommend such programs.

When pain develops in response to stress, exercise also can help relieve muscle tension. Such exercises can consist of brisk walking, jogging, rope skipping, tennis playing, or other appropriate sports. When an individual feels tension mounting, simply walking for 5 to 10 minutes—even indoors—can help considerably in relieving muscle tension.

Preventive measures for migraine sufferers are many. Often, modifying one or two aspects of a stressful lifestyle can result in reduced headache symptoms. Although there is much debate among headache experts regarding the importance of diet, many clients have benefited from restricting foods that contain tyramine and other substances that relax or contract blood vessels, as well as decreasing their caffeine intake. Clients can also be prescribed a "migraine diet" (Diamond & Ebstein, 1982), which recommends that no more than two caffeine-containing beverages be consumed per day. Smoking is considered to be a precipitating factor in headaches; therefore clients are encouraged to stop smoking or at least to limit their intake to half a pack of cigarettes a day.

Specific foods that have been found to trigger migraine headaches are chocolate, aged cheese, onions, yogurt, canned figs, avocados, hot dogs, bacon, dry soup mixes, chicken liver, fermented sausage, Chinese food (which contains MSG), citrus fruits, tea, bananas, nuts, and alcohol. Diamond and Epstein (1982) found that these food substances tend to lower the migraine threshold and can precipitate a migraine attack. Clients are counseled to stay on an elimination diet for at least 2 months and told that any improvement in their headache condition is an indication that at least some of the foods are implicated. Clients can then add one of the restricted foods in intervals of 2 days to 2 weeks to note any improvement or deterioration in the pattern of the attacks.

Finally, headaches can be avoided by refraining from oversleeping on weekends. It seems that sleeping late increases levels of carbon dioxide in the blood, which decreases blood sugar levels and precipitates headaches.

An aspect of prevention not often recognized concerns events that turn otherwise short-term problems into long-term ones. The case of chronic back pain is such an example. For those who suffer from back pain, both medical strategies and public policies have operated to make the condition persist longer than need be the case. As Fordyce (1985) points out, the striking increase in long-term and permanent disability as a result of Social Security Disability Insurance (SSDI) began in the mid-1950s. Although the benefits were not intended to be automatic or to continue indefinitely, once awarded, they are not often terminated. Fordyce notes that the rate of awards of SSDI for back pain is increasing at a rate of more than 10 times the growth of the population.

The award rate also indicates that eligibility for wage replacement, duration of benefits, and percentage of wages replaced all seem to encourage the persistence of the disability. In short, public policy and those physicians who make disability determinations appear to have unwittingly reinforced chronic illness behavior as well as the disincentive to return to normal functioning at home, in relationships, and on the job. A systematic approach to prevention of chronic pain would truly call for a reevaluation of the SSDI criteria.

CONCLUDING NOTE

This chapter reviewed the biopsychosocial factors involved in the experience of chronic pain. It described various theories and emphasized pain as a biopsychosocial formulation. Several biological, psychological, and social—particularly behavioral—methods of assessment of chronic pain were described, as were several intervention methods. Intervention strategies for both group and individual treatment of chronic pain conditions were elaborated. A discussion of treatment adherence and relapse was followed by case examples involving the two most common forms of chronic pain: headache and back pain. A section on prevention measures for chronic pain completed this chapter, with a reference to the specific public policy—SSDI—that actually reinforces rather than prevents chronic pain.

RESOURCES

Organizations

- *The National Headache Foundation,* 820 N. Orleans, Suite 217, Chicago, IL 60610; (888) NHF-5552—www.headaches.org—This foundation, previously called the National Migraine Foundation, is an organization for both professionals and laypersons. Its mission is to provide educational resources for headache sufferers and their families and to sponsor research on headaches and to serve as a research clearinghouse. It publishes a quarterly newsletter that provides articles of interest for the headache sufferer.
- *The National Foundation for the Treatment of Pain,* P.O. Box 70045, Houston, TX; (713)

This foundation is a not-for-profit organization dedicated to providing support for individuals who are suffering from intractable pain, their families and friends. Their Pain Care Bulletin Board is a chat room for corresponding with members, pain patients, experts, and physicians. The foundation is also a resource for medical professionals and attorneys concerned with legal issues regarding the legitimate treatment of pain. Their website can be accessed at www.paincare.org.

Professional References

- Diamond, M., Solomon, G., Diamond, S., and Dalessio, D. (Eds.). (1999). *Diamond and Dalessio's the practicing physician's approach to headaches* (6th ed.). Baltimore: Williams & Wilkins.—This classic handbook on headache pain and its treatment is now in its sixth edition. Although the title suggests that this book is for physicians, or is basically medical in orientation, it is not. Clinicians will find this reference indispensable because the authors achieve an expert and practical synthesis of biological and psychological treatments
- Gatchel, R. J., and Turk, D. C. (1996). *Psychological approaches to pain management: A practitioner's handbook.* New York: Guilford.—Emphasizes the role of psychosocial factors in pain and provides extensive coverage on various psychological approaches to pain management. The roles of mental health specialists in pain con-

sulting, 862-9332. prevention, and outcome are addressed. The book includes secondary prevention and treatment for specific syndromes and considers issues of special populations, including children and olderadults.
- Loeser, J. D., Butler, S. D., Chapman, C. R., and Turk, D. C. (2001). *Bonica's management of pain* (3rd ed.). Philadelphia: Lippincott/Williams & Wilkins.—A compendium on pain management with a largely biopsychosocial perspective; it contains 110 contributions that address the fundamental aspects of pain, its assessment, and its treatment.
- Turk, D. C., & Melzack, R. (2001). *Handbook of pain assessment* (2nd ed.). New York: Guilford.—Emphasizes pain assessment, behavioral expressions of pain, diagnostic methods, and psychiatric disorders in individuals with pain, with a particular focus on diagnosing and assessing acute pain.

■ Wall, P. D., and Melzack, R. (1999). *Textbook of pain* (4th ed.). New York: Churchill Livingstone.—An encyclopedic textbook (1,588 pages) covering all aspects of pain management from basic science to clinical treatment protocols; it emphasizes the biological perspective.

REFERENCES

Ansari, A. (2000). The efficacy of newer antidepressants in the treatment of chronic pain: A reviews of current literature. *Harvard Review of Psychiatry, 7,* 257–277.

Bandura, A. (1977). Self-efficacy: Toward a unifying theory of behavior change. *Psychological Review, 84,* 191–215.

Banks, S., M., & Kerns, R. D. (1996). Explaining high rates of depression in chronic pain: A diathesis-stress framework. *Psychological-Bulletin, 119,* 95–110

Blackwell, B. (1989). Chronic pain. In H. Kaplan & B. Sadock (Eds.), *Comprehensive textbooks of psychiatry* (5th ed.). Baltimore: Williams & Wilkins.

Blackwell, B., Galbraith, H., & Dahl, D. (1984). Chronic pain management. *Hospital and Community Psychiatry, 35,* 999–1008.

Blanchard, E. G., & Andrasik, F. (1985). *Management of chronic headaches: A psychological approach.* New York: Pergamon.

Brannon, R. (1976). The male sex-role: Our culture's blueprint of manhood and what it's done for us lately. In D. S. Brannon & R. Brannon (Eds.), *The forty-nine percent majority* (pp. 1–45). Reading, MA: Addison-Wesley.

Castillo, R. J. (1997). *Culture & mental illness: A client-centered approach.* Belmont, CA: Brooks/Cole Publishing.

Chaplin S. L. (1997). Somatization. In W. Tseng & J. Streltzer (Eds.). *Culture and psychopathology: A guide to clinical assessment* (pp. 67–86). Philadelphia: Brunner-Routledge.

Chapman, C., Cassey, K., Dubner, R., et al. (1985). Pain measurement: An overview. *Pain, 22,* 131.

De La Cancela, V., Jenkins, Y., & Chin, J. (1998). Psychosocial and cultural impact on health status. In V. De La Cancela, J. Chin, & Y. Jenkins (Eds.), *Community health psychology: Empowerment for diverse communities* (pp. 57–84). New York: Routledge.

Diamond, S., & Ebstein, M. (1982). *Coping with your headache.* Madison, CT: International Universities Press.

Diamond, M., Solomon, G., Diamond, S., & Dalessio, D. (Eds.). (1999). *Diamond and Dalessio's the practicing physician's approach to headaches* (6th ed.). Baltimore: Williams & Wilkins.

Fordyce, W. (1985). Back pain, compensation, and public policy. In J. Rosen & L. Solomon (Eds), *Prevention in health psychology.* Hanover, NH: University Press of New England.

Gatchel, R., & Turk, D. (1999). *Psychosocial factors in pain: Critical perspectives.* New York: Guilford.

Helmen, C. (1985). *Health, culture, and illness.* Boston: Wright.

Holzman, A., Turk, D., & Kerns, R. (1986). The cognitive-behavioral approach to the management of chronic pain. In A. Holzman & D. Turk (Eds.), *Pain management: A handbook of psychological treatment approaches.* New York: Pergamon.

Hullard, L. (1954). The Munkfors investigation. *Acta Orthopedia Scandinavia, 42,* 174–175.

Jamison, R. N., Rudy, T. E., Penzien, D. B., & Mosley, T. H. (1994). Cognitive-behavioral classifications of chronic pain: Replication and extension of empirically derived patient profiles. *Pain, 57,* 277–292.

Jensen, M. P., Nielson, W. R., Romano, J. M., Hill, M. L., & Turner, J. A. (2000). Further evaluation of the Pain Stages of Change Questionnaire: Is the transtheoretical model of change useful for patients with chronic pain? *Pain, 86,* 255–264.

Jensen, M. P., Turner, J. A., & Romano, J. M. (1994). What is the maximum number of levels needed in pain intensity measurement? *Pain, 58,* 387–392.

Johansson, E., & Lindberg, P. (2000). Low back pain patients in primary care: Subgroups based on the Multidimensional Pain Inventory. *International Journal of Behavioral Medicine, 7,* 340–352.

Johnson, A. (1978). *The problem claim: An approach to early identification.* Department of Labor and Industries, State of Washington.

Jung, A., Staiger, T., & Sullivan, M.(1997). The efficacy of selective serotonin reuptake inhibition for the management of chronic pain. *Journal of General Internal Medicine, 12,* 384–389.

Karoly, P., & Jensen, M. (1987). *Multimethod assessment of chronic pain.* New York: Pergamon.

Keefe, F. J., & Van Horn, Y. V. (1993). Cognitive-behavioral treatment of rheumatoid arthritis pain: Maintaining treatment gains. *Arthritis Care and Research, 6,* 213–222.

Kerns, R. D., & Payne, A. (1996). Treating families of chronic pain patients. In R. J. Gatchel & D. C. Turk (Eds.), *Psychological approaches to pain management: A practitioner's handbook* (pp. 283–304). New York: Guilford.

Kerns, R. D., & Rosenberg, R. (1999). Predicting responses to self-management treatments for chronic pain: application to the pain stages of change model. *Pain, 84,* 49–56.

Kerns, R. D., Rosenberg, R., Jamison, R. N., Caudill, M. A., & Haythornthwaite, J. (1997). Readiness to adopt a self-management approach to chronic pain: The Pain Stages of Change Questionnaire (PSOCQ). *Pain, 72,* 227–234.

Kroenke, K., & Swindle, R. (2000). Cognitive-behavioral therapy for somatization and symptom syndromes: A critical review of controlled clinical trials. *Psychotherapy and Psychosomatics, 69,* 205–215.

Lutz, R. W., Silbret, M., & Olshan, N. (1983). Treatment outcome and compliance with therapeutic regimens: Long-term follow-up of a multidisciplinary pain program. *Pain, 17,* 301–308.

Marlatt, G., & Gordon, J. (1985). *Relapse prevention.* New York: Guilford.

Melzack, R. (1975). The McGill Pain Questionnaire: Major properties and scoring methods. *Pain, 1,* 277–299.

Morley, S., Eccleston, C., & Williams A. (1999). Systematic review and meta-analysis of randomized controlled trials of cognitive behavior therapy and behaviour therapy for chronic pain in adults, excluding headache. *Pain, 80,* 11–13.

O'Neil, J. M. (1981). Patterns of gender role conflict and strain: Sexism and fear of femininity in men's lives. *Personnel and Guidance Journal, 60,* 203–210.

Paniagua, F. A. (2001). Culture-bound syndromes. In I. Cuellar & F. A. Paniagua (Eds.), *Handbook of multicultural mental health* (pp. 142–170). San Diego: Academic.

Pearce, S., & Erskine, A. (1989). Chronic pain. In S. Pearce & J. Wardle (Eds.), *The practice of behavioral medicine.* Oxford: BPS Books/Oxford University Press.

Pernia, A., Mico, J., Calderon, E., et al. (2000). Venlafaxine for the treatment of neuropathic pain. *Journal of Pain and Symptom Management, 19,* 408–410.

Pilowsky, L., Spence, N. Rousefell, B., et al. (1995). Outpatient cognitive-behavioral therapy with amitriptyline for chronic non-malignant pain: A comparative study with 6-month follow-up. *Pain, 60,* 49–54.

Pleck, J. (1995). The gender role strain paradigm: An update. In R. Levant & W. Pollack (Eds.), *The new psychology of men* (pp. 11–32). New York: Basic.

Price, D. (1999). *Psychological mechanisms of pain and analgesia: Progress in pain research and management,* Vol. 15. Seattle: IASP Press.

Rainville, P., Duncan, G. H., Price, D. D., Carrier, B., & Bushnell, M. C. (1997). Pain affect encoded in human anterior cingulate but not somatosensory cortex. *Science, 277,* 968–971.

Sanders, S. (1985). Chronic pain: Conceptualization and epidemiology. *Annals of Behavioral Medicine, 7,* 3–5.

Silverman, J. T. (2001). Catastrophizing and coping with chronic pain. *Dissertation Abstracts International, 61*(9-B), 0419–4217.

Sindrup, S., & Jensen, T. (1999). Efficacy of pharmacological treatments of neuroleptic pain: An update and effect related to mechanism of drug action. *Pain, 83,* 389–400.

Sternbach, R. A. (1968). *Pain: A psychophysiological analysis.* New York: Academic.

Svensson, H., & Anderson, G. (1982). Low back pain in 40–47-year-old men: Frequency of occurrence and impact on medical services. *Scandinavian Journal of Rehabilitation Medicine, 14,* 47–53.

Turk, D. (1996). Psychological aspects of chronic pain and disability. *Journal of Musculoskeletal ain, 4,* 145–153.

Turk, D., & Feldman, C. (2000). A cognitive-behavioral approach to symptom management in palliative care: Augmenting somatic interventions. In H. Chochinov & W. Breitbart (Eds.), *Handbook of psychiatry in palliative medicine* (pp. 223–239). New York: Oxford University Press.

Turk, D. C., & Flor, H. (1999). Chronic pain: A biobehavioral perspective. In R. J. Gatchel & D. C. Turk (Eds.), *Psychosocial factors in pain: Critical perspectives* (pp. 18–34). New York, NY: Guilford.

Turk, D., & Holzman, A. (1986). Commonalities among psychological approaches in the treatment of chronic pain: Specifying the meta-constructs, In A. Holzman & D. Turk (Eds.), *Pain management: A handbook of psychological approaches.* New York: Pergamon.

Turk, D., Kerns, R., & Rosenberg, R. (1992). Effects of marital interaction on chronic pain and disability: Examining the down side of social support. *Rehabilitation Psychology, 37,* 259–274.

Turk, D., Meichenbaum, P., & Genest, M. (1983). *Pain and behavioral medicine: A cognitive-behavioral perspective.* New York: Guilford.

Turk, D., Okifuji, A., Sinclair, J. D., & Starz, T. W. (1996). Effects of type of symptom onset on psychological distress and disability in fibromyalgia syndrome patients. *Pain, 68,* 423–430.

Turk. D., & Okifuji, A. (2002). Psychological factors in chronic pain: Evolution and revolution. *Journal of Consulting and Clinical Psychology, 70*(3), 678–690.

Unruh, A. (1996). Gender variations in clinical pain experience. *Pain, 65,* 123–167.

Wall, P. D., & Melzack, R. (1999). *Textbook of pain* (4th ed.). New York: Churchill Livingstone.

Webb, W. (1983). Chronic pain. *Psychosomatics, 1,* 1053–1063.

. . . . . ▬▬▬▬▬▬▬▬▬▬▬▬▬▬▬▬▬▬▬

CHAPTER ELEVEN

CHRONIC DISEASE AND OTHER ILLNESS-RELATED CONCERNS

In the midst of winter I finally learned that
there is within me an invincible summer.
—Albert Camus

Programs designed to promote health and prevent illness have become more and more prevalent in recent years. An increasing variety of strategies has been implemented, encouraging people to engage in health-protective behaviors and training them in the skills they need to achieve a higher degree of health and well-being. The resulting lifestyle changes have helped countless individuals maintain their health and reduce their risk for the development of serious health problems.

Reality tells us, however, that everyone is subject to illness at some time in his or her life. Whether the illness is chronic or acute, mild or life-threatening, some degree of adaptation has to occur. There are several such conditions for which health counseling can be enormously valuable, including the following:

- Helping individuals manage and cope with chronic diseases
- Helping social systems (e.g., families) adapt to the special needs of those with health problems
- Helping individuals cope with psychological reactions to illness
- Helping individuals cope with anxiety associated with aversive medical procedures
- Helping individuals adhere to medical regimens that may require lifelong behavioral changes
- Working to prevent or minimize the long-term effects of illness

This chapter describes background information and treatment considerations for each of the six conditions and provides illustrations for some.

Since the incidence and prevalence of chronic diseases are by far the most common of these conditions and increasingly seen in health counseling, this chapter emphasizes chronic disease. An understanding of the biopsychosocial factors involved in these conditions is indispensable in their treatment. The discussion begins with a brief consideration of the biopsychosocial factors, followed by a discussion of the basic terminology and epidemiology regarding chronic disease, the cultural context of chronic illness in the United States, and the phases of chronic illnesses. A subsequent section addresses issues of the counselor–client relationship and engagement and focuses on countertransference. Assessment is next discussed. This is followed by a detailed discussion of treatment intervention of each of the six conditions noted earlier. Next, maintenance is discussed. The chapter ends with a consideration of prevention. The appendix contains resources for these health counseling issues.

BIOPSYCHOSOCIAL FACTORS
IN COPING WITH ILLNESS

Each biological illness affects and is affected by psychological and social factors. The individual's psychosocial well-being can be challenged—even jeopardized—by his or her physical illness. At the same time, the person's ability to mobilize personal and social resources can have major implications for his or her success in combating or coping with a disease or disability.

The client dealing with an illness or disability faces a number of tasks that must be performed effectively for adaptation to occur (Moos & Tsu, 1977). First, the individual must cope with a health problem's physical aspects—pain, discomfort, and/or incapacitation—while at the same time being forced to make personal and social adaptations to a major life change. Also, medical treatments may be invasive or uncomfortable, requiring still more adaptive efforts. The individual's psychological well-being must be preserved; emotional balance and a new, but satisfactory, self-image have to be sought.

While these intrapersonal tasks are being addressed, new interpersonal challenges develop. The individual must forge new relationships and/or accept the reality of changes in the existing social network. Health-care professionals become a new part of the social network, and communication concerning medical issues becomes a necessity. Finally, some clients need to cope with the loss of good health; the loss of physical abilities; and, probably most important, the loss of a sense of certainty about the future.

It is important to note that even the concept of illness and the views of disease causation vary across cultures. Without an appreciation of the role of culture in the perception and manifestation of health and illness, health counselors run the risk of misinterpreting and misdiagnosing illnesses due to ethnocentric biases (Angel & Williams, 2001). Western views of disease causation are often based on naturalistic views such as infection, stress, organic deterioration, accidents, and acts of overt aggression. In contrast, non-Western views of disease causation sometimes have components of supernatural views such as mystical causation (i.e., impersonal views such as fate, ominous sensations, contagion, etc.), animistic causation due to personalized forces of soul loss and spiritual aggression, and theories of magical causation such as witchcraft (Murdock, 1980, as cited in Marsella & Yamada, 2001). Non-Western notions of disease are seldom considered in Western-professional settings, which can lead to compliance problems with those not adhering to the Western conceptualization of disease. In general, however, it is important to recognize that there are no set rules to determine if responses to perception, to treatment, and for coping with illness will be more culturally specific than ones that appear to some as culture-bound, or more Western. To simply categorize responses as Western or non-Western does not allow for the understanding of other factors, including belief systems, acculturation, socioeconomic status, and other salient cultural variables (Arredondo, 1996).

The interaction of biological, psychological, and social factors has a major impact on the process of adaptation, whether the problem being faced is acute or chronic. The sudden onset of an illness may throw an individual into a crisis situation, requiring new ways of behaving and living with altered perceptions of the world. His or her success in coping with a crisis can have long-term implications for both physical and mental health. Focusing attention narrowly on the physical aspects of the newly diagnosed disease, without equally intense regard for psychological and social variables, may jeopardize the individual's stabilization or recovery. One's worldview and cultural orientation also influence coping behavior. For example, among Latino/Hispanic populations is *fatalismo*—the belief that a divine providence governs the world and that an individual cannot control or prevent adversity (Neff & Hoppe, 1993). Fatalism can imply both a sense of vulnerability and a lack of control in the presence of adverse events (e.g., chronic illness; see Paniagua, 1998). In terms of treatment, this could lead clients to believe that they are powerless in creating better outcomes or in developing coping skills.

In addition to helping people survive the acute phases of illnesses, improvements in medical techniques also tend to prolong the lives of individuals with chronic diseases so that they need to cope with their conditions for longer periods of time than was true in the past (Kendall & Turk, 1984). Now more than ever, millions of people find themselves trying to cope with unrelenting health problems. According to Friedman and DiMatteo (1989), among the special problems they face are the need to be vigilant in checking for signs that medical problems may reappear or accelerate; the need to manage treatment regimens that may be complex, time-consuming, uncomfortable, and demanding; the need to control symptoms; and the need to manage social relationships that have been jeopardized by the uncertainty of the prognosis and the behavioral limitations brought on by the illness. Because individuals' experience of illness is as salient as the physical symptoms, "the biopsychosocial model proposes that medical diagnosis should always consider the interaction of biological, psychological, and social factors in order to assess a person's health and to make recommendations for treatment" (Schwartz, 1982, p. 1047).

CHRONIC DISEASE

The Centers for Disease Control and Prevention (CDC) reports that nearly three quarters of adults age 65 years and older have one or more chronic illnesses, and nearly half report two or more. With an aging population, chronic diseases will increase proportionately. Moreover, children and young people who have chronic diseases, such as juvenile-onset diabetes, can expect to live longer and, therefore, will have a need to manage their health conditions over a longer lifespan than in the past. With an increasing lifespan, older individuals will require more health services longer for chronic health conditions. Every year, chronic diseases claim the lives of more than 1.7 million Americans; diseases are responsible for 7 out of every 10 deaths in the United States (National Center for Chronic Disease Prevention and Health Promotion, 2000).

What accounts for this increase in chronic diseases? Many reasons have been suggested including the standard U.S. diet, which is characterized by a high intake of simple carbohydrates (e.g. sugar) and other unhealthy food choices; environmental factors (e.g. exposure to heavy metals such as mercury, cadmium, and aluminum); as well as improvements in medical care itself, as Friedman and DiMatteo (1989) note:

> Better emergency treatments allow many patients to now survive the initial critical stages of acute illnesses or trauma (e.g., stroke, accident, or heart attack). Patients live with the effects of these acute illnesses and trauma and thus face chronic illness from which they will never recover. . . . Thus better medical care, coupled with demographic trends that produce an increase in the elderly population, contributes to an increase in chronic illness (p. 222).

So, what exactly are chronic diseases? Which are the most common types? What role can health counseling play with regard to these conditions?

Defining Chronic Diseases

Chronic disease can be defined as illnesses that are prolonged, do not resolve spontaneously, are rarely cured completely, and may involve some type of long-term disability that is irreversible. The National Center for Chronic Disease Prevention and Health Promotion defines chronic diseases as those illnesses that are preventable, and that pose a significant burden in mortality, morbidity, and cost. The health problem can be stabilized and controlled, but the affected individual cannot expect to return to the level of health enjoyed before the onset of the illness (National Center for Chronic Disease Prevention and Health Promotion, 2000).

Costs of Chronic Diseases

The United States cannot effectively address escalating health-care costs without addressing the problem of chronic diseases, since more than 90 million Americans—approximately one third of all men, women, and children—live with chronic diseases. Chronic diseases account for 70 percent of deaths in the United States and for one third of the years of potential life lost before age 65 (Robert Wood Johnson Foundation, 1994). The cost of health care for individuals with chronic illnesses does not typically consider the personal, occupational, and financial costs related to self-management or disabilities. Nor does it account for the social and psychological burdens placed on the individual, the family, and society as a whole by the 90 million Americans with one or more chronic diseases. The medical care costs for individuals with chronic diseases total more than $400 billion annually, which is more than 60 percent of total expenditures for medical care.

Prevalence in Women and Ethnic Groups

Chronic disease disproportionately affects women and the racial minority population. Women comprise more than half of the people who die each year of cardiovascular disease.

Deaths due to breast cancer are decreasing among White women but not among African American women. The death rate from cervical cancer is more than twice as high for African American women as it is for White women. The 5-year survival rate for men with colon cancer is 51 percent for African Americans and 63 percent for White men. The prevalence of diabetes is about 1.7 times more among non-Hispanic African Americans, 1.9 times more among Hispanics, and 2.8 times more among Native Americans and Alaskan Natives than among non-Hispanic White Americans of similar age. The death rate from prostate cancer is more than twice as high for African American men than it is for White men. African Americans are more likely than Whites to get oral or pharyngeal cancer, half as likely to have the diseases diagnosed early, and twice as likely to die of these diseases.

Some Common Chronic Diseases

Although there are more than 100 chronic diseases, only five are quite common among adults in the United States. Not surprisingly, the progression of each of these diseases can be greatly attenuated, particularly in the early stages, with effective health counseling. The following epidemiological data on disease conditions is from *Chronic Diseases and Their Risk Factors: The Nation's Leading Causes of Death, 1999* (National Center for Chronic Disease Prevention and Health Promotion, 2000).

Arthritis.   Arthritis and other rheumatic conditions affect nearly 43 million Americans, which is about one of every six individuals. As the nation's population ages, arthritis is expected to affect 60 million people by 2020. Arthritis is the leading cause of disability in the United States. It is estimated to cost almost $65 billion annually in medical care and lost productivity. Although prevailing myths have portrayed arthritis as an inevitable part of aging that can only be endured, effective interventions are available to prevent or reduce arthritis-related pain and disability.

Cardiovascular Disease.   Cardiovascular diseases, such as high blood pressure, heart disease, and stroke, are the cause of almost one million deaths in the United States each year; they are the leading cause of death among both men and women, and across all racial and ethnic groups. About 58 million Americans live with some form of cardiovascular disease. In 1999 alone, these diseases cost the nation an estimated $287 billion in health-care expenditures and lost productivity, and this burden is growing as the population ages. Three health behaviors—cigarette smoking, lack of physical activity, and poor nutrition—are major risk factors for the onset of cardiovascular diseases.

Cancer.   Cancer is the second leading cause of death among Americans—approximately 550,000 U.S. deaths in 2000. It is estimated that 8.4 million Americans alive today have a history of cancer; and that 1.2 million new cancer cases were diagnosed in 2000, together with an estimated 1.3 million new cases of nonmelanoma skin cancer and numerous new cases of preinvasive cancer. Cancer costs this nation an estimated $107 billion annually in health-care expenditures and lost productivity. Reducing the incidence of cancer requires addressing the behavioral and environmental factors that increase cancer risk and making screening and health counseling services available and accessible in its early, most treatable stages.

Chronic Obstructive Lung Disease. Chronic Obstructive Lung Disease (COLD) is characterized by nonreversible airflow impairment or obstruction, which is often diagnosed as emphysema or chronic bronchitis. COLD is responsible for more than 100,000 U.S. deaths each year. Cigarette smoking is a major contributor to these conditions.

Diabetes. An estimated 16 million Americans have diabetes, and about one third of them are unaware of it; about 1,700 new cases are diagnosed every day in the United States. Diabetes is the seventh leading cause of death among Americans, and is the leading cause of new cases of blindness, kidney failure, and lower extremity amputations. It also greatly increases a person's risk for heart attack or stroke. Diabetes accounts for more than $98 billion in direct and indirect medical costs and lost productivity each year. Diabetes could be prevented with early detection; improved delivery of care, and, of course, health counseling.

THE CULTURAL CONTEXT OF CHRONIC ILLNESS

Chronic illness cannot be understood apart from its cultural context. Although many uses the terms *disease* and *illness* and *impairment* and *disability* interchangeably, they actually have quite different meanings; and disease represents an objective process, illness is a subjective process. Similarly, although *impairment* is an objective limitation of function, limitation of function in *disability* is socially defined. Table 11.1 offers formal definitions of these and others terms.

Disease and sickness do not occur within a vacuum. Rather culture exerts a profound influence on how individuals in subcultures and in the dominant culture think about disease and its treatment. Certain aspects of the dominant culture positively support and respond to people experiencing chronic illnesses, but other aspects of the culture make living with chronic illnesses very difficult. Fennell (2001) discusses the following six cultural factors—in the dominant U.S. culture—that are nonsupportive and even harmful to individuals with chronic illnesses:

- *Intolerance of suffering*—Suffering is perceived as having no value to America and society frowns on the public expression of grief and sorrow, especially among males.
- *Intolerance of ambiguity*—Because of scientific bias, Americans dislike the unknowable and much about chronic illness is unknown. This intolerance fosters feelings of powerlessness, fear that chronic diseases are contagious, and the belief that the chronically ill are somehow responsible for their condition.
- *Intolerance of chronic illness*—Because of their action and achievement-orientation, Americans accept acute diseases because they have a distinct cause, course, treatment, and eventual cure while chronic diseases do not. Furthermore, Americans have come to expect miraculous cures and technological marvels, but that the nontreatability of chronic diseases represents a failure of the health-care system and modern medicine.
- *Current cultural perceptions of disease*—Americans fear new diseases—for example, recall the public hysteria surrounding AIDS in the 1980s—and those who are ill even with "acceptable" diseases are considered "outsiders" who tend to arouse suspicion.
- *Disease enculturation*—There is a definable process in which a new disease entity is recognized and met with fear and foreboding. Later it becomes identified and named

TABLE 11.1 Definitions of Chronic Illness Terms

TERM	DEFINITION
Disease	An *objective* and medically definable process characterized by pathophysiology and pathology
Acute disease	A disease entity with a single cause, a specific onset, identifiable symptoms, which are often treatable with a single biological intervention (e.g. drug or surgery), and which is usually curable
Chronic disease	A disease entity, which usually does *not* have a single cause, a specific onset, nor a stable set of symptoms. While cure may be possible for a mild level, it is unlikely for moderate and advanced levels of disease process. The disease course tends to be marked by periods of exacerbation and remission as well as progressive degeneration. Biopsychosocial interventions are commonly used to achieve treatment goals of coping, management, or palliation. The levels of the chronic disease process are: ■ Mild ■ Moderate ■ Advanced
Illness	The *subjective* experience of a disease
Chronic illness	The *subjective* experience of a chronic disease
Impairment	The *objective* limitation of capacity or functional ability
Disability	The *social* definition of limitation of capacity or functional ability based on degree of impairment

and after being studied and treated sufficiently, the disease entity becomes accepted as part of everyday social reality. This entire process of disease enculturation can extend over several years and individuals who are diagnosed with the disease earlier in the process are more likely to be negatively impacted by others than if they contracted the disease later in the enculturation process.

■ *Influence of the media*—While the mass media can educate the public by conveying medical findings on chronic diseases, it can significantly influence and reinforce social stereotypes and cultural biases. Moreover, feature stories about a given chronic illness can result in an invasion of privacy, as "friends and coworkers have access to intimate details of your illness which you may not really want to share with them. You may not have even experienced aspects of the disease that are dramatized, but people will be convinced that you must have" (Fennell, 2001, p. 25).

A PHASE MODEL OF CHRONIC ILLNESS

Fennell (2001) describes a phase model of chronic illness. She uses the term *phase* rather than *stage* because stages imply a forward moving progression whereas phase implies that both progression and regression are possible. The descriptions of the four phases that follow are based on Fennell's clinical research with several hundred clients with a variety of chronic diseases.

- *Phase one: Crisis*—The onset of illness triggers a crisis for which individuals seek relief through medical diagnosis and treatment, spiritual help, or substance abuse. Family, coworkers and caregivers can respond with disbelief, revulsion, and rejection. In this phase, the basic task is to deal with the immediate symptoms, pain, or traumas associated with this new experience of illness.
- *Phase two: Stabilization*—A plateaus of symptoms is reached, and individuals become more familiar with their illnesses. Individuals attempt to carry on their pre-illness activity level, which overtaxes them and contributes to relapses and the ensuing feelings of upset and failure. The basic task of this phase is to stabilize and restructure life patterns and perceptions.
- *Phase three: Resolution*—Amidst plateaus of symptoms and relapses, individuals understand their illness pattern and others' response to it. There is initial acceptance that a pre-illness sense of self will not return. In this phase, the basic task is to develop a new self and to seek a personally meaningful philosophy of life and spirituality consistent with it.
- *Phase four: Integration*—Despite plateaus and relapses individuals are able to integrate parts of their old selves before the illness into their new selves. The basic task in this phase is to find appropriate employment if able to work, to reintegrate or form supportive networks of friends and family, and to integrate the illness into a spiritual or philosophical framework.

Not every individual with a chronic illness manages to journey through all four stages. As Fennell points out, many chronically ill individuals get caught in a recurring loop of cycle between phase one and phase two wherein each crisis produces new wounding and destabilization of their biopsychosocial system. Such crises tend to be followed by a brief period of stabilization and, without intervention, a new crisis invariably destabilizes the system again. With appropriate health-focused counseling, chronically ill individuals can be assisted to break this recurring cycle and move on to phases three and four.

Some people, particularly those on the margins of society with almost no sources of support, never escape phase one. "They are buffeted from crisis to crisis, some relieved only by alcohol and drugs. These individuals often lose everything they have . . . simply because they are sick and have not received the care and help they need" (Fennell, 2001, pp. 40–41).

Thus, appropriate and competent health-focused counseling can help chronically ill individuals find a new meaning in life and be encouraged to develop coping skills to live that life with a measure of dignity and a sense of wellness. The following case, adapted from Fennell (2001), illustrates the phases.

Case Example

Betty is in her late 30s, is married with two children. She works part-time at a bank in her suburb while her husband, a computer consultant, travels 1 to 2 weeks a month.

- *Phase one*—Over several weeks she notices that she has become increasingly fatigued with blurry vision and, at times, has trouble walking. She pushes herself with her regular family and work responsibilities despite not feeling well. At a certain point she consults with her family physician who cannot find objective evidence of a disease process but suggests that she cut back on work, relax more, and join an exercise class. She is unable to follow these suggestions since her symptoms worsen and now she has difficulty driving. Her doctor responds by ordering a full medical evaluation which yields a presumptive diagnosis of multiple sclerosis (MS). Having a diagnosis provides Betty with a way to make sense of and explain her symptomatic experiences to others. Nevertheless she experiences feelings of shame, self-hatred, fear, and depression. She wonders if she is losing her mind or even dying. She also feels increasingly isolated from her husband, family, and coworkers. Although her supervisor is supportive, she fears that others will reject her, so she is very cautious about expressing both her pain and her fears at work and at home.

- *Phase two*—Betty's physical symptoms begin to stabilize and she recognizes a pattern in her energy level, pain threshold, and mood swings. She experiences two physical relapses with a sudden, increased intensity to her symptoms, which are relieved with prescribed steroid medication. She reads and talks widely to learn as much as she can about MS, yet she is unable to find someone who will guarantee a cure, remove her symptoms, or effectively cope with her situation. There is growing conflict with her family and a loss of patience among some of her care providers. Persistence of symptoms is increasingly frustrating for everyone. Her coworkers are annoyed that she can't "pull herself together" and her husband gives her the ultimatum to get well or get divorced. She experiences stigma for the first time in her life, but silently accepts others' labeling, misinformation, and nastiness. On the other hand, Betty has developed a support system of a few loyal friends, a nurse practitioner, and a social worker whom she began seeing about her family, friends, and job concerns.

- *Phase three*—She is now experiencing longer periods of stability and occasionally slight improvement, which is short-lived and followed by relapses. Betty recognizes that efforts to return to being her old, productive self inevitably lead to relapse. As a result, she focuses less on finding a cure and more on grieving the loss of her old self. With the help of the social worker, she struggles to find a new sense of meaning in life, and begins keeping a journal of this new journey. She is overwhelmed with the prospect of a divorce but is able to reach an amicable agreement about custody, finances, and health insurance for herself and the kids. Slowly and painfully, a new self begins to emerge as she begins to consider and pursue new roles and new friends in her life. As time passes, she also feels increasingly empowered and assertive in confronting others' bias and stigmatizing comments.

- *Phase four*—Betty has become better at recognizing and accepting the cyclic nature—plateau, improvement, and relapse—of her illness and comes to view relapse as inevitable but no longer as a failure. She is also more able to incorporate salvageable parts of her pre-illness self with her newly emerging sense of self, as well as to integrate her suffering with a greater sense of compassion and respect. Fortunately, she has also been able to reintegrate some of her formerly alienated family and friends. She befriended another student in an evening writing course and they have dated a few times during the past month. Whether this will lead to a committed relationship remains to be seen. Finally, because of the increasing difficulty she has experienced in working outside the home, she sought and found a home-based position running a MS Web site and chat room.

This case example is an accurate portrayal of how an individual with a chronic and progressively debilitating condition such as MS can achieve a reasonably high level of wellness despite the ravages of an noncurable disease process.

■ ■ ■ ■ ■

RELATIONSHIP AND ENGAGEMENT ISSUES: COUNTERTRANSFERENCE

In Chapter 1, countertransference was described as a relational phenomenon referring to all the emotional reactions, positive or negative, elicited in a health-care provider by a client or patient (Goodheart, 1997; Fennell, 2001). Because of the very nature of chronic illness, countertransference may be more common in health-focused counseling and health-focused psychotherapy provided those with chronic diseases than to most other forms of health counseling.

Fennell (2001) lists a number of reasons why countertransference is so common in health care and, particularly, health counseling, including the following:

- *Disbelief*—Because of the waxing and waning nature of chronic illness symptoms, providers may be hesitant to believe symptom patients' reports that are not apparent or do not match the findings of a physical examination or lab reports at the time of their appointment. This may result in patients misreporting symptoms in order to please providers whom they are fearful of offending.
- *Intolerance of suffering*—While most providers feel competent and successful in their efforts to relieve pain and suffering in acute disease patients, they often feel much less successful and competent attempting to relieve pain and suffering in those with chronic illnesses. Despite their best efforts providers may be become quite intolerant of patients' suffering, which "makes it even more difficult for patients to learn to work with their suffering" (Fennell, 2001, p. 222).
- *Intolerance of chronicity and ambiguity*—Since cure is associated with success in U.S. health care, health providers may feel they have failed in their efforts to treat chronic illness. Patients and their families may also feel that providers have failed them. As a result some providers refuse to be involved in the treatment of chronic diseases. Moreover, because little is known about them and symptoms seem to constantly change, providers perceive chronic diseases as ambiguous.
- *Avoidance of chronic illness patients*—Because chronic diseases do not fit the acute illness–cure model of Western medicine in which most providers have been trained, chronic illness symptoms are easily perceived as psychological in nature or as malingering (i.e., falsifying or faking a symptom or illness). This leads to avoiding such

patients through refusal to treat them or referral to other providers. Similarly, providers who are committed to treating chronic disease may be regarded as having lower professional status than those treating acute disease.

Suggestions for Dealing with Countertransference

First, effectively dealing with countertransference begins with the recognition that the phenomenon does exist in health counseling situations. Second, contrary to the view that it is always harmful, countertransference can potentially aid providers in their professional work with patients and clients. Third, providers must recognize countertransference feelings, both positive and negative, when they arise and then process them, as Fennell (2001) notes:

> They must listen attentively to their patients to hear on all levels what [they] have to say. They've also got to "listen" to themselves. Later, when they have time to reflect, [providers] must examine their feelings and develop insight and understanding as to why they've had these feelings with this patient in this situation, On the basis of this insight, they must try to see whether and how they can use what they've learned about themselves to help their patients. (p. 223)

Fourth, providers may also find it useful to consult with a supervisor or senior colleague who is experienced with countertransference issues.

ASSESSMENT

If counselors are to help people cope effectively with illness, they need to recognize that the medical examination and the diagnosis are only the first steps in assessment. Successful treatment planning requires a clear understanding of the kinds of personal, behavioral, and social factors that might affect clients' success in managing illness and limiting its effects.

Williamson, Davis, and Prather (1988) suggest several assessment techniques that can help in treatment planning for people affected by certain health disorders. Behavioral assessment, for example, has obvious relevance for clients with coronary heart disease. Behavioral risk factors, including the Type A behavior pattern and lifestyle-related behaviors (e.g., eating habits, exercise regimen, and smoking and drinking behaviors), play a part in the origin and control of heart disease. Once a medical diagnosis has been made, procedures for assessing the behavioral factors can be implemented.

The Type A personality profile, which involves time urgency, aggressiveness, hostility, competitiveness, and restlessness, can be measured through use of a structured interview (Rosenman et al., 1964), the Jenkins Activity Survey (Jenkins, Rosenman, & Friedman, 1967), or the Framingham Type A Scale (Haynes et al., 1980). These data, along with information regarding the client's participation in health risk activities, can help in treatment planning by identifying behaviors that should be targeted for change.

Personality and behavioral factors may also affect outcomes for cancer patients, so interviews and inventories that measure psychological characteristics and emotional states can be useful. Because a diagnosis of cancer is very stressful and because the side effects of its treatments are often severe, a number of psychological and physiological symptoms can appear. The Psychological Adjustment to Cancer Scale (DiClemente & Temoshok, 1986), the Health Survey (Frank-Stromborg & Wright, 1984), and symptom checklists (McCorkle & Young, 1978) can give some indication of the physical and psychosocial changes associated with the cancer diagnosis.

Williamson and his colleagues cite asthma as an additional example of a disease with strong psychosocial components. Careful assessment can help identify the role of emotional factors in precipitating or exacerbating attacks and pinpoint the psychological effects of symptoms. The Asthma Symptom Checklist (Kinsman et al., 1977) measures subjective reports of asthmatic symptomatology, and the Creer, Marion, and Creer (1983) Asthma Problem Behavior Checklist (APBC) identifies specific behavior problems that may exacerbate asthma and that should be addressed. The APBC also illuminates issues related to family systems, which appear to play a major role in affecting the severity of the disease.

Finally, the notions the patient or client has about illness can be as important as a health professional's own perception of the means to provide comfort and care. Careful assessment of biological, psychological, social, and cultural factors all comprise a comprehensive assessment of coping behaviors.

Assessment Tools

Efforts to develop specialized, disease-specific assessment tools continue. Just as promising are efforts to develop and validate instruments that address more general health issues. Among those that can help in a biopsychosocial assessment are the following.

- *Health and Daily Living Form* (Moos, Cronkite, Billings, & Finney, 1984)—The HDL form is a 200-item instrument that can be self- or interviewer-administered. It assesses health-related functioning, social functioning and resources, family functioning and home environment, children's health and functioning, life-change events, and coping responses. This form is one of the few instruments that takes life circumstances and events outside of the treatment milieu into account.
- *Psychosocial Adjustment to Illness Scale* (Derogatis, 1977)—The PAIS self-report assesses the client's adjustment to his or her illness. The instrument yields a score for overall adjustment to the illness as well as subscores in several related domains.
- *Health Locus of Control Inventory* (Wallston, Wallston, & Devellis, 1978)—This inventory assesses the individual's attributions concerning health outcomes. Given the importance of the cognitive factor of control in individual health behaviors, this inventory can help the counselor anticipate problems in the client's progress.
- *Millon Behavioral Medicine Diagnostic* (MBMD) (Millon, Antoni, Millon, Mengher, & Grossman, 2001) and *Millon Behavioral Health Inventory* (MBHI) (Millon, Green, & Meagher, 1982)—The MBMD is the revision of the MBHI. Both are designed for use with clients dealing with medical problems. This self-administered instrument yields scores on a number of variables associated with health behaviors and outcomes. Eight scales identify coping styles, six measure the existence of psychosocial stressors

associated with illness, and six assess emotional factors that might be associated with psychosomatic illnesses or complications. The scales were designed to assess the presence of factors that are shown by research to relate to health outcomes (e.g., chronic tension, recent stress, pre-illness pessimism, social alienation). Several scales were designed for use with patients diagnosed with allergy, gastrointestinal problems, or cardiovascular disease; they compare a client's responses with those of patients whose illnesses have been complicated by psychosocial factors or whose course of treatment was unsatisfactory.

- *Symptom Check List-90, Revised* (Derogatis et al., 1983). This 90-item checklist has been used with patients in medical settings, although it was originally designed for use with psychiatric patients. Clients are asked to record the degree of difficulty they currently feel—are experiencing—with regard to each problem.

The use of these assessment instruments, as well as others that might focus more directly on an individual client's needs, can lead the way toward treatment planning that addresses issues beyond the medical diagnosis. Ideally, client evaluation in any medical setting should take personal and environmental dimensions, as well as biological factors, into account (Schwartz, 1982).

INTERVENTION ISSUES AND STRATEGIES

A client who is coping with an illness may need assistance in making emotional, behavioral, and social adaptations. Health counseling strategies can address each of these needs, whether services are provided in a medical setting or in the context of ongoing personal counseling. The sections that follow review some promising approaches and discuss some pressing issues related to illness. It is, of course, far beyond the scope of this chapter to address any more than a small sampling of the health problems with which people are forced to cope in contemporary society. For this reason, specific illnesses are used only as examples to illustrate various types of interventions.

Managing Chronic Diseases

Managing or coping with chronic disease has been the basic intervention strategy used over the past several decades. Recently, the concept of managing chronic disease has been changing—a more proactive self-management role is being promoted. The traditional approach was for a health-care provider to give instructions and hope individuals would adhere to them; the hope was to delay disease progression. There was no realistic expectation that the disease could be cured or even reversed.

Today, however, individuals with a chronic disease are being encouraged to take a more active role in the treatment process. Effective interventions now include a broad range of health, lifestyle, and self-assessment and treatment behaviors by the individual, often with the assistance and support of others. The promotion and maintenance of a healthful and satisfying life in the presence of chronic disease requires individuals to assume a more proactive role with health-care providers, particularly those providing health counseling.

The personal and social costs of chronic disease can be decreased by improving and supporting a healthy lifestyle and self-management behaviors of those affected by chronic disease. Researchers have developed several effective interventions, including *lifestyle management* and *self-management,* for chronic diseases. Many interventions, however, were developed in one chronic disease population and not adequately tested in other chronic disease populations (Lorig et al., 2000; Goodheart, 1997; DiLima, 1997). Interventions involving social support, improved self-efficacy, problem-solving or coping skills, and certain follow-up activities have a positive impact on self-management and health outcomes for specific chronic diseases. This has impacts on both affected individuals and significant others.

Not surprisingly, among health professionals there is growing interest in interventions that can be applied across chronic diseases. Standard health counseling interventions requiring minimal adaptation to a particular disease have the potential to be more cost-effective and less complicated to translate into practice than those requiring extensive adaptation to each health condition. Nevertheless, more research is needed before such effective interventions will be identified for chronic diseases. The next sections describe the lifestyle management and self-management intervention strategies for chronic illnesses.

Lifestyle Management.   Lifestyle management is a health-promotion counseling strategy useful in dealing with clients who have a mild level of chronic disease. Also called a subclinical conditions (i.e., mildly symptomatic conditions), this level of chronic disease typically has not yet progressed to clinical or diagnosable conditions. For example, type II diabetes is a clinical condition increasingly diagnosed in middle-age and older adults. Also known as adult-onset or noninsulin-dependent diabetes, type II diabetes afflicts some 95 percent of the 16 million diabetics in the United States. It is estimated that there are another 60 million with prediabetes or subclinical forms of type II diabetes.

There are three subclinical forms of type II diabetes. The first and easiest to reverse is insulin resistance; the second is hyperinsulinism, also called Syndrome X; while the third is blood sugar abnormalities. Because it is a subclinical condition, symptoms such as fatigue and signs (e.g., weight gain and high triglycerides and low HDL cholesterol) are often not recognized as indicators of insulin resistance. Unlike advanced level chronic disease for which the goal is to achieve a sense of integration (i.e., phase four) and a higher level of wellness, the goal for mild level chronic disease is improved health functioning and possibly cure, or something close to cure, as well as a higher level of wellness. The following case study involves treatment considerations for insulin resistance and another subclinical condition—joint pain associated with early osteoarthritis.

Case Example

Jack T was referred by his family physician for health counseling for stress reduction and weight management. Over a period of 3 months Jack had been given a diet plan and exercise by his physician, followed by weekly diet and stress-management "counseling" sessions by the clinic's nurse practitioner. Because these efforts had made little difference, the referral was made to a psychologist with expertise in health counseling. Jack is a building contractor and has six construction workers and one estimator who report to him. He is also an avid part-time soccer coach at his children's private school. He is 41, has been married for 14 years, and has a 12-year-old daughter and a 10-year-old son. For the past year, his energy and stamina have declined. He admits his job is stressful, but no more so than it has been for several years. In addition to his declining energy levels, and occasional periods of moodiness and irritability, he took 11 sick days for various maladies, compared with no more than 1 or 2 sick days in previous years. Because Jack is the boss and coordinates the work of employees, missed days mean lower productivity for his company. Being away from work only increased his stress level. He has been eating more and gaining weight.

The initial health evaluation assessed this client's energy pattern, stress response pattern, body type and weight gain pattern, as well as personality and relational patterns. With some focused questioning, the psychologist learned that Jack's diet consistently contains mostly complex carbohydrates, no red meat, and only occasional fish and chicken. Jack said he was embarrassed to admit that he craves snack foods—chocolate covered nuts, donuts, and chocolate chip cookies—but added that he also snacked on apples, grapes, and bananas. Except for an occasional glass of wine, he used no other alcohol or recreational drugs, and had never smoked. He took a number of vitamins, some minerals and herbs, but no prescription medicines.

Jack indicated that the nurse practitioner had him start on a high-carbohydrate, low-fat diet. He agreed to it because his wife had used such a diet to return to her ideal weight for the first time since the birth of their first child. Jack noted that it was ironic: she had lost weight but he had actually gained an additional 15 pounds on the diet despite his 4 hours of exercise a week! He had been jogging for 20 years, even though his knee joints were becoming increasingly painful and arthritic. Jack made it clear that he was not interested in taking prescription medicine for either stress or weight loss; however, he agreed to a medical evaluation.

Before they met again, the psychologist referred Jack for a comprehensive medical evaluation. It had been more than 3 years since his last physical and lab tests. The extensive lab testing, given a family history of heart disease, included a cardiac stress test. The report of that evaluation indicated that Jack was approximately 32 pounds above an optimal weight for someone his age and level of conditioning. His cardiac stress test was in the normal range and exhibited a level of exercise conditioning usually seen in amateur athletes. He was noted to have chronic sinusitis and mild to moderate levels of osteoarthritis in both knees and the right hips. Two treatment recommendations were provided.

To reduce sinus symptoms, it was recommended that he reduce sugar and eliminate dairy products from his diet. In addition, a trial glucosamine sulfate, an extraordinarily effective natural remedy, was suggested for 12 weeks; and a referral to a joint specialist would be made if the trail was not successful. The diagnosis of insulin dependence, which the examining physician said was the first stage of adult-onset or type II diabetes, was also given along with the recommendation for an initial trial of either weight loss or medication. Overall, the physician assessed Jack's health status as being average to above average for individuals his age and gender.

Jack met with the psychologist 2 weeks later to review the medical evaluation and continue the health assessment. An important focus of that session was on assessing client strengths and motivation for change as well as establishing an intervention plan. His current readiness for change was assessed as at the decision level. In short, Jack appeared to be a good candidate for health counseling given that he had target symptoms and was reasonably motivated in terms of readiness for change.

The psychologist suggested a 10-session course of counseling over a 6-month period. Sessions would be 45 minutes a week for 5 weeks, followed by biweekly and then monthly sessions. Two health-promotion target goals were proposed: stress reduction and weight loss and maintenance (i.e., to be within 10 percent of his ideal weight). Three intervention strategies would be involved: an individualized diet plan, an individualized stress-management plan, and an individualized exercise program. A contract was made in which Jack agreed to the goals and made the personal and time commitment to the intervention strategies.

Their next session focused on increasing readiness for change and identifying reasons why his recent efforts at weight loss and stress reduction with the nurse practitioner had failed. Not surprisingly Jack noted his discouragement at gaining weight on the prescribed diet and the increase in his cravings for sweets. The psychologist described the concept of biological individuality and the difference between one-size-fits-all health programs and individualized diet, exercise, and stress-management prescriptions.

A profile of health concerns, health status, health behaviors, personality patterns, and body type was shared with Jack. The psychologist noted that his energy level was inconsistent throughout the day; that he craved sweet and starchy food, he was creative, impatient, irritable and easily angered; and that he appeared to be carrying most of his weight around his waist and hips (i.e., love handles). Psychosocially, Jack had a variety of friends and colleagues and was most attracted to individuals who were original thinkers and stimulating conversationalists, and he seemed energized and exhilarated when initiating new projects but most stressed when finishing projects and engaging in work that was repetitive, detailed, and tedious. The process of describing and explaining Jack's unique dietary needs and his stress pattern, a key strategy in motivational counseling, fostered a shift from the decision to the action level of readiness.

They talked about the health patterns that Jack exhibited and they talked about ways to optimize his diet in order to both reduce his food cravings and lose weight. It appeared that the high-carbohydrate diet he had been on was a poor match for him. The nutritional strategy that better matched him was one with more protein, emphasizing eggs, poultry, fish, with some complex carbohydrates but limited nonstarchy vegetables.

It appeared that Jack's exercise plan needed fine-tuning too. A more optimal exercise strategy would emphasize strength training with some aerobic conditioning. Jack expressed interest in working with a personal trainer who could design and monitor a strength training program for him. It is interesting to note that given his joint pain and damage, the trainer urged Jack to replace jogging with lap swimming. Another key part of the recommended changes involved stress reduction and management. As was noted, Jack was overly stressed by job functions that required extensive involvement in detail-oriented oversight of ongoing construction sites. The psychologist asked whether it was possible to shift much of this activity to one of his employees. Jack indicated that this was actually one of his foreman's duties, but though it was not one of his stated job functions, he had believed he needed to roll up his sleeves and show employees his personal commitment to projects. It had become even clearer that he was a "big picture" person rather than a "detail" person, so delegation increased Jack's job-fit considerably. It was mutually agreed to try the recommendations for 4 months and evaluate the outcomes.

A major focus of the third, fourth, and fifth sessions was on Jack's operating belief that "if you want something done right, you have to do it yourself." His underlying schema of perfectionism came under therapeutic scrutiny. Through the use of cognitive-restructuring and reframing, this operating belief was sufficiently modified so that Jack felt increasing comfortable in reducing his micromanagement at each construction site. Decreasing his level of involvement in a job function, which was actually not his but that of his foreman, was a strategic part of the stress-reduction prescription.

During their eighth session, Jack indicated he was feeling considerably better. He felt less pressured and irritable since he had successfully delegated many onsite management responsibilities to his foreman. Now he was simply monitoring progress at various sites on a weekly basis. Using his creativity to conceptualize and plan new projects was not only immensely gratifying for him, but also more energizing and less stressful. Furthermore, being on the new diet plan, exercise routine, and glucosemine sulfates seemed to be working. He was now within 5 pounds of his ideal weight, and his sinus and joint symptoms were considerably lessened. His physician indicated that his lab tests revealed no indication of diabetes or insulin resistance.

At 6 months Jack continued to do well. For the first time since college, he was at his ideal weight. He enjoyed lap swimming and strength training workouts with his trainer and was able to exercise without joint pain. The elimination of dairy products from his diet had nearly eliminated sinus congestion. He had taken only one sick day in 10 months.

■ ■ ■ ■ ■

Self-Management.   Cardiac rehabilitation provides a good example of the importance of a behavioral self-management approach. People who are recovering from myocardial infarction (MI) are faced with the need to make major lifestyle changes at the same time that they are trying to cope with the stress of their illness. If rehabilitation is to be successful and recurrences prevented, patients need to: (1) change health risk behaviors such as smoking, high-cholesterol diets, and lack of physical activity; (2) alter Type A behavioral patterns; and (3) learn how to manage stress without eliciting heightened cardiovascular responses (Langosch, 1984). Several projects have demonstrated success in bringing about behavioral changes and thereby avoiding multiple acute episodes.

The Recurrent Coronary Prevention Project (Thoresen & Eagleston, 1985), for instance, focused on altering Type A behavioral responses through group interventions using discussion, modeling, relaxation training, and practice. Clients learned how to alter the cognitions, behaviors, and environmental and physiological factors associated with the Type A personality; Thoreson and Eagleston note:

> In the cognitive area, treatment covered such topics as self-instructional training, evaluation of basic beliefs, active listening skills, and mental relaxation. Behaviorally, participants learned to alter certain speech patterns (such as interrupting others), psychomotor actions (such as excessive or abrupt emphatic gesturing), and other physical activities (such as reducing hurried walking [and] fast eating, and increasing smiling and complimentary comments). . . . The basics of social problem solving were used to help participants alter stressful environmental factors, such as revising work routines cooperatively with a supervisor or scheduling time to practice relaxation. Physiologically, participants were informed how biochemical processes appear to function in chronic stress reactions. . . . The feelings of anger,

> irritation, aggravation, and impatience . . . were equated with potential increases in a variety
> of biochemical and cardiovascular variables. (pp. 60–61)

These interventions were found to have a positive impact on rehabilitation. Participants had significantly fewer repeat infraction than did those in a control group. The best results in terms of recurrence were shown by the clients who had shown the most substantial changes in their behaviors.

Razin (1984) also reported good results for a cardiac stress-management training program that focused on psychosocial rehabilitation for a group of post-MI patients. The program's weekly sessions included: (1) discussion of risk factors and their modifiability; (2) progressive relaxation training; (3) cognitive-behavioral approaches to stress management, including the use of stress diaries and "self-talk" practice; (4) work on modification of Type A behaviors, including the use of videotapes to provide feedback on individual behaviors; and (5) anger-management training. Favorable results were reported for behavioral, physiological, and self-report measures.

An interesting aspect of Razin's study was the active involvement of spouses who participated with the patients in the training program. This approach reflects an important trend in the health field. Regardless of the particular disease or disability being addressed, family members are always deeply affected. Any attempt to help individuals cope with illnesses brings with it the need to work with their families as well.

Dealing with the Impact of Illness on the Family

Of course, the illness of a family member has a major impact on the family unit as a whole; Turk and Kerns (1985) report:

> Few health professionals or family scholars challenge the proposition that illness or impairment in a family member has adverse effects on family functioning. Most agree that families of ill people generally function more poorly than families in which all the members are healthy. With the onset of an illness, the family's social life contracts and becomes primarily family centered. Within this circumscribed existence, the patient often becomes the focus of the family, with other family members forced into the background. . . . The more severe and long-lasting the illness or impairment, the greater the potential for family disruption. (p. 15)

Illness can be highly disruptive to a family's functioning, but many families do manage to cope with this stress and even become more cohesive in the process. Families that have shown a general ability to function well can continue to do so even in the wake of a serious health crisis; they can effectively cope with the disruption of illness and, at the same time, play an important role in supporting and assisting the affected family member. Family-focused interventions should have a dual emphasis: (1) supporting and strengthening family units as a means for enhancing the adaptation of the individual patient, and (2) helping the family system as a whole maintain its functionality despite illness-related crises or challenges. Most efforts have tended to focus on the family's role in helping the affected individual achieve health stabilization or improvement.

A good example of a chronic illness that can act as a major family stressor is diabetes mellitus, as Hamburg, Elliott, and Parron (1982) note:

> Despite medical advances, following the diagnosis of diabetes the patient and family still must adapt to a radically altered life. There are continuing stresses such as living with the foreboding of a shortened lifespan for the patient; the specter of severe complications that may result in coronary disease, blindness, stroke, amputation, or other major physical handicaps; apprehension over unpredictable occurrence of insulin reactions or life-threatening crises related to ketoacidosis; and pervasive concern over ability to handle these crises. At best, there are [the] daily problems of fitting a personal and family lifestyle around monitoring and regulating the diet, exercise, and medication of the diabetic patien. (p. 147)

The family as a whole must make major adaptations, as would be the case with any serious illness. In the case of diabetes, an additional challenge is created by the urgent need for adherence to a complicated medical regimen involving a high degree of self-care.

The individual affected with this disease has major health-related tasks to perform, including careful, long-term self-assessment and adherence to self-administered medical regimens, which can be complex. "The diabetic patient really needs to be his or her own physician" (Hendrick, 1985, p. 521). For an affected individual, compliance with treatment may involve monitoring blood sugar levels; making decisions concerning insulin injections; using oral medications; and maintaining ongoing health behaviors (e.g., a carefully regulated diet, a weight-control regimen, and an exercise program). According to Hendrick (1985), the family's success in adapting to the challenges of the disease may have a major affect on the individual's success with self-treatment:

> The family plays an especially important role in adherence for children. The family is an important ingredient in treatment. If the diabetic's parents are educated about the disease, offer help and support, encourage independence, stress a "health-care" orientation to the disease . . . and in general focus on the child rather than the disease, normal family development and interaction should ensue. However, this optimum level of behavior is extremely difficult to achieve. . . . Obsessive concern with diabetic control by parents can result in either rebelliousness or in almost overcompliance by a child, neither extreme a healthy one. On the other hand, denial of or uninvolvement with the diabetes by parents can be disastrous. (p. 127)

As the health counselor works with the diabetic child to enhance the likelihood of adherence to treatment regimens, he or she should also work with other family members. Although knowledge of the disease is important, awareness of the challenges of self-care may have even greater significance. The more that family members understand about the nature of the self-care skills required, the more they will be able to help and support the child's efforts. Family members may also need assistance in examining their own reactions to the child's health problems so that they can balance positive concern with recognition of the child's need for control. This process is further complicated by the need to make changes in response to the child's development. As Johnson (1985) points out, the disease of a young child is best controlled through active parental involvement and "giving the youngster too much responsibility too early may prove disastrous" (p. 225). In contrast, adolescents show better results if they control their own regimens. Families may need ongoing help and support if they are to adapt to constant changes in the disease itself and in the patient's psychosocial needs.

One helpful approach is to provide assistance in the context of family support groups, which can furnish mutual nurturance along with skill development. This type of intervention may be especially useful in helping families cope with illnesses that tend to exacerbate feelings of helplessness. For example, family support groups have been used for dealing with health problems such as adult cancer (Dunkel-Schetter & Wortman, 1982; Euster, 1984), childhood cancer (Chesler & Yoak, 1984), Alzheimer's disease (Kapust & Weintraub, 1984; Kerns & Curley, 1985), spinal cord injuries (Eisenberg, 1984), and multiple sclerosis (Pavlou, 1984)—all of which tend to be intensely crisis-provoking.

Case Example

Mark T was told after his bypass surgery at age 48 that he would have to make major changes in his lifestyle. Mark was a hard-driving executive, dedicated to his work but also intensely involved in competitive sports. In his youth, he had concentrated on team sports: football and hockey. Now, his focus was on handball and golf; his country club trophies provide evidence of his success.

Mark's wife, Ellen, was desperately concerned about his health. She felt that the bypass surgery had given him a new chance for longevity. She thought that this experience, which had come as a surprise after what they had thought was a routine checkup, should have jolted him into reality and forced him in the direction of more health-oriented behaviors. She has tried to help him maintain a low-cholesterol diet; in fact, she and their two teenage children have begun to eat differently because of her attempts to prepare healthful meals that Mark might enjoy. She became more and more upset because, despite her efforts, Mark has failed to bring his cholesterol under control. She knew that he ate correctly at home but consumed whatever he wanted at restaurant lunches and during business travel. She also realized that, although her reminders had stopped him from smoking in the house, he continued to "sneak" cigarettes at his office. Mark insisted that he was, in fact, healthy and that his continued athletic success proved it. He worked as hard as he ever had and tended to lose his temper when Ellen confronted him.

Mark was referred for health counseling by the coronary rehabilitation unit because follow-up checks showed no change in his cholesterol levels or in his stress tests. The Jenkins Activity Survey indicated a clear tendency toward a Type A behavior pattern. Mark's wife indicated that this result was accurate and that time urgency, competitiveness, and restlessness continued to be his most obvious characteristics both at work and in his leisure time.

The counselor's first intervention for Mark and Ellen T involved short-term counseling for the couple. The focus of this counseling process was placed on the question of responsibility for Mark's health risk behaviors. Ellen had become overly responsible for his behavior; the more responsibility she took, the less Mark accepted. As long as this pattern of interaction continued, Ellen felt frustrated and powerless and Mark ignored the problem. The couples' counseling helped bring this process to Mark and Ellen's awareness so that both could begin to interrupt their circular pattern. Ellen tried to turn the responsibility for his health back over to Mark, although she was able to do this only through the support of a group of women whose husbands had had either myocardial infarctions or surgery.

Mark was referred to a training group that focused on helping heart patients regain their health through behavioral changes. He and the other participants learned behavioral self-management strategies to change Type A patterns and eliminate high-risk behaviors such as smoking and eating foods high in cholesterol.

The educational component of the program helped Mark identify the differences in effect between aerobic exercise and the kind of sports involvement to which he was accustomed. In reality, however, Mark was a highly educated person who already possessed this information on a cognitive level. Individual counseling helped him explore his reactions to the health crisis he had endured and understand that his denial of the need to change his behavior was in part related to his reluctance to face the fact of his mortality.

■ ■ ■ ■ ■

Dealing with Psychological Reactions to Illness

The onset of serious illness represents one of the most disruptive crises an individual can endure. When an illness has been diagnosed, the client must ready himself or herself to cope with what may be a staggering number of separate problems. Among the many nagging questions—some conscious and some unconscious—for which the client must seek answers are the following:

- Will I be completely incapacitated?
- Do I face a life of pain?
- Will I be able to make the changes that the doctor has said I have to make?
- Will I have to be dependent on others to take care of me?
- What will this mean for my family and my relationships with family members?
- Can I still see myself as a sexual being?
- How will this affect my relationships with friends and colleagues?
- Will I be able to participate in any kind of recreation?
- Will I have to give up my job or my career plans?
- Will my family and I be wiped out financially?
- Will I be completely isolated?
- Is this my fault?
- Is there a God?
- Will I live?

These questions are particularly important in the context of the anxiety and fear brought about by diagnosis of a life-threatening illness. Consider, as an example, the plight of the individual whose illness has been diagnosed as Acquired Immune Deficiency Syndrome (AIDS).

Persons with AIDS (PWAs) can be expected to go through stages of adaptation similar to those experienced by people who have received diagnoses for other life-threatening illnesses (Macks & Turner, 1986; Mandel, 1986; Mejta, 1987). At the earliest stage, when the diagnosis is first received, a client may respond with denial or with strong emotions such as shock, anxiety, depression, fear, and anger. As the reality of the diagnosis becomes engrained in the person's perception, he or she may continue to experience these emotions and may also develop feelings of worthlessness, self-devaluation, social withdrawal, and isolation; suicidal ideas may intensify. As the individual moves toward acceptance of the AIDS diagnosis, he or she may become ready to take more responsibility for participation in decisions and behaviors related to treatment. If the PWA is able to deal with fears and concerns about impending death, he or she can make emotional and practical preparations.

Not all clients move in an orderly way through these stages however. Recognizing the existence of the stages can help the counselor become aware of the individual client's issues. Often, however, clients move in and out of stages in reaction to changes in symptoms or treatments (Mejta, 1987).

The adjustment of a client diagnosed with AIDS is further complicated by the effects of prejudice, discrimination, and blame. The phenomenon of blaming the victim for bad outcomes in his or her life is exacerbated by society's view of people who have a diagnosis of AIDS, as Mejta (1987) notes:

> This tendency, prodded by panic, fear, and misinformation about AIDS and already existing prejudices toward groups particularly at risk for contracting AIDS, is especially strong when attributing responsibility or blame for contracting AIDS. Furthermore, it lays the groundwork for unfounded prejudices and discriminatory behaviors toward those with or at risk for AIDS. The stress already experienced . . . is exacerbated by society's reactions toward them. (p. 2)

Thus, people may be denied social support at the time in their lives when they need it the most. They may be targets of prejudice and irrational hatred at the point when their self-esteem is at its lowest point. Those diagnosed with AIDS may be forced to cope with practical problems (e.g., job discrimination and lack of funds for medical treatment) at the very time when their energy should be focused directly on self-care.

Coping processes are also complex and challenging for HIV-positive persons. As Cramer (1989) says, people who have been tested and whose blood shows antibodies to the human immunodeficiency virus (HIV) may be as highly stressed as PWAs.

> This seems to be a result of feeling like one may be a walking time bomb—knowing one is not completely healthy and yet not having any serious signs of illness. People who are HIV-positive carry similar stressors to people with AIDS, yet they must also live with the uncertainty of it—when and how their infection will progress (p. 63).

Counseling interventions for clients who have been diagnosed with AIDS or whose blood tests have shown them to be HIV-positive should include helping them come to terms with the diagnosis and its meaning, helping them improve the quality of their lives, and helping them feel more in control of their lives and their illness (Mejta, 1987; Namir, 1986). According to Mejta (1987):

> Psychological interventions should be sensitive to the individual's feelings, reactions, and experiences related to the AIDS diagnosis, the process of adjusting to it, and self-reported concerns and needs. Typically, both emotional and practical support is needed. (p. 5)

Assisting clients with an illness crisis may involve helping them sort out the kinds of coping mechanisms that are most likely to be useful. Active, problem-focused coping behaviors are generally considered to be healthier than passive efforts that focus on emotional adaptation or distancing from the problem. In fact, however, when situations are beyond individuals' control, denial or resignation may be healthy options. The counselor has to be sensitive to clients' perceptions of the situation, offering support for any efforts to make the decisions affecting their destiny. Whether clients' need is for practical problem-solving assistance or for an opportunity to vent emotion, the counselor needs to be able to adapt.

Whereas health professionals may choose to not intervene at supernatural or non-Western levels, they cannot ignore the power these beliefs may have in shaping a client's expression of illness, perceived coping skills and abilities, and the actual course and duration of an illness (Marsella & Yamada, 2001). This reality suggests that counselors may need to be open to alternative forms of treatment, which may include consulting or involving culturally relevant healers in the effort to bring a complete cure or treatment for members of a particular cultural tradition (Lee & Armstrong, 1995). Lee and Armstrong (1995) add that traditional healers, such as shamans, may provide a different orientation to healing and coping with illness that includes holistic health, alternative realities, and an emphasis on the spiritual realm of one's personality.

Coping with Aversive Medical Procedures

Clients also vary in the kinds of coping styles they use to deal with anxiety-provoking situations such as surgery or other aversive medical procedures. Such variations are associated both with personality differences and with differences in the demands of a particular situation. Some patients use a vigilant coping style, seeking information and taking active steps to maintain control of the situation, while others use an avoidant style in an effort to lower their anxiety. As Matthews and Ridgeway (1984) state, which coping style is more adaptive may depend on the nature of the situation:

> Presumably, nonanxious avoidant patients are naturally using strategies related to cognitive distraction, which facilitate their adaptation to surgery. . . . Whether this natural style is beneficial or detrimental may depend on whether distraction or related avoidant methods hold up during or after the actual stressful event. We would suggest that with low level or slowly rising pain, or when other anxiety-elevating stimuli are not too intrusive, this strategy is indeed an effective one. Generally speaking, a vigilant or monitoring style would be clearly preferable only when aversive stimuli or external threats cannot be ignored, either because they are too intense or because the threat demands some action requiring rehearsal or planning. (p. 256)

The success of the health counseling process depends on the counselor's sensitivity to the needs and coping styles of the individual client. Even given this assumption, however, the counselor can develop general strategies to help anyone prepare for medical procedures.

Mathews and Ridgeway (1984) reviewed a number of experimental studies that focused on the effects of processes used to help patients prepare psychologically for surgery. The types of *preparation* measured were categorized as follows: (1) procedural information (describing pre- and postoperative procedures, whether to reassure or to forewarn the individual); (2) sensation information (telling patients what they are likely to feel); (3) behavioral instructions (telling patients what they should do after surgery or during a medical procedure to facilitate recovery); (4) modeling (providing information through methods such as filmed models); (5) relaxation (using hypnosis or other methods to reduce patient anxiety and ability to cope with pain); and (6) cognitive coping training (encouraging the individual to identify fears or worries and counter them with positive self-statements). The measures used to assess patient recovery included (1) performance of recovery-relevant behaviors such as ambulation; (2) clinicians' ratings of recovery or adjustment; (3) length of stay from surgery to discharge; (4) amount of analgesics and other medications; (5) self-reported mood; (6) self-reported pain; and (7) physical indices, including medical complications.

This metaanalysis led Mathews and Ridgeway to note that psychological preparation for surgery was clearly associated with positive outcomes in terms of the recovery variables measured. Despite some individual differences, such as the likelihood that patients already using avoidant coping styles with some success might find unsought information disruptive, these researchers were able to generalize that "the evidence clearly favors the efficacy of sensation information, behavioral instructions (including relaxation), and cognitive coping methods in promoting recovery" (Mathews & Ridgeway, 1984, p. 256). Cognitive strategies were found to be consistently effective, but the successful methods probably interact with one another. Cognitive methods may help give the client a sense of the possibility of control, which in turn motivates him or her to use relaxation methods and follow other behavioral instructions. Sensation information, too, may enhance patients' sense of control by helping them avoid the anxiety and alarm associated with unexpected sensations; again, cognitive preparation may play an important role.

Some differences exist between the outcomes sought from preparatory strategies for surgery and the results desired when the client is being prepared for other procedures. Although other medical procedures may be painful or aversive, "physical recovery variables are less relevant and the main targets of psychological intervention are the reduction of anxiety during the procedure itself and facilitation of the patient's active cooperation" (Mathews & Ridgeway, 1984, p. 248).

Cognitive-behavioral strategies have proved equally successful in achieving these goals. For example, Kendall, Williams, Pechacek, Graham, Shisslak, and Herzoff (1979) reported on the use of cognitive-behavioral strategies in preparing patients for cardiac catheterization. These researchers compared the effectiveness of a cognitive-behavioral treatment and a patient-education treatment for reducing the stress of undergoing this diagnostic procedure. Their design also included the use of two control groups—one that received attention and one that was treated in accordance with current conditions. The cognitive-behavioral strategy used was an adaptation of stress inoculation (Meichenbaum, 1985), which involves helping people deal with stressful situations through preparation, skills training, and application and practice.

Kendall and his colleagues trained cardiac catheterization patients to identify aspects of the situation that they found stressful and to identify and apply the cognitive coping strategies that they found most helpful in lessening their anxiety. Cognitive and behavioral coping techniques were practiced in response to stress cues. The results of the study indicated that the people who received this cognitive-behavioral intervention adjusted to the procedure more effectively than did patients in any of the other groups. In a 1984 follow-up study, Kendall and Turk report:

Physicians and technicians independently rated the patients' behaviors during catheterization, and these ratings indicated that the patients receiving the cognitive-behavioral treatment were [the] best adjusted—that is, least tense, least anxious, most comfortable. . . . The patient-education group was rated as better adjusted than the two control groups but significantly less well adjusted than the cognitive-behavioral group. (p. 399)

Evidence has also been accumulating to indicate that cognitive and behavioral strategies may be useful in preparing people for other medical procedures, including endoscopy, sigmoidoscopy, electromyography, and dental surgery (Caplan, 1982, p. 187).

MAINTENANCE AND TREATMENT
ADHERENCE ISSUES

One of the most important functions of health counseling is to help clients develop the kinds of self-management skills that they can use to work toward their own health goals. When clients are forced to cope with illness, they frequently need to engage in new behaviors to stabilize their condition or to move toward optimal health. Chronic illnesses provide a special challenge in this regard, forcing clients first to learn new health-oriented behaviors and then to permanently integrate these behaviors into their lifestyles. Although treatment regimens may be clearly delineated, clients are affected by a number of factors that can complicate their behavior-change attempts. For the counselor, the effort to encourage clients to adhere to treatment regimens can be frustrating.

Adherence to medical regimens involves behaviors such as staying in treatment programs, keeping appointments, taking medication as prescribed, making suggested lifestyle changes, performing home-based therapies correctly, and avoiding health risk behaviors (Meichenbaum & Turk, 1987).

People jeopardize their health, their recovery, and even their lives by failing to adhere to medical advice concerning appropriate behaviors; yet nonadherence is normative. Approximately a third to a half of all medical patients fail to follow through on the regimens that have been prescribed for them (Stone, 1979; Meichenbaum & Turk, 1987), and levels of adherence are even poorer for certain medical problems. The people who are most likely to follow through on recommended behaviors are individuals whose illnesses are serious and acute and those who show distressing, overt symptoms. Clients whose illnesses are chronic and of long duration show very low adherence rates, as do individuals whose treatment regimens are complex. For instance, Stone (1979) cites studies showing that patients whose diabetes had lasted for more than 20 years had much higher rates of medication dosage errors than patients whose diabetes had been diagnosed less than 5 years earlier. Furthermore, the number of dosage errors made by diabetes patients increased with the number of different drugs involved. Adherence rates are lowest when no symptoms are present, especially when regimens are essentially preventive.

Although the nature of the illness and the form its treatment takes are important factors that affect adherence, additional variables also come into play, including the individual's beliefs about the threat posed by noncompliance and the benefits of adherence Janz & Becker, 1984), the nature of the relationship between the individual and the health-care provider (Stone, 1979), and the client's perceptions concerning the quality of the care provided by the clinical setting.

Meichenbaum and Turk (1987) suggest that there are a number of possible reasons for nonadherence. Sometimes, clients really do not understand what they are supposed to do. Frequently, they lack the skills, resources, or self-confidence needed to carry out the treatment protocol; may believe the regimen is too demanding, too difficult, or too unpleasant; and/or may think that carrying out required behaviors will not make enough difference to make the effort worthwhile. Sometimes, the problem lies in the relationship between the client and the helper or in the shortcomings of the health-care system.

Traditionally, medical transactions have been based on the assumption that it is the role of the physician to decide the course of treatment, and that it is the role of the client to take the responsibility for complying. This has been ineffective in ensuring compliance. In fact, "physicians systematically overestimate the extent to which their patients [will] adhere to their recommendations" (Stone, 1979, p. 48). Health counseling can play an important role as an adjunct to the medical transaction. Clients' performance of behaviors that conform to medical recommendations can be improved through psychoeducational and counseling approaches designed to solidify self-management.

One important aspect of a self-management approach is recognition of the client's role in determining the goals and methods for treatment. Although health-care professionals may have expert knowledge of the positive and negative aspects of various regimens, they are not necessarily aware of the individual client's values and priorities. Selection of a regimen to which a client can be expected to adhere depends on a combination of the helper's knowledge about the illness and its treatment and the client's self-knowledge. According to Friedman and DiMatteo (1989):

> Rational selection of a course of treatment requires that the patient take (and the health professional give) some responsibility when the treatment course is being selected. The health-care professional must be willing to take advice from the patient, who, after all, is the only person who really knows what manner of treatment he or she will be able and willing to follow. (p. 98)

If the client is to be held responsible for carrying out a course of action, he or she must be involved in selecting it. Although involving the client in negotiating the goals and methods of the regimen is time-consuming, this involvement increases the likelihood of adherence far beyond what could be expected if the client were simply instructed in or advised about appropriate behaviors.

The clients' commitment to a health-enhancing regimen is an important first step in their long-term adherence. Ideally, clients can develop intervention plans that they can use to develop new, health-oriented behaviors. Once clients have set realistic behavioral goals, they can learn to monitor their performance of these health-oriented activities. A behavioral contract—either with others or with themselves—can be used by clients to identify desired levels of performance and to schedule personally designed reinforcements.

Because individuals differ in the kinds of rewards they find reinforcing, each client needs to identify his or her own reinforcers. Reinforcement can then be made contingent on completion of the specific activity as contracted. As this plan is implemented, clients can continue to maintain careful records so that improvements in their performance levels can be identified. At the same time that clients maintain their reinforcement schedules, they can also attempt to identify and manipulate the internal and environmental cues associated with their health-oriented behaviors. This approach establishes a collaborative relationship between client and counselor, with the counselor's efforts concentrated on (1) helping the client select realistic and measurable goals, (2) coaching the client in his or her use of self-management techniques, (3) supporting the client's efforts, and (4) providing feedback to ensure that prescribed behaviors are implemented correctly.

The sense of self-efficacy that accompanies self-management training increases the likelihood of long-term adherence. Self-efficacy is also enhanced by training in the specific skills associated with the practice of health-associated behaviors. Carrying out new behaviors may require the development of skills that have not previously been part of the individual's repertoire. Informing a client about the need to change behaviors does not encourage adherence unless the individual has specific knowledge about the new behaviors, possesses the skill to implement the behaviors, and believes in his or her ability to carry out the recommended action. The client's ability to adhere to treatments may depend on his or her opportunity to participate in carefully designed training sessions. If these sessions are carried out in group settings, the client may enjoy the added benefit of mutual support.

PREVENTION

Efforts to prevent illnesses generally need a broad focus because of the difficulty of identifying a single, linear relationship between a definitive cause and a specific disorder. Health problems result from the interplay of numerous factors, and the same high-risk behaviors can place people in jeopardy for a number of disorders. Health-promotion programs that encourage self-management, enhance people's sense of control over their health, and support the development of new behaviors tend to serve a preventive function that is not necessarily associated with a specific disease. They also appear to be cost-effective.

Cost-Effectiveness of Preventing Chronic Diseases

Practical interventions exist for controlling and preventing many chronic diseases. Implementing proven clinical smoking-cessation interventions would cost an estimated $2,587 for each year of life saved—the most cost-effective of all clinical preventive services. Each $1 spent on diabetes outpatient education saves $2 to $3 in hospitalization costs. Mammography screening, when performed every 2 years for women 50 to 69 years old, costs between $8,280 and $9,890 per year of life saved. The cost of this screening compares favorably with other widely used clinical preventive services. Cervical cancer screening among low-income older women is estimated to save 3.7 years of life and $5,907 for every 100 Pap tests performed. The cost of preventing one cavity through water fluoridation is about $4, far below the average $64 cost of a simple dental restoration. For every $1 spent on preconception care programs for women with preexisting diabetes, $1.86 can be saved by preventing birth defects among their offspring. Participants in an arthritis self-help course experienced an 18 percent reduction in pain at a per-person savings of $267 in health-care system costs over 4 years.

Outcomes of Prevention Efforts

Some illnesses do have a clear enough relationship with specific behavioral risk factors to make the design of preventive programs a realistic endeavor. For example, increasing success is being reported for community-based programs aimed at the prevention of heart disease. The Stanford Three Community Study (Farquhar, Maccoby, & Solomon, 1984; Farquha et al., 1977) examined the results of an educational program aimed at two communities; the study used a third, comparable community as a control group. Citizens of Gilroy, California, received education through mass media, including TV and radio programming, newspaper advertisements and stories, billboards, and a mailing of printed materials. In Watsonville, the mass media program was supplemented by more intensive instruction for groups of people at high risk. Tracy, California, citizens received no education programs. Both Gilroy and Watsonville residents showed general improvement in comparison with the no-treatment community. The success of the program in bringing about changes in risk behaviors led to an expansion of the project to include five cities.

A comparable effort in Finland also brought about clear behavior changes (Puska et al., 1980). Residents of North Karelia, Finland, received a comprehensive program aimed at improving hypertension detection and treatment, reducing smoking, changing dietary habits, and generally lowering mortality rates. In comparison with residents in the control community of Kuopio, North Karelia residents showed a greater decrease in smoking, an improvement in average cholesterol levels, and a decrease in blood pressure.

Such comprehensive campaigns can also be adapted for the prevention of other diseases associated with specific risk factors. New cases of AIDS, for example, can be prevented through efforts to change risky behaviors that have been very clearly identified. Albee (1989) notes:

> The strategy [for] prevention of HIV transmission through education and the modification of behaviors is clearly the most hopeful approach to the prevention of AIDS. Educating persons with information that leads to changed behaviors that reduce or eliminate high-risk, unprotected sexual encounters constitutes effective prevention. Safer sexual practices, particularly if one partner has been infected, reduce the likelihood of transmission. Educating intravenous drug users about the use of clean needles and techniques for sterilizing needles and injection paraphernalia can reduce this form of [HIV] transmission . . . and thereby reduce the infection of IV drug users' sexual partners and many of the babies born within this social network. (p. 19)

Clearly, a combination of wellness-oriented health-promotion programs and comprehensive efforts to address identified risk behaviors provides the most promising available avenue to illness prevention.

CONCLUDING NOTE

Coping with a chronic illness can be a major challenge to the well-being of the individual and his or her family. Dealing with a sudden, acute disease can throw an individual into a crisis situation that requires new ways of behaving and of perceiving oneself and the world.

Chronic disease and impairment can be even more challenging as people try to cope with unrelenting health problems over long periods of time. As noted in this chapter, culture impacts chronic diseases and impairment "transforming" them into chronic illnesses and, often, later into disabilities.

Helping clients cope with acute and chronic diseases and other illness-related conditions requires careful assessment, and a number of general and disease-specific tools are currently available. Based on information about the individual, family and its cultural context as well as the disease or illness-related condition, the health counselor can focus on tailoring lifestyle management or self-management interventions for chronic diseases or other illness-related issues. Such interventions include helping the client deal with his or her psychological reactions to the illness, helping the client cope with aversive medical procedures, and enhancing the client's ability to adhere to recommended treatments. The goal of these interventions is to improve health status and/or wellness, whichever the client is capable of achieving. Emphasis should also be placed on working with the family, since the functionality of the family system can have a major impact on the individual's coping success and treatment adherence. Finally, the chapter noted that prevention, particularly regarding chronic diseases, is not only cost-effective but significantly reduces suffering and increases overall well-being.

RESOURCES

Organizations

Clients may benefit by contacting centers that provide information about a specific disease; examples include the following:

- American Burn Association, New York Hospital–Cornell Medical Center, 525 E. 68th Street, New York, NY 10021
- American Cancer Society, 90 Park Avenue, New York, NY 10016; 800-ACS-2345

- American Lung Association, 61 Broadway, New York, NY 10006
- National AIDS Hotline, 1-800-342-AIDS (www.ashastd.org/nah/)
- National Cancer Institute, Cancer Information Service, 6116 Executive Boulevard, Bethesda, MD 20892; 800-4-CANCER

Self-Help Groups

People dealing with health problems frequently find self-help groups highly beneficial as a means for obtaining emotional and social support. Self-help groups, each focused on a specific illness, are available in most communities. Among them are the following:

- AMEND (for mothers experiencing neonatal death)

- Candlelighters (for parents of children with cancer)
- Compassionate Friends (for bereaved parents)
- Epilepsy Foundation
- Heart to Heart (a visitation program for people with problems related to coronary heart disease)
- Make Today Count (for persons with cancer and their families)

- Muscular Dystrophy Association
- Phoenix Society (for burn victims)
- Reach to Recovery (for women who have had mastectomies)

- Spina Bifida Association
- United Cerebral Palsy
- United Ostomy Association

Suggested Readings

- *Patient education for common chronic diseases:* DiLima, S. (Ed.). (1998). *Chronic disease patient education manual.* Gaithersburg, MD: Aspen.—A patient education resource for the five diseases most commonly targeted for chronic disease management programs: asthma, diabetes, hypertension, coronary artery disease, and stroke. Presented in a three-ring binder, the manual contains large-print handouts concerning each disease state. Each section contains 30 to 100 or so sheets. It also includes a chapter on promoting wellness and addresses interventions common to many disease states such as smoking cessation and nutrition.
- *Bilibiotherapy:* Lorig, K., Holman, H., Sobel, D., Laurent, D., Minor, N. and Gonzalez, V. (Eds.). (2000). *Living a healthy life with chron-*

ic conditions: Self-management of heart disease, arthritis, diabetes, asthma, bronchitis, emphysema and others. San Francisco: Bull Publishing.—A client-friendly, easy-to-read account about facing the challenges of everyday coping with heart disease, diabetes, emphysema, asthma, and arthritis, and so on. This book includes information gathered in a 5-year study at Stanford University's Center for Disease Prevention. It is based on the input of hundreds of study participants with long-term health conditions. The focus is on nutrition, exercise, mind–body strategies, and working with the health-care system and its professionals. The goal of this book is to help individuals live the best possible life with a long-term condition.

REFERENCES

Albee, G. W. (1989). Primary prevention in public health: Problems and challenges of behavior change as prevention. In V. M. Mays, G. W. Albee, & S. F. Schneider (Eds.), *Primary prevention of AIDS: Psychological approaches* (pp. 15–20). Newbury Park, CA: Sage.

Angel, R. J., & Williams, K. (2001). Cultural models of health and illness. In I. Cuellar & F. A. Paniagua (Eds.), *Handbook of multicultural mental health* (pp. 25–44). San Diego: Academic.

Arrendondo, P. (1996). MCT theory and latina(o)-American populations. In D. W. Sue, A. E. Ivey, & P. B. Pedersen (Eds.), *A theory of multicultural counseling and therapy* (pp. 217–235). Pacific Grove, CA: Brooks-Cole.

Caplan, R. M. (1982). Coping with stressful medical examinations. In H. S. Friedman & M. R. DiMatteo (Eds.), *Interpersonal issues in health care* (pp. 187–206). New York: Academic.

Chesler, M. A., & Yoak, M. (1984). Self-help groups for parents of children with cancer. In H. B. Roback

(Ed.), *Helping patients and their families cope with medical problems: A guide to therapeutic group work in clinical settings* (pp. 481–526). San Francisco: Jossey-Bass.

Cramer, D. (1989). The HIV-positive individual. In C. D. Kain (Ed.), *No longer immune: A counselor's guide to AIDS* (pp. 55–76). Alexandria, VA: American Association for Counseling and Development.

Creer, T., Marion, T., & Creer, P. (1983). Asthma Problem Behavior Checklist: Parental perceptions of the behavior of asthmatic children. *Journal of Asthma, 20,* 97–104.

Derogatis, L. R. (1977). *Psychological Adjustment to Illness Scale.* Baltimore: Clinical Psychometric Research.

Derogatis, L. R., Morrow, G. R., Fetting, J., Penman, D., Piasetsky, S., Schmale, A. M., et al. (1983). The prevalence of psychiatric disorders among cancer patients. *Journal of Behavioral Medicine, 7,* 171–189.

DiClemente, R. J., & Temoshok, L. (1986). Psychological adjustment to having cutaneous malignant melanoma as a predictor of follow-up clinical status. In *Proceedings of the Seventh Annual Society of Behavioral Medicine Meeting* (p. 13). New York: Plenum.

DiLima S. (Ed.). (1997). *Chronic disease management: Clinical pathways and guidelines.* Gaithersburg, MD: Aspen.

Dunkel-Schetter, C., & Wortman, C. B. (1982). The interpersonal dynamics of cancer: Problems in social relationships and their impact on the patient. In H. S. Friedman & M. R. DiMatteo (Eds.), *Interpersonal issues in health care* (pp. 69–100). New York: Academic.

Eisenberg, M. G. (1984). Spinal cord injuries. In H. B. Roback (Ed.), *Helping patients and their families cope with medical problems: A guide to therapeutic group work in clinical settings* (pp. 107–129). San Francisco: Jossey-Bass.

Euster, S. (1984). Adjusting to an adult family member's cancer. In H. B. Roback (Ed.), *Helping patients and their families cope with medical problems: A guide to therapeutic group work in clinical settings* (pp. 428–452). San Francisco: Jossey-Bass.

Farquhar, J. W., Maccoby, N., & Solomon, D. S. (1984). Community applications of behavioral medicine. In W. D. Gentry (Ed.), *Handbook of behavioral medicine* (pp. 437–478). New York: Guilford.

Farquhar, J. W., Maccoby, N., Wood, P. D., Alexander, J. K., Breitrose, H., Brown, B. W., et al. (1977). Community education for cardiovascular health. *Lancet, 1,* 1192–1195.

Fennell, P. (2001). *The chronic illness workbook: Strategies and solutions for taking back your life.* Oakland, CA: New Harbinger Publications.

Frank-Stromborg, M., & Wright, P. (1984). Ambulatory cancer patients' perception of the physical and psychosocial changes in their lives since the diagnosis of cancer. *Cancer Nursing, 7,* 117–130.

Friedman, H. S., & DiMatteo, M. R. (1989). *Health psychology.* Englewood Cliffs, NJ: Prentice-Hall.

Goodheart, C. (1997). *Treating people with chronic conditions.* Washington, DC: American Psychological Association.

Hamburg, D. A, Elliott, G. R, & Parron, D. L. (1982). *Health and behavior: Frontiers of research in the biobehavioral sciences.* Washington, DC: National Academy Press.

Haynes, S., Feinleib, M., Levine, S., Scotch, N., & Kannel, W. (1980). The relationship of psychosocial factors to coronary heart disease in the Framingham Study. III. Eight-year incidence of coronary heart disease. *American Journal of Epidemiology, 111,* 37–58.

Hendrick, S. S. (1985). Behavioral medicine approaches to diabetes mellitus. In N. Schneiderman & J. T. Tapp (Eds.), *Behavioral medicine: The biopsychosocial approach* (pp. 509–531). Hillsdale, NJ: Erlbaum.

Janz, N. K., & Becker, M. H. (1984). The Health Belief Model: A decade later. *Health Education Quarterly, 11*(1), 1–47.

Jenkins, C., Rosenman, R., & Friedman, M. (1967). Development of an objective psychological test for the determination of the coronary-prone behavior pattern in employed men. *Journal of Chronic Diseases, 20,* 371–379.

Johnson, S. B. (1985). The family and the child with chronic illness. In D. C. Turk & R. D. Kerns (Eds.), *Health, illness, and families: A life-span perspective* (pp. 220–254). New York: Wiley.

Kapust, L. R., & Weintraub, S. (1984). Living with a family member suffering from Alzheimer's disease. In H. B. Roback (Ed.), *Helping patients and their families cope with medical problems* (pp. 453–480). San Francisco: Jossey-Bass.

Kendall, P. C., & Turk, D. C. (1984). Cognitive-behavioral strategies and health enhancement. In J. D. Matarazzo, S. M. Weiss, J. A. Herd, N. E. Miller, & S. M. Weiss (Eds.), *Behavioral health: A handbook of health enhancement and disease prevention* (pp. 393–405). New York: Wiley.

Kendall, P. C., Williams, L., Pechacek, T. F., Graham, L., Shisslak, C., & Herzoff, N. (1979). Cognitive-behavioral and patient education interventions in cardiac catheterization procedures: The Palo Alto medical psychology project. *Journal of Consulting and Clinical Psychology, 47,* 49–58.

Kerns, R. D., & Curley, A. D. (1985). A biopsychosocial approach to illness and the family: Neurological diseases across the life span. In D. C. Turk & R. D. Kerns (Eds.), *Health, illness, and families: A life-span perspective* (pp. 146–182). New York: Wiley.

Kinsman, R., Dahlem, N., Spector, S., & Staudenmeyer, H. (1977). Observations on subjective symptomatology, coping behavior, and medical decisions in asthma. *Psychosomatic Medicine, 39,* 102–119.

Langosch, W. (1984). Behavioural interventions in cardiac rehabilitation. In A. Steptoe & A. Mathews (Eds.), *Health care and human behaviour* (pp. 301–324). London: Academic.

Lee, C., & Armstrong, K. (1995). Indigenous models of mental health intervention. In J. G. Ponterotto, J. M. Casas, L. M. Suzuki, & C. M. Alexander (Eds.), *Handbook of multicultural counseling* (pp. 441–456). Thousand Oaks, CA: Sage.

Lorig, K., Holman, H., Sobel, D., Laurent, D., Minor, N., & Gonzalez, V. (Eds.). (2000). *Living a healthy life with chronic conditions: Self-management of heart disease, arthritis, diabetes, asthma, bronchitis, emphysema and others.* San Francisco: Bull Publishing.

Macks, J., & Turner, D. (1986). Mental health issues of persons with AIDS. In L. McKusick (Ed.), *What to do about AIDS* (pp. 111–124). Berkeley: University of California Press.

Mandel, J. (1986). Psychosocial challenges of AIDS and ARC: Clinical and research observations. In L. McKusick (Ed.), *What to do about AIDS* (pp. 75–86). Berkeley: University of California Press.

Marsella, A. J., & Yamada, A. M. (2001). Culture and mental health: An introduction and overview of foundations, concepts, and issues. In I. Cuellar & F. A. Paniagua (Eds.), *Handbook of multicultural mental health* (pp. 3–24). San Diego: Academic.

Mathews, A., & Ridgeway, V. (1984). Psychological preparation for surgery. In A. Steptoe & A. Mathews (Eds.), *Health care and human behaviour* (pp. 231–259). London: Academic.

McCorkle, R., & Young, K. (1978). Development of a symptom distress scale. *Cancer Nursing, 1,* 373–378.

Meichenbaum, D. (1985). *Stress inoculation training.* New York: Pergamon.

Meichenbaum, D., & Turk, D. C. (1987). *Facilitating treatment adherence: A practitioner's guidebook.* New York: Plenum.

Mejta, C. L. (1987). Acquired Immune Deficiency Syndrome (AIDS): Implications for counseling and education. *Counseling and Human Development, 20*(2), 1–12.

Millon, T., Antoni, M., Millon, C., Mengher, S., & Grossman, S. (2001). *Millon Behavioral Medicine Diagnostic Manual.* Eagan, MN: Pearson Assessments.

Millon, T., Green, C., & Meagher, R. (1982). *Millon Behavioral Health Inventory manual.* Minneapolis: National Computer Systems.

Moos, R. H., Cronkite, R. C., Billings, A. G., & Finney, J. W. (1984). *Health and Daily Giving Form Manual.* Palo Alto: Social Ecology Laboratory, Veterans Administration and Stanford University Medical Centers.

Moos, R. H., & Tsu, V. D. (1977). Overview and perspective. In R. H. Moos (Ed.), *Coping with physical illness.* New York: Plenum.

Namir, S. (1986). Treatment issues concerning persons with AIDS. In L. McKusick (Ed.), *What to do about AIDS* (pp. 87–94). Berkeley: University of California Press.

National Center for Chronic Disease Prevention and Health Promotion (2000). *Chronic diseases and their risk factors: The nation's leading causes of death, 1999.* Washington, DC: Author.

Neff, J. A., & Hoppe, S. K. (1993). Race/ethnicity, acculturation, and psychological distress: Fatalism and religiosity as cultural resources. *Journal of Community Psychology, 21,* 3–20.

Paniagua, F. A. (1998). *Assessing and treating culturally diverse clients.* Thousand Oaks, CA: Sage.

Pavlou, M. (1984). Multiple sclerosis. In H. B. Roback (Ed.), *Helping patients and their families cope with medical problems: A guide to therapeutic group work in clinical settings* (pp. 331–365). San Francisco: Jossey-Bass.

Puska, P., Tuomilehto, J., Nissinen, A., Salonen, J., Maki, J., & Pallonen, U. (1980). Changing the cardiovascular risk in an entire community: The North Karelia project. In R. M. Lauer & R. B. Shekelle (Eds.), *Childhood prevention of atherosclerosis and hypertension* (pp. 441–451). New York: Raven Press.

Razin, A. M. (1984). Coronary artery disease. In H. B. Roback (Ed.), *Helping patients and their families cope with medical problems: A guide to therapeutic group work in clinical settings* (pp. 216–250). San Francisco: Jossey-Bass.

Robert Wood Johnson Foundation (1994). *Annual report: Health in the United States, 1994.* New York: Author.

Rosenman, R., Friedman, M., Straus, B., Wurm, M., Kositchek, R, Hahn, W., & Werthesson, N. (1964). A predictive study of coronary heart disease: The Western Collaborative Group Study. *Journal of the American Medical Association, 189,* 103–110.

Schwartz, G. E. (1982). Testing the biopsychosocial model: The ultimate challenge facing behavioral medicine? *Journal of Consulting and Clinical Psychology, 30,* 240–253.

Stone, G. C. (1979). Patient compliance and the role of the expert. *Journal of Social Issues, 35*(1), 34–59.

Thoresen, C. E., & Eagleston, J. R. (1985). Counseling for health. *Counseling Psychologist, 13*(1), 15–87.

Turk, D. C., & Kerns, R. D. (1985). The family in health and illness. In D. C. Turk & R. D. Kerns (Eds.), *Health, illness, and families: A life-span perspective* (pp. 1–22). New York: Wiley.

Wallston, K. A., Wallston, B. S., & Devellis, R. (1978). Development of the Multidimensional Health Locus of Control (MHLOC) scales. *Health Education Monographs, 6,* 160–170.

Williamson, D. A., Davis, C. J., & Prather, R. C. (1988). Assessment of health-related disorders. In A. S. Bellaek & M. Hersen (Eds.). *Behavioral assessment: A practical handbook* (3rd ed., pp. 396–440). New York: Pergamon.

HEALTH COUNSELING VIDEOTAPES

APA Psychotherapy Video Series III on Behavioral Health and Health Counseling presents distinguished psychologists illustrating how to work with patients who have specific health problems. These videos are designed for clinical training and are appropriate for health-care practitioners.

Each video is practical, informative, and provides more than 100 minutes of insight into the use of specific treatments including:

1. Provocative discussion between the host and guest expert about treatment for clients with a health issue
2. An actual therapy session with a real client
3. A lively question-and-answer exchange with the expert and host about the therapy session

The videos include

- Chronic Illness *with Len Sperry*
- Sleep and Sleep Disorders *with Edward J. Stepanski*
- Drug and Alcohol Abuse *with William Richard Miller*
- Smoking Cessation *with Bonnie J. Spring*
- Sexual Health *with Lisa Firestone*
- Weight Loss and Control *with Ann Mary Kearney-Cooke*
- Pain Management *with Robert J. Gatchel*
- Exercise *with Kate F. Hays*
- Breast Cancer *with Suzanne M. Miller*
- Cardiac Psychology *with Robert Allan*
- Childhood Asthma *with Bruce G. Bender*
- Genetic Issues *with Andrea Farkas Pantenaude*

For more information about the purpose of this series, the therapist's orientation, notes about the client, suggested readings, and/or to purchase videos, please visit www.apa.org/videos/series3.html; or contact American Psychological Association, 750 First Street, NE, Washington, DC 20002. To purchase books, go to www.apa.org/books or call the APA toll free—1-800-374-2721.